RECORDING HISTORY

The British Record Industry, 1888–1931

PETER MARTLAND

THE SCARECROW PRESS, INC.
Lanham • Toronto • Plymouth, UK
2013

Published by Scarecrow Press, Inc.
A wholly owned subsidiary of The Rowman & Littlefield Publishing Group, Inc.
4501 Forbes Boulevard, Suite 200, Lanham, Maryland 20706
www.rowman.com

10 Thornbury Road, Plymouth PL6 7PP, United Kingdom

British Library Cataloguing in Publication Information Available

Library of Congress Cataloging-in-Publication Data

Martland, Peter.
  Recording history : the British record industry, 1888–1931 / Peter Martland.
    p. cm.
  Includes bibliographical references and index.
  ISBN 978-0-8108-8252-2 (cloth : alk. paper) — ISBN 978-0-8108-8253-9
  (ebook) 1. Sound recording industry—Great Britain—History. I. Title.
  ML3790.M3507 2013
  384—dc23   2012024446

∞™ The paper used in this publication meets the minimum requirements of
American National Standard for Information Sciences—Permanence of Paper
for Printed Library Materials, ANSI/NISO Z39.48-1992.

Printed in the United States of America

CONTENTS

LIST OF FIGURES

LIST OF TABLES

FOREWORD

I first met Peter Martland in the mid-1990s. At the time I was nearing the end of a thirty-year career in the music business, twenty of which would be spent at EMI in a series of widely differing responsibilities, including nearly ten years for the EMI archive, culminating in the task of celebrating the company's centenary in, as I had been told, 1998.

Peter had already availed himself of some of the unique and extraordinary archive resources for a detailed business history of The Gramophone Company from 1897 to 1918 that he was writing for a Cambridge University doctoral thesis. When, some time later, it became apparent that an EMI history book needed a second opinion, it was Peter to whom I was recommended to turn, and thank goodness I did. Not only did he quickly and tactfully realise that the manuscript with which he had been presented needed substantial extra work, but he also alerted us to one crucial error— our centenary would be a year earlier than we expected! This chopped twelve vital months off our timetable, causing momentary panic, offset by the realisation that at least EMI's centenary would come ahead of that of Deutsche Grammophon, the oldest part of EMI's strongest rival.

The net result of Peter's hawkeyed diligence was that he was commissioned to start again with EMI's history, and the result, *Since Records Began*, though sadly now out of print, remains the prime source for an ever-growing number of researchers into the history of recorded music.

Now, some fifteen years later, the circle has been completed by Peter's new work, based on his original doctoral thesis but expanded to not only take the story forward to 1931—the year financial circumstance forced The Gramophone Company to merge with its greatest rival, The Columbia Graphophone Company—but add the rise (and fall) of many other early competitors.

Peter is scrupulous and dedicated to the accuracy of his research yet has the enviable added talent of turning detailed company history into an absorbing and satisfying read. The music industry is unique in its combination of successfully nurturing, protecting and exploiting the creative talent of its artists, on the one hand, while never quite managing to grasp the pitfalls of the carriers of their music, from 78-rpm shellac through cassette and compact disc to digital download, on the other. Notwithstanding, it is rapidly moving through its second century and will continue to survive whatever the technology wizards throw at it.

This is the start of that story and I heartily commend it to you.

David Hughes
Chairman, EMI Group Archive Trust

ACKNOWLEDGMENTS

During the course of my research I was fortunate in locating a vast array of archival material in Britain and the United States, much of it previously unused. Without question The EMI Group Archive Trust and its unique archive proved the single most important British source. Rupert Perry, the former European head of EMI Music Ltd and its former archivist Ruth Edge were most generous in opening up this extraordinary collection to me and this support has continued through David Hughes, the present chairman of the Trust. The importance of this treasure house cannot be overstated and its preservation (despite an uncertain business environment) as part of our industrial and cultural heritage is a credit to the Trust and The EMI Group plc. Other EMI figures past and present contributed to the research and writing of this book; these include Richard Abram, Michael Allen, Claire Enders, Tony Locantro, Guy Marriott and Sir Colin Southgate. Other archives and libraries were liberally trawled, especially in the United States of America. The success of this large scale research depended on the help and enthusiastic support of a number of individuals who generously gave of their knowledge and time. Amongst these were Professor Paul Israel at the University of Rutgers, the State University of New Jersey, Lenny DeGraaf at The Edison National Historic Site, West Orange, New Jersey, Dr. John R. Bolig and Ann Horsey of The Johnson Victrola Museum, Dover, Delaware. The latter opened its archive of Eldridge Johnson and Victor papers to me and both listened patiently to my questions over many long hours. The Camden Historical Society, Camden, New Jersey also allowed me access to its considerable holding of papers and artefacts relating to The Victor Talking Machine Company, while the Rodgers and Hammerstein Collection at New York Public Library provided me with unique access to The Lawrence Collection with its insights into the various Columbia businesses. In addition,

I was able to examine a number of sources based in and around Washington, DC, including The United States National Archives and Records Center at College Park, Maryland, The Volta Laboratory, The Smithsonian Institution Archive Center and The Motion Picture, Broadcast and Sound Recording Division of The Library of Congress. It was there that I met its then reference librarian Samuel S. Brylawski to whom I am deeply indebted for his encouragement and friendship. It was he who urged me to work on the papers of Emile Berliner in The Robert Sanders Collection and who introduced me to a number of Emile and Cora Berliner's surviving grandchildren then resident in and around Washington, DC.

In Britain I had the pleasure of working with many enthusiastic and interested friends and colleagues. Among these were Peter Adamson formerly of the University of St Andrews, Dave Roberts, Mike Field and Richard Taylor of the City of London Phonograph and Gramophone Society, Eliot Levin of Symposium Records, Tom Stephenson, Tim Wadey, Nigel Howarth, Russell Church, Liam Denning and most especially Christopher Proudfoot and Frank Andrews, whose detailed insight and knowledge kept me on the straight and narrow. Thanks must also go to my first editor Bruce Phillips who commissioned the book on behalf of Scarecrow Press. Among the many individuals who kindly assisted in the course of my original research are a number who have since sadly passed on. These include George Frow (sometime President of the City of London Phonograph and Gramophone Society, whose understanding of the Edison phonograph business remains unsurpassed), Janet Lord MBE (formerly manager of the EMI photographic archive), Robert Sanders (the grandson of Emile Berliner and son of industry pioneer Joseph Sanders), Kathleen Darby (the daughter of sound engineer William Sinkler Darby), Sir Anthony Burney OBE (the son of Theodore Birnbaum, the second managing director of The Gramophone Company), Gwendolyne McCormack-Pyke (the daughter of tenor John McCormack), Kathleen Fryer-Homer (the daughter of contralto Louise Homer), Charlotte Erickson (emeritus professor of American history at Cambridge University) and Frederick Manning. Others too assisted, including Michal Hambourg and Nadine Marshall, the daughters of concert pianist and early Gramophone Company recording artist, Mark Hambourg. All of these gave generously of their time with patience and forbearing and as a consequence added much needed insights and context.

I also benefited from the encouragement and patient assistance of current and former Cambridge academics including Clive Trebilcock, Professor J. M. Winter, Professor Christopher Andrew, Dr Nick Hiley,

Dr. Patrick Zutshi, Professor Hyman Gross and, not least, by my doctoral supervisor Professor Barry Supple FBA, whose enthusiasm, interest, guidance and wisdom has meant so much to me. In addition, I have relied on a generation of Cambridge undergraduates and graduates who, knowingly or otherwise, helped more than they could ever know. Most recently I have had the assistance of Ross Moody, formerly of UCLA and now Pembroke College, Cambridge, who patiently read the manuscript and made positive and helpful comments. To all the institutions and individuals named and many others, I offer my grateful thanks for their patience, time and interest. I also take this opportunity to acknowledge all copyrighted sources used by me.

INTRODUCTION

The British and broader international record industry has had a pretty miserable start to the twenty-first century, which saw its more than one hundred year old system of manufacturing and selling collapse under the weight of technological change, a revolution in communications and a wildly fluctuating world economy. If that were not enough, the industry has also experienced serious structural problems and failed to keep pace with fundamental changes to consumer habits. All of this has combined to destabilise and plunge the industry into one of its periodic bouts of crisis and painful reinvention. Fortunately, crisis and reinvention is familiar territory for the record industry and ever since its late-nineteenth-century beginnings these hazards have occurred with monotonous regularity. These early ups and downs form the core of this book.

        ★   ★   ★

The scope of this book is ambitious, providing as it does a business, economic, social and cultural history of the British record industry from its beginnings in 1888 to the 1931 depression-led integration that created Electric and Musical Industries Ltd (EMI Ltd). Although a new medium, sound recording formed a part of a wider series of late-nineteenth-century technological advances such as the safety bicycle, the Kodak camera, moving pictures, the mass circulation popular press and the automobile. From a cottage industry to industrial formation, the record industry grew with amazing speed to the point that, by the early twentieth century, it had become a popular medium capable of delivering the very best music and entertainment of the day into the home. As a consequence, by the outbreak of war in 1914 British domestic life had been transformed as records and

xviii   *Introduction*

talking machines replaced the piano as the main method of home-based music-making and entertainment. Records also transformed audience-performer relations as, previous to the coming of this industry, public entertainment (whether sporting or other forms of leisure activity) involved artists appearing at premises to which access was gained through the payment of a fee. It involved a direct and highly personal relationship for both artist and audience. Records challenged these traditional methods of public entertainment and revolutionised the entertainment and music industries. In changing both the venue and the method by which a performance was heard, the new medium triggered a mass-communications revolution, shifting the venue for much entertainment and leisure activity away from the public into the domestic (or at least the private) domain. Today the importance of this shift is evident as most leisure activities and therefore much art and musical culture is distributed through such largely domestic (or at least portable) electronic technologies as radio and television, computers, iPods and an array of other devices playing media such as CDs, DVDs and most notably music downloads (often MP3 files) from the internet. The effect of this fundamentally altered the relationship between performer and audience to the point that today it is largely impersonal. One purpose of this book is to give context to this shift in social habits.

The infant record industry attracted its fair share of hucksters and get-rich-quick merchants who attempted to make easy money either by exhibiting phonographs at fairgrounds and other locations or by dubious business practices; their story provides a great deal of light relief in early chapters of this book. The initial success of the British record industry was due to a number of factors, including important innovations in the art of sound recording and rapidly falling prices, both of records and the machines to play them. As a result, by the outbreak of the First World War in 1914 annual sales were fifteen million records and 500,000 machines and more than one in three British households boasting a record collection and a talking machine. This upward trend continued in the decade or so after the war to the point that, by 1931, more than 60 percent of households had a gramophone and annual record sales were sixty million; a figure not repeated until the late 1950s. This work explains how record companies moved from engaging established artists and existing musical forms to promoting new artists and new musical forms. This began in 1902 when the young Italian tenor Enrico Caruso made his first records; in 1917 the first jazz records were made, which crossed the Atlantic by means of recordings at the end of the First World War. Also examined is the long-term viability of the record industry, how it dealt with wartime disruptions and why, after the depression years of 1921 to 1923 and despite the economic dislocations of that decade, it experienced an unparalleled boom.

This history surveys the processes of invention and innovation, how mass production and market formation occurred in the United States and its importance to later developments in Britain and continental Europe; British industrial and market formation is also discussed. However, because of the number of record companies (and foreign companies selling into Britain) it has proved impossible to enter into a discussion of every one. This is resolved by use of case studies of important industry pioneers. Of course these businesses did not begin at the same time and not all survived to the end of the period, but they do exemplify the new industry and the different sectors of the market they sold into.

The main business case study is provided by The Gramophone Company Ltd, which was an important multinational business. Developments such as its changing organisational and structural needs, together with evidence of transaction cost economies, internal markets, management methods and the role played by the executives and directors are examined. In addition, a range of time line statistical data is deployed and compared to both its competitors and US partner. Also highlighted are the key pioneers like Alfred Clark, The Gramophone Company's managing director from 1909 to 1930 and subsequently chairman of Electric and Musical Industries Ltd (EMI); Louis Sterling, managing director of The Columbia Graphophone Company Ltd and, from 1931, of EMI Ltd; and James Edward Hough, the dominant figure in the history of Edison Bell. These backroom figures were responsible for company finances and the long-term viability of their respective businesses. The book also examines the degree of initial monopoly profits enjoyed by industry pioneers, their response to competition and the reaction of the market to movements in the broader economy. Marketing and advertising methods and competition strategies are both examined, particularly during the format-divided period in the early 1900s. This allows for an assessment of the various elements market and explains how and why the Berliner-Johnson zigzag or lateral-cut disc record became the industry standard.

Throughout the pre-1914 period several British record companies retained important relations with American affiliates. The Gramophone Company and its partner The Victor Talking Machine Company provides an excellent basis for a discussion of these alliances, as both exploited the Berliner-Johnson disc patents and based their relationship on a number of mutually beneficial agreements. It would not be possible to understand record industry developments without insight into these links. They also provide an opportunity for a comparison between the British and American record markets. From its earliest days the British record industry was engaged in a lucrative domestic and overseas trade and was itself attractive to foreign record companies and machine manufacturers. These dynamics provide opportunities to look at the problems faced by early-twentieth-century multinational businesses, for example, how to control overseas branches. It also examines the distinction between ventures dependent on the purely domestic and those which developed an overseas trade. The pre-1914 fight for an industry standard format and its influence on British and continental Europe markets (but significantly not in the United States) is also scrutinised.

Central to this book is an assessment of the art of sound recording and the technical limitations that determined the kind of music recorded in the first quarter of the twentieth century. Also examined are changes following on from the introduction of electrical recording in 1925 and how the industry used the new technology to remake and broaden its catalogues, particularly (but not exclusively) in the field of classical works. Other issues explored include the methodology used to persuade new and established performing artists to make records, the fees they could earn and new relationships recording artists formed with the public. To place all this into perspective, the earning potential of recording artists is contrasted with those of other professionals. The industry is also fitted into the broader revolution in communications; for example the development of a world transport network which enabled performers to undertake world tours, the impact of which, and the role played by records in promoting and spreading their art, is also reviewed.

The impact of the First World War is examined from business and cultural angles. The loss of the previously dominant German record and machine manufacturers is assessed with its impact in accelerating the development of a British talking machine industry. Further, the underlying strength of the industry is revealed in its ability to ride out serious postwar economic problems and emerge as one of the new and modern high-tech industries of the 1920s and become one of the great glamour industries of its day. Finally, the industry's successful transition from light engineering to electrical engineering in the mid-1920s is examined; by 1931 the main concerns also manufactured radios, radiograms and domestic electrical goods.

★ ★ ★

The publication of this book represents something of a milestone both for me and for the subject. For much of the present work started life as my

1993 Cambridge University doctoral dissertation and it has taken many years of on-and-off work to get it finally to press. This absurdly drawn-out period of gestation is down to many factors, not least the writing of several other books and the need to earn a living. As to the subject, until this present work few historians have attempted to either chronicle or assess the early British record industry. The puzzle is not just the lack of publications but until comparatively recently the paucity of research into the subject, despite the availability of sources. The consequences have been unfortunate; for instance, having failed to recognise its importance, historians have attributed to more recent media precedence that rightly belongs to the record industry. This work seeks to redress the balance.

1

INVENTING THE RECORD INDUSTRY: 1877–1903

"Mary Had a Little Lamb Its Fleece Was White as Snow"

It was ludicrous in the extreme to see ten people grouped about a phonograph, each with a tube leading from his ears, grinning and laughing at what he heard.

—Fred Gaisberg describing how people
listened to records in the 1890s[1]

Prominent singers, speakers, or performers, may derive an income from royalties on the sale of their phonautograms [Berliner's word for records], and valuable plates may be printed and registered to protect against unauthorised publication. Collections of phonautograms may become very valuable, and whole evenings will be spent at home going through a long list of interesting performances.

—Emile Berliner speculating on the
future of his invention,[2] 1888

The world reacted with astonishment when, in December 1877, the great American inventor Thomas Edison demonstrated his latest invention, a speaking machine he called the phonograph. It was a small uncomplicated mechanism, which he claimed could both record and reproduce the human voice. It was a remarkable invention and proved so important in transforming communications, art and culture that Paul Israel, a recent Edison biographer, suggests it was the most significant of his career.[3] After the initial demonstrations and many subsequent sound recording patents there developed an utterly new industry, first in the United States then in Britain and continental Europe before spreading to the rest of the world. To feed this industry, many business ventures were created and

1

performing artists persuaded to make records. A number of these ventures also made what were known at the time as "talking machines" on which to play records, together with related products for use in what became a revolution in home entertainment.

Just as the invention of sound recording was an American phenomenon, American ideas provided many subsequent innovations and improvements to the art, and it was mainly American businessmen who founded the industry and guided the spread of the technology. Therefore to understand British and European developments in the field of record making, manufacturing and market formation it is essential to grasp happenings in the United States during the pioneering years 1877 and 1903, as these proved critical to the establishment of important British and European record companies in the years immediately before and after 1900. These same years also saw Americans enter the new industry as sound engineers, businessmen, salesmen and entrepreneurs. However, as with all new technology industries, it also attracted crooks, conmen and get-rich-quick merchants anxious to make a quick buck before the bubble burst: usually they went bust but the bubble didn't, though these people did play an important role introducing sound recording to the masses. In fact many American industry pioneers stayed for the long haul, enjoying long and distinguished careers creating and developing the British and European record industry. Therefore, by describing the key developments in the United States between 1877 and 1903, this chapter sets the scene for the opening of British and European markets after 1888.

★   ★   ★

The invention of sound recording during the last quarter of the nineteenth century was a by-product of research into the nature of sound and its transmission by telephone. The three figures who came to hold fundamental sound recording patents, Thomas Edison, Alexander Graham Bell and Emile Berliner, were all prominent inventors and innovators in the art of relaying sound by telephone. In part their work built on research conducted during the 1850s by Lord Rayleigh in Britain and Hermann von Helmholtz in Germany. These men of science examined the nature of sound and its practical application to scientific problems. Their seminal work on acoustics encouraged others to explore the possibilities of utilising the properties of sound in overcoming problems of communication.

One of the most important precursors of the phonograph was the phonautograph, a device that made sound waves visible. Invented in 1857 by a French scientist Édouard-Léon Scott de Martinville, the Phonauto-graph was a purely mechanical device. It traced sound waves in a zigzag or sinuous fashion on a revolving cylinder mounted on a feed-screw. To do this the cylinder was covered with a sheet of paper coated with lampblack and the sound waves were traced by a hog's bristle attached to a diaphragm, which was in turn fixed to a horn. The principle underpinning the device was simple enough; if the bristle was traced in silence a straight line was produced, but if someone spoke into the horn the sound vibrated the dia-phragm and its stylus to create a sound wave in the form of a zigzag trace.[4] Scott and others demonstrated this phenomenon, but never attempted to make a sound record capable of being reproduced.[5]

Alexander Graham Bell was drawn to the science of acoustics as a teacher of the deaf. He saw the Phonautograph as a useful tool, which he used to illustrate his lectures.[6] In 1876 Bell's work on acoustics led not to the invention of sound recording but rather to the development of a practical telephone. The following year a machine capable of storing and reproducing sound emerged from the laboratory of his great rival, Thomas Edison. In late 1877 Edison was undertaking experiments to improve and develop Bell's original telephone concept.[7] He stumbled upon the idea of recorded sound while working on a telephone-repeating device aimed at assisting long-distance voice transmissions.[8] Historian Andre Millard argued, "[It] was one of the few inventions that had not been visualized before it was made. In Edison's argot the phonograph was more a *discovery* than an *invention*."[9] The machine Edison called the phonograph integrated many of the Phonautograph's features. It employed a grooved metal cylin-der mounted on a hand-cranked feed-screw, the action of which turned the cylinder and moved it laterally. The recording medium was tinfoil wrapped around the cylinder and the sound signal was created by bringing a stylus attached to a diaphragm connected to a horn into contact with the revolv-ing cylinder. When speech or other sounds were played into the horn it caused the diaphragm and stylus to vibrate. As the stylus passed over the revolving cylinder its vibrations created an indented analogue sound signal in the tinfoil. To play back, the process was simply reversed using a blunt stylus to reproduce the sound record. Years after the event Edison claimed the first words he spoke into the phonograph were the nursery rhyme "Mary had a little lamb."

Edison's remarkable invention received enthusiastic international press coverage, complete with futuristic speculations as to its use and im-ages of future concertgoing audiences listening to recordings of musical performances. However, due to the limitations of the technology, these proved fanciful and listening to records developed as a domestic rather than a public activity. Interestingly, a study of the newspaper coverage suggests that Edison struck a chord with the mid-Victorian obsession with death. A decade later the inventor Emile Berliner struck that same chord, when he observed that listening to a record would be like "holding communion even with immortality."[10] Nothing characterised this reaction better than a *Scientific American* editorial:

> It has been said that Science is never sensational; that it is intellectual not emotional; but certainly nothing that can be conceived would be more likely to create the profoundest of sensations, to arouse the liveliest of human emotions than once more to hear the familiar voices of the dead. Yet Science announces that this is possible, and can be done. That the voices of those who departed before the invention of the wonderful apparatus . . . are forever stilled is too obvious a truth; but whoever has spoken or whoever speaks into the mouthpiece of the phonograph . . . has the assurance that his speech may be reproduced audibly in his own tones long after he has turned to dust. . . . Speech has become immortal.[11]

Although providing a fascinating insight into the late-Victorian mind-set the editor had somewhat gilded the lily, as the phonograph Edison demonstrated was little more than a crude laboratory instrument. The indented tinfoil created an imperfect and impermanent record and the problems inherent in the tinfoil technology were obvious. Ten years later Edison recalled them in an interview,

> It weighed about one hundred pounds; it cost a mint to make; no one but an expert could get anything back from it; the record made by the little steel point upon a sheet of tin-foil lasted only a few times after it had been put through the phonograph. I myself doubted whether I should ever see a perfect phonograph. . . . But I was perfectly sure that if we did not accomplish this, the next generation would.[12]

Alexander Graham Bell reacted to the invention with anger and bitterness, writing to his father-in-law in February 1878, "It is a most astonishing thing to me that I could have possibly have let this invention slip through my fingers when I consider how my thoughts have been directed to this subject for so many years past. So nearly did I come to the idea that I had stated again and again in my public lectures the fundamental principles of the phonograph."[13] Whatever Bell felt about the unfairness of it all the laurels were with Edison who, in early 1878, obtained the first of his many US and British phonograph patents. These fundamental patents created a new art, embodying the principle of storing sound signals on cylinders, discs or tape.[14] Edison had clear opinions as to the potential of his phonograph, which he expressed in an 1878 *North American Review* article. They included "letter writing, and other forms of dictation, education, reader, music, family record; and such electrotype applications as books, musical boxes, toys, clocks, advertising and signal apparatus, speeches, etc."[15] Surprisingly, although he organised The Edison Speaking Phonograph Company he failed to develop the invention and, between 1879 and 1887, abandoned work on the phonograph altogether.

Commenting on the imperfections inherent within new inventions, such as the tin-foil phonograph, and the importance of innovation to bring new processes successfully to market, the historian of technology Nathan Rosenberg observed, "New techniques frequently require considerable *modification* before they can function successfully in a new environment. This process of modification often involves a high order of skill and ability, which is typically underestimated or ignored. Yet the capacity to achieve these modifications and adaptations is critical to the successful transfer of a technology."[16] Such was the case with the phonograph, and Edison's failure to improve and develop his remarkable invention permitted others to enter the field.

★   ★   ★

Between 1881 and 1885 Alexander Graham Bell and others developed many of the innovations needed to move Edison's concept towards commercial exploitation. Using the $10,000[17] French government Volta Prize awarded for the invention of the telephone, Bell created the Volta Laboratory in Washington, DC. There, with two partners known as Associates, Chichester A. Bell, a British chemist who was also Bell's cousin and Charles Sumner Tainter, a precision engineer and instrument maker, they examined a broad range of sound related problems. The Volta Laboratory was not a philanthropic enterprise; the whole idea was to engage in work that would show a profit. Bell summed up the situation, "We fully decided . . . to devote our time to something that would pay. . . . Upon looking over the ground Dr. C. A. Bell, Mr. Tainter and I decided that the most promising field of *joint* work would be to perfect the 'Phonograph' or 'Graphophone' or whatever we decide to call it."[18] The pioneering research by the Volta Associates is largely beyond the scope of this book.[19] Its principal achievements were the creation of permanent records by cutting sound signals into wax and a new kind of phonograph they called the Graphophone. The Volta Associates recognised the deficiencies of the

Edison tinfoil phonograph and undertook a complete rethink. The Volta laboratory and home notebooks chronicle wide-ranging activity including experiments with magnetic recording and photography; they also tried the Phonautograph method to cut sound signals on to discs, a process later taken up by Emile Berliner. As the recording medium they substituted a wax-coated card cylinder for tinfoil and, rather than indenting, they incised a sound signal into the wax material, thus creating a permanent sound record. Furthermore, the Associates devised more sensitive recording and reproducing mechanisms. In 1886 the Bells and Tainter were granted six patents, which became the foundation for the practical art of sound re-cording and upon which subsequent industrial formation was developed. Their US patent 341,214 *Recording and Reproducing Speech and Other Sounds* contained the key concept of cutting or engraving sound signals into wax tablets. It became central to the recording process and was the most litigated patent in the industry.[20]

In 1886 the Associates sold their patents to The Volta Graphophone Company for $200,000. Tainter and Chichester Bell each received $50,000, whilst Alexander Graham Bell retained the remaining $100,000; half for his original investment and half as an associate. Of this sum, Bell used $50,000 to create The Volta Bureau as an educational facility for the deaf and hard of hearing located at the Volta Laboratory site in Washington, DC, where its important work continues to the present. In the meantime, the overseas Bell-Tainter patents were sold for shares and $175,000 cash to a business called International Graphophone.[21] In 1887 The Volta Graphophone Company licenced the US Bell-Tainter patents to The American Graphophone Company by means of a stock exchange. This venture had been created to manufacture Graphophones as office-dictating machines. In January 1889 The Columbia Phonograph Company was established as a selling agency in Washington, DC, Delaware and Maryland. It had a share capital of $125,000, of which just $30,000 was actually subscribed.[22] Among its found-ers were two highly experienced stenographers, Edward Easton and Frank Dorian, who became major figures in the early recording industry on both sides of the Atlantic. As stenographers, Easton and Dorian also saw the utility of the technology to their profession and marketed it as an office-dictating machine. The Columbia Phonograph Company encountered initial success and had, by May 1890, rented out 372 machines. Although Columbia's ac-counts and rental data for this period have not survived, *The Phonogram,* an early trade journal, claimed its January 1889 revenue amounted to $110. In comparison, January figures for 1890 and 1891 stood at $1,563 and $3,720 respectively.[23] The overall effect of the Volta Associates innovations was to kick-start the processes of invention and innovation and with it was born a new industry. In an 1896 affidavit Charles Sumner Tainter, who alone of the Associates continued to work at improving the Graphophone observed, "In the eight years prior to our patents, there were but five patents issued in the USA relating to the recording and reproducing of sounds. In the eight years following the issue of our patents about 200 patents for improvements in this art were granted."[24] According to record industry historian, Allen Koenigsberg, "between 1877 . . . and 1912 . . . the US Patent Office granted more than 2,000 inventive (utility) patents to about 1,000 inventors in the sound recording field."[25]

Thomas Edison was outraged at the Bell-Tainter developments, referring to the Volta associates as "pirates" who were going to "deprive me of the honour of the invention."[26] During 1887 he angrily rebuffed a proposal to create a joint Edison-Graphophone venture. Edison realised he had been outmanoeuvred by the Bell-Tainter patents and was determined to regain the initiative. To this end he began developmental work on an improved phonograph, which came to fruition in 1888. The new Edison technology was a tremendous advance on the tinfoil phonograph of 1877, incorporating cylinder records of solid wax (rather than wax-coated card) and a battery-driven electric motor. Thereafter, Edison's output was prolific and he filed a total of 81 phonograph patents between 1887 and 1891.[27] These included a solid wax cylinder with a tapered internal bore (to allow the safe mounting and removal of the cylinder), improved engraving and reproducing styluses, more sensitive diaphragms and better design and engineering of the phonograph itself. These important contributions to the art allowed him to reenter the field as a manufacturer of records and phonographs, which helped market formation on both sides of the Atlantic. With greatly improved technology he too eschewed the potential of the phonograph as a medium for entertainment and instead saw it joining the telephone, telegraph, ticker tape, electric light and typewriter in the developing office revolution. Like the Graphophone it was to be put to use as an office dictating machine. However, to achieve this Edison needed a manufacturing and sales organisation capable of beating American Graphophone.

★ ★ ★

During the latter part of 1888 the Edison and American Graphophone ventures created rival manufacturing plants and marketing organisations. The products were designed for office rather than entertainment use, though this is unsurprising given the limitations of making and reproducing music records. Until the start of the twentieth century there was no moulding or cheap duplicating capacity and the narrow range of sound capable of being reproduced and low volume forced listeners to use rubber listening tubes resembling a physician's stethoscope. In addition, Edison did not pursue the music side to the business because he was unconvinced of the potential market and Easton and Dorian's original profession led them to see the Graphophone solely as an amanuensis. To match The American Graphophone manufactory at Bridgeport, Connecticut, Edison built his own $500,000 factory adjacent to his laboratory at West Orange, New Jersey, with machines and cylinder blanks in production at both plants by the autumn of 1888. According to American Graphophone annual reports for the years 1888 to 1890, 300 machines were made in 1888, 992 plus 126,715 cylinder blanks in 1889 and 2,817 during the first ten months of 1890. At this stage American Graphophone was profitable, making $2,010 in 1888, $43,270 in 1889 and on a turnover of $167,430, $68,263 in 1890.[28] Unfortunately there was trouble afoot for both parties. By July 1888 Edison's finances became overstretched due to production problems and to raise ready cash he sold his marketing rights for $500,000 to The American Phonograph Company. This was subsequently renamed North American Phonograph Company, and its assets were then acquired by venture capitalist Jesse Lippincott.[29] Prior to the deal Lippincott had paid $200,000 for the Graphophone marketing rights, which gave him monopoly selling rights to both the Edison and Bell-Tainter technologies in the US. North American Phonograph did not itself trade; rather it franchised local companies to lease machines for a fee of $40 per year.[30]

As it turned out neither the Edison phonographs nor the Bell-Tainter Graphophones proved sufficiently robust to withstand everyday office use and most were returned after the leases ran out. Industry pioneer Alfred Clark, who worked for North American in 1889, later wrote of this period and its problems, "Business firms would rent them for a year, at the end of which time they were almost invariably sent back, and of course, the one year's rent was not nearly sufficient to enable Mr Lippincott to pay the factory for the cost of the machine. So things went from bad to worse."[31] Both Edison and Tainter worked to improve their respective products, but to little avail. Quite simply they had been marketed too soon, victims of a desire to obtain a quick return on capital and to dish the competition. Failure to iron out the bugs resulted in a fiasco for both manufacturers and a disaster for North American Phonograph and most local franchisees. In November 1890 Lippincott became seriously ill, left the business and subsequently died. His successor was Thomas Edison, who was also chief creditor. Beset by bugs, the Graphophone soon went out of production, leaving the Edison phonograph the only product in the field. At this point, surviving local companies turned from leasing to selling phonographs for entertainment purposes, although for reasons described above the machines were unsuited to this purpose. Nonetheless, despite the initial scepticism, Edison responded to demand by producing up to 200 music cylinders per day. This all ended in January 1891, when Edison closed the West Orange recording room and dismissed the staff.[32] In this vacuum the surviving local franchisees began producing their own music records and, in the process, brought into the fledgling industry several key figures who later became recording engineers and artist and repertoire managers.

On 6 August 1894, in the midst of a deep economic recession and in a move that dogged him for years, Edison threw North American into receivership, though by this time most franchisees had gone out of business. Paradoxically between 1894 and 1896, a number of bankruptcy court orders prevented Edison from selling phonographs and records in the United States. In 1895 Edison acquired the remaining North American assets and, in January 1896, formed a marketing organisation he called National Phonograph Company Inc.[33] The primary market for this venture was not the office-dictating machine, but rather the by now profitable coin-in-the-slot and home entertainment music cylinder business. With this new venture and almost twenty years after his original invention Edison was in a position to manufacture and sell phonographs and cylinder records in the USA and, as a consequence, cut out local franchisees. This and moves made by the Graphophone interests left the US market once again controlled by patent holders and it remained largely that way until 1921.

The formation of National Phonograph Company Inc committed Edison to the home entertainment market. To this end he made music records and created an inexpensive phonograph called, appropriately, the "Home." Initially the "Home" cost $40.00 but was reduced to $30.00 in 1897. It incorporated a clockwork motor and a black japanned metal horn. This replaced the cumbersome rubber listening tubes, which had limited the number of people able to listen to the record at any one time and therefore the utility of the instrument for home entertainment.[34] Although Edison marketed phonographs and music cylinders in the US, he was unable to do so in Britain because he had sold his overseas recording patents in 1890. This subsequently became the source of much vexation to him.[35]

In the wake of the North American collapse, American Graphophone needed what proved to be the first of many financial reconstructions. In May 1894 a new venture was created, the clumsily named Columbia

Phonograph Company General, as a joint venture with the Washington, DC–based sales company Columbia Phonograph Company, which pre-dated and had survived the North American fiasco. The new management team was Edward Easton, Frank Dorian and other Columbia Phonograph Company executives and although the business had a $100,000 capital, in fact only $4,000 was actually subscribed. Thus, although it was an impressive paper company, there was and remained an underlying financial weakness. In 1901, for example, Columbia was losing large amounts of money which it stemmed by severe cost cutting, dismissing staff and offering special discounts to dealers. Columbia also milked its profitable European branch.[36] Whatever the long-term weaknesses, Columbia Phonograph Company General, based in New York, had become sole selling agent for American Graphophone and with a range of new products it looked to develop the lucrative market in home entertainment.

Although North American failed, its period of activity had a number of positive effects. Of key importance to industrial development it was, through its franchised subcompanies, the first to create markets for music records. It also created a market for instruments and by doing so heightened public awareness of the technology. As a consequence, this shallow but broadly based market quickly revealed technical deficiencies to manufacturers, which forced them to develop better and more reliable machines and improve the sound quality of records. Furthermore, as exclusive selling agent to both Edison and American Graphophone, the North American setup avoided patent litigation between the rivals. Of lasting importance, North American attracted into the business many of the men and women who went on to dominate the early-twentieth-century record industry as entrepreneurs, businessmen, performers or engineers. In the final analysis, North American's greatest contribution to the industry it helped form was the creation of the music record business.[37]

The survival of Columbia Phonograph and other local North American franchisees can be accounted for by a combination of high quality machine servicing, and by the increasingly important entertainment market.[38] Initially, music records were sold as a coin–in–the–slot barroom entertainment, though no detailed data as to the number of such phonographs have survived. Record industry historian Tim Brooks has suggested that by November 1890 Columbia had rented more than one hundred such machines with figures of one hundred and twenty-six in April 1891 and one hundred and forty in November.[39] Edward Easton writing in an early trade journal *The Phonogram* in November 1890 said, "We have more than one hundred nickel-in-the-slot phonographs on exhibition in the various drug stores, hotels, depots etc, in our territory, and find these machines profitable."[40] Brooks also suggests that by late 1892 or early 1893 machines were being offered for rental at $150 per annum or outright sale for $250. As the North American franchisees went bust, phonographs were sold at rock-bottom prices and found their way into the burgeoning entertainment market on both sides of the Atlantic. It has proved possible to locate record lists or catalogues from as early as 1889, suggesting the willingness of the more enterprising North American Phonograph franchisees to diversify into what was clearly a more profitable area of commerce; for more on how this point applied to Britain see chapter 2.[41]

Writing in the mid-1940s Fred Gaisberg,[42] a pioneer recording engineer, performer and maker of early music records, wrote about Columbia's offices on Pennsylvania Avenue, Washington, DC. Of the ground floor, he said it was a "nickel-in-the-slot audition room" where customers could listen to and select records, the other rooms were used as offices and a recording studio. He also claimed that this business was very successful.[43] By the early 1890s, therefore, sound recording wasn't simply a part of the downtown Columbia office or its barroom "jukebox" customers, it featured in fairgrounds, was touted around the United States by hucksters and could be found in that short-lived vogue, the phonograph parlour. Gaisberg recalled those days in his memoirs:

> Showmen and fairs demanded records of songs and instrumental music. Phonographs, each equipped with ten sets of ear-tubes through which the sound passed, had been rented to these exhibitors. It was ludicrous in the extreme to see ten people grouped about a phonograph, each with a tube leading from his ears, grinning and laughing at what he heard. It was a fine advertisement for the onlookers waiting their turn. Five cents was collected from each listener, so the showman could afford to pay $2 or $3 for a cylinder to exhibit.[44]

The failure of manufacturers to innovate in the crucial growth area of the music record business affected industrial development. Critically, until 1901, there was no effective process for making multiple copies of cylinder records.[45] That said, from the early 1890s, it was possible to duplicate cylinders mechanically by transferring the vibrations from a recorded cylinder with a pantograph-like device on to a blank cylinder running parallel to the first. It was slow, clumsy and limited, as both Edison and American Graphophone needed large numbers of duplicating machines to meet growing demand for music records. In 1901 it was reported that American Graphophone had around five hundred such duplicating machines at its Bridgeport factory.[46] Until mass production of moulded cylinders began at the turn of the twentieth century, the cylinder market was severely limited by the number of copies available from an original record. Of the performing artists who were prepared to make records at this time, Alfred Clark wrote:

> The companies were unable to supply records at a popular price and at the same time by reasonably good artists. At this stage of development only one record would result from an artist singing one song into the horn. By dint of careful arrangement, four horns were later arranged with four machines in front of a singer and a maximum of four records was the result. Obviously artists willing to accept such fees and put up with the tiresome experience of singing the same song over again, could hardly be classified as "stars." On the contrary, they were selected less for their artistic ability than for the strength of their voice, for the recording machines were not very sensitive and the best records were those made by singers who could make the most noise.[47]

Fred Gaisberg described his experiences and those of his friend Charles Gregory working for Columbia, "We have many memories of those Washington days in common: memories deeply embedded in our youthful minds. Often we meet for lunch and recall the great names of those cylinder days—to us they were stars without equal: George J. Gaskin, Len Spencer, Billy Golden, Johnnie Myers, Dan Quinn, George W. Johnson and the prince of all, Russell Hunting."[48] Russell Hunting was indeed another key American and later European industry pioneer, whose presence enlivens the early pages of this book. He made the transition from actor to self-taught recording engineer and performer working for a while at The New England Phonograph Company, one of the North American franchisees, and then other companies. Fred Gaisberg described him as "the star attraction of the phonograph parlours." He recorded a number of rapid-fire crosstalk comedy monologues, playing a host of different characters; the best remembered being Michael Jeremiah Casey, the deaf cantankerous old Irish-American judge with an eye for the ladies. Casey also appeared in other guises, such as "Casey taking the census."[49] Gaisberg claimed "Thomas A. Edison became very fond of Hunting and Berliner found his company a tremendous tonic."[50] There was another side to Russell Hunting, who had a nice line in homemade risqué (and to some obscene) recordings which he sold to bars and taverns in New York and elsewhere for $1.50 apiece. This product line was very successful, though it got him into serious trouble. In 1896 he fell foul of Anthony Comstock, the secretary of

The New York Society for the Suppression of Vice. In what was possibly the first example of record censorship the case was reported in the *New York Times* and other local newspapers. Comstock claimed he spent two years clamping down on people exhibiting phonographs playing such records and trying to find the record maker. On 24 June 1896, having identified Hunting and an associate, Charles M. Casson, he had both of them arrested and arraigned before a New York police court. During what was a sting operation the police seized a total of fifty-three "obscene" recordings. The pair were charged with producing records "containing vile songs and stories" and sent for trial to a superior court. The case was heard on 30 June 1896, and although newspaper reports claimed Hunting was sentenced to three months in prison, the court records tell of a quite different outcome. In fact he and Casson pleaded guilty, were given suspended sentences and discharged. Russell Hunting continued his career as a recording engineer and was for a time editor of the trade journal *The Phonoscope*. He then went on to a successful career not just in the US, but also in Britain and France.[51]

There are few surviving details of individual record sales at this stage of industrial development. US record industry historian Tim Brooks suggests that in 1892 one best-selling artist accounted for sales of about 5,000 cylinder records. The Library of Congress has an 1894 copyright sheet music deposit called *The Whistling Coon* which claims sales of 50,000 recordings of this song; it is however quite impossible to verify that or any other claims.[52] *The Phonoscope* advertised cylinder records by named artists, claiming the number of "original" records made; the November 1896 edition carried an advertisement claiming "Russell Hunting *original records* 80 cents each. There have been over 50,000 manufactured and shipped to all parts of the English speaking world." In the same issue another advertisement asserted "Dan W. Quinn made over 300 records for the US Phonograph Co each week for two years . . . made 1,500 records for the New England Company . . . made 5,000 records for the Ohio and other Companies."[53]

In 1895 Thomas Hood MacDonald, the chief engineer at American Graphophone designed a home entertainment Graphophone known as the "Eagle," which retailed at $10.00; the ten-dollar US gold coin is emblazoned with an eagle. The "Eagle" was powered by a spring motor and like the Edison "Home" phonograph it sported a horn so it could be heard by everyone in a room. It was also capable of playing both Edison and Columbia cylinders. The transformation of sound recording equipment from an office-dictating into a domestic entertainment machine was complete. Although they looked different, the "Eagle" and other Graphophones were technically similar virtually from Edison's "Home" and later range of phonographs. Both utilised Edison's solid wax cylinder principle. As a result, both Graphophone and phonograph cylinders could be played on either machine, creating an industry standard. These developments did not end the manufacture of office dictating equipment, but the sector was tiny compared to the music record industry. Both Edison and American Graphophone continued to manufacture and market the "Ediphone" and "Dictaphone," which used cylinder technology, until the 1940s. Although the "Ediphone" business was sold on, the "Dictaphone" brand continues to manufacture office-dictating and other office equipment, but neither is associated with the entertainment record industry.[54]

The post North American period ended the uneasy truce between the Edison Phonograph Works and American Graphophone. As the domestic record business grew and profits were realised, each company engaged in bruising litigation with the intent of driving the other from the field. This litigation tested not just the Bell-Tainter master patent for cutting sound signals into wax cylinders, but also Edison's solid wax cylinder patents and other important innovations. In the end little was achieved, beyond the enrichment of lawyers. The litigation finally ended in 1901 with consent decrees and cross-licensing agreements, which created a patent pool, an outcome that recognised the interlocking nature of the Bell-Tainter and Edison patents and entrenched the industry in the hands of the patent holders. This outcome avoided what would have been a costly and uncertain resolution of the differences, and it enabled both businesses to develop markets in the USA and Europe.[55] However, by this time the potentially lucrative market for music recordings was being successfully challenged by a totally new system of sound recording, Emile Berliner's disc Gramophone.

★   ★   ★

The invention of sound recording during the last quarter of the nineteenth century was mainly achieved by men with established scientific records in the field of acoustics and access to research laboratories. However, the development of what became the industry standard of recording for much of the twentieth century was achieved by someone with little scientific standing, who worked alone and without the benefit of a well-equipped laboratory; he was Emile Berliner. This apparently marginal figure demonstrated the limitations of the Edison process of indenting sound signals on to tin foil and the Bell-Tainter process of cutting a vertical or hill-and-dale sound signal into wax cylinders. He then created the principles of a simple and effective recording technology that was used until the end of long playing record production in the late 1980s, and a method of duplication by pressing still used in the manufacture of CDs and DVDs.

Emile Berliner was born in Hanover, Germany, in 1851 and emigrated to the United States where, in 1871, he became a citizen. He attended school in Germany till he was fourteen and although he spent some time at Cooper Union in New York (it is uncertain whether he was a student or simply taught himself using its facilities), that was as far as his formal education went. In the United States he found employment as a shop worker and came to the science of acoustics by the same route as Bell and Edison, the telephone. In 1877, this remarkable man, working alone in a Washington, DC, boarding house, and with little more than the self-taught rudiments of electricity and physics, invented the "loose contact" microphone which was used in the Bell telephone, transforming that invention into a commercially viable proposition. As Berliner could not afford the lawyers' fees, he drafted the patent specification. The Bell Telephone Corporation paid him $50,000 for this innovation. Between 1879 and 1884 Berliner worked for Bell Telephone as an experimenter, overseeing the manufacture of his microphones.

Back in Washington, DC, Berliner turned his attention to the problems of sound recording.[56] Over the next four years he developed those elements of the system that dominated much of the twentieth century record industry. These incorporated a disc record with a spiral groove of even depth that contained the sound signal and was strong enough to carry the weight of a reproducing stylus, sound box and horn. The latter innovation obviated the need for a separate feed-screw, as used in the phonograph and Graphophone. The Berliner record had a zigzag sound signal (as did the Phonautograph) cut into the walls of the groove. Most importantly, and a decade and a half before cylinders could be produced from moulds, it was possible to apply the existing art of electrotyping to turn Berliner's original recordings into metal negatives from which copies could be printed into plastic material on a steam press. Until 1925, when microphones and electrical amplifiers were introduced into the recording studio, cutting disc and cylinder records remained a purely mechanical process requiring a performer to sing or play into a horn, which focused the sound on to a diaphragm connected to the cutting stylus. This stylus cut both the groove and the sound into the revolving wax. The machine on which his discs were played Berliner called the Gramophone.[57]

Berliner came to these developments by reevaluating the fundamental principles of sound recording. Unfortunately his laboratory notebooks have not survived, and without these it is difficult to assess Berliner's method of working.[58] However, by reference to accounts in contemporary news-papers, journals and other literature it is possible to gain insights into his process of reasoning and invention.[59] From these it is clear Berliner realised the fundamental flaws in both the Bell-Tainter method of cutting sound signals, the vertical or hill-and-dale cut, and the original Edison process of indenting signals into the floor of the recording material. As he observed in a November 1887 interview in *The Electrical World*:

> The resistance of any material to indentation increases faster than the depth of the indentation, it follows that a vibration of greater amplitude of the stylus meets with a disproportionately greater resistance than a vi-bration of smaller amplitude. . . . With a view of overcoming this defect, attempts have been made to engrave, instead of indent, a record of the vibrations by employing a stylus, shaped and operated like a chisel . . . even in this case the disturbing causes . . . are still present.[60]

On the same occasion Berliner described how these difficulties could be overcome by employing the lateral or zigzag sound wave principles of The Scott Phonautograph. In early experiments Berliner tried fixing the sound signal by a process of photoengraving on glass discs.[61] He later developed a more effective method, using an acid etching process on wax-covered zinc plates. Berliner was forced to adopt this method to avoid in-fringing the impregnable Bell-Tainter master wax-cutting patent 341,214, though he recognised that cutting sound signals into wax discs was the way forward in the art.

Berliner's Gramophone was launched at the May 1888 meeting of The Franklin Institute, which was a learned society based in Philadelphia. On that occasion he gave a paper entitled *The Gramophone: Etching the Hu-man Voice*.[62] In it Berliner described and demonstrated how he created an etching ground by cutting a zigzag sound signal laterally on to the surface of a highly polished zinc plate covered with wax in a benzene-based suspen-sion. He then immersed the exposed plate into etching fluid, observing that "The lines will be eaten in and the result will be a groove of even depth, such as is required for reproduction."[63] Berliner then described his other innovations, concluding his paper with a prophetic speculation as to the future of the record industry (cited at the start of this chapter).

In 1889 Berliner visited Germany where he exhibited his Gramo-phone and records and tried unsuccessfully to raise capital for its develop-ment. While in Germany he demonstrated his invention to men of science and commerce, conducted experiments and, with others, overcame some of the problems relating to precision electrotyping of master records. The only apparent commercial gain was a contract with a firm of toy makers, Kämmer und Reinhardt in Waltershausen, to manufacture and market Gramophones, records and a talking doll. During the 1890s these were the first Berliner records and Gramophones to be sold in Britain; there is evidence of disc records and Gramophones being hired out for public entertainment in Britain.[64] He returned to the USA without the hoped-for capital. Berliner had a brilliant concept, but undercapitalised and with a crude technology found it frustratingly difficult to make progress. Expressing this in an 1890 paper to the American Institute of Electrical Engineers, the inventor said, "The work of gradually bringing the Gramophone up to the present state has been exceedingly tedious. Working out telephones or transmitters is child's-play in the face of the traps and Jack-o'-lanterns which beset the experiments in talking machines."[65] The same year, according to Alfred Clark, Berliner offered the Gramophone to North American Phonograph but was turned down. In 1892 he formed The American Gramophone Company, which appears never to have conducted business.[66] In the following year The United States Gramophone Company appeared as a vehicle to hold his patents and market his Gramophones and discs. With inadequate capital and a deficient hand-cranked Gramophone, he experienced little success. In the autumn of 1894 Berliner estimated he sold a mere 1,000 machines and 25,000 disc records.[67] In 1895, after a further Franklin Institute demonstration, he interested a group of Philadelphia venture capitalists sufficiently to form The Berliner Gramophone Company to manufacture and market machines and records. The United States Gramophone Company sold on its rights to The Berliner Company in return for cash, stock and royalties; it was not a success.[68]

According to Alfred Clark, The Berliner Gramophone Company was poorly capitalised and not particularly competent. Of them, Clark said, "The management of The Berliner Company was so backward that we had despaired of any progress coming from that quarter."[69] Furthermore, it had inadequate products and no marketing strategy. The business tried The North American Phonograph formula of franchising subcompanies, but in the end only two were taken up. One failed but the other, The New York Gramophone Company, selling into the lucrative New York and New Jersey markets, proved successful. This business was owned by an advertising executive, Frank Seaman, and in October 1896 he and The Berliner Company concluded an agreement giving Seaman an exclusive contract to sell Berliner products throughout the United States. In the short term this agreement undoubtedly saved The Berliner Company, though it proved disastrous in the longer term.

By the mid-1890s, the evidence suggests Berliner had hit the limits of his engineering skills. He was incapable of effecting the innovations required to develop the Gramophone and a more satisfactory recording process; the only commercial Gramophone available was his original hand-cranked model.[70] Furthermore, the ingenious zinc etched process of recording had serious shortcomings; the acid that ate into the etching ground had a habit of seeping into the adjoining wax-covered surface, resulting in an erosion of sound quality. As it turned out help was at hand. In 1896 The Berliner Company, in a move that had dramatic long-term implications for the Gramophone and the industry on both sides of the Atlantic, approached Eldridge Reeves Johnson, a Camden, New Jersey, jobbing machinist,[71] to help redesign the Gramophone. He wrote of his first encounter with the machine, "The little instrument was badly designed. It sounded much like a partially educated parrot with a sore throat and a cold in the head. But the wheezy instrument caught my attention and held it fast and hard. I became interested in it as I had never been interested before in anything."[72] Johnson had the precision engineering skills necessary to provide the breakthrough. He was so prolific that, between 1898 and 1921, his innovations resulted in seventy-two US patents. Within a decade, the combination of Johnson's engineering skills, business flair and an uncanny ability to hire and delegate to able subordinates, enabled him to create mass markets for talking machines and disc records. His contribution to industrial formation on both sides of the Atlantic was substantial.

In 1896 Johnson, with the help of an engineer called Levi Montross, redesigned the Berliner Gramophone with an improved clockwork motor and, with help from Alfred Clark, a new and more sensitive sound box. In 1897 The Berliner Company placed its first order for 200 instruments, which they paid $4.00 each. This Gramophone gained an altogether unexpected immortality when, two years later, the British artist Francis Barraud adopted it for the painting of *His Master's Voice*, which eventually became an important international record industry trademark. In 1897 Emile Berliner sent William Barry Owen[73] (sales director of Seaman's National Gramophone Company) to London to begin a British and European trade in gramophone products. The venture he created became The Gramophone Company Ltd and is discussed in chapters 2 and 5. This chapter examines the impact this business had on US happenings before 1903. It was during this period that the first and determining relationships between the British and American companies were formed.

In 1898, despite the innovations, production of the new Gramophone remained focused on the tiny Johnson workshop in Camden, New Jersey.

An early employee was Harry O. Sooy, who later recalled the trouble he encountered trying to find the workshop and of getting a job there:

> I had the price for the ferry in my jeans and reached Front and Federal streets, Camden, N.J—it was then I found there was no south Front street in the city—so I started north, reading every sign in sight on both sides of the street. The first block was covered and no sign of "Johnson's Shop." I started on the second block still going north on Front street, I had not gone far beyond Market street when I saw a sign which read "Eldridge R. Johnson's Machine Shop, 108 North Front Street." The sign was surely large enough to be seen all right, but on arriving at this number I found it was [the Collings] carriage factory, and upon making inquiry as to where the shop was located, I learned it was a little building in the rear of this carriage factory; then, I wasn't very much surprised I didn't find it on my first trip.[74]

Sooy believed he was only the eighteenth employee of the Eldridge R. Johnson Machine Shop. As he remembered, "And, after sizing up the place for a couple of days, I could not see how it could possibly exist very long. The shop was a one storey building about 25' × 70' in which were the Machine Shop and Boiler and Engine Room." It was a hand-to-mouth existence. Sooy's starting wage was $12.00 per week, raised after ten weeks to $14.00. By the end of the year Sooy was doing more specialist work for which he was paid piece rates adding an extra $6 to $10 to his regular wage, making his an average skilled US engineering wage of the time.[75] Sales of the new Gramophone grew rapidly and quickly outgrew the workshop. In 1899 Johnson built a four-storey brick factory on the same site. He used the fourth storey as a recording studio and an experimental machine shop, described by Sooy as "a place he could have his mechanical ideas worked out under his own supervision."[76] These facilities were used to develop Johnson's own recording method using wax rather than Berliner's zinc-etching process. It was here he built the cutting lathes, matrix plant and other technology required to make the new records. Johnson did not apply for patents, which he was unlikely to gain because of the priority of the Bell-Tainter patents; rather he maintained the process as a trade secret.

The United States Gramophone Company's 1898 annual report claimed Johnson was manufacturing 600 Gramophones per week for The Berliner Gramophone Company.[77] As a result, The Berliner Gramophone Company earnings grew from $12,240 for the seven months to March 1897 to $40,000 for the year ending March 1898. It seemed that the

Gramophone and its disc records had reached takeoff. As a bullish Berliner wrote to Alfred Clark, who was working for Edison's export business, "if we don't knock out wax cylinder records by our latest Gramophone discs then your name ain't Clark."[78] Table 1.1 provides a consolidation of Gramophone and Berliner-Victor record sales data for the decade 1893 to 1903 and compares it with Edison phonograph and cylinder production for the same period. Unfortunately, comparable data relating to The Columbia Phonograph Company General has not survived, nor do these figures indicate whether exports are included.

The lack of American Graphophone figures is problematic, though evidence suggests that, at least in 1901, production figures were comparatively low. In a letter to William Edgar Gilmore, president of Edison's National Phonograph Company Inc, American Graphophone's weekly production figures were put at no more than one hundred Disc Graphophones and a mere 7,000 discs and 65,000 cylinder records, and the business was in deep financial trouble.[79] As the data in table 1.1 suggest, despite the lack of firm American Graphophone data or the size of its export markets, it has been possible to examine American record industry production figures for the closing years of the nineteenth and start of the twentieth century. There are in addition data in *The United States Census of Manufactures for 1900.* These show an enormous growth in production during that year,

Table 1.1.   United States Production Figures, 1893–1903: Edison Phonographs and Cylinder Records and Berliner-Victor Gramophones and Disc Records

Year	Edison Phonographs	Berliner/Johnson Gramophones	Edison Records	Berliner Records
1893–95	NA	1,000[a]	NA	27,000
1896	1,239	NA	NA	100,000
1897	5,167	12,420	87,690	248,652
1898	14,255	10,651[b]	428,310	713,753
1899	46,097	14,348	1,886,137	569,154
1900	41,894	3,054[c]	2,080,132	255,784
1901	41,381	7,570	1,976,645	256,908
1902	80,257	42,110	4,382,802	1,696,296
1903	113,151	46,601	7,663,142	1,966,036

Source: Data relating to pre-1900 disc production are derived from *Frank Seaman v Berliner Gramophone Company,* US Circuit Court, Western District of Virginia, 1 Nov 1900. Phonograph production figures are taken from Raymond Wile *Antique Phonograph Monthly,* March 1973. Disc machine sales compiled from Benjamin L. Aldridge, "Sales by Class of Product," in *The Victor Talking Machine Company* (New York: RCA, 1964), 109. Disc sales data post-1901 cited in Michael W. Sherman, *The Paper Dog* (New York: APM Press, 1987), 43.

[a]Autumn of 1894 only.
[b]Nine months only.
[c]January to April only.

with the industry employing $3.3 million in capital; production volumes of $2.2 million and employment standing at 1,411. Total production for 1899 stood at 151,403 talking machines of all kinds with a value of $1.2 million, and the number of records at 2,763,277 records, valued at $539,370.[80] The number of machines manufactured by Edison and Johnson in 1899 was 60,445, leaving 90,458 machines accounted for by the export trade, American Graphophone and other minor manufacturers. Similarly, if the 2,455,291 records manufactured by Berliner and Edison in 1899 are subtracted from the census figures, then the 307,986 records remaining must be the American Graphophone production, plus records sent for export and other manufacturers.

Table 1.1 figures reveals the impact of the years between 1899 and 1901, when the US disc record and Gramophone business unravelled in a sea of bitter recrimination, sharp practice and costly litigation, the resolution of which saw the integration of the Berliner-Johnson enterprises and the creation of a new patent-based oligopoly with the two other manufacturers, which kept the US industry in its hands until 1921. It must be remembered that Johnson had a contract with The Berliner Gramophone Company to manufacture Gramophones. The Berliner Gramophone Company created the original disc recordings and made the metal negatives, which were sent to contract pressers who manufactured the records. In turn, The Berliner Gramophone Company had an exclusive marketing contract with Frank Seaman, who established The National Gramophone Company in New York in 1896 as a selling and distributive business. Thus both Berliner and Johnson were dependent on Seaman's orders for Gramophones and records to keep their respective businesses going.

In 1899 Seaman, having failed to obtain better margins from The Berliner Company, created The Universal Talking Machine Company (and later The Universal Talking Machine Manufacturing Company) to manufacture and sell patent-infringing machines and disc records under the mark "Zonophone."[81] Interestingly, the Zonophone talking machine was designed by Levi Montross who had previously helped Johnson create the improved Gramophone. In 1901 Frederick Marion Prescott formed The International Zonophone Company GmbH in Berlin.[82] Prescott was another American pioneer record industry entrepreneur and International Zonophone was largely owned and acted as the export arm of Universal. In May 1900 The Berliner Gramophone Company responded to these challenges by cutting off Seaman's supply of Berliner discs and Gramophones and started their own marketing organisation. To force The Berliner Gramophone Company to comply with the earlier agreement, Seaman

entered suit against them.[83] Seaman also strengthened his position, concluding a licensing deal with American Graphophone, which manufactured
cylinder records using the wax-cutting Bell-Tainter patents but wanted to
break into the disc market.[84] In the summer of 1900, Seaman and American
Graphophone obtained judgments preventing Berliner from marketing his
invention in the United States. This left Johnson, who had invested heavily
in factory extensions and was totally dependent on orders from Berliner,
high and dry. To overcome this, Johnson created his own US selling organisation, The Consolidated Talking Machine Company. The marketing
situation in the USA, and by extension Britain and continental Europe,
reached a critical point in the spring of 1901. The Berliner Company was
subject to an injunction from Seaman, and Johnson was the subject of legal
action by both Seaman and American Graphophone.[85] Johnson wrote a
long and thoughtful letter to Owen in London.

> I don't believe from your letters that you thoroughly appreciate the
> condition of the talking machine business on this side and its relation
> to your side. . . . I am in the midst of a most desperate fight which is
> made all the more difficult for me because I am looking out for your
> interests as well as the others. I could make terms with Seaman and
> the Graphophone Co which would relieve me of all my important law
> suits, but such an action . . . would be fatal to the Berliner interests
> on this side. It would also increase your troubles as to the invasion of
> your territories.[86]

In 1900, The Berliner Company circumvented the Seaman injunction
by various means, including confusion, reorganising as The Consolidated
Talking Machine Company *of America* (author's italics). At the same time
The Berliner Gramophone Company merged with the nontrading United
States Gramophone Company. It may well be that Johnson colluded with
his partners in this confusion of names. Also in 1900, Eldridge Johnson
hired Leon Forrest Douglass as general manager of Consolidated.[87] In 1900,
according to Douglass, Johnson told him the machine shop and record
plant was worth about $60,000 and Johnson had $5,000 in cash. With these
slender resources Douglass restarted the business, advertising in national
weekly and monthly mass circulation magazines including *McClure's*, *Cos-
mopolitan* and *Munsey's*. This extensive campaign included the offer of free
records.[88] Years later Douglass recalled the heady days of 1900:

> In the beginning Mr. Johnson left everything pertaining to sales, ad-
> vertising, and recording to me. Mr. Johnson came over to Philadelphia

every day and for many years we lunched together. At that time he was a shy man but had the most brilliant mind I have ever known. . . . When we first started the business, I had only one helper, Oliver Jones. For $15 a week he kept the books and wrote my letters. . . . When we received an order we rushed into the shed that we used as a packing room, packed the goods, rushed back to the office, billed and did other office work. The next month we rented a small office in Philadelphia in the Stephen Girard Building, Room #1313 on the 13th floor. We employed a stenographer, Miss Alice Hargraves, who stayed with us 25 years. We also hired a man as shipping clerk for the shed in Camden.[89]

These moves caused strains between Johnson and Berliner, and to exploit them Seaman tried to bring an injunction against Johnson. Although Seaman's attempt at preventing the new venture selling its products failed, he did succeed in one important aspect, preventing Johnson from using the term "Gramophone" to describe his products. As a consequence the term fell from use in the United States but not elsewhere, specifically in Britain.

★   ★   ★

Between 1898 and 1903, and in the midst of the increasingly confused legal situation, a number of unsuccessful proposals were made to consolidate the various US and the new British gramophone interests. All were made at the instigation of the American businesses, which wished to capitalise on London's strength and resolve the impasse in the United States. All failed, because the British partner proved an unwilling suitor. In these years The Gramophone Company enjoyed a number of clear advantages over the various US enterprises. It had record pressing facilities, wealthy directors with ready access to additional capital and a strong effective management and marketing team, something conspicuously absent from the American businesses in the 1890s.[90] The first merger attempt occurred in 1898, against the collapsing Seaman and Berliner marketing agreement. The British manager William Barry Owen and his British investor visited America where they acquired a licence from Berliner and an option on his European patents. Berliner needed cash, which he gained from the sale of products to the British venture together with the stock and dividend payments. It was not just the financial gain, for by this arrangement he and Johnson had, at little cost or risk, succeeded in breaking into a new and valuable market. During the same visit, Seaman and his associate Orville La Dow tried to persuade Owen to abandon Berliner and enter into an association with their business. This move failed, as did Seaman's attempt to kill the London business by cutting off supplies of products and persuading a rival cylinder record manufacturer to initiate patent-infringement proceedings against them. These issues are discussed in chapters 2 and 5.[91]

This bid to consolidate all the elements of the transatlantic Gramophone business (which consisted of the Johnson factory and business, The Berliner Company and The Gramophone Company), was made in 1900. Details of the negotiations have not survived. However, comments in his letters to his wife explain his attitude towards the business. In February 1900 he observed:

> [I] am under the impression that the consolidation has none too good a chance to go through. I have suggested that I might sell if the price was made satisfactory to me, and Owen seemed much pleased. It would no doubt be better all around and relieve me of the danger of losses in case things should go smash. Mr Seaman and his crowd are with Williams and Owen. They are willing to come in but I think it is a case of coming in out of the wet.[92]

Why this consolidation failed remains a mystery. Had it gone through, The Gramophone Company would have acquired an instrument-manufacturing capacity, together with Johnson's services and access to the potentially inexhaustible US market, without paying punitive import taxes. With greater financial assets and a proven marketing team the British business was immeasurably stronger than the US concerns. Adding to the pressure on The Gramophone Company was the appearance at this time of Zonophone imports in Europe.[93] A combination would have given the new enterprise additional strength to fight this competition on both continents.

Although Leon Douglass's selling strategy worked, the overall marketing situation in the USA and Europe reached a critical point in the spring of 1901 with The Berliner Company subject to an injunction from Seaman and Johnson to legal action by both Seaman and American Graphophone. Johnson wrote to Owen:

> I note . . . that you are interested in the proposition you cabled me sometime ago concerning my selling departments and US patents. . . . I shall never separate my talking machine patents from the factory, for if I dispose of one I must dispose of both. . . . If you wish to get control of the talking machine business on this side, I can sell you the key, which would be composed of three things. First, the factory, second my patents and laboratory, and third, my selling department.[94]

Johnson was also thinking beyond his present impasse, "If I could, I would like to purchase the stock of The Berliner Company but I have so far formulated no plan."[95] The Seaman injunction against The Berliner Gramophone Company left Johnson seriously exposed. Previous to it the bulk of his output had been purchased by The Berliner Company, the balance being exported to The Gramophone Company. Johnson was confident he controlled the key patents and, with Leon Douglass, had the organisation to develop the business.[96] He wrote to Owen, "I believe that eventually I can make it very difficult for anyone to manufacture a good gramophone in this country. . . . I believe I can do a big business."[97]

If the early attempts at consolidation did not succeed, neither did Seaman's and American Graphophone's attempts at stifling the Johnson-Berliner enterprises. Matters were finally resolved in July 1901. Johnson cabled to Owen "Berliner Company thrown over Seaman injunction dissolved appeal dismissed. Seaman completely defeated. I must decide on policy quickly. If you have any suggestions to make it must be prompt and decided to meet the new situation. Disaster however if business leaves my control."[98] This development brought the British executives back to the United States. They offered The Consolidated Talking Machine Company of America 25 per cent of the stock in a proposed new Anglo-American Gramophone enterprise in exchange for the US Berliner patents and other assets. Johnson responded, offering Consolidated a 40 per cent stake in a new venture, The Victor Talking Machine Company. This offer was accepted, thus combining the US Berliner-Johnson patents.[99] Details of these negotiations survive only in the Johnson letters to his wife for August and September 1901. In one he remarked, "It looks as if I shall be a gentleman in about thirty days. . . . This business is going to be a magnificent enterprise and I find that I have drifted into the habit of being very proud of it."[100] Of his discussions with The Gramophone Company, "there is a big contract to close covering the manufacture of foreign goods and it may not be completed. There is little doubt that things will go through and E. R. Johnson Machinist will be a thing of the past."[101]

The European manufacturing contract was a key building block on which Johnson secured the new business. This consolidation created a new venture called the Victor Talking Machine Company. Eldridge Johnson became president and Emile Berliner received stock for his patents and withdrew from the US business, but he did retain a controlling interest in The Berliner Gramophone Company of Canada and was a shareholder in The Gramophone Company Ltd.[102] The Victor consolidation provided the springboard, launching the Gramophone and disc records into mass markets. In its first full year of trading, net sales amounted to $1.9 million and profits stood at $618,252, whilst dividends of $129,000 were paid and assets stood at $2.85 million.[103]

Thus within the space of a year, Johnson achieved forward and backwards integration of the US disc record and talking machine business and held a contract with The Gramophone Company for half the output of his greatly enlarged machine factory at Camden. Holding 55 per cent of Victor stock and the positions of president and chief executive gave him a commanding position in the industry. Yet it was not a position he wanted, and at this critical juncture he attempted to sell Victor to The Gramophone Company. The deal would have left him in charge of manufacturing and product development, but not of the business. The failure of these moves and the subsequent collapse of his health, suggest that Johnson was a reluctant captain of industry. His natural role was, after all, Eldridge Johnson, Manufacturing Machinist.[104]

Reviewing the evidence it is probable that the Victor consolidation was intended as the first step towards the amalgamation of Victor and Gramophone interests for, in early 1902, British executives were again exploring the possibility of consolidation. At the time Johnson's personal 55 per cent holding of Victor stock was valued at £130,000; of this he offered to sell half for £52,000 cash, which would have given The Gramophone Company a 27.5 per cent stake in Victor. Although it had previously attempted to gain a more substantial stake, The Gramophone Company saw this as an opportunity to create a position in the new company. Unfortunately, failure to agree terms ended this opportunity.[105] In 1903, in what turned out to be The Gramophone Company's final bid for the whole of the Victor Company's stock, company accountant Colin Cooper and managing director William Barry Owen acted as intermediaries. Victor was offered for sale at £350,000. Cooper valued the Victor Company at £380,000 and The Gramophone Company at £464,000.[106] This move like the others ended in failure, probably precipitating Owen's withdrawal from the business and return to the United States.[107] This failure proved a watershed in Victor-Gramophone relations. For within a short time Victor, with its integrated manufacturing and marketing organisation, serving a single continental market and protected from domestic and foreign competitors by a patent-based oligopoly, experienced dramatic growth, which by 1910 made it the dominant venture in the US record industry.[108] The 1901 Victor consolidation also brought financial success to the US gramophone interests and for Johnson personally.

When he sold his then 50 per cent Victor holding to New York bankers in 1926 he received $26 million.[109]

The commercial success of the Gramophone and the disc record was secured by the technological improvements of Johnson and Leon Douglass. These included the switch from zinc etching to wax as a medium of recording, the creation of a better electrotype process for turning wax masters into metal matrices, the introduction of 10- and 12-inch records, which increased the maximum playing time to four-and-a-half-minutes, and the development of a tone arm supported separately from the horn, which lightened the pressure bearing down on the record, reducing wear. Another innovation was the adoption of an internal horn, which proved an important design feature, making talking machines a more acceptable piece of domestic furniture. It was known in the United States as the "Victrola." Furthermore, Johnson and Douglass brought flair to marketing and, with the new Victor products ensured the dominance of the Berliner-Johnson processes and its future in the mass markets of the United States, Britain, Europe and beyond.

★   ★   ★

By the end of 1901, Johnson and Victor had joined American Graphophone and Thomas Edison's National Phonograph Company as principal players in the American sound recording business. In 1903 the three ventures established their ascendancy and control of the market, settling outstanding patent litigation and concluding a licensing agreement between American Graphophone and Victor, which matched a number of key Berliner-Johnson and Graphophone patents. This was similar to the earlier agreement between the American Graphophone and National Phonograph Companies.[110] The effect of all this was to create a patent-based oligopoly, controlled by the three major players in the American industry. It enabled them to use their fundamental patents in the courts to exclude and eliminate would-be competitors and force out any existing competition. They did this with ruthless efficiency. Under these circumstances, these businesses controlled the market by regulation of a dealership system and strict adherence to retail price maintenance; that is until 1917 when the US Department of Justice obtained anti-trust judgements against them. However, it took a 1921 court case, which successfully challenged the last major patent, to end this distortion of the market.

The development of the talking machine from Edison's invention in 1877 to its realisation as a domestic entertainment device took twenty years.

Delays were caused by such factors as patent disputes, premature marketing attempts and consequent company failures, as well as the failure of the first inventors to foresee that the future lay more with entertainment than with office dictation. Despite these problems, the latter part of that twenty-year period, and the ensuing five years, saw rapid advances as shortcomings were recognised and overcome. All the protagonists adapted existing techniques; for example Berliner in his experiments tapped into the well-known arts of photography and precision etching, and Johnson used the existing process of precision electrotyping in developing a process of matrix making from wax originals. These innovators achieved success despite difficulties obtaining finance, pressures to market products before their time, poor marketing and on occasion crooked associates. They were able to do this because they absorbed these parallel technologies, then changed and applied them to their own creative work. With these innovations in place, the interlocking patents acknowledged and supply lines created, the pioneering phase ended. Thereafter the way was clear for the establishment and development of mass markets on the American continent and throughout the world. How this market was created in Britain is the subject of the next several chapters.

NOTES

"Mary had a little lamb" was a popular nursery rhyme composed in 1830 by Sarah Josepha Hale. The American inventor Thomas Edison claimed to have recited when he spoke for the first time into the phonograph.

1. F. W. Gaisberg, *Music on Record* (London: R. Hale, 1946), 11.

2. Emile Berliner, "The Gramophone: Etching the Human Voice," *Journal of the Franklin Institute* 125, no. 6 (June 1888): 435–47.

3. For an excellent account of the events leading up to Edison's invention of the phonograph and its initial reception, see Paul Israel, *Edison, a Life of Invention* (New York: Wiley, 1998), especially chapter 9, "The Wizard of Menlo Park." See also the accounts in George L. Frow and Albert F. Sefl, *The Edison Cylinder Phonographs 1877–1929* (Sevenoaks: Frow, 1978), and George L. Frow, *Edison Cylinder Phonograph Companion* (Woodlands Hills, CA: Stationary X-Press, 1994).

4. For a contemporary description of the Phonautograph, see Adolphe Ganot, *Elementary Treatise on Physics*, trans. Edmund Atkinson (London: Wood, 1870), 239–42.

5. In 2008 sound engineers scanned and reproduced the sounds preserved on an 1860 phonautograph recording, making it the oldest playable sound recording in the world (see "Oldest Recorded Voices Sing Again," http://www.BBCNews.co.uk, 28 March 2008). Unlike the cylinder instrument described above, the sound was inscribed on a 15-foot-long paper tape.

6. R. V. Bruce, *Alexander Graham Bell and the Conquest of Solitude* (Boston: Little, Brown, 1973): 110–11.

7. For an account of the phonograph's invention, see Paul Israel, "Telegraphy and Edison's Invention Factory," 63–83, and Edward J. Pershey, "Drawing as a Means of Inventing: Edison and the Invention of the Phonograph," 110–15, in *Working at Inventing: Thomas A. Edison and the Menlo Park Experience*, ed. William S. Pretzner (Dearborn, MI: Henry Ford Museum and Greenfield Village, 1989).

8. Israel, "Telegraphy," 73.

9. Andre Millard, *Edison and the Business of Innovation* (Baltimore: Johns Hopkins University Press, 1990), 63.

10. Berliner, "The Gramophone."

11. Editorial, *Scientific American* 37 (17 November 1877). The first phonograph was constructed in early December 1877 and demonstrated to the editor on 7 December 1877; clearly, the masthead date did not coincide with actual publication dates.

12. News report *New York World*, 6 November 1887.

13. Alexander Graham Bell to Gardiner G. Hubbard, 18 March 1878. "G. G. Hubbard File," 255 (Bell papers, Manuscript Division, Library of Congress, Washington, DC).

14. The complexity of the international patent system defeated Edison in his attempts at protecting his invention. For more on this issue, see Raymond Wile, "The Seventeen Year Itch: The Phonograph and the Patent System," in *The Patent History of the Phonograph 1877–1912*, ed. Allen Koenigsberg (New York: APM Press, 1990).

15. Thomas A. Edison, "The Phonograph and Its Future," *North American Review* 176 (1878): 526–36.

16. Nathan Rosenberg, *Perspectives on Technology* (Cambridge: Cambridge University Press, 1976), 174.

17. During the period covered by this work, with the exception of the First World War and its immediate aftermath, the US dollar British exchange rate was $4.85 to the pound. This work follows the contemporary custom of business accounts, which used a rounded-up rate of $5 to the pound. For a pound-dollar conversion table, see the appendix.

18. "Volta Laboratory Notes," 4:55–56 (Bell papers).

19. The work of the Volta Associates has never been adequately assessed. Fortunately, many of the Volta Laboratory papers and two sets of log notes have survived. "The Volta File" (Bell papers) holds drawings, laboratory notes, patents and other documents. The Charles Sumner Tainter papers (Archives Center, Museum of American History, Smithsonian Institution, Washington, DC) hold ten of the thirteen Tainter Home Notebooks, many drawings and a manuscript entitled "The Talking Machine and Some Little Known Facts in Connection With Its Early Development" (circa 1929). For an account of the Volta Associates' recording activities, see Raymond R. Wile, "The Development of Sound Recording at the Volta Laboratory," *Association for Recorded Sound Collections Journal* 21, no. 1 (1990): 208–25. Charles Sumner Tainter's account of his work at the Volta Laboratory, together with relevant parts of the surviving Volta Laboratory notebooks and extracts from his manuscript "The Talking Machine," was published in *For the Record* (the journal of the City of London Phonograph and Gramophone Society Ltd), nos. 17–19 (2006).

20. "Notice to Stockholders: Volta Graphophone Co," 6 July 1887; "Phonograph: Litigation," 256 (Bell papers).

21. For details of this transaction and its consequences for the British industry, see chapter 2.

22. The certificate of incorporation is held at the Sony Music Archive, New York.

23. *List of Users of the Phonograph and Phono-Graphophone in the District of Columbia, Maryland and Delaware: The Territory of Columbia Phonograph Co.* "Phonograph: Printed Matter," 256 (Bell papers). "Columbia Phonograph Co, Washington, DC," *The Phonogram* 1, no. 4 (1891): 88–92.

24. "Affidavit of Charles Sumner Tainter," 14 February 1896. *American Graphophone Co v Edward H. Amet*, US Circuit Court, Northern District of Illinois.

25. Koenigsberg, *The Patent History of the Phonograph*, 5.

26. Thomas Edison to E. H. Johnson, undated ("1888 Phonograph Folder," Edison National Historic Site, West Orange, New Jersey).

27. Data compiled from Koenigsberg, *The Patent History of the Phonograph*, 49–51.

28. "Phonograph: Printed Matter," 256 ("American Graphophone," 255; Bell papers).

29. For accounts of these manoeuvres, see Raymond Wile, "Introduction," *Proceedings of the 1890 Convention of Local Phonograph Companies* (reprint; Nashville, TN, 1974), and Millard, *Edison and the Business of Innovation*, 79. See also Raymond Wile, "Growing Hostilities Between Edison and the Phonograph and Graphophone Developers," *Association for Recorded Sound Collections Journal* 22, no. 1 (1991): 8–34.

30. See Wile, "Introduction," xxx.

31. Alfred Clark (1873–1950), "His Master's Voice: A Record," 7 (unpublished, EMI Music Archives, Hayes, London; hereafter, EMI). Alfred Clark was a prosperous middle-class New York engineer and businessman. His record industry career began in 1889 with North American Phonograph, and following its collapse, he worked for The Edison Kinetoscope business, taking charge of film production and sales. He returned to the sound recording industry in 1895. Clark became involved with Emile Berliner and Eldridge Johnson in 1896 and partnered Johnson in the redesign of the gramophone sound box. In 1899 he came to Europe establishing with The Gramophone Company a joint venture in Paris, Cie Française du Gramophone. In 1909, Clark became managing director of The Gramophone Company, restructuring the business and turning it into a major manufacturing concern. In 1930, he became company chairman and in 1931, the founding chairman of EMI and then in 1941, chairman and managing director. In 1946 he became life president of EMI, only to resign six months later after a fierce boardroom row. Clark was an extraordinary record industry survivor and was probably the most important figure in the development of the recording industry outside the USA. Furthermore, he made important contributions to the creation of the British electronics industry and television. See "Alfred C. Clark," in *Dictionary of Business Biography*, ed. David J. Jeremy and Christine Shawe (London: Butterworth, 1985), 1:671–76; Peter Martland, *Since Records Began* (London: Batsford, 1997), 24; Peter Martland, "Alfred Clark," in *Oxford Dictionary of National Biography: From the Earliest Times to the Year 2000*, ed. H. C. G. Matthew and Brian Harrison (Oxford: Oxford University Press, 2005); entry in *Who Was Who*, 1943; F. W. Gaisberg, "Emile Berliner Picks a Winner," *The Gramophone* 19, no. 8 (December 1943): 97–98; F. W. Gaisberg, "He Was a Man," *The Gramophone* 27, no. 4 (August 1950): 41–42; "Obituary," *The Times* (19 June 1950); obituary circular, "Edison Pioneers" (19 July 1950) (Alfred Clark file, Edison National Historic Site).

32. During 1890 at least three lists (or catalogues) of records were published. One, with Edison-type cylinders, consisted of recordings made by The American Graphophone Company in New York and sold by North American. This was followed by a second four-page list, which was published in June 1890. In November 1890 The Columbia Phonograph Company of Washington, DC, published a catalogue, which included seventy-seven record-

ings by the US Marine Band. Further Columbia-derived catalogues appeared in 1891. I am grateful to Frank Andrews for his assistance with the chronology of these catalogues.

33. For an account of these moves, see Millard, *Edison and the Business of Innovation*, 163.

34. The 1898 British price was £15.15s.0d. For a description of the "Home" and other Edison phonographs, see Frow and Sefl, *The Edison Cylinder Phonograph*, 40–50, and Frow, *Edison Cylinder Phonograph Companion*, 83–98.

35. For further discussion of these moves and the consequences, see chapters 2 and 3.

36. For details of this, see chapters 2 and 3. See also Howard W. Hayes to William Edgar Gilmore, 27 November 1901 (phonolegal files 1901, Edison National Historic Site). In this letter, Hayes set out the miserable financial state that the business had fallen into. He also observed, "The Washington newspapers had been full of accounts of the loss of money by the Graphophone Company."

37. I am grateful to the British record industry historian Frank Andrews for his help with this section, particularly the North American chronology.

38. Sound recording technology was used for other purposes—for example, after 1890, ethnographers and anthropologists used office dictating machines to make field recordings of indigenous American music and language, at a time when these were still practiced and taught. See: J. W. Fewkes, "On the Use of the Phonograph in the Study of the Language of American Indians," *Science* 15 (1890): 267–69, and "A Contribution to Passamaquoddy Folk-Lore," *Journal of American Folk-Lore* 3 (1890): 257–80. See also the publications of The Library of Congress, American Folklife Center, "Federal Cylinder Project" and contemporary anthropologists Francis La Flesche, Alice Cunningham Fletcher and Frances Densmore. Densmore enjoyed a unique career beginning in 1907 when she began work for the Smithsonian Institution's Bureau of American Ethnology. She dedicated her long life to making sound records of the indigenous American populations, resulting in more than 3,500 cylinder records. Early twentieth-century composers Béla Bartók, Ralph Vaughan Williams, Percy Grainger and others also used the technology to collect folk melodies, which was often interpolated into their compositions. Many of these cylinders are held at the English Folk Dance and Song Society, Cecil Sharp House, and the British Library, National Sound Archive, both in London; at the Australian National Museum, Canberra, Australian Capital Territory; and at the Library of Congress, Washington, DC. See also Percy Grainger, "Collecting With the Phonograph" *Journal of the Folk Song Society* 12 (1908): 147–242; Michael Yates, "Percy Grainger and the Impact of the Phonograph," *Folk Music Journal* 4, no. 3 (1982): 265–75; C. J. Bearman, "Percy Grainger, the Phonograph, and the Folk Song Society," *Music & Letters* 84, no. 3 (2003): 434–55.

39. Tim Brooks, "Columbia's Recording in the 1890s: Founding the Recording Industry," *Association for Recorded Sound Collections Journal* 10, no. 1 (1978): 5–38.

40. Edward D. Easton letter to the editor, "How It Works," *The Phonogram* (November 1890).

41. See Allen Koenigsberg, *Edison Cylinder Records 1889–1912* (New York: APM Press, 1987). See also the holdings of record catalogues in the Bell papers and in the Motion Picture, Broadcast and Recorded Sound Division of The Library of Congress, Washington, DC, and at The BMG-Sony Music Archives, New York.

42. Gaisberg, *Music on Record*, 11. Frederick William Gaisberg (1873–1951) was born in Washington, DC. A gifted musician and skilled precision engineer, he began his career with Charles Sumner Tainter and later served an apprenticeship with American Graphophone; he subsequently worked with Emile Berliner, who trained him as a recording engineer. In

1898 he came to London as The Gramophone Company's first recording engineer, and he recorded for that company around the world; he made the first recordings of celebrities such as Caruso, Melba, Patti, Kreisler, Paderewski and many other great performing artists. His natural sympathy and understanding of artistic needs, together with a highly developed appreciation of music, enabled him to manage performers in the often-difficult circumstances of the recording studio. With the coming of electrical recording in 1925, Gaisberg's career changed focus, and he became an artist and repertoire manager. Gaisberg maintained contact with the industry until his death in 1951. His memoirs *Music on Record* and his writings in *The Gramophone* provide enormously important, though highly romanticised, insights into the pioneering of the industry. See also Jerrold Northrop Moore, *A Voice in Time* (London: Hamilton, 1976); Martland, *Since Records Began*, 21; and Martland, "Frederick William Gaisberg," *Oxford Dictionary of National Biography*. The Pennsylvania Avenue premises of Columbia have survived to the present and must qualify as the site of the oldest recording studios in the world.

43. F. W. Gaisberg, "Charlie Gregory's Fifty Years of Talking Machines" (typescript, n.d., Charles B. Gregory file, EMI).

44. Gaisberg, *Music on Record*, 11. Easton was clearly trying to identify the business with other icons of efficiency and modernity. He wrote, "In Washington our inspectors go from place to place on bicycles. This system enables us to attend to calls with great promptness. Our Baltimore and Washington offices are manned days, nights and Sundays, and telephone calls are always promptly answered." *The Phonogram* (November 1890).

45. For an account of Edison's development of a moulding process, see Thomas F. Gillen, "Thomas A. Edison and the Process of Duplicating Wax Cylinder Records" (unpublished manuscript, Edison National Historic Site).

46. "Howard W. Hayes to William Edgar Gilmore," 27 November 1901 (phonolegal files 1901, Edison National Historic Site).

47. Alfred Clark, "A Record," 80.

48. Gaisberg, "Charlie Gregory's Fifty Years of Talking Machines." See also Martland, "Charles Gregory," *Since Records Began*, 93.

49. Gaisberg, *Music on Record*, 14–15.

50. Gaisberg, *Music on Record*, 14–15

51. American-born actor, journalist, recording artist and engineer Russell Hunting (1864–1944) entered the record industry in the early 1890s as an artist and later a self-taught recording engineer. In 1898 he came to Britain first as chief engineer for Edison Bell and, subsequently, with Louis Sterling, establishing his own record company, which failed. Thereafter, he worked for the Pathé company first in Britain, then in Asia and finally in the United States. See "Russell Hunting," in *Encyclopedia of Recorded Sound in the United States*, ed. Guy A. Marco (New York, 1993), 330–31. See also *Actionable Offenses: Indecent Phonograph Recordings From the 1890s* (Archeophone Records 1007, 2007)—in particular, the case notes by Patrick Feaster and David Giovannoni. See also "Comstock Arrests an Actor," *New York Times*, 26 June 1896. For more about the career of this fascinating figure, see chapters 3–7. See also the New York Court of Special Sessions records, 27 June 1896 (New York City Archives, New York). I am grateful to Alex Orquiza, who took time from his own researches to locate the records, and Ms. Tobi K. Adler of the New York, Municipal Archives, whose work locating the court records went way beyond the call of duty.

52. Brooks, "Columbia's Recording in the 1890s," 15.

53. *The Phonoscope*, November 1896 (New York). The companies referred to were surviving North American franchisees.

54. The "Ediphone" and other Edison brands were eventually sold to Lanier Business Systems. "Dictaphone" survived into the modern era and has, since 2007, been a division of Nuance Communications.

55. The settlement is cited in Raymond Wile, "The American Graphophone Company and Columbia Phonograph Company Enter the Disc Record Business, 1897–1903," *Association for Recorded Sound Collections Journal* 22, no. 2 (1991): 207–21.

56. For an account of Berliner's telephone work, see Frederic William Wile, *Emile Berliner: Maker of the Microphone* (Indianapolis, IN: Bobbs Merrill, 1926): 55–155.

57. Raymond Wile, "Etching the Human Voice: The Berliner Invention of the Gramophone," *Association for Recorded Sound Collections Journal* 21, no. 1 (1990): 208–25.

58. His grandson the late Robert Sanders believed that all Berliner's notebooks and drawings were destroyed in an 1897 fire at his Washington, DC, laboratory.

59. Among these sources are the series of lectures Berliner gave to The Franklin Institute in Philadelphia between 1888 and 1913, the 1926 biography by F. W. Wile, his scrapbooks (which now form a part of "The Robert Sanders Collection" at the Motion Picture, Broadcast and Recorded Sound Division, LC), together with the recollections of the Berliner family given to the present author in 1990—especially those of the late Robert Sanders, who worked for the inventor as a boy during the 1920s.

60. News report, "Berliner's Gramophone," *The Electrical World* (November 1887): 255–56.

61. See Berliner manuscript note on the flyleaf of Johann Muller, *Physik und Metriologie*: "Today I succeeded for the first time to get articulate speech, plainly audible from a stereotype copy of a photoengraved phonautographic record. Washington, DC May 17 1887. E Berliner, Cora Berliner" (Berliner papers, Manuscript Division, Library of Congress). There is a curious postscript to Berliner's attempts at photoengraving sound signals. Some years after his own formative work, Berliner discovered the writings of Charles Cros, a French poet, philosopher and photographer. In 1877 Cros had proposed to the French National Academy of Science a system for fixing Scott's sound signals by means of photoengraving. He never reduced the idea to a practical art; nonetheless, Berliner always acknowledged his parallel contribution to the process of invention.

62. Berliner, "The Gramophone."

63. Berliner, "The Gramophone," 438.

64. For an account of these years, see Wile, "Etching the Human Voice," 14–16. Also Wile, *Emile Berliner*, 202–16.

65. Berliner, "The Improved Gramophone," *Electrical Engineering* (16 December 1890): 27–28.

66. Clark, "A Record," 87.

67. Cited in Wile, "Launching the Gramophone in America, 1890–1896" (unpublished), 11.

68. Wile, "Etching the Human Voice," 17.

69. Clark, "A Record," 100.

70. There is evidence to show that the Waltershausen factory produced a 7-inch disc and a Gramophone utilising a clockwork motor, even an electrically powered model. I am grateful to Peter Adamson for drawing this to my attention.

71. See "Eldridge Reeves Johnson," in *Biographical Dictionary of American Business Leaders*, ed. John N. Ingham (Westport, CT: Greenwood, 1983), 668–69. Eldridge Reeves Johnson (1867–1945) was a precision engineer and jobbing machinist based in Camden, New Jersey. He designed and manufactured a new gramophone, which gained him lucrative contracts with Berliner and his British licencees. Johnson created a recording process using wax tablets, which resulted in better sound quality and longer-playing times. After furious court battles, he fused his and the Berliner assets to form The Victor Talking Machine Company, which he turned into the premier US record company. His skill was in hiring able subordinates, which paid off when ill health prevented him dealing with day-to-day business. He sold Victor to US bankers in 1926 earning $26 million for his stake.

72. Cited in E. R. Fennimore Johnson, *His Master's Voice Was Eldridge R. Johnson* (Dover, DE: E. R. Fennimore Johnson, 1974): 36.

73. William Barry Owen (1860–1914) was born in Vineyard Haven, Massachusetts. Although he read law at Amherst, he never practised; rather than a lawyer, Owen was a natural salesman and a compulsive gambler. He was sales director of National Gramophone Co, though never supported Seaman in his disputes with Berliner and Johnson. He came to London in 1897 to start a trade in gramophone goods and find investors. The Owen venture became The Gramophone Company Ltd, which (with him as managing director) expanded across continental Europe, Russia, the British Empire and the Far East. He left in 1904 to undertake an unsuccessful agricultural venture in Vineyard Haven. His fortune dissipated, he lived on a pension provided jointly by The Gramophone and Victor Companies. See "William Barry Owen" in *Dictionary of Business Biography*, ed. David J. Jeremy and Christine Shawe (London: Butterworth, 1985), 4:507–9; Martland, *Since Records Began*, 36; and the "William Barry Owen file" (EMI).

74. Harry O. Sooy, "Memoir of My Career at Victor Talking Machine Company" (Sooy memoir and that of his brother Raymond can be accessed via http://www.davidsarnoff.org).

75. Sooy, "Memoir of My Career."

76. Sooy "Memoir of My Career."

77. Copy with the Berliner papers. In addition, Johnson was manufacturing substantial quantities of machines for the European market.

78. Berliner to Alfred Clark, 8 November 1898 (legal files, box 121, "American Graphophone Co v United States Phonograph Co et al," correspondence, Edison National Historic Site).

79. "Howard W. Hayes to William Edgar Gilmore," 27 November 1901 (phonolegal files, 1901, Edison National Historic Site).

80. "Manufactures," in *Twelfth Census of the United States Taken in the Year 1900* (Washington, DC: GPO, 1901), 10:181–85.

81. Sometimes Zonophone and Gramophone were referred to as Zon-o-phone and Gram-o-phone. For the sake of consistency, the former is used throughout.

82. Frederick Marion Prescott (1869–1923) was an American businessman and record industry pioneer, having previously been engaged in the film industry and the import-export trade. He was, after 1898, largely a European-based record industry entrepreneur. He created International Zonophone GmbH, importing machines from the US but manufacturing records. In 1903 this venture was sold, and he formed International Talking Machine GmbH and, with it, labels including Odeon and Jumbo. In 1911 that business was sold, and he returned to the United States.

83. See *Frank Seaman v Berliner Gramophone Co* and Berliner's countersuit *Berliner Gramophone Co v Frank Seaman*. Both in US Circuit Court, Western District of Western Virginia, Harrisburg, 1900 and 1901.

84. For an account of these manoeuvrings, see Wile, "The American Graphophone Company and the Columbia Phonograph Company Enter the Disc Record Business, 1897–1903," *Association for Recorded Sound Collections* 22, no. 2 (1991): 207–21.

85. American Graphophone's key Bell-Tainter patents expired in 1901. To maintain its preeminent patent position, it acquired an untested patent for cutting sound signals into wax, essentially a parallel to Johnson's own unpatented wax process—the so-called Jones patent.

86. Eldridge Reeves Johnson to William Barry Owen, 12 March 1901 (Victor papers, EMI).

87. Inventor, businessman and record industry pioneer, Leon Douglass (1869–1940) came to sound recording after working in the telephone business. He wrote in his unpublished memoirs, "In 1888 I saw my first phonograph and was fascinated with it. I made one and took it to Seward [Nebraska] to show my old friends. . . . I went to Omaha to see E. A. Benson, President of Nebraska Phonograph Co. [one of the North American franchisees], and he gave me the agency for the western part of the State." In 1889, he invented a coin-in-the-slot attachment for the phonograph and went to work for Benson's Chicago Phonograph Co. In 1892 Douglass patented a method of duplicating cylinder recordings, which he sold to American Graphophone. In 1900 Douglass began his association with Johnson and became his and, later, Victor's sales director. See "Leon Douglass," *Encyclopedia of Recorded Sound*, 217. See also http://www.gracyk.com/leon.shtml.

88. Eldridge Reeves Johnson to The Gramophone Company," 5 June 1900 (Victor papers, EMI).

89. See http://www.gracyk.com/leon.shtml.

90. Although The Gramophone Company began integrating manufacturing and marketing functions in 1899, the US gramophone business remained fragmented, with manufacturing and marketing functions undertaken and owned by different ventures. Although the formation of Victor in 1901 began the process of integration, it was not completed until 1904, when Victor built its own record-pressing facilities.

91. For details of this development, see chapter 2.

92. Eldridge Reeves Johnson to Elsie Johnson, February 1900 (Elsie Johnson file, Johnson Victrola Museum).

93. For details, see chapter 2.

94. Eldridge Reeves Johnson to William Barry Owen, 12 March 1901 (Victor papers, EMI).

95. Johnson to Owen.

96. For details concerning this, see Eldridge Reeves Johnson to William Barry Owen and Edmund Trevor Lloyd Williams, 5 June 1900 (Victor papers, EMI).

97. Eldridge Reeves Johnson to William Barry Owen, 24 January 1901 (Victor papers, EMI).

98. Eldridge Reeves Johnson to William Barry Owen, 9 July 1901 (Victor papers, EMI).

99. "Memorandum of Evidence," *US v Victor Talking Machine Co et al.* Department of Justice Anti-Trust file, 60-23-0, Southern District of New York (US National Archives, College Park, MD).

100. Eldridge Reeves Johnson to Elsie Johnson, 6 August 1901 (Elsie Johnson file, Johnson Victrola Museum).

101. Eldridge Reeves Johnson to Elsie Johnson, 30 August 1901 (Elsie Johnson file, Johnson Victrola Museum).

102. For details of ownership, organisation and structure of the Victor Company, see Eldridge Reeves Johnson to William Barry Owen and Edmund Trevor Lloyd Williams, 18 November 1901 (Victor papers, EMI).

103. Data compiled from "E. R. Johnson financial files" (Johnson Victrola Museum).

104. For an account of Johnson's career and the illness that dogged him, see Johnson, *Eldridge R. Johnson*.

105. British accountant Colin Cooper assessed the respective values of the Victor and Gramophone businesses in his "Report to the Directors," 20 February 1902 (board papers, EMI).

106. Both sides were worried as to how the merger could be financed; however, Colin Cooper pointed out that the combined assets of the two companies would amount to more than double the necessary bond issue needed to cover the purchase. Highlighting the problems the fledgling industry faced in raising capital, Cooper wrote, "I think you should have the issue underwritten. In this connection it is well to remember that the general investor looks upon the Gramophone business as anything but a permanent one." Colin Cooper to William Barry Owen, 7 December 1903 (board papers, EMI).

107. The progress of these protracted negotiations is chronicled in The Gramophone Company board minutes for 1903–1904.

108. The 1910 *United States Census of Manufacturing*, "Manufacturing," reported 8.57 million discs manufactured, whilst Sherman, *The Paper Dog*, 43, cited Victor sales at 4.63 million discs, giving Victor 54 per cent of the US market, although what proportion of these were exported is unknown. The census also reported the manufacture of 191,990 disc machines, whilst Aldridge, *The Victor Talking Machine Company*, 109, cited 1909 Victor instrument sales of 68,231, to which must be added the 58,368 machines manufactured for the British company and an unquantified number manufactured and exported to Canada, South America and the Far East. This gave Victor, excluding machines manufactured by Columbia and also exported, at least 66 per cent of the US disc instrument market.

109. Thomas R. Navin's assessment of leading US industrial companies in 1917 placed Victor 174 of 278. See *Business History Review* (Autumn 1970). Cited in Alfred D. Chandler, *The Visible Hand* (Cambridge, MA: Harvard University Press, 1977), 510.

110. Copy in "Agreements File" (Victor papers, EMI).

2

PIONEERING THE BRITISH RECORD INDUSTRY: 1888–1903

"I'll Sing Thee Songs of Araby"

When can I get some of the 125 machines ordered from you some time ago? I am really afraid to meet my customers as I have put them off so long.

—British Gramophone dealer,[1] Christmas 1897

The dramatic story of Edison's invention of a talking machine soon reached Britain. On 17 January 1878 Henry Edmunds, a young British engineer who knew Edison and had attended one of the December 1877 phonograph demonstrations, wrote a letter to *The Times* newspaper describing the invention.[2] This was reprinted by other newspapers and its impact provoked commentaries and editorials similar to those in the United States. Within days of publication William Henry (later Sir William) Preece, the chief engineer and electrician at the General Post Office, constructed a tinfoil phonograph from drawings prepared by Edmunds. He later demonstrated the instrument to a Society of Telegraph Engineers meeting held on 1 February 1878 at the Royal Institution in London; the first ever demonstration of recorded sound in Britain. This and later demonstrations were so successful that The London Stereoscopic and Photographic Company, having acquired the British patent rights from Edison for £1,500, began manufacturing and selling tinfoil phonographs. However, just as phonograph development in the United States languished, so did its exploitation in Britain. In fact, the invention became little more than a scientific curiosity and commercial exploitation did not begin again until Edison's improved phonograph appeared in 1888. How the improved phonograph was exploited provides one of the more colourful episodes in the early history of the British record industry.[3]

★ ★ ★

The British promotion and marketing of the improved phonograph was in the hands of Edison's British agent, Colonel George Edward Gouraud. An American Civil War veteran and holder of the prestigious Medal of Honor awarded for bravery under fire, Gouraud was a businessman and company promoter. A great admirer of the Edison, he named his house "Little Menlo" after Edison's Menlo Park laboratory. Gouraud was also a ceaseless self-publicist, social climber and eccentric. Photographs show him at Edison's West Orange laboratory in June 1888, when the improved phonograph was first displayed. He brought one back to Britain and demonstrated it to the press, men of science and anyone else who would listen.[4] On 29 June 1888, Gouraud, with his uncanny eye for publicity, took the phonograph to the annual Handel Festival at the Crystal Palace and made recordings of excerpts from the oratorio *Israel in Egypt* on three wax cylinders: these are the first known recordings of an actual performance. Gouraud also established The Edison Phonograph Company and appointed Jonathan Lewis Young as manager.[5]

Between 1888 and 1892 Gouraud, Young and others toured the country demonstrating the phonograph to audiences of press and public. There were tangible results from these demonstrations; among them were a series of recordings of eminent Victorians including Liberal Prime Minister William Ewart Gladstone, heroine of the Crimean war Florence Nightingale, composer Sir Arthur Sullivan, actor manager Sir Henry Irving[6] and poets Robert Browning and Alfred, Lord Tennyson. Several of these recordings were made when celebrities visited Little Menlo where making records formed part of Gouraud's after dinner entertainment. The recordings later passed into the hands of James Edward Hough, Gouraud's eventual successor in business. Fortunately for posterity, a surprising number of these sound autographs, or at least copies of them, survive at The Edison National Historic Site, West Orange, New Jersey, and in The National Sound Archive at the British Library, London. Many are well recorded, providing a unique window into the late Victorian age.

The formation of The North American Phonograph Company in 1888 and Thomas Edison's need for capital focused the attention of the inventor on overseas markets. In 1890 Edison and Stephen Fossa Moriarty[7] the manager of International Graphophone, owners of the foreign Bell-Tainter patents, pooled all the overseas sound recording patents they controlled and vested them in The Edison United Phonograph Company, a US-based international marketing organisation. Edison held 50 per cent of the equity and Moriarty became its head with power of attorney in all overseas dealings.[8] Edison United was committed to purchasing phonographs and cylinder blanks exclusively from the Edison Phonograph Works, though at the time manufacture of the Graphophone had ceased. Paradoxically this move gave Edison an interest in the Bell-Tainter patents, the very patents he later challenged in the United States.[9]

Meanwhile, back in London, Gouraud began selling as The Edison United Phonograph Company and Young left the business. Moriarty clearly detested Gouraud and Edmunds and soon got rid of them, claiming their sound recording demonstrations were little more than a circus. In November 1892, Edison United formed The Edison Bell Phonograph Corporation Ltd in London, with a share capital of £60,000 as a sales outlet for Edison talking machine products. In turn Edison United sold the British Edison and Bell-Tainter patents to Edison Bell for £20,000 cash, plus 4,000 of the £5 shares in the business. The indenture of sale had provision for Edison United to participate further in profit as well as restating the earlier commitment to purchase phonographs and cylinder blanks from the Edison Works. Edison United thus became a major shareholder in the British venture. Essentially it was Moriarty's show, as he was managing director and sole purchasing agent of the business.[10] Any dispassionate review of Edison United and Edison Bell financial and business papers together with other evidence shows that even by the standards of the time Moriarty was a crook who saw in Edison Bell a cow, which he milked dry. Moriarty, in stark contrast to Gouraud and Edmunds, saw the technology as purely an office-dictating machine and committed the Edison Bell business to developing this market to the exclusion of entertainment.[11] Because of his decided views and financial trickery, The Edison Bell Phonograph Corporation was not a success and it took six years to lease or sell 1,500 phonographs.

Edison Bell was a monopoly and engaged in a highly restrictive marketing policy, which ignored growing demands of the potentially lucrative entertainment market. As a result, a clandestine transatlantic trade in phonographs intended for entertainment purposes began, breaching the Edison Bell monopoly. Following the collapse of North American and many of its franchisees in and after 1893, large numbers of phonographs came on to the US market at knockdown prices, which increased the flow. Those coming into Britain ended up with hucksters, showmen, fairground entertainers and others. It was not just enterprising individuals who broke the Edison Bell monopoly; fed up with its miserable performance Thomas Edison began his own clandestine export of entertainment phonographs to Britain. Furthermore, in 1896, the inventor disposed of his remaining Edison United shares and lost whatever residual control he had over Edison Bell's activities. One of these illegal importers was Jonathan Lewis Young, whose London shop traded in phonographs obtained from former North American franchisees and middlemen. The British Edison historian Frank Andrews suggests Young sold more than two hundred of these monopoly-busting phonographs, before an Edison Bell injunction ended his activities.[12] Young also made music records some of which were fakes (the earliest cover versions) supposedly made by public figures like Gladstone, though several genuine recordings were made by music hall performers Dan Leno, Charles Coborn and others.

One of the most successful Edison Bell infringers was James Edward Hough, who later styled himself the "father of the British trade." Previous to his recording business Hough had been a manufacturer of sewing machines and, according to Edison, an early infringer of his moving picture Kinetoscope.[13] Hough traded as "The London Phonograph Company," entering the business as a showman and illegal importer of Edison phonographs and cylinder records. He also made own-brand cylinder records, which he sold to showmen and others. One of his associates, Harry Bluff, featured on many of these cylinders. It was a rough-and-ready business and his recordings included yet more imitations of Gladstone and other political figures, together with comic songs, recitations and other short musical pieces of the kind that could be contained within a two-minute cylinder record.[14]

The British public was therefore introduced to sound recording as a fairground sideshow amusement rather than as a device for home entertainment. In a 1922 interview Hough recalled those pioneering days, explaining how he first heard a phonograph while in North America. He immediately realised its potential as a moneymaker and bought an instrument and thirty-six records, which he exhibited in Dublin. Hough said people flocked to see this "wonder of the age," claiming that in five days he had made £200. With admission at one penny, this improbable figure would have required nearly 50,000 patrons. Whatever the truth, the experience persuaded him to make a further phonograph and record buying trip to the United States. Hough claimed he sold one instrument for £200, while the records were sold at £1 apiece.[15] The sale of these illegally imported phonographs was blatant, with advertisements appearing in British popular and trade magazines. One, in 1897, invited offers for an "Exhibition phonograph, spring motor and fifteen ear tubes," which it was claimed had cost £28.[16] By the mid-1890s profits like this created a flourishing clandestine trade that Edison Bell with its office dictating machine marketing strategy failed lamentably to capitalise on.

Evidence of lost opportunities appeared in an 1898 letter from Frederick Marion Prescott, then in Britain, published in the American trade journal *The Phonoscope*. Entrepreneur and salesman Prescott commented unfavourably on Edison Bell's business methods, contrasting the differences between the US and British markets and compared the US high volume low margins with the British low volume and high margins, noting:

> I have been surprised in visiting all the large cities not to find any phonograph parlours. . . . I think the fault can be traced to the door of the company who own the patent rights for Great Britain. . . . It is the exorbitant prices they ask and the excessive royalty demanded for the use of machines which prevents the general adoption of the phonograph here. . . . The Edison Standard phonograph which sells in America for $20 sells here for 6 guineas, 10 shillings [*sic*; he probably means £6.10s or 15s], and musical records sell here for 5s or $1.25, and are of a very poor grade at that.[17]

In 1898, having sold or leased 1,500 phonographs as per the original contract with Edison United, Edison Bell was reconstructed as the Edison Bell Consolidated Phonograph Company Ltd, with a £110,000 capital made up of £100,000 preference shares and 10,000 ordinary £1.00 shares. Edison United and Moriarty held half the shares in the new enterprise and Moriarty became a director. It was a typical late-1890s British company with a board of directors stashed with aristocratic names like Lord Denbigh, Lord Farquhar and Count de Torre Diaz, whose presence acted as a lure to entice the investing public.[18] Unsurprisingly the crooked Moriarty feathered his nest for a second time, though his fellow directors soon worked out his scam and got rid of him, taking the opportunity to end the Edison United supply monopoly.[19] In a letter to Edison, Charles A. Stevens (who ran Edison's export business) summed up the whole sorry business, "Moriarty has left the country [Britain], and they [Edison Bell] do not expect him to return. He has 'sandbagged' them all, and they are all on to it."[20] Unfortunately for Edison Bell, Moriarty left the business with crippling debts and disappeared with £100,000: at least that sum is unaccounted for in the accounts. As Edison observed, "The English Company is nearly wrecked by Moriarty, and they finally got rid of him and I am cooperating with the English Company to put it on its feet." In a further note Edison commented, "Moriarty is an extremely dangerous adventurer."[21] Although his name appeared as a director until 1906 Stephen Fossa Moriarty had no further dealings with the business having moved to continental Europe, where he died in 1907.[22]

Edison Bell finally put Hough and "The London Phonograph Company" out of business in 1896, but he bounced back the following year forming Edisonia Ltd to manufacture and sell cylinder records under an Edison Bell licence. Later in 1897 Hough wrote to "The Gramophone Company," which had just started trading in London, suggesting Edisonia might become exclusive sales agents for its products; nothing came of this move. In 1898 Hough sold the Edisonia business to Edison Bell, which then became its record manufacturing and selling arm with Hough as general manager. In the autumn of 1898 both The Gramophone Company and Edison Bell issued music record catalogues, signalling the start of a competitive British market between cylinder and disc records.

Edison clearly disliked the bluff and blustering Hough as much as he distrusted Moriarty, and as events unfolded he was quite right to do so.[23] The move into the music business saw Edison Bell take sales offices and establish recording studios in Charing Cross Road with the services of a top American recording engineer, the ubiquitous Russell Hunting. He was paid the impressive salary of $7,000 per year, making him by far the best paid recording engineer in the business.[24] He made significant contributions to the art of sound recording, developing an effective and high-quality mechanical system for duplicating cylinder records. In a 1900 letter to William Barry Owen in London, Alfred Clark (then manager of Cie Française du Gramophone) alluded to a conversation he had with Russell Hunting. According to Clark, Hunting told him Edison Bell was using various mechanical duplicating processes to produce between five and six thousand cylinder records per week.[25] Illustrating this freewheeling pioneering period, Clark described Hunting as "absolutely crooked."[26]

A review of late-1890s Edison Bell record catalogues suggests they took the form of a prospectus rather than a conventional "off-the-shelf" record catalogue. Apparently clients made a selection and Edison Bell made the record, with either a performer coming into the studio or as a copy cloned from a master. Whether a copy or an original recording the price was the same, 5s.0d, though later catalogues indicate copied records priced at 2s.6d. Edison Bell also sold a range of phonographs from the Edison Phonograph Works at West Orange and Graphophones from the American Graphophone factory at Bridgeport, retailing at prices from £7.10s to £27.10s. To the dismay of the British wholesale and retail trades, these were significantly higher than those in the United States.[27] Edison Bell Consolidated continued to press its monopoly, though its belligerent attitude made few friends in the trade. In an 1899 letter to his London headquarters Peter Bohanna (The Gramophone Company's travelling salesman) cited instances of "bullying tactics" used by Edison Bell salesmen, particularly against smaller retailers. British dealer correspondence in *The Phonoscope* (responding to Prescott's earlier letter) also claimed Edison Bell salesmen used combative and bullying tactics. Finally, in a September 1898 letter to Thomas Edison, Liverpool importer Bunney's Ltd complained that Edison Bell retail prices were one third higher than in the United States, and wholesale discounts were only fifteen to 20 per cent compared to 30 per cent in America.[28] Inevitably, sales were poor. A letter from the Edison Phonograph Works suggested that Edison Bell machine purchases for the period September 1899 to the end of February 1900 (covering the main Christmas selling period) amounted to a mere $7,979.26.[29] Lacking capital, this second Edison Bell venture was not a success, although it did have several positive achievements, among them getting rid of Moriarty's Edison United supply channel, establishing a music record capacity and forming new commercial links with Edison.

Late 1900 letters between Edison Bell and Thomas Edison show the former trying to persuade the inventor to stop selling in what Edison Bell claimed as its overseas territory. Edison rejected these claims, spelling out the cost of his relationship with Moriarty.[30] The third Edison Bell concern was formed on 3 December 1901, injecting much needed capital into the ailing business, though this too was unsuccessful. The core problem remained a weak financial and capital structure. The company inherited the £100,000 debt Moriarty made off with, which carried annual dividend payments of £5,000. This was a crippling burden when capital was desperately needed to reconstruct the business and take advantage of the rapidly growing market in records and phonographs. The business also had to deal with the expiry of the British Edison patents, and therefore of its monopoly of Edison products.[31] Until 1903 when these patents expired, Edison Bell was bound by contract to purchase its machines from the Edison factory at West Orange, though all its records were made at the London recording studio. In fact Edison Bell breached its agreement with Edison by importing cheap bottom-of-the-market German phonographs, which they passed off as "Edison phonographs."[32] In 1902 a London wholesaler wrote to Edison complaining bitterly that Edison Bell was advertising "the cheap German made phonograph known in the trade as the Puck model . . . [as] the genuine Edison Bell machine." This made the point that the name of Edison was being linked with the cheapest German phonographs.[33] Knowledge of this chicanery did not improve the already poisonous relations between Thomas Edison and Edison Bell, which was accurately summed up in by George Croydon Marks, Edison's London patent agent, "I have no doubt . . . that the Edison Bell Co are injuring the name of Edison and that they are working for all they are worth to exploit their own goods under the name of Edison, or any other goods they can get hold of, so as to get in the market against the time when they may think you will likely to be dealing in this country yourself."[34]

The year 1902 proved to be Edison Bell's year of opportunity and despair. On the one hand, the new process of moulding cylinder records boosted sales and opened up mass markets for its products. Cheap to manufacture, Edison Bell cylinder record prices fell from 5s.0d to 1s.6d. However, its most pressing problem was the expiry of the British Edison patents and future relations with Thomas Edison. Recognising its impossibly weak position, Edison Bell spent much of the year trying to make terms. In June 1902 James Hough wrote to William E. Gilmore, the head of Edison's American phonograph business, "It remains for your Company, who control the issue of the goods, whether we remain worthy of the business of distributing Edison phonographs or not."[35] Gilmore and Edison were having none of it; after ten years working with the dishonest Moriarty, Edison United and Edison Bell, they were determined to create their own operation in Britain. How Edison Bell and National Phonograph Company Ltd fared is the one of the subjects discussed in chapter 3.

★   ★   ★

In 1888 Henry Edmunds, the British engineer who witnessed one of Edison's earliest phonograph demonstrations, acquired a licence to exploit the British Bell-Tainter patents. Like Colonel Gouraud, Edmunds demonstrated the Graphophone at learned gatherings and gave commercial exhibitions. Occasionally, this brought the two men on to the same platform or at least together as one gave a demonstration.[36] Just as Gouraud made recordings of great Victorian figures, it has been claimed that Sydney Morse, one of Edmunds colleagues, made a recording of the voice of Queen Victoria.[37] The 1890 sale of the British Bell-Tainter patents to Moriarty's International Graphophone and creation of Edison United ended Edmunds's and Gouraud's association with sound recording. Thereafter, until the expiry of the main Bell-Tainter patents in 1900, it was not legally possible to import Graphophones other than through the Edison Bell monopoly and its strategy to buy Edison phonographs.[38]

In 1897, Frank Dorian, a top Columbia Phonograph Company General executive, left New York for Paris where he established Columbia's European headquarters selling the new range of "Eagle" home Graphophones and records. Dorian opened a supply line importing Graphophones and barrel loads of cylinder records from the American Graphophone manufacturing plant at Bridgeport, Connecticut. He also established Columbia's presence in Germany, Russia and other European locations, though in France he had to contend with competition from Pathé Frères. By the time Dorian arrived in Paris, this company was already manufacturing its own versions of the American Graphophones and music records as, according to local law, patents had to be worked in France within two years of their grant or they fell into the public domain. This happened to the French Edison and Bell-Tainter patents, enabling Pathé Frères to establish itself well before the arrival of American competition. The Pathé Frères trade was significant, leaving its factory unable to fulfil demand. To bridge the gap, Dorian obtained large orders for American Graphophones and records. Interestingly Charles A. Stevens, the head of Edison's export business, claimed Pathé Frères was full of praise for Edison and contemptuously dismissive of both Columbia and Edison Bell.[39] Although the patent situation prevented Columbia trading in Britain until 1900, the Edison Bell and Stephen Moriarty papers at the Edison National Historic Site suggest a clandestine cross-channel trade in Columbia Graphophones and records. Furthermore, the Sony Music Archive holds an 1898 English language trade circular produced by the French branch advising British customers of the availability of Columbia products (which were being imported to a Dutch free port). It also gave details of trade discounts.[40] Unfortunately, information does not survive to indicate the extent of this illicit trade.

In May 1900, the last major British Bell-Tainter patent expired and Dorian immediately moved his operation to London where he traded as an unregistered business, the foreign branch of an American company. The new venture was purely a marketing organisation based at offices and showrooms in Oxford Street, importing a range of Graphophones and cylinder records from the United States. In an attempt to prevent Columbia trading, Edison Bell initiated proceedings alleging patent infringement, but it led nowhere. As the trade journal *The Phonoscope* noted, "The Columbia Phonograph Co. opened their London office on May 5 in a blaze of glory and law suits under the management of Frank Dorian formerly in charge of the Paris office. The Edison Bell Consolidated Phonograph Company Ltd jumped on them with both feet before they got comfortably settled."[41] Although designed to assert its monopoly, the Edison Bell moves showed the extent to which it had already lost control of the cylinder trade. Furthermore, it soon faced yet another competitor, Pathé Frères. Columbia sold a range of Graphophones into the British market retailing at prices ranging from £2.5s for the "Eagle" (compared to the Edison Bell price of £7.50) to £30.00. Columbia moulded cylinder records sold for 2s.0d. In 1902 Columbia introduced its first disc records and machines, again imported from the US.[42] With a product range extending across both cylinder and disc technologies, Columbia participated in the rapidly developing British mass market. However, despite the outward appearance of growth and business efficiency, the operation was subject to the financial travails of its American parent. In 1901 The Columbia Phonograph Company General experienced one of its recurrent financial crises and used Dorian's European business as a source of ready cash. Dorian managed this crisis with heavy discounting and he cut costs by moving to cheaper premises and by a series of layoffs. Though the British business survived, its reputation was seriously tarnished.

★ ★ ★

On 13 July 1897, shortly after Frank Dorian's departure for Paris, William Barry Owen, formerly general manager of Frank Seaman's National Gramophone Company, also left New York though his destination was London, where as emissary to Emile Berliner he had the twin tasks of restarting the British market for Gramophone goods (after the Waltershausen venture of the early 1890s) and finding capitalists willing to invest in a European Gramophone venture. Owen succeeded in both and in doing so created The Gramophone Company, which eventually grew into The EMI Group plc, which was one of the most important record companies in the world. Of all the British record companies founded in the late nineteenth century, The Gramophone Company and its successors have left the most significant imprint. Continuity of business from 1897 to the present provides a unique chronicle and establishes The EMI Group Archive Trust as the most important resource of its kind in the world. The record is by no means complete, but fortunately sufficient data have survived to enable this analysis to be made of the company's activities in the years leading up to 1903.

Prior to his departure, Owen and Emile Berliner agreed a strategy for the British and continental European markets. Owen was to trade in his own right, purchasing goods through National Gramophone Company in New York and paying Berliner a royalty of 15 per cent of the retail selling price.[43] He was also to find investors willing to invest in the business. Berliner wrote to Owen, "A good way would be to start a syndicate of say 20 equal shares of say £5,000 each. . . . The syndicate then buys the patents and processes from me and organises a company, reserving say 60 per cent of the stock for themselves, with the money on hand which can be paid in as necessary."[44]

Upon arrival and believing there was an effective supply line with National Gramophone Company, Owen began trading from the Hotel Cecil in The Strand. His products were 7-inch Berliner discs with a sound signal printed on one side retailing at 2s.6d and the Johnson Improved Gramophone retailing at £5.10s.[45] On 3 August 1897 Orville La Dow, Owen's successor at National Gramophone, wrote, "We have on hand orders for about 250 and we have 5 machines in the place. . . . I send you 2 machines. . . . I was in hopes also of getting off some new records, but . . . find that demand has eaten up the supply."[46] As the letter suggests, Owen had been overoptimistic, supply line failures quickly appeared and irritated customers began complaining. One wrote, "We regret . . . that you are not in a position to supply gramophones. We have sold quite a number." These shortages and complaints continued for several months.[47]

The second stage of Owen's commission was to find investors. Of his strategy, Berliner wrote on the 23 August 1897, "Your plan seems comprehensive enough. . . . You say nothing of stock. Of course if we could sell out at $100,000 we could waive stock, but how otherwise?"[48] This first and a subsequent attempt at forming a syndicate failed, though Berliner wrote encouragingly, "You have met with a bad snag. I trust that you will not become discouraged as you have a good thing to put before the people there."[49] In December 1897, Owen consulted a solicitor Edmund Trevor Lloyd Williams about a new proposal.[50] Williams counselled against the contract and expressed interest himself. Owen wrote to Berliner, "I have been taking Mr Williams' advice professionally, and have each day seen the growing interest which always comes. . . . He said to me today that he would assist me in getting up a syndicate."[51] According to the 1897 edition of *The Directory of Directors* Williams held no directorships though he did have extensive American business interests and visited the United States in February 1898. He was followed by an increasingly desperate Owen who introduced him to Berliner, Johnson and Seaman. In his unpublished memoirs Alfred Clark wrote of Owen's difficulties, "When he returned to America on the same ship as Williams, his funds were completely exhausted and it was Calvin G. Child . . . who joined with me in advancing the money necessary to enable Owen to return once more to England."[52]

These remarks contrast with Owen's apparent trading success. Little by way of financial data for this period has survived either at The EMI Group Archive Trust or among the Berliner papers at the Library of Congress, apart that is from a statement of monthly royalty payments paid to

**Table 2.1.   William Barry Owen's Trading Account,
September 1897 to February 1898**

Retail sales	£48,763	[$243,815]
Cost of product	£9,752	[$48,760]
Royalty	£7,314	[$36,570]
Gross profit	£24,381	[$121,905]

Berliner by Owen for the period September 1897 to August 1899.[53] The royalty was based on 15 per cent of the retail selling price. Owen bought his goods at 20 per cent of the retail selling and sold them to retailers at 70 per cent. This left him with a gross profit of 50 per cent, out of which he paid Berliner his 15 per cent royalty. From this it is possible to compute Owen's trading activities for the six months of September 1897 to February 1898 and these are shown in table 2.1, which suggests that Owen was buying on average £1,625 worth of product each month. Furthermore, after paying Berliner a total of £7,314 out of gross profit he was left with £17,067 to pay his expenses and purchase new product. The difference between Clark's analysis and the above calculation must lie in National Gramophone's insistence on cash for goods.

In February 1898 Berliner and Williams concluded two agreements. The first gave Williams an option to purchase the British and European Berliner patents, whilst the second was a licence to exploit the Gramophone business in Britain and Europe. The deal was conditional on Williams forming a partnership willing to invest £5,000 in the Gramophone business, a continued royalty payment of 15 per cent on retail prices and the employment of Owen as manager.[54] Berliner and Williams further agreed to the immediate delivery of 3,000 machines and 150,000 records.[55] On his return to London, Williams formed a partnership with the self-styled title "The Gramophone Company" and Owen became manager with a quarter share in the business. Williams also introduced Edgar Storey to the venture. Storey was an old friend from his Cambridge days, a wealthy colliery owner and Liverpool businessman. Between them, they held the remaining three quarters share. At first Storey's involvement was substantial but, unfortunately, in 1906 ill health forced him to abandon his business career and he died shortly after. In contrast, it was the beginning of Trevor Williams's long association with The Gramophone Company, which only ended with his death in 1946.

The partnership procured offices at 31 Maiden Lane, just off The Strand. Owen then engaged Theodore Bernard Birnbaum, an experienced businessman who understood British and European business methods. He had been director of a manufacturing concern B. Birnbaum and Sons, was an outstanding salesman and especially knowledgeable of the import-export trade. Furthermore, he had contacts with the upper echelons of British society and in 1903 married Gertrude Lewis, the daughter of society solicitor Sir George Lewis, the personal lawyer to King Edward VII.[56] The two nonexecutive partners did not invest capital, but rather arranged bank guarantees so Owen could purchase product from America. As no accounts or ledgers have survived, the Berliner royalty statement provides the only clue to the growth of the business during this second and most crucial period for the European gramophone business (table 2.2).

During the partnership period product purchases averaged £1,364 per month and after deducting the Berliner royalty £42,947 was retained as gross profit. A dealership network was created following an extensive 1898 British sales tour by Birnbaum and the business developed. Interestingly, the partnership eschewed the wholesaler network and instead dealt directly with retailers, a practice that continued into the modern era. The following year company salesman Peter Bohanna who wrote a series of on-the-road letters to Owen made positive allusions to Birnbaum's earlier tour, the creation of dealerships and the good relations formed with retailers.[57]

A review of the payments in table 2.2 show monthly purchases lower than the period of Owen's solo trading. This apparent paradox is explained by two serious attacks on the business designed to drive it from the field. The first sign of difficulties came from National Gramophone in New York. Seaman's office might write, "We shipped you our regular weekly order of 100 machines and 50,000 records," but underlying this apparent harmonious arrangement there remained a continuing supply problem.[58] The issue surfaced at the end of May 1898 when Berliner wrote to Frank Seaman of National Gramophone, "You are trying your best to interfere with my European Gramophone ventures. Mr La Dow told me the other day that you would fight me in France. . . . You made a contract with Parisian parties and Williams refused to recognise it."[59] At the same time Berliner wrote to Owen, "Now I believe that owing to the unbusiness-like blunders made in New York the business in the United States has not

Table 2.2.   "The Gramophone Company": Accounts, March 1898–August 1899

Retail sales	£122,707	[$613,535]
Cost of product	£24,541	[$122,705]
Royalty	£18,406	[$92,032]
Gross profit	£61,353	[$306,765]

Note: For details of this calculation see page 48.

gained ground but that Mr Seaman relies on the export business to keep up his orders to the Berliner Co and that explains his desperate efforts to get hold of a slice of the European business."[60]

The second threat to The Gramophone Company came from The Edison Bell Consolidated Phonograph Company Ltd. Owen knew that Edison Bell, in importing Seaman-supplied Gramophones, Zonophones and records, was seeking ways to eliminate The Gramophone Company. As early as 1897, Edison Bell's solicitors had written, "I have to say that we claim the gramophone is an absolute and complete infringement of our patents."[61] Owen told Joseph Berliner,[62] brother to Emile and manager of Berliner Telephon Fabrik of Hanover, Germany:

> We are having heaps of trouble with The National Gramophone Co of New York, who are making direct efforts to interfere with our trade here. Indeed The National Gramophone Co have actually been in correspondence with Edison-Bell Phonograph Co, informing them that if they would attack our patents and bring a suit to restrain us from selling gramophones here in London that they would engage to sell Gramophones in England subject to a royalty to the Edison people.[63]

Owen had too high an opinion of the efficiency of Edison Bell, as it took till February 1899 to serve a writ on The Gramophone Company and a further ten months before settling and withdrawing its claims. Nonetheless Owen complained bitterly to Joseph Berliner about the debilitating effect that Edison Bell's publicity campaign had on the trade, which characterised The Gramophone Company as patent infringers. Joseph Berliner also learned of the threats Edison Bell were making to the dealership network. While Williams was in New York in early 1898, Frank Seaman and Orville La Dow pressed him to form a combination against Emile Berliner and his refusal appears to have been the trigger for the Seaman attack. In June 1898 Orville La Dow wrote to Williams, "We have told you over and over again that the claims of Mr Berliner in foreign countries are practically worthless. We made this point in our arguments as to the desirability of an amalgamation of interests."[64] In June 1898 Frank Seaman cut supplies. An angry William Barry Owen said, "They want to put us in the position of not being able to do any business in Germany France or any other foreign country where the language is different from English."[65]

In order to remain in business the partners first had to break Seaman's embargo and then secure their own European-based recording and manufacturing facilities. On 20 June Emile Berliner wrote, "You must go ahead with manufacturing in Europe as quickly as possible, rather than keep on buying in New York. . . . I am ready to send both [Joseph] Sanders[66] and [Fred] Gaisberg over to Europe to start things. This would give you at once a vantage ground from which you can sweep over Europe in spite of all the machinations on the part of Seaman or the Edison Bell crowd."[67] Frank Seaman realised time was of the essence, as Eldridge Johnson commented, "[Seaman] thinks he can cripple you by refusing to fill your orders and said that he will not send you any more goods. . . . Mr Seaman says that it will take a year for you to get your factory started and that he is the master of the situation."[68] The Hanover telephone factory was an obvious location for a pressing plant, as Joseph Sanders knew the German language, the factory and trusted Joseph Berliner with the matrix and record compound secrets. Sanders arrived in Europe at the end of July 1898, and in October Owen reported, "I have been over to Germany . . . and I found that they can send us records now at the rate of about 500 per day, and within a week they will be able to send us 2,000 a day."[69]

Working on behalf of the London partners Johnson broke Seaman's embargo, surreptitiously buying and shipping US-sourced records.[70] Until the Hanover record production was secure he continued this clandestine buying for what had become his most valuable cash customers. The maintenance of this perilous supply line enabled London to weather the storm, though the disruption damaged and disrupted the trade as the Berliner royalty statement indicates. In May 1898, the last full month of supplies from Seaman, the royalty was $6,283, about the average for the six previous months. In June and July this had fallen to $3,400 almost half the previous average and between August and October 1898 monthly royalties averaged $4,500, whilst November and December (with Hanover running to capacity and the Christmas trade boosting sales), royalties amounted to $6,415 and $8,402. Between January and July 1899, the period of the Edison Bell attack, royalties fell back and averaged under $4,000 per month.[71]

Chapter 1 discussed the July 1898 long-term agreement between Johnson and the London business, which encompassed Gramophone manufacturing, shipping and assembly in Britain. It proved the beginning of a long and fruitful trans-Atlantic association that lasted nearly sixty years. The same month Belford G. Royal, a long-time associate of Johnson, came to London to take charge of machine assembly and assist in the recording studio.[72] In November 1898 Joseph Sanders, together with Emile Berliner's brothers Joseph and Jacob, formed Deutsche Grammophon Gesellschaft. It had a capital of M20,000 [£1,000] and functioned as a matrix maker and record manufacturer.[73] Initially the Hanover plant charged London 3s.9d per dozen records, which was later reduced to 3s.6d per dozen.[74] Despite supply problems, correspondence for the second half of 1898 indicates the growth of British business. In July 1898, Owen wrote, "We could undoubtedly use 75–100,000 American records between now and the 1st January. . . . I am not overstating it when I say that by the 1st October we could easily dispose of 3–400 machines a month."[75] On 30 July Owen revised his machine order, telling Johnson, "I shall cable you to send along at least 400 machines per week. . . . At present we can use 300 without any doubt."[76] In September 1898 Owen ordered 100,000 machines, a third of Johnson's annual capacity at his newly enlarged factory. Johnson commented, "You must be selling machines very fast. We had no idea that you would sell that lot of machines so soon."[77]

With supplies of records secure, the second key to The Gramophone Company's survival strategy was the creation of a recording studio in London, though making recordings for local markets meant it had to have mobile recording facilities capable of moving around Britain, continental Europe and beyond. To establish this first disc recording studio in Europe, Emile Berliner sent his finest recording engineer, Fred Gaisberg, to London with Joseph Sanders and Belford Royal.[78] On his departure from New York, Owen noted, "Sanders and Geysberg [sic] are both leaving New York today. . . . I am simply getting Geysberg [sic] over here to get the lab started, make some tests, and get things prepared for someone else."[79] It proved a crucial decision for both Fred Gaisberg and the British record industry. In fact he spent the rest of his career in Britain and remained until his death in 1951. Gaisberg was the first and most influential recording engineer and artist and repertoire manager The Gramophone Company and later EMI ever had.

Fred Gaisberg wasted no time in constructing a recording studio in a basement room at 31 Maiden Lane. On 6 August 1898 Owen noted, "Gaisberg will commence to take records tomorrow. . . . We hope to have matrices turned out from English records within two weeks from today."[80] To help bridge the gap between the making of these first London recordings and their appearance in the shops, Berliner sent Sanders metal plates from his laboratory which were used to get record production started in Hanover. Gaisberg spent the rest of the year creating a British catalogue to supplement existing American record lists, all in the 7-inch Berliner process zinc-etched disc format. In February 1899 the recording technology took a significant leap forward when the London business purchased Eldridge Johnson's process for recording on "wax tablets." Johnson built a wax disc-cutting lathe for his British associates and, according to Harry Sooy, it incorporated innovations such as stationary horn connections and a capability for cutting 10-inch records. It cost The Gramophone Company £3,000, but proved a sound investment. These new discs provided a greatly improved sound quality and the capacity to make records of longer duration on first 10-inch and then, in 1903, 12-inch discs.[81] Unfortunately, published use of this technology was delayed until the impregnable British Bell-Tainter patent for cutting sound signals into wax expired in May 1900; the first releases bore that date.

By 1899, the small marketing organisation envisaged by Williams and his partners had been transformed into a business engaged in disc record making, the assembly of Gramophones and the marketing finished products not just in Britain, but also in continental Europe, the wider British Empire and beyond. This very success posed problems. Under the terms of the partnership, the entire business was carried out in Williams's own name and on a cash basis. With the rapid growth of the enterprise, the sums involved became sizeable. Of the suppliers Johnson appeared satisfied with cash on delivery. By contrast Joseph Berliner was worried and wrote to Williams in January 1899, "Who is *The Gramophone Co*? I am *personally* aware that *you* made up this Company with the intention to work the Gramophone business, but up to this date you never confirmed this in any way, that is to say you never wrote to me that you were identical with The Gramophone Co, as you really are."[82] The status of the London partnership required rethinking. In March 1899 Emile Berliner wrote to Owen, "I am willing to sell out simply so to clear the field for you. I have other schemes under way though you all will have my hearty cooperation for the glory of the gramophone at any time–and I want you all to make money."[83]

Other factors also made a change to the business relationship essential, for example the Berliner-owned Deutsche Grammophon Gesellschaft, conscious of the weak intellectual property laws in many European states, tried to establish recording facilities independently of London. In March 1899 Joseph Berliner secured the services of William Sinkler Darby, a Berliner sound engineer, and a set of disc recording equipment. Darby came over to Germany and went to Russia where he made the first disc records.[84] The secrecy surrounding this venture, unauthorised by London, is revealed in his diary. He wrote of his arrival in Hanover, "*Wed March 22, 1899:* I went to Mr Berliner's house . . . in Hanover and we talked over matters and the situation. . . . Hawd [The Gramophone Company's representative at the pressing factory] had been sent over to London the day before and they do not know in London that I am here but they have found out through Mr Royal [Johnson's representative in London] I suppose I was coming."[85] By the time Darby returned to Germany word of Joseph Berliner's plans and the unauthorised Russian expedition had reached London. Clearly very angry, Owen wrote to Joseph Berliner in which he said, "We are absolutely the proprietors of all the German rights under the contract of which you have knowledge with your brother Emile Berliner; we are making plans for the development of the Continental rights especially Scandinavia, Belgium, France, Germany, Russia, Austria and Italy and the Far East."[86] This cut no ice with Joseph Berliner, who responded:

> I do not know how it came to your knowledge that I had engaged a "Flying operator" for this Company but I really had at no times any reason to keep it secred [sic] before you. . . . I have not yet determined at all to which country I shall send the operator first, but you will never prevent this Company [going] to any country which is not protected by valid patents and to take records there! You are speaking from your "Continental rights" especially in Scandinavia, Holland, Russia and the Far East. Which are your rights in these countries? None whatever, and nobody will prevent this Company . . . of manufacturing and trading in these countries.[87]

These moves evidently worried the London partners and when, in May 1899, Emile Berliner came to London he accepted Williams's offer to purchase all the European Berliner patents outright for £10,000 plus an allotment of 10,000 shares in a new company.[88] This resolution of the patent issue did not prevent prevarication on the part of Joseph Berliner, who was selling gramophone goods in Germany through the Orpheus Musikwerke of Leipzig, a wholesale and retail business managed by his brother-in-law. Between May and August 1899 an aggressive correspondence continued over this and other issues, creating much ill feeling.[89] In August, under the threat of litigation and at the insistence of his brother Emile, Joseph Berliner withdrew from marketing and agreed to be the record-manufacturing arm of The Gramophone Company. For its part the partnership purchased a 60 per cent controlling interest in a reconstructed Deutsche Grammophon Aktiengsellschaft and Darby joined Gaisberg as a London employee. Under these arrangements Birnbaum went to Germany to organise and manage the German, central European and Russian selling branches, which became the largest in The Gramophone Company's domain.[90]

Having resolved the German question, the partnership was converted into a limited liability company called The Gramophone Company Ltd[91] with a nominal capital of £150,000. In the sale agreement the takeover was backdated to 1 May 1899, and Williams and his two partners became directors of the concern.[92] Under its terms, the partners received any remaining cash in excess of £20,000 working capital, plus profit from the old business and were allotted the bulk of the shares in the new company.[93] No firm financial data survives concerning the partners' business dealings or how much they took out of the business, though a balance sheet for the fifteen months to 30 June 1899 does exist. This indicates cash and assets totalling £40,711, giving the partners a potential return of £20,711 on their original investment.

The Gramophone Company Ltd traded between May 1899 and 30 June 1900 and during this period a multinational structure took shape, with subcompanies or agencies formed in Italy, France, Germany, Holland, Belgium and Scandinavia. To serve the musical needs of these culturally diverse states, Gaisberg, Darby and Birnbaum undertook a major continental European and recording tour. During the course of this and a subsequent tour of Russia and also one of Britain and Ireland, a total of 1,800 new recordings were made. These tours were mentioned by G. Morrison of Edison Bell in a 10 June 1899 letter to Moriarty in which also he related it to the suit Edison Bell was pursuing against The Gramophone Company. As he observed, "It looks as if Owen and the others felt more confident [about the Edison Bell suit] if they are taking records in the different languages, and going to that expense, and it is worthy of note that Johnson is now over here."[94] The recording and pressing facilities together with a multinational base proved the springboard to growth. This growth was chronicled in reports from Britain and the overseas branches; for example, in December 1899 Theodore Birnbaum writing from Berlin said monthly business had increased from £1,000 in September 1899 to £4,850 in November 1899.[95] Emile Berliner wrote of this to company chairman Trevor Williams, "We are all a hustling."[96]

In the very early days of the business, Theodore Birnbaum designed a trademark for use on Gramophone Company products. It took the form of a cherub seated on a disc record holding a quill pen and was known as "The Recording Angel." In November 1899, The Gramophone Company acquired a second and, as it proved, a more important and enduring trademark, the picture of "His Master's Voice."[97] This showed a fox terrier called Nipper listening to the sound of "His Master's Voice" on one of the new Johnson Gramophones. The artist was Francis Barraud RA and he was paid £50 for the picture and a further £50 for the copyright. The Gramophone Company Ltd secured the copyright of this image and the words "His Master's Voice" in Britain, Europe and much of the rest of the world, except in the Americas where Emile Berliner registered its use. When The Victor Talking Machine Company was formed in 1901 these rights passed into its hands.

The Recording Angel continued in use on all Gramophone Company records until 1910, when the company lost the right to use the word "Gramophone" as a proprietary term in Britain. As a consequence the Recording Angel was dropped and the picture of "His Master's Voice" substituted, with the words "His Master's Voice" replacing "Gramophone" as the main title on record labels.[98] Subsequently, Victor and The Gramophone Company promoted the image in aggressive advertising campaigns which turned it into one of the world's most iconic manufacturing images. The Recording Angel trademark fell into relative disuse until the 1950s, when EMI Ltd began trading on its own account in the USA. As RCA Victor owned the American rights to the "His Master's Voice" trademark EMI turned to its old mark, trading as "Angel Records." In the modern era the rights to the HMV trademark have fallen to the HMV international chain of record stores, though the Recording Angel trademark is still in use.

A balance sheet for the first six months of trading indicates liquid assets totalling £40,600.[99] In December 1899 a 10 per cent dividend was paid, and when in December 1900 this company was sold its assets were valued at £180,000. Two-thirds of these assets were liquid and one third goodwill, patents and holdings in foreign companies. Thus, during its life, Gramophone Company shares earned 50 per cent of their face value, and were bartered for all 500,000 £1 ordinary shares in the 1900 reconstruction.[100] The shareholders also received £60,000 cash for their shares, of which £38,885 was used to buy almost half the allotted preference shares. The balance was taken out of the business by Owen, Williams and Storey.[101]

In June 1900, shareholders of The Gramophone Company voted to form an entirely new venture to purchase the existing business, acquire the remaining 40 per cent of shares in Deutsche Grammophon Aktiengsellschaft and purchase the rights to manufacture and market the Lambert typewriter.[102] Although the new company, called The Gramophone and Typewriter Ltd, was formed in December 1900, for accounting purposes it took over the assets and business from 30 June 1900. This venture exists to the present day, trading as EMI Music Ltd, though for continuity The Gramophone Company Ltd will be used throughout this book.[103] The new business had a nominal capital of £600,000, divided into 500,000 £1 ordinary shares and 100,000 £1 preference shares. To provide working capital and acquire the Lambert typewriter rights, about 20,000 of the preference shares were sold. In his 1903 "Address to shareholders" Trevor Williams confessed, "Of the £80,000 original working capital, £60,000 was composed of stock in trade and sundry debtors."[104] Initially there was no market for Gramophone Company shares, although in June 1901 Owen wrote to Joseph Berliner, "We are preparing here to make a market in Gramophone shares and I think we shall be extremely successful and be able to get in the end, about 25s to 30s a piece. . . . It will be necessary to make some arrangements with all the principal stockholders, to pool their shares so that they will not put on the market the shares any faster than the public can be induced to take them up."[105] Until April 1903 there was a slow turnover in shares, thereafter, monthly share transfer data amounted to seventy pages; though by the time Owen left the company at the end of 1903 he had sold nearly all of his shares.[106]

The directors of the new company were chairman Trevor Williams together with three executives; managing director William Barry Owen, Theodore Birnbaum and Joseph Berliner. The remaining nonexecutive directors were Edgar Storey and two of Trevor Williams's brothers-in-law, Ernest (later Sir Ernest) de la Rue (a former vice chairman of printers Thomas de la Rue Ltd)[107] and Romer Williams a solicitor and director of several insurance companies. Owen, Birnbaum and Joseph Berliner were paid salaries and held substantial blocks of shares.[108] At first Williams and Owen made the important decisions, for example the board was not consulted on investment strategies for the large sums of surplus cash generated during the early days. This suggests the close relationship between Owen and Williams continued at least until the board developed a greater knowledge of the business. By 1904, this stage had evidently been reached as Owen's then assistant Sydney Dixon[109] wrote to Birnbaum in Germany, "The board are now taking a much more active role in the whole business than at any previous time."[110]

The new company made important changes to the structure of the business. Owen, Storey and Williams had formed the earlier directorates, with Owen and Birnbaum comprising the executive. In contrast the new board was larger and had the potential to be stronger in two significant ways. First, the presence of three executive directors kept the board in close touch with manufacturing and marketing conditions. Second, the three nonexecutive directors together with chairman Trevor Williams provided the board with an overview of the market and strategy.

To manage a multinational business in the days before instant communications required trust between managers and the board, together with an organisation capable of controlling domestic and overseas manufacturing and marketing. In the case of The Gramophone Company, the organisation also had to maintain strong links with Johnson in the US, on whom they were dependent for mechanical components. The multinational management was divided into three, with Berliner based in Hanover managing record manufacturing, Birnbaum based in Berlin managing the central and eastern European and Russian markets and Owen in London managing the rest of the business including relations with America.[111] There was no executive department in Owen's time or a separate British branch. It seems as though Owen, the guiding spirit of the business for its first seven years, was incapable of creating an organisation controlled by subordinates capable of being managed by a chief executive. The need for these organisational changes and the board's growing supervisory role, may well have spurred Owen's departure.

By November 1902 the strain on Owen was showing, and he told Johnson said he would leave the following year because the board refused to pay him 5 per cent of profit instead of a salary. Owen confessed, "I do not care to have the wear and tear upon my health that I see to be necessary in the next two or three years unless I am certain that at the end of the time I shall have more money than I have at the present."[112] The fact that he stayed for only a further eighteen months suggests a balance between the strain of his position and his own financial reward was never achieved. In his memoirs, Fred Gaisberg described Owen as "an opportunist, of quick decision and a bold gambler. . . . He brought to London an infectious enthusiasm and energetic leadership."[113]

★   ★   ★

In the years between its formation in 1900 and the departure of William Barry Owen in 1903, The Gramophone Company Ltd experienced phenomenal growth. In 1900 the business employed capital amounting to £80,000 and by 1904 new capital employed in Russia and Germany alone accounted for £160,000.[114] To keep track of developments Owen wrote regular reports, which survive in sufficient quantity to analyse the company's growth during his period of office.

Table 2.3 shows the remarkable growth in turnover, net profit and record sales. This is further highlighted in table 2.4 below by the use of indexed figures. The most significant figures are those for 1903–1904, which indicate a reduction in record sales because of the appearance of European disc competition and the impact of a short recession. That year was of great importance for The Gramophone Company, marking as it did the end of its European near monopoly in the disc record market and the beginning of effective competition.

Table 2.3. The Gramophone Company Ltd: Performance (British and International), 1900–1904

Year	Turnover	Net Profit	Record Sales	Gramophone Sales	New Capital
1900– 1901	NA	£79,348 [$396,740]	1,989,504	12,589[a]	£14,391 [$71,955]
1901– 1902	£342,218 [$1,711,090]	£137,268 [$686,340]	2,750,178	25,178	£61,543 [$307,715]
1902– 1903	£685,593 [$3,427,965]	£253,285 [$1,266,425]	5,414,269	19,823	£72,339 [$361,695]
1903– 1904	£500,505 [$2,502,525]	£211,750 [$1,058,750]	3,908,889	71,453	NA

Source: Compiled from "Managing Directors' Reports to the Board 1901–1904." Data relating to unit sales of records and Gramophones are compiled from "Nominal Ledger No 1" (board papers, EMI).

[a]Six months only.

When in December 1903 William Barry Owen retired to keep chickens on Martha's Vineyard he left behind a cash rich business. The balance sheet for 1903–1904 show £115,578 cash and investments, £61,253 in unpaid overseas profits, plus £367,332 carried forward from the previous year. Furthermore between 1901 and 1904 shareholders received dividends of 30 per cent on ordinary shares and 20 per cent on preference shares.[115] The annual report for 1904 indicates a cash surplus after dividends of £544,161.[116]

In 1901, the company moved its offices and recording studio to 21 City Road, in the City of London. This enabled the venture to expand its recording and Gramophone assembly facilities and develop an office management system capable of controlling the dispersed manufacturing, marketing, purchasing, credit and accounts. To fund the central office a rudimentary internal market was created, with Hanover and the London Gramophone assembly plant charging the company for their products and the centre adding an administration cost to the price the branches paid for product.[117] All this moved the business out of its pioneering phase, which had clearly ended when Owen left.

Table 2.4. The Gramophone Company Ltd: Profits and Sales, Indexed Figures (1900–1904)

Year	Turnover	Net Profit	Record Sales	New Capital
1900–1901	NA	100	100	100
1901–1902	100	169	138	428
1902–1903	200	262	272	510
1903–1904	146	267	196	NA

Despite the phenomenal growth after 1899, Owen worried about the competitive incursions made by Frank Seaman's Zonophone. In November 1899 he wrote to Johnson, "The Zonophone has arrived in England."[118] Imported by Edison Bell and others, Owen received reports from Birnbaum in Berlin about the Zonophone machines and records. Of greatest concern was the fact that they were being offered for sale at substantially lower prices than Gramophone Company products. Owen said, "We cannot see how Frank Sieman [*sic*] . . . can win at the game he is playing as . . . the prices which he is preparing will be beaten, and his trade lost if it comes to a question of necessary competition."[119] Seaman employed American businessman Frederick Marion Prescott as his European agent. Prescott had not been secretive in his activities, and his early progress was chronicled in the American trade journal *The Phonoscope*.[120]

The entry of Zonophone into the European disc record business was quickly followed by Columbia in 1902. Together, these ventures provided an important check on The Gramophone Company's British and European disc record monopoly. Reacting to these moves and in an attempt to preserve this monopoly (and at the same time gain a position in the mass disc and machine markets developing in Germany), The Gramophone Company bought International Zonophone GmbH in 1903.[121] In that same year Theodore Birnbaum, aware of the growing competitive threat, wrote ominously, "The whole of the German Musical Industry, represented by the large Leipzig Manufacturers, are turning their attention to talking machines and are devoting their extensive mechanical facilities to the manufacture . . . of ordinary Gramophone motors and are now about to make a determined onslaught on our, up to now unassailable position."[122] Despite the warning the board failed to develop a European-based Gramophone manufacturing capacity; as the following chapters show, this proved its most serious strategic error.

Between 1897 and 1903, The Gramophone Company created an international market in gramophone goods and founded the British and European disc record industry. Initially a marketing organisation, it quickly learned the importance of controlling its products back to the point of manufacture. To this end The Gramophone Company, in 1898, established recording facilities and the following year acquired a controlling interest in Deutsche Grammophon Gesellschaft. These moves allowed it to meet better the needs of local markets and were achieved at modest outlay. They gave the company both a strength and subtlety in its various markets and provided important economies of scale. It allowed, for example, records with a universal appeal to be sold throughout Europe and beyond for the cost of a single recording session.

The initial prime mover advantages enjoyed by The Gramophone Company earned it windfall profits. Rather than use the cash to pay large dividends they instead funded capital developments and built a surplus against future needs. In the circumstances this cautious approach was sensible. On the other hand the company failed to anticipate the growth of competition, particularly from German and Swiss manufacturers. These were well established in the field of mechanical musical devices such as clocks and musical boxes, and they quickly moved into the market for cheap clockwork-driven talking machines. This failure left William Barry Owen's successors dependent on much more expensive American components and a shrinking market share. His legacy to his immediate successor, Theodore Birnbaum, was therefore mixed. Although the company had large cash surpluses its management structure was inadequate and its disc record monopoly had ended. Unlike Owen, Birnbaum faced a fiercely competitive market with effective competition from all quarters. The following chapters analyse it and other players in the burgeoning British record industry under these new conditions.

★   ★   ★

By 1903 the new British record industry was established in many of its constituent forms. There was still much working out to be done. For instance there was still no British industry standard format for records. However, in comparison to the closed patent-based oligopoly in the United States, the British and European trade took place within a vibrant free market that drew on manufactured goods priced increasingly within the pocket of the British skilled and semiskilled working classes. Also by the end of 1902, the days of the Edison Bell and Gramophone Company monopoly of cylinder and disc markets was over, the pioneering period was at an end and the motor of growth set to accelerate. How the record industry fared in the decade before the outbreak of the First World War is the subject of the next chapters.

NOTES

Written in 1879, "I'll Song the Songs of Araby" was a successful late-Victorian ballad by Frederick Clay. It was a popular choice of early record companies on both sides of the

Atlantic, and in 1901, The Gramophone Company Ltd made its most prestigious recording of the song with the tenor Ben Davies (G&T 2-2501).

1. American Talking Machine Company London to William Barry Owen, 20 December 1897 (Formation, 1897, EMI).

2. Henry Edmunds, "Letter to the Editor of *The Times*, 17 January 1878." Later in his career, Edmunds became a motoring pioneer and, in 1904, introduced Charles Rolls to Henry Royce. See Paul Tritton, *The Godfather of Rolls Royce: The Life and Times of Henry Edmunds MICE, MIEE* (Academy Books, 1993).

3. The early development of Edison's phonograph in Britain is chronicled in V. K. Chew, *Talking Machines* (HMSO, 1967); Frank Andrews, *Edison Phonograph the British Connection* (Rugby: City of London Phonograph and Gramophone Society, 1986), and chapter 9, "The Wizard of Menlo Park," in Paul Israel, *Edison: A Life of Invention* (New York: Wiley, 1998).

4. After the phonograph venture, Gouraud became involved in a private enterprise flight of fancy; the so-called Kingdom of the Sahara, holding the self-styled post of "Governor-General." See James White to William Edgar Gilmore, 5 February 1904 (document files, 1904, phonomanufacturing, Edison National Historic Site).

5. For more information, see Andrews, *Edison*, xvi, 1–2. Jonathan Lewis Young (1859–1940) was a British record industry pioneer associated with several early businesses. In 1893, he published *Edison and His Phonograph*, and in 1903, just before the British Edison patents (held by Edison Bell) expired, he established National Phonograph Company Ltd, which was quickly acquired by Edison as a vehicle to exploit his products in Britain. Young went on to form The English Record Company, but that business failed in 1913.

6. For more on the Irving recording, see Wes Folkerth, "Then Play On: Listening to the Shakespearean Soundscape" (unpublished PhD thesis, McGill University, Montreal, Canada, 1999), 1–3. See also Richard Bebb, "The Voice of Henry Irving," BBC radio 4 recording, 1974 (copy in my collection). See also Richard Bebb, "The Voice of Henry Irving: An Investigation," in *Recorded Sound: The Journal of the British Institute of Recorded Sound*, no. 68 (1977): 727–32.

7. Stephen Fossa Moriarty (d. 1907) was an American businessman and British record industry pioneer. He formed International Graphophone and Edison United, jointly with Thomas Edison, which acted as the export arm of his phonograph business. A key figure in the creation of the first two Edison Bell businesses, Moriarty milked them both dry and was eventually dismissed though he remained a director. He lived in continental Europe until his death in 1907.

8. See Andrews, *Edison*, 3–12. Also see Paul Tritton, *The Lost Voice of Queen Victoria* (London: Academy Books, 1991), which reviews this venture.

9. "International Graphophone and Edison United Transferring Bell-Tainter Patents Indenture," 31 December 1892 (Edison phonograph works, phonograph file, 1900, Edison National Historic Site).

10. See "Edison Bell Phonograph Corporation Ltd," company registration file BT31/5448 (The National Archive, Kew, London).

11. Although Edison's involvement with Edison United ended in 1896, quantities of Edison United, Edison-Bell and Stephen Moriarty's personal and business papers relating to the years after that date are held at Edison National Historic Site. Current research has not revealed the provenance of this deposit. The collection contains two long and detailed letters written by Moriarty to Senator Orville H. Platt setting out the history of the business from his

perspective. One is dated 4 March 1896, and the other is undated but appears to have been written a little earlier. In them Moriarty denounced George E. Gouraud, the entertainment phonograph and Thomas Edison.

12. Andrews, *Edison*, 16–17.

13. A note by Edison described Hough as "the pirate who is infringing and making bogus kinetoscopes in Europe" (Edison phonograph works, 1895, Edison National Historic Site).

14. For an account of Hough's early activities, see *The Story of Edison Bell* (City of London Phonograph and Gramophone Society, reprint, 1969). See also Andrews, *Edison*, 9–10.

15. Ogilvie Mitchell, *The Talking Machine Trade* (London, 1922).

16. See *English Mechanic and World of Science*, no. 1 (22 October 1897): 700.

17. Frederick M. Prescott, *The Phonoscope* (September 1898): 10.

18. For further information about the complex financial deals that led to the creation of Edison Bell Consolidated Phonograph Co Ltd, see Andrews, *Edison*, 27–30.

19. As principal shareholder, Moriarty benefited financially from this reconstruction. For details and agreements, see company registration file, Edison Bell Consolidated Phonograph Co Ltd, BT31/7861 (The National Archive, Kew), and *The Phonoscope* (March 1898): 7–9.

20. C. A. Stevens to William Edgar Gilmore, 1 September 1899 (Edison phonograph foreign files, July-September 1899, Edison National Historic Site).

21. Undated note, circa 1899, by Thomas Edison (Edison general files, phonograph-foreign, July-September 1899, Edison National Historic Site).

22. J. E. Hough reported Moriarty's death in the British trade journal *Talking Machine News* 5, no. 4 (August 1907): 272. Details of Moriarty's death in Europe and the removal of his body to the United States can be found in the Moriarty papers at the Edison National Historic Site.

23. Andrews, *Edison*, 26.

24. For more about the early career of Russell Hunting, see chapter 1. G. Morrison to Stephen Moriarty, 16 December 1898 (Moriarty papers, Edison National Historic Site).

25. Alfred Clark to William Barry Owen, 26 April 1900 (company formation papers, 1900, EMI).

26. Alfred Clark to William Barry Owen, 26 April 1900.

27. See Prescott's letter cited above and "Edisonia Price List, 1898" (Columbia file, EMI).

28. See Peter Bohanna letters (company formation papers, 1899, EMI), *The Phonoscope* (December 1899): 10, and Bunney's Ltd to Thomas Edison, 28 September 1908 (phonograph foreign files July-September 1898, Edison National Historic Site).

29. William Edgar Gilmore to Howard W. Hayes, 22 November 1901 (Phono-National Phonograph Co-Dealers, 1901, Edison National Historic Site).

30. Edison Bell to Thomas Edison, 11 September 1900, and Edison's reply, n.d. Edison Bell to Thomas Edison, 16 October 1900 (phonograph-foreign, Edison Bell Phonograph Co, 1900, Edison National Historic Site).

31. In 1901 the patent-based monopoly for the sale of phonographs operated by Edison Bell expired. All that remained of the Edison Bell patent portfolio were minor patents, which expired in 1903, and a patent for the tapered mandrel used to accommodate the tapered bore of cylinder records. I am grateful to Frank Andrews for explaining this important point.

32. These German phonographs were described by Edison export manager Charles A. Stevens as "cheap infringements . . . [with] prices [varying] from 15 to 30 marks [£0.60p to £1.20]." Stevens to William Edgar Gilmore, 28 September 1899 (phonograph-foreign files, July-September 1898, Edison National Historic Site).

33. Symonds to Thomas Edison, October 1902 (document files, 1902, phonolegal, Edison National Historic Site).

34. George Croydon Marks to William Edgar Gilmore, 2 December 1902 (document files, 1902, Phono-NPC-Foreign, Edison National Historic Site).

35. Hough to William Edgar Gilmore, 7 June 1902 (document files, 1902, Phono Pats/ Schools and Colleges, Edison National Historic Site).

36. For accounts of these demonstrations, see Henry Edmunds, "The Graphophone," *Transactions of the British Association for the Advancement of Science*, Bath Meeting (September 1888). Henry Edmunds, "The Graphophone," *Journal of the Society of Arts* (7 December 1888): 39–48.

37. See Tritton, *Lost Voice*.

38. In 1891 US production of Graphophones ceased, and as far as Edison Bell was concerned, the key Bell-Tainter assets were the patents—specifically, the floating sound box principle and the incising of sound signals into wax.

39. Charles A. Stevens to William Edgar Gilmore, 6 September 1899 (phonograph foreign files, July-September 1899, Edison National Historic Site). For similar remarks about Columbia, see Alfred Clark to William Barry Owen, 11 November 1901 (French files, EMI).

40. "To Our Dealers," Columbia trade circular to British dealers, Paris, 25 August 1898 (Sony Music Archive, New York). Edison Bell also sold Pathé machines as Graphophones, which, from the British patent point of view, they were. I am grateful to Christopher Proudfoot for pointing this out.

41. *The Phonoscope* (March 1900): 8. The publication dates of these early trade journals often failed to match the masthead date.

42. Cited from a Columbia catalogue, 15 December 1902 (Columbia catalogue files, EMI).

43. Emile Berliner to William Barry Owen, 23 November 1899 (Berliner papers, EMI).

44. Emile Berliner to William Barry Owen, 13 July 1897 (Berliner papers, EMI).

45. The retail price is cited in Brian Oakley and Christopher Proudfoot, *His Master's Gramophone* (Kent, 2011): 2–3.

46. National Gramophone Co to William Barry Owen, 3 August 1897 (company formation papers, 1897, EMI).

47. R Wylie Hill and Co, Glasgow to William Barry Owen, 10 August 1897 (Formation, 1897, EMI).

48. Emile Berliner to William Barry Owen, 23 August 1897 (Berliner papers, EMI).

49. Emile Berliner to William Barry Owen, 15 September 1897 (Berliner papers, EMI).

50. Born into a wealthy Welsh landowning family, Edmund Trevor Lloyd Williams (1859–1946) was educated at Marlborough College and Trinity College, Cambridge. When he met Owen, Williams was in practice at a city law firm and married into wealth. See Barbara Gibbs, "Trevor Williams 1859–1946" (unpublished manuscript, 1968, Trevor Williams file, EMI). In this work, Barbara Gibbs pointed out that many of her father's early business papers relating to the formation of The Gramophone Company had been accidentally destroyed. Williams was chairman of The Gramophone Company till 1930, when Alfred Clark succeeded him, but was a director of EMI until his death in 1946.

51. William Barry Owen to Emile Berliner, 20 December 1897 (Berliner papers, EMI).

52. Alfred Clark, "His Master's Voice: A Record" (unpublished, circa 1939), 124.

53. Emile Berliner to William Barry Owen, 23 November 1899 (Berliner papers, EMI).

54. Williams and Berliner Agreements (Formation papers, 1898, EMI).

55. Emile Berliner to Jack Watson Hawd (Hawd was an American employee of Owen's in London; for more on Hawd, see chapter 4), 19 April 1898 (Berliner papers, EMI).

56. For more on this, see chapters 5 and 6. Information given to me by the late Sir Anthony Burney OBE, Theodore Birnbaum's son.

57. Bohanna file (Formation, 1899, EMI).

58. National Gramophone Co New York to Edmund Trevor Lloyd Williams, 6 May 1898 (Formation, 1898, EMI).

59. Copy of a letter sent by Emile Berliner to Frank Seaman, 30 May 1898 (Berliner papers, EMI).

60. Emile Berliner to William Barry Owen, 31 May 1898 (Berliner papers, EMI).

61. Edison Bell to Messrs Ashurst Morris and Crisp and Co, Music Dealers, undated copy (Formation, 1897, EMI).

62. Joseph Berliner (1858–1938) was the brother of Emile. Previous to his record industry career, he and his two brothers formed The Berliner Telephon Fabrik in Hanover. In late 1898, the first European matrix-making and disc record–pressing plant was established at that factory. Also in 1898, Emile Berliner and his brothers formed Deutsche Grammophon Gesellschaft and in 1900 merged it with The Gramophone Company Ltd. Joseph Berliner became an executive director and managed the company's European manufacturing facilities. When war broke out in 1914, Berliner lost his seat on the London board, and when, in 1917, the German government seized and sold the German assets, Berliner went with them. Dismissed by his new employers in 1921, Berliner tried but failed to mend his fences with London. He left the business and died in 1938.

63. William Barry Owen to Joseph Berliner, 8 June 1898 (Formation, 1898, EMI). See Edison Bell File (Formation, 1899, EMI). See also Frank Andrews, "Edison Bell in 1899" (unpublished manuscript).

64. Orville La Dow, National Gramophone Company, New York to Edmund Trevor Lloyd Williams, 10 June 1898. Entered as evidence in *Berliner Gramophone Co v Frank Seaman*, United States Fourth Circuit Court of Appeals for West Virginia, Harrisburg, 7 February 1901. (Copy of trial transcript in *Supreme Court of the United States Files, 1901*, US National Archives, College Park, Maryland). The letter forms part of Seaman's attack on the Berliner patents in the USA and is a comment on the minefield of pre-1914 European intellectual property rights.

65. William Barry Owen to Emile Berliner, 1 June 1898 (Formation, 1898, EMI).

66. German-born Joseph Sanders (1877–1960) was the nephew of Emile Berliner (who married Berliner's daughter). Sanders emigrated to the USA in 1885, lived in Washington, DC, and worked in his uncle's laboratory. A naturalised US citizen, he returned to Germany in 1892 to serve an apprenticeship at the Berliner factory. He returned to Washington and his uncle's employment in 1895, where he learned the art of matrix making and the skills of record production—particularly, the formulae for record compounds. In 1898 Sanders established the Hanover record pressing factory: the first such dedicated plant in the world. He later formed the Standard Materials Company, which supplied both the Victor and Gramophone companies with the mixture used for record making. In 1907 he was offered the post of manager at the Hayes record-pressing factory but turned it down when he was refused a directorship; he subsequently left the sound recording business. Joseph Sanders's son, the late Robert Sanders, gave much of this information to me. He also made available Joe Sanders's diaries for the years 1907–1908, together with a series of letters concerning this period written by his father to RCA in the 1950s and a copy of the 1960 service in memory

of his father; all this material is now in the Library of Congress, where it forms a part of The Robert Sanders Collection.

67. Emile Berliner to William Barry Owen, 20 June 1898 (Berliner papers, EMI).

68. Eldridge Reeves Johnson to William Barry Owen, 11 July 1898 (Formation, 1898, EMI).

69. William Barry Owen to Eldridge Reeves Johnson, 16 October 1898 (Formation, 1898, EMI).

70. See letters from Eldridge Reeves Johnson to William Barry Owen, July-October 1898, in which he chronicles purchases of records for London (Formation, 1898, EMI).

71. Emile Berliner to William Barry Owen, 23 November 1899 (Berliner papers, EMI).

72. William Barry Owen to Eldridge Reeves Johnson, 22 June 1898 (Formation, 1898, EMI). Writing of this event, Harry O. Sooy said, "Everything seemed to be flourishing at this time, and, I am quite sure, it was late this year that Mr. Royal, an old and confidential employee of the shop having every detail of the business at his finger ends, was appointed by Mr. Johnson to go to Europe and establish the Johnson processes and methods of work for the European trade" (Sooy, "Memoir of My Career at Victor Talking Machine Company," http://www.davidsarnoff.org).

73. Copy of Deutsche Grammophon Gesellschaft company registration papers in translation (German file, EMI).

74. J. Berliner to Edmund Trevor Lloyd Williams, 24 January 1899 (Formation, 1899, EMI).

75. William Barry Owen to Eldridge Reeves Johnson, 6 July 1898 (Formation, 1898, EMI).

76. William Barry Owen to Eldridge Reeves Johnson, 30 July 1898 (Formation, 1898, EMI).

77. Eldridge Reeves Johnson to William Barry Owen, 9, 13 and 16 September 1898 (Formation, 1898, EMI).

78. Harry Sooy's memoirs reveal something of the close relationship between the Johnson and British organisations at this critical stage in the trade:

Mr Royal, although located in England, would make frequent trips back to the US, and, naturally, would spend a lot of time around the Recording Laboratory and Experimental Machine Shop, which were the departments he was interested in, being in the line of his duties in Europe.

They were always a little sceptical of Mr Royal around the plant on his return visits to the US, because we had heard he usually brought a large trunk with him to be filled before starting back to England. And, by gosh, we realized this to be true later on, as Mr Royal, on one of his early trips, had a big trunk delivered to the Laboratory—just why this trunk was delivered to this department we did not know, although Mr Royal would make daily visits to the Laboratory. Sometime later we began to miss some of the working parts of the department, and upon investigation, we had the courage to open his trunk, we found the parts all nicely packed ready to start for England, comprising especially of mechanical parts for making records. Mr Royal was, of course, most particular to get the parts which he knew to be working good, and he didn't hesitate to slip in a good recording box that he knew to be working well.

After we located this paraphernalia in Mr Royal's trunk, it was then we (Reinhart, Nafey and I) abused his thought by unloading his entire trunk, which he had so nicely packed, and filled it with all the old scrap iron we could find in the department. Well, just before Mr Royal's departure, he opened his trunk to see if all of his collection was there, and to his surprise he found the trunk had been emptied of his choice mechanical parts, and that it contained only scrap iron. But, as we always found Mr Royal good natured, he thought it a huge joke, and, after he had explained the many difficulties he was working under in Europe, we, of course, fell for the line of talk, and returned all the parts we had taken from him, wishing him the best of luck. (Sooy, "Memoir of My Career")

79. William Barry Owen to Eldridge Reeves Johnson, 16 July 1898 (Formation, 1898, EMI).

80. William Barry Owen to Eldridge Reeves Johnson, 6 Aug 1898 (Formation, 1898, EMI). For an account of Gaisberg's preparations and first recording session, see Peter Adamson, "The First London Disc Recordings," *Hillandale News* 207 (December 1995): 411–22.

81. Details of the process are examined in chapter 1. See "E. R. Johnson and The Gramophone Company 1899 Agreements" (Eldridge Reeves Johnson–Victor agreements, Victor papers, EMI).

82. J. Berliner to Edmund Trevor Lloyd Williams, 14 January 1899 (Berliner papers, EMI).

83. Emile Berliner to William Barry Owen, 8 March 1899 (Berliner papers, EMI).

84. In 1990 the late Kathleen Darby, daughter of William Sinkler Darby, passed his diaries and photographs for this period to The EMI Music Archive Trust. In addition she gave a number of sound records he sent in 1899 as messages to his parents and friends in the USA. These now form part of The Darby collection at EMI.

85. Entry from The Darby Diaries, 1899 (Darby collection, EMI).

86. William Barry Owen to J. Berliner, 17 March 1899 (Formation, 1899, EMI).

87. J. Berliner to William Barry Owen, 19 March 1899 (Berliner papers, EMI).

88. Emile Berliner to Edmund Trevor Lloyd Williams, 9 to 25 May 1899 (Formation, 1899, EMI).

89. See Formation papers, March-August 1899, EMI.

90. The development of the European trade is discussed in chapter 5.

91. Only 100,000 shares were issued. See "Statutory Meeting," 11 December 1899 (Formation, 1899, EMI).

92. See "The Gramophone Company Ltd," company registration file, BT31/8687 (The National Archive, Kew).

93. Initially, the ownership of the 500,000 ordinary shares was entrenched in the board of directors. Williams and his family owned just under 30 per cent, Owen and his family 11 per cent, Joseph Berliner and his family 12 per cent (Emile Berliner owned a further 11 per cent), Birnbaum owned 5 per cent, as did Storey and his family; de la Rue and Romer Williams had nominal holdings. In addition Gaisberg, Royal and the company secretary held 1 per cent each, with existing company servants allocated shares in blocks of less than 200.

94. G. Morrison to Moriarty, 10 June 1899 (Moriarty collection, Edison National Historic Site).

95. See managing directors reports, 1899 to 1900 (Formation, 1899–1900, EMI). Theodore Birnbaum to William Barry Owen, 3 December 1899 (Formation, 1899, EMI).

96. Emile Berliner to Edmund Trevor Lloyd Williams, 18 May 1900 (Berliner papers, EMI).

97. Initially, a small "Angel" trademark appeared on the discs; it was later enlarged to make it more visible. The "Angel" trademark was also added to existing metal masters by means of an

embossing process. I am grateful to Peter Adamson for pointing out these developmental steps. See also Leonard Petts, *The Story of Nipper and the His Master's Voice Picture* (Bournemouth, UK: Talking Machine Review, 1983).

98. The Recording Angel continued to feature on the blank side of many single-sided records till the 1920s and never entirely disappeared from record labels.

99. "Assets and Liabilities Sheet," 30 September 1899 (Formation, 1899, EMI).

100. Data compiled "Share and Dividend Files" (board papers, EMI).

101. Data compiled from "Liquidator's Report" (board papers 1903, EMI).

102. The typewriter was a hedge against the failure of the Gramophone. Lacking the universal keyboard, it was not successful and proved a poor seller. Some 10,000 were manufactured, and, in 1903, the unsold balance was disposed of for £2,000. No definite figure can be allocated to the losses of capital and revenue incurred by this disaster (typewriter file, EMI).

103. Until 1907, the company traded as The Gramophone and Typewriter Ltd; it then reverted to The Gramophone Company Ltd and traded as such until 1974, when the name was changed to EMI Music Ltd. For details see BT31/68,172: EMI Music Ltd (Companies House, London).

104. "Annual Report, 1903" (meeting file, EMI).

105. William Barry Owen to J. Berliner, 14 June 1901 (Berliner papers, EMI).

106. For details of share transfers, see "Board Meetings," April and May 1903 (board papers 1903, EMI).

107. Sir Ernest de la Rue was educated at Rugby School and King's College, Cambridge. He was, until 1898, a director of Thomas de la Rue, the family printing firm. Knighted in 1921, de la Rue was treasurer of the Royal Albert Hall, a member of the Syndicate, Royal Opera House Covent Garden and, with others, developed the rules of bridge and the starting rules for horse racing. See *Who Was Who*, 1929, and *The Voice* (September 1929): 2.

108. For details of the initial share ownership, see note 93. See EMI Music Ltd file (Companies House, London).

109. Sydney Wentworth Dixon (1868–1921) was born in Manchester. His father was editor of *The Athenaeum*, his brother a Manchester University academic and his sister the novelist Ella Hepworth Dixon. Dixon's first career was journalism; he edited a sporting journal before turning to advertising, and prior to joining The Gramophone Company, he advised and undertook advertising commissions for Owen. In 1902, after military service in the South African War, he joined the company as assistant manager and company secretary. Between 1904 and 1909, he was British branch manager and, from 1909 to 1912, joint managing director with a seat on the board; in 1912, he became sales director. Dixon saw further military service during the First World War, returning to the company in 1919; though suffering serious illness, he ran the recording department until his death. See Peter Martland, *Since Records Began* (London: Batsford, 1997), 64; "Boers, Gramophones, Mr. Jas. McKay, Captain S. W. Dixon and Other Matters," *Talking Machine News* 4, no. 8 (December 1906): 664–67; and Alfred Clark, "In Memoriam, Major Sydney Wentworth Dixon OBE," *The Voice* (April 1922): 2.

110. Sydney W. Dixon to Theodore Birnbaum, 18 January 1904 (Dixon papers, EMI).

111. Relations with the US were not just hard-nosed business, and in his memoirs, Harry Sooy noted a visit by Owen to the Johnson factory:

> The model "C" machine was built and demonstrated during March 1900, which pleased Mr Johnson very much, and, on a visit of Mr Barry Owen to Camden one warm spring day, Mr Owen, clothed in a beautiful white flannel suit, was brought to the Laboratory

by Mr Johnson for a demonstration of the aforementioned "C" reproducing machine [which would run and play records whilst being wound], which, of course, was cheerfully given in the Experimental Machine Shop. Mr Owen became so highly interested in the performance he unconsciously sat down in a pan of black grease, which did not add any to the beauty of his dress. (Sooy, "Memoir of My Career")

112. William Barry Owen to Eldridge Reeves Johnson, 12 December 1902 (Johnson Victrola Museum).

113. F. W. Gaisberg, *Music on Record* (London: R. Hale, 1946), 28–29.

114. William Barry Owen, "Report to the Board," June 1904 (board papers, EMI).

115. See "Annual Reports: The Gramophone Company Ltd, 1901 to 1904" (meetings file, EMI).

116. "The Fourth Annual Report, The Gramophone Company Ltd" (meetings file, EMI).

117. The workings of this internal market are analyzed in chapter 5.

118. William Barry Owen to Eldridge Reeves Johnson, 4 November 1899 (Formation, 1899, EMI). See chapter 1 for details of the Seaman Zonophone developments in the USA.

119. William Barry Owen to Eldridge Reeves Johnson.

120. For more on this, see chapter 4.

121. See "A History of the International Zon-o-phone Company, New York and Berlin," in *The Zonophone Record: A Discography*, ed. Ernie Bayly and Michael Kinnear (Victoria, Australia: Kinnear, 2001).

122. Theodore Birnbaum, "Report: Year Ending 30 June 1903" (board papers, 1903, EMI).

3

THE BRITISH DISC AND
CYLINDER INDUSTRY: 1902–1914

"Let's Have a Song on the Phonograph"

> The talking machine is firmly established in the homes of
> the people. Its admirers are numbered by the millions. . . . It
> has come to stay. It is a means to music, which was before
> unobtainable except to the leisured and wealthy classes. It has
> brought the treasures of the song within the reach of all.
>
> —British trade press commentary,[1] 1908

In April 1902 the last important British Edison record patent expired, taking with it the final vestiges of the restrictive, overpriced Edison Bell monopoly.[2] In its wake competitive markets quickly emerged, which grew rapidly down to the outbreak of the First World War in 1914, by which time more than one third of British households owned a phonograph or Gramophone and some records. It was during these same years that records and talking machines joined other new popular lifestyle pastimes like spectator sports, the safety bicycle, photography, the cinema, the automobile and mass circulation national newspapers and magazines to bring about a revolution in British social and cultural habits.

Chapter 2 showed how the British record industry was formed at the turn of the twentieth century, as American and European manufacturers realised the commercial possibilities of recorded music. The ventures they created are examined in this chapter. They came from three distinct sources: first, overseas branches of American enterprises associated with the inventors of sound recording and others; second, European manufacturers importing products either directly through their own marketing organisations or via agents or wholesalers; and third, British manufacturers. The first took two specific forms. Some were ventures exporting capital, manufactured goods, specific skills and entrepreneurial ability, as in the case of

Edison's National Phonograph Company Ltd, while others simply exported skills relying on British capital and entrepreneurship, as in the case of The Gramophone Company Ltd. Furthermore, this chapter not only examines developments in the broader record and talking machine industry, but also the curious rise and collapse of the cylinder record and the fate that befell those businesses engaged in the cylinder phonograph trade.

★   ★   ★

Britain at the start of the twentieth century was a good business environment to trade in. As the richest country in the world it was also highly industrialised and overwhelmingly urban, with workers enjoying the highest per capita incomes in Europe.[3] As music historian Cyril Ehrlich has written, "In the second half of the 19th century real national income per head had more than doubled and real wages increased by more than 80%. This left some disposable cash to be spent on leisure, which became increasingly commercialised during this period."[4] The rapid take-up of records and instruments is a testimony to this disposable income and the development of a highly organised professional leisure industry. Other evidence supports this view, for example a 1911 industry memorandum to British members of parliament considering the extension of copyright protection to records and the creation of composer royalties for records of their work asserted, "About eight million talking machine records are sold per year in the UK, with an average retail price of 2s.6d. . . . [The] total spent by the public [in a year amounts to] one million pounds."[5] They claimed around £1,000,000 was invested in the British talking machine industry, which directly employed between 2 and 3,000 people with a further 15,000 supported in the wholesale and retail trades, plus an uncountable number of performing artists, travelling salesmen and advertisers. It cited annual machine sales of 500,000, with retail prices of records ranging from 9d to £1.10s. All this suggests records and machines entered the homes of the urban industrial working classes at a phenomenal rate.[6]

No other industry-wide machine sales data survive, though the 500,000 estimate appears realistic.[7] On the eve of war therefore there were, excluding those purchased before 1909, perhaps as many as three million talking machines in British homes, or one for every three households.[8] This remarkably rapid spread was helped by its high visibility in the home and made it, like the piano, a status symbol.[9] In rapidly growing highly competitive markets record sales topped fourteen million on the outbreak of war. This steep upward competitive trend was noted as early as 1904 in a letter from William Edgar Gilmore (the president of National Phonograph Company Inc) to Thomas Edison, written during a European visit to test the market potential of Edison products. Startled at what he found in Britain, he observed, "There is a great deal more competition here than in the United States."[10]

Other aspects of the trade also appeared during these years, including a British, continental European and American trade press. Among the English-speaking titles were the British *Talking Machine News* (first published in 1903) and the American *Talking Machine World*, which appeared in 1904 and had strong British connections. These were supplemented by other British trade papers like *The Phono-Trader and Recorder* and *Sound Wave,* together with a number of company in-house magazines, to which must be added the vibrant continental European trade press. These both provide the contemporary trade and subsequent historical research with an essential pulse on the industry.

The seasonality of the pre-1914 talking machine industry was highlighted in 1905 by American John Schermerhorn of Edison's National Phonograph Company Ltd (hereafter NPC), "Past history of the business here shows very conclusively that in England the phonograph trade is purely seasonal and the season is somewhat short. The best business is done in the months of November, December, January and February. During the summer months in the past there has been practically no business."[11] Seasonality also defined the retail trade and was noted in a May 1907 Gramophone Company report by British branch manager, Sydney Dixon, "The . . . trade . . . is very largely handled by the cycle trade, hardware trade and sports and games trades. The abnormally fine weather at Easter led the trades above mentioned to give up the talking machine earlier than usual to get out their bicycles, their gardening implements and their athletic appliances."[12]

Although The Gramophone Company and some other record companies engaged in a high-class trade (see chapters 5 and 6), the bulk of consumers were from the skilled and semiskilled working classes. Of the retailers engaged in this sector, Dixon said they were mainly general dealers, tobacconists, sports goods and cycle shops.[13] Critically, Dixon was British and understood the complexities and subtleties of this kind of trade. In contrast his American competitors found them alien and baffling, with structures and retail outlets quite different to those back home. As a 1909 NPC report noted, "The tone of our dealers on the whole is not as high as in America, and there are many dealers whose places of business are very objectionable."[14] Further, there were the prescient observations of NPC manager Schermerhorn, "Over here it is the small shops that do the aggregate business, whereas in America most of the business is done in the large shops. . . . They have four or five small shops here to every one in America."[15]

British markets developed from bottom up, mirroring the equally infant movie industry.[16] Initially, the British talking machine industry developed as a dual-format market based on cylinder and disc. However, after 1908, the market changed rapidly into a single-sector using the Berliner-Johnson zigzag-cut disc, as pioneered in Britain by The Gramophone Company Ltd and later adopted by International Zonophone GmbH and The Columbia Phonograph Company General. These important changes forced consumers with cylinder phonographs to buy their records from the dwindling number of cylinder manufacturers and retailers, or stop buying records altogether or, alternatively, move over to the disc record. With disc machines available from 15s upwards, entry costs were low and when compared to the cylinder disc records enjoyed manifold advantages. For example, after 1903, discs had a playing time of up to four and a half minutes and could be manufactured with a recording on both sides. In contrast, until 1908, the playing time of a cylinder was two minutes. Discs were easier to store and, with the exception of a small number of cylinders made from celluloid, were more robust. Developments in technology meant that the sound quality of disc records was superior to that of the wax cylinder and disc Gramophones and records were simpler and cheaper to manufacture. There was also a more diverse range and quality of music available on disc than on cylinder records. To understand this market, table 3.1 lists the major manufacturers and their technologies.

Table 3.1. Major Record Companies Active in Britain between 1903 and 1914

Major Record Companies Active in Britain 1903–1914	Technologies Employed
The Gramophone & Typewriter Ltd to 1907 then The Gramophone Company Ltd.	Pioneered the Johnson-Berliner zigzag-cut discs. Had recording and instrument assembly facilities in London and from 1907 a pressing factory; previously records were manufactured in Germany. It had licencing agreements with The Victor Talking Machine Company and imported Victor components from the United States. In 1902 it introduced a celebrity catalogue and in 1903 acquired International Zonophone, as a vehicle to enter mass markets. This label was supplemented first in 1908 by The Twin and in 1913 by The Cinch.

Columbia Phonograph Company General to 1913, then Columbia Phonograph Company, New York and London.

Manufactured cylinder records until 1909 and discs from 1902. Had a British recording studio from 1899 and record manufacturing facilities (with access to US Columbia recordings) from 1905. Machines were imported from the United States. In 1909 it acquired Rena Manufacturing Co and until 1914 its records were sold as Columbia-Rena. It also had the subsidiary labels Phoenix and Regal.

Pathé Frères (London) Ltd, through two successor companies. Then in 1911 Pathé Frères Pathéphone Ltd.

Made cylinder records until 1906, then centre start vertical-cut (hill-and-dale) discs. Machines and records were manufactured and imported from France.

Edison Bell Consolidated Phonograph Company Ltd to 1909 then succeeded by J. E. Hough Ltd.

Manufactured cylinders and vertical-cut discs until 1911, thereafter zigzag-cut disc records. It manufactured a small number of cylinder machines in Britain. Machines imported from US, Germany and Switzerland. J. E. Hough owned Bell discs, The Winner and Velvet Face labels.

National Phonograph Company Ltd 1902 to 1913 then renamed Thomas A. Edison Ltd.

Formed in 1902. It had a London recording studio but also drew on US recordings. Manufactured records in Belgium then London. In 1908 it introduced a four-minute Amberol cylinder. Imported phonographs from the United States.

Originally The Sterling Record Company Ltd, The Russell Hunting Record Company Ltd was formed in 1905. In 1906 Sterling and Hunting Ltd was formed to act as British agents for German importers.

Manufactured Sterling cylinder records 1904 to 1908 and was British agent for the International Talking Machine Co GmbH, owners of the Odeon, and Fonotipia labels until bankruptcy in 1908.

Carl Lindström AG and after 1911 Carl Lindström (London) Ltd.

This major German business manufactured instruments from 1904 and records after 1909. Between 1909 and 1914 Carl Lindström AG integrated much of the German industry and by 1914 the record labels it used in Britain included: Beka, Decapo, Coliseum, Favorite, Jumbo, Lyric, Fonotipia, Odeon and Scala.

These important ventures were joined by other often transient medium and small businesses together with a number of matrix makers and disc pressing contractors who are discussed in the next chapter. One list of British ventures (that is manufacturers, agents for foreign manufacturers and wholesalers) survives as a "Telephone directory of UK talking machine companies" published in the March 1907 edition of *Talking Machine News*. In all there were twenty-eight, though some like British Zonophone were subsidiaries of larger concerns.[17]

★ ★ ★

The years between 1902 and 1907 saw the British market for cylinder records and phonographs grow rapidly. This had the effect of drawing often small poorly capitalised ventures into the field. The trade also benefited from turn-of-the-century innovations, including a cheap cylinder moulding process which brought with it mass production and dramatically reduced prices. For example, the retail price of an Edison Bell record fell from 5s to as little as 9d, but averaged 1s. This, together with the free market, encouraged German and Swiss manufacturers to produce cheap machines, reducing entry costs to a few shillings or around a dollar.[18] This busy period created what proved to be the false belief that the manufacture of cylinder records was an easy business to break into and profit from.

The lack of firm figures makes it difficult to estimate the size of the cylinder trade, though some runs of Edison Bell, Sterling, Pathé Frères (which is considered in chapter 4) and National Phonograph Company Ltd (NPC) data exist. The data suggest Edison Bell sold an average of 2.4 million records annually in the years 1903 to 1907, while NPC averaged 1.8 million per annum. During these same years NPC claimed one third of the total market.[19] If this is true then at its peak the British cylinder market was an impressive 5.4 million records, comprising some 25 different brands.[20] These ventures created a low-cost, high-volume market providing access for the masses to this new technology. The expansion continued, with fresh entrants appearing as late as 1908 when the trade was in terminal decline. The paucity of data means that assessing manufacturing and selling costs can only be tentative. One problem is the failure of some companies, particularly Pathé, Edison Bell and Columbia, to maintain coherent price structures. Because these companies were chronically cash-strapped, they engaged in secret discount deals to obtain whatever business they could. Of this William Gilmore wrote in 1903, "Pathé is selling his records wholesale at from nineteen cents down, according to the quantity ordered. Columbia is badly crippled, and it looks as though they will have to quit. Both Pathé and Columbia cylinder records are being sold by dealers to the public as low as 25 cents."[21] There is some data at the Edison National Historic Site that gives an insight into price structures. For example, in 1906, John Schermerhorn the head of the NPC wrote, "Hough [of Edison Bell] says his records are manufactured at 3d each." It is uncertain whether Hough's figures, if they are true, included artist and mould-making oncosts.[22] However, if correct, they contrast sharply with NPC's own costs, which were as high as 5d each.[23]

Cylinder records and phonographs were largely distributed through the wholesale trade (known to Americans as jobbers or factors). Trade circulars from 1905 reveal The Russell Hunting Record Company dealer prices at 8s per dozen records, whilst The Lambert Company (a medium-sized cylinder manufacturer), charged wholesalers 4s.9d per dozen, 6s.6d to dealers.[24] In 1905 James Henry White, the founding manager of NPC, wrote, "Columbia and Edison Bell sell to factors [wholesalers] at 6d. NPC sell to factors at 10d, who sell to dealers at 1s."[25] NPC records retailed at 1s.6d. This was reduced to 1s in 1907. In contrast, from 1905 Sterling, Edison Bell, Pathé Frères (London) Ltd and Columbia records were generally sold for 1s each, though in reality they often retailed well below this price.

Sales of cylinder records and phonographs boomed until 1907, with consumers drawn almost exclusively from the skilled and semiskilled urban industrial working classes. As NPC manager Thomas Graf noted, "the cotton district with Manchester and Liverpool is the best field for our products in England."[26] Edison's British-based business associates continually bemoaned this dependence on working-class consumers. One was George Croydon Marks[27] who wrote disparagingly, "Unfortunately, the masses buy the records in this country, and they are not the most critical in musical quality, and they do not always differentiate between a record which is well produced, for they have the same entertainment or laugh out of each, irrespective of the actual quality or refinement of the sound reproduced."[28]

To support sales of 5.4 million cylinder records required annual sales of perhaps 200,000 cylinder phonographs. NPC never sold more than 50,000 machines in any one year and Edison Bell's manufacturing efforts produced derisory numbers. In these circumstances, sales of German and Swiss machines together with those domestically manufactured but incorporating foreign-made mechanisms must have been phenomenal.

The sale of 50,000 NPC phonographs in its best year suggests there was a strong market for Edison's well-made and robust machines. In part it was pricing. His phonographs were sold at prices as low as £2.2s. In sharp contrast The Gramophone Company had no comparable machine and its US supplier had neither the skill nor incentive to provide one. Not only did Edison manufacture and export phonographs to Europe, he also made a profit, a feat that eluded The Gramophone Company for a number of years before 1914. The success of cheap NPC phonographs is explained by an examination of Edison's American trade. According to James van Allen Shields, a British-based American businessman and Columbia executive, Edison consumer strength lay in the American rural heartlands whereas Victor dominated the wealthier more musically sophisticated urban centres.[29] Evidently Edison's rural American customers had incomes and musical tastes comparable with his British working-class customers. The crucial difference was the presence of cheap German and Swiss made machines and a strong competitive British cylinder record market, whereas the US was a tariff protected market insulated from competition by the manufacturers' patent-based oligopoly.

Throughout its existence and despite the outward appearance of prosperity and seemingly well established position in the marketplace, the cylinder record and phonograph trade was unstable. As early as 1904 Gilmore was explaining why competitors failed to make an impact, "Columbia seem to be dead here and Pathé has killed himself with the English trade by turning out the worst kind of product. The only people we have to compete with therefore is The Gramophone Company."[30] As chapter 4 shows the impact of German manufacturer's records and machines in the European free market was decisive and by 1908 the cylinder phonograph trade was practically dead, superseded by the disc record and machine.

★   ★   ★

Turning from a survey of the cylinder phonograph trade, it is now appropriate to look at case studies of three business ventures engaged in this trade. Formed in 1904, The Sterling Record Company Ltd (the venture was renamed The Russell Hunting Record Company Ltd) traded from 81 City Road (part of the talking machine industry's enclave in the City of London dubbed "phonoland" by the trade press).[31] Plugging into the cylinder record trade, the business was a sizeable record manufacturer with a creditable catalogue of quality recordings. Its founders were two Americans,

Russell Hunting (the ex-actor and former Edison Bell recording engineer) and record entrepreneur and salesman Louis (later Sir Louis) Sterling,[32] with British-born William Manson acting as his deputy (he later enjoyed a long career with The Gramophone Company Ltd). The Russell Hunting Record Company Ltd manufactured the Sterling, which was a quarter of an inch longer than the standard cylinder and therefore played slightly longer. It was a well recorded and manufactured product. The brand was backed by a strong sales team and experienced initial success, replicating Edison Bell's marketing success without the financial burdens or managerial weaknesses. In 1906 the venture formed Sterling and Hunting Ltd to act as British agents for Fonotipia and Odeon discs. This business was also agent for Sterling records and for The International Linguaphone Company Ltd records. Ever the salesman, Louis Sterling embarked on an extensive advertising campaign, which included floating a hydrogen balloon emblazoned with the company's advertisements across London.

Plugging into a rapidly rising market The Russell Hunting Record Company was successful, with accounts for the years 1905 to 1907 showing profits of almost £19,000.[33] The Sterling catalogue had records by several well-known artists like music hall star Florrie Ford, who was also a shareholder, and the young Irish tenor John McCormack. Sterling trumpeted the success, claiming sales of 1.8 million records between July 1905 and January 1906.[34] This was probably the high point, for price deals between Columbia, Edison Bell and Pathé undermined the price structure of cylinder records, which hit hardest on poorly capitalised businesses like The Russell Hunting Record Company Ltd. In September 1906, NPC chief John Schermerhorn, noted, "During the past three or four months the business of Sterling records has fallen off very materially, particularly due to the fact that the Edison Bell Co. are selling to dealers considerably cheaper than are the Sterling people with the consequent effect that the dealer gets a larger profit. The price of Edison Bell records is 6s.3d per dozen, whereas the Sterling price is 8s per dozen."[35]

The end of 1907 saw the economy in recession and the business in crisis. In an attempt to regain market share, retail prices were reduced from 1s to 9d. This was a mistake which further destabilised the price structure in an already overstocked market and helped bring about the collapse of the business. NPC's manager Thomas Graf told his boss in America, "Whilst we are suffering ourselves the dissolution of the other cylinder concerns is rapidly progressing. The Edison Bell and Sterling Companies are at their wits end and the coming months will bring interesting developments."[36] In 1908 The Russell Hunting Record Company Ltd went into liquidation. In an attempt to recover some cash, the receiver dumped the remaining stock of 500,000 records on the wholesale market at the knockdown price of 2s.6d per dozen, retailing at 5s per dozen; eventually the retail price went as low as 2d each.[37] This further undermined an already unstable market. It was the end of the road for The Russell Hunting Record Company Ltd, but not for its remarkable founders who went on to greater things in the industry.[38]

★   ★   ★

The Edison Bell Consolidated Phonograph Company Ltd was the most interesting and certainly the most colourful of early record companies. Chapter 2 showed how between 1892 and 1897 the original Edison Bell business controlled the British phonograph market, emphasising its use as an office-dictating machine. As a consequence music records developed by means of illegally imported phonographs and records, which were exhibited by showmen and others. In 1898 the business was reconstructed as The Edison Bell Consolidated Phonograph Company Ltd, a move that lined the pockets of its manager and encumbered the new venture with huge debts. This firm embraced the music record business, entering into partnership with former infringer James Edward Hough. Hough became general manager and his business Edisonia Ltd merged with Edison Bell, becoming its record-manufacturing arm. In 1902, so as to attract new capital to its debt burdened balance sheet, Edison Bell underwent a third reconstruction. This company inherited a £100,000 debenture, which carried with it annual payments of £5,000.[39] Between 1902 and 1909 and trading in the new free market Edison Bell experienced a revival and restored its terrible reputation with the trade. It also survived the rupturing of relations with Thomas Edison and succeeded in opening mass markets for cylinder records. Unfortunately, its ability to develop a strong market share was fatally hampered by a hopelessly weak financial and capital structure, which proved crippling when the business desperately needed capital. In 1903 Edison Bell cut all its prices. James White, head of The National Phonograph Company Ltd (NPC), who had blacklisted Edison Bell and refused to supply it with phonographs, said this was proof of NPC's success in throttling its rival. In an overly optimistic letter to West Orange he said it "indicates the last desperate stand, and if you can only keep me supplied with sufficient goods to meet all the requirements of our customers in Great Britain, I think this winter will see the finish of the Edison Bell."[40]

It is difficult to work out what was happening in the Edison Bell accounting office. For although balance sheets survive, they show little more than the use of legal but dubious accounting methods to hide the true nature of its finances. Edison Bell disguised and protected profit from debenture holders, with cash, profit and other assets, for example, concentrated in its wholly owned subsidiary Edisonia Ltd, the effect of which was to hide true profit and tangible assets. It also used accounting devices to diminish profit further, including the maintenance or writing down of patent rights in the balance sheet. The published accounts show Edison Bell's principal assets as stock-in-trade, book debts and the declared Edisonia profits. *The Stock Exchange Year Book* provides additional though gnomic evidence of Edison Bell's poor financial position and its financial decline. In the 1900 entry the company reported losses of £7,970, whilst the 1903 entry indicated a credit balance on profit and loss of £4,920; the following year the balance stood at £11,273. No further credit balances were reported and in the decade prior to 1909 little by way of dividend was paid. The 1905 edition of the *Stock Exchange Year Book* entry contains little helpful information but noted ominously "further information has been refused by the company." The previous year the Edison Bell directors told investors the company could not pay the debenture interest and the following year it borrowed £15,000 in short term bonds simply to continue trading.[41] Edison Bell took drastic measures to raise cash. In August 1906 it raised wholesale prices of records from 6s.6d to 7s per dozen. In February 1907, Hough declared there was "a decided slump after Christmas though he claimed to have sold 186,764 cylinder records during Christmas week 1906, which would have grossed almost £40,000."[42] The recession finally claimed Edison Bell. At first Hough tried to improve cash flow by sacking staff, abandoning the wholesale network and dealing directly with retailers; and he adopted that old stand-by offering a 3d discount to customers exchanging an old Edison Bell cylinder record for a new one. However it all came to naught, and in early 1909 bond holders put the business into receivership for failing to redeem the 1905 bonds.[43] Unit sales of Edison Bell records but not machines together with turnover and profit as declared in the company accounts are set out in table 3.2.

Until National Phonograph Company Ltd (NPC) began its British trade in 1903 Edison Bell had purchased most of its phonographs from the Edison factory at West Orange, though it produced its own-brand records.[44] By 1903 relations between Edison Bell, its manager J. E. Hough and the Edison camp had become so poisonous that when the patent position allowed, Thomas Edison dumped Edison Bell and commenced trading

Table 3.2.   Edison Bell Consolidated Phonograph Company Ltd: Performance, 1900–1908

Year	Unit Sales of Records	Turnover	Profit
1900–1901	80,000	NA	−£7,970 [−$39,850]
1901–1902	200,000	NA	£4,290 [$21,450]
1902–1903	1,500,000	NA	£11,273 [$56365]
1903–1904	1,500,000	NA	NA
1904–1905	2,456,000	£56,548 [$282,740]	−£10,710 [−$53,550]
1905–1906	2,467,000	£48,064 [$240,320]	£9,064 [$45,320]
1906–1907	2,280,000	£48,193 [$240,965]	£13,943 [$69,715]
1907–1908	1,396,644	NA	NA

Source: Data compiled from "Edison Bell Consolidated Phonograph Co Ltd v National Phonograph Co Ltd," Chancery Division 1907, cited in *Talking Machine News* 5, no. 10 (February 1908): 767; accounts of Edison Bell Consolidated Phonograph Co Ltd, 1903 to 1908; "Evidence of Mr J. E. Hough," *Law on Copyright Committee*, Cmd. 4976 (London: HMSO, 1909): 104–15. In a 1903 *Talking Machine News* interview, Hough claimed a turnover of £80,000 in the fiscal year 1900–1901, £200,000 for 1901–1902 and an incredible £1.5 million in the seven months to January 1903. This is incorrect as they are exactly the same figures as unit sales of records cited in the table, which were derived from the 1907 court enforced accounting.

on his own account. This created the curious spectacle of two competing British businesses each claiming association with the inventor of the phonograph! As NPC controlled the supply of phonographs fortune favoured it. It also left Edison Bell with a critical supply problem. To continue in the Edison phonograph trade it had to obtain machines. Unfortunately, the sole British importer and distributor of Edison products was its avowed competitor National Phonograph Company Ltd, who wanted to crush Edison Bell. As soon as NPC started trading it cut supplies to Edison Bell and placed it on a published blacklist. Edison Bell retaliated by playing the anti-American card, accusing NPC of using "American marketing tactics" tying dealers in NPC products to exclusive contracts (for more on this see below). This was perfectly true and contracted dealers were forbidden to trade with any other firm trading in cylinder products (for this read Edison Bell) under pain of blacklisting. Hough tried various means to circumvent the ban, including using third parties and having supplies delivered to an outhouse of his home.

Depriving Edison Bell of phonographs proved the opening round in a bitter trade war between the two companies. The letters between NPC and West Orange reveal a determination to drive Edison Bell from the field and deprive its manager J. E. Hough of the right to use the name Edison on Edison Bell products. The six years 1903 to 1909 were littered with lawsuits for conspiracy and trade libel. It involved ferocious advertising campaigns, characterised by the use of vicious anti-American insults (at a time when trading relations between Britain and the United States were very bad owing to prohibitive American import tariffs), and Edison Bell even attempted to manufacture what were essentially fake Edison machines in Britain. In 1906 NPC was offered an opportunity to extinguish Edison Bell. The Edison Bell business was in such dreadful financial straits that Hough offered to sell it to NPC. Its American chairman John Schermerhorn told his boss in West Orange that Edison Bell wanted an incredible £120,000 for the venture. This was made up of £100,000 for the debenture holders and £20,000 for the business.[45] Schermerhorn was instructed to tell Hough, "We have no money to spend buying up rotten defunct corporations, so the next time Mr Hough comes in to see you . . . simply turn him down cold and tell him it would not be considered."[46] The battle ended in 1909 with Edison Bell in receivership, by which time the British cylinder trade was all but finished.[47]

Receivership presented NPC with a second more favourable opportunity to extinguish Edison Bell and its brand name. The receiver offered the concern to NPC director George Croydon Marks for £5,000, but Marks's derisory offer of £1,000 was rejected and he accepted a better offer from Hough.[48] By this means, and for an additional payment of £15,000, Hough acquired the assets of Edisonia Ltd and then those of Edison Bell Consolidated Phonograph Ltd. In its essentials this was the name, factory site, cylinder moulds, recording studios and stock in trade. At the same time Hough purchased the plant and cylinder moulds of The Russell Hunting Record Company Ltd. The £100,000 debenture stock and other debt was finally repudiated and freed from this crippling debt the business was relaunched as J. E. Hough Ltd.[49] Having spent so much time and money trying to extinguish the name Edison Bell, it seems incredible that Marks allowed this opportunity to slip through his fingers. It is clear that this reflected a deeper malaise afflicting the Thomas Edison empire (see below).

As a pioneer of the British mass market in records and phonographs, Edison Bell with an excellent record catalogue was an important competitor to the British branch of The Gramophone Company Ltd, National Phonograph Company Ltd, The Russell Hunting Record Company and other early businesses. It was Edison Bell's post-1903 low cost cylinder records and phonographs that attracted the British urban industrial working classes to this new form of entertainment. By offering higher quality records both in terms of music and price Hough helped create mass markets and broaden the base of this new industry. That Edison Bell was beset by so many financial problems does not detract from its achievement, nor did bankruptcy drive Hough and the business to the sidelines.

Even before the bankruptcy Edison Bell was beginning to respond to the rapidly changing market and released its first discs as a 2s.6d 10¼-inch zig-zag cut record in June 1908; in November 1908 it released a series of 8½-inch Pathé-type vertical cut discs known as the Phona, all of which were transcriptions derived from the existing cylinder catalogue. This transition to disc records ended with the bankruptcy of the Edison Bell business, but continued with the J. E. Hough Ltd reconstruction; and aided by a convenient late 1909 fire at the Edison Bell record factory which destroyed the plant. Hough was able to restart, first with the existing vertical-cut Phona disc and then a series of zigzag-cut discs with recordings printed on each side. Introduced in December 1910 as Velvet Face, these records retailed at 3s later reduced to 2s.6d (with a 12-inch record in 1913). Velvet Face records were later joined by the 2s.6d Genuine Edison Bell Gramophone Records and, in 1912, J. E. Hough Ltd created The Winner Record Company Ltd to launch its The Winner disc retailing at 2s.6d later reduced to 2s and in 1913 to 1s.6d.[50] This reductive pricing competed with The Gramophone Company Zonophone, The Twin and the many new German labels. The Winner label was launched with a catalogue of fifty-five titles, all of which were cover (or stencilled) records derived from the earlier disc catalogue. All this suggests the primary role of The Winner was to recycle existing recordings but at a cheaper price (in the manner of the first Zonophone and Rena records). The label did not release its own recordings until 1913.

The Winner label was aimed at the burgeoning low cost, high volume market. It was also an important new competitor, this time not with the American cylinder trade but with the growing cheap German disc record competition. Sales data indicate its prewar success in this rapidly growing sector of the market. By August 1912, after five months of trading, a total of 118,832 had been sold. In September 1912 Hough claimed he had received a single order for 40,000 of The Winner records. This growth continued to the war and in the selling year July 1912 to June 1913 sales of 678,681 were achieved and during the same period to June 1914, 874,265. New buildings were needed for the manufacture of Ebonitis, the mixture used in the pressing of these records and in keeping with previous practice Hough created another internal market with Ebonitis Ltd (like The Winner Company Ltd a wholly owned subsidiary of J. E. Hough Ltd).[51]

★   ★   ★

In 1903 Thomas Edison entered the British market trading as The National Phonograph Company Ltd (NPC).[52] Like The Gramophone

Company Ltd, NPC was a British registered business engaged in a multinational trade, with factories and selling branches in several European centres. Unlike The Gramophone Company, NPC was a wholly owned subsidiary of National Phonograph Company Inc, of New Jersey, and the company name highlighted the prime aim of the venture. Until 1908, when the movie business took over as its main engine of profit, phonograph goods dominated its activities. NPC was unique among early record manufacturers for it had, in addition to phonograph goods exclusive rights to market a range of Edison products including Kinetoscopes (film projectors), movies from the Edison film studio, storage batteries, electric fans, x-ray equipment and the Ediphone office-dictating machine. NPC was never a retailer; rather it manufactured and distributed records and imported phonographs. Initially the firm dealt through wholesalers, but it later traded directly with retailers bound by exclusive, enforceable contracts whose main purpose was to prevent Edison Bell obtaining products but it was also used to maintain retail prices.

The NPC war with Edison Bell had the unfortunate side effect of drawing the business into the broader dispute between Britain and the United States over its protectionist policies. British Free Trade manufacturers saw American protectionism as a grossly unfair trading practice. It meant US manufacturers could import goods into Britain free of taxes but British goods exported into the United States paid punitive tariffs which made them uncompetitive. This policy effectively excluded most British manufactured goods from US markets, causing strong anti-American feeling in Britain, especially in the manufacturing districts. Furthermore, many record retailers saw NPC contract and pricing policies as reflecting these trading practices and deeply resented it. One angry London retailer pasted the unsigned NPC contract and a defiant notice of his own in his shop window. It read:

> Here is a fine object lesson for you in Free Trade. These Yankee trust mongers have, and are, daily bringing millions of these records into this country free of any duty, which no other country permits them to do, and they are now trying to put a tax on record buyers up to the tune of 75 per cent [referring to the premium prices]. They are not going to force us retailers to do their dirty trust tax collecting work for them. Some weak-kneed invertebrate sellers have knuckled down and signed their highwayman-like agreement to sell at their enhanced price. We have decided not to do so, and defy them. Twelve thousand records in stock for you to choose from. We hope you will support us in our defiance of these Yankee bluff merchants. The precious agreement hangs beside this.[53]

Trade was booming and in the circumstances NPC did not care about the bad publicity. Management believed the superior quality of NPC products enabled them to ride out any storm and maintain premium prices. Sales evidence suggests they were right, as manager James White told Gilmore in the US, "I cannot impress on you too strongly the necessity of having goods rushed forward to me with all possible haste; orders are coming in from all directions, and I firmly believe I can sell all the goods you can possibly ship this Winter and still have orders in hand."[54] In an October 1903 interview, White claimed trade during the first selling season was such that NPC would be unable to fill orders for about two million records, despite a stock of 500,000 and round-the-clock record production.[55] In this rapidly rising market dealers queued at its doors with orders and those, such as the writer of the notice, were sued, blacklisted and bypassed.

Like other record companies NPC had a recording studio staffed by an American engineer. He was William Hayes and his duties involved travelling to Europe to make records for local markets.[56] NPC imported a range of phonographs and were continually improving the technology. Retail prices ranged from £2.2s to £6.6s, with record retail prices at 1s.6d until 1907, when they were reduced to 1s. Until 1903 when NPC began its British trade, Edison products were shipped to its European distribution centre at the free port of Antwerp in Belgium, where it had a record factory. To supply its British market NPC opened larger facilities in Brussels and in 1908, in what proved a disastrous decision, record manufacturing moved to London (see below). The market potential for Edison goods was described in a 1903 letter to Edison from Gilmore in Europe and he noted the labour situation in Antwerp: "The labor market over here is very good indeed, and very cheap. Such help as porters, or people in the wax plants can be obtained readily at $4.00 a week for men, and boys for practically nothing. So that the cost of records will be very low indeed. These same remarks will apply all over Europe, as well as in the British Isles. We should therefore be able to make plenty of money."[57]

Despite the range of NPC products and the multinational nature of its business, sufficient data have survived to give a relatively clear picture of the British record and phonograph operation and include unit sales of records and machines, turnover and profit as set out in tables 3.3 and 3.4.

Despite the relatively late entry into this market, the problems with Edison Bell and the premium price of its records, the figures in table 3.3 indicate a strong early showing. The declining trend in record sales after 1904–1905 reflects the growing strength of competition, with Sterling and other 1s brands eating into NPC market share. The incomplete figures for 1907–1908 indicate the effect of the economic recession, the reduction of

Table 3.3.   National Phonograph Company Ltd: Unit Sales, 1903–1912

Year	Records	Phonographs
1903–1904	2,009,475	27,224
1904–1905	2,368,846	41,372
1905–1906	1,417,167	35,443
1906–1907	1,647,015	54,668
1907–1908	1,943,486[a]	22,617[b]
1908–1909	1,276,371[c]	12,767[d]
1909–1910	NA	NA
1910–1911	401,725	2,491[e]
1911–1912	499,661	1,906[f]

Sources: Compiled from monthly sales returns (document files, 1903–1912: phonograph-foreign and sales files, Edison National Historic Site).

[a]Eleven months only.
[b]Ten months only.
[c]Nine months only.
[d]Eight months only.
[e]Six months only.
[f]Eight months only.

prices to 1s and the failure of its new product, the four-minute Amberol cylinder record. 1910 to 1912 figures, though compiled from incomplete data, illustrate in a dramatic manner the collapse of the phonograph and cylinder record business.

Sufficient data exist to reconstruct much of the NPC turnover and profit accrued from its record and phonograph business and is shown in table 3.4. In revealing these figures, it is worth noting that a secret 1904

Table 3.4.   National Phonograph Company Ltd: Record and Phonograph Performance, 1902–1911

Year	Turnover		Profit/Loss	
1902–1903	£106,116	[$530,580]	£8,125	[$40,626]
1903–1904	£121,828	[$609,140]	£5,708	[$28,540]
1904–1905	£97,857	[$489,285]	£11,248	[$56,240]
1905–1906	£136,357	[$681,785]	£4,365	[$21,825]
1906–1907	£95,069	[$475,345]	£11,278	[$56,390]
1907–1908	£96,236	[$481,180]	£4,387[a]	[$21,935]
1908–1909	£62,910	[$314,550]	£7,435[b]	[$37,175]
1909–1910	£44,159	[$220,795]	£240[c]	[$1,200]
1910–1911	£21,291	[$106,455]	–£2713[a]	[–$13,565]

Source: Figures are for full years unless noted for profit. Table compiled from monthly returns, letters and reports (document files, 1901–1911, Edison National Historic Site).

[a]Six months only.
[b]Seven months.
[c]Nine months only.

correspondence between West Orange and the London directors indicates a tax avoidance scheme. This was achieved by inserting additional charges for the use of Edison's name. In this way nearly £10,000 annually was creamed off the top of phonograph profits.[58]

The manipulation of taxable profit makes this component of the data tentative, though turnover figures are firm and comparable to that achieved by the British branch of The Gramophone Company and Edison Bell. This further supports the view that between 1903 and 1907 and despite its late entry turnover roughly equalled that of its main competitors. It also shows that after 1907 business fell away, while the turnover of its disc competitor grew dramatically.[59] By selling quality goods at premium prices into this important market, NPC was able to develop, during the years 1903 to 1907, a medium cost, high volume market for its products much faster than its rivals.

Despite the initial success, NPC was handicapped by organisational failures largely outside its control. The US parent company was the creature of Thomas Edison, whose idiosyncratic business methods resulted in a high turnover in executives.[60] Between 1904 and 1911 the US concern had two chief executives and NPC had four managing directors, of whom three were Americans with no prior experience of the record industry or of British trading methods. The first, James White, had worked for a North American franchise in the early 1890s but then became a filmmaker at the Edison film studios before starting the British venture.[61] Alfred Fenner Wagner, the fourth and first British-born (and most successful) managing director, wrote in his memoirs of his frustration at this instability and its impact on policy.[62] The problem was recognised and mitigated by the appointment of Edison's British patent attorney George Croydon Marks MP as a nonexecutive director; however, his involvement was slight and limited to crisis intervention.

Leaving aside the Edison Bell fiasco, three issues highlight the vulnerability of NPC as a foreign company trading in Britain. The first was the question of artist contact and relations with The Gramophone Company. The second was the creation of a British record manufacturing base and the third was NPC's response to the collapse of the cylinder trade. Although NPC engaged a creditable list of artists on contracts exclusive to cylinder technology, it appears to have botched a 1904 offer by The Gramophone Company for a joint tie-up of talent.[63] Such a deal would have created an artist monopoly able to control recording fees. This would have allowed NPC and The Gramophone Company to dominate their respective sectors of the market and maintain prices and costs. The process would have helped both enterprises to develop, particularly the building of the British NPC and Zonophone catalogues. However, nothing came of it and the opportunity lapsed. In 1908 NPC consolidated European record manufacturing at a new factory in North West London. Among the many advantages justifying this move was the size of the British business compared to continental operations. There was also a need for the quick release of highly profitable but ephemeral popular music records. Letters to West Orange and Alfred Wagner's memoirs cite the problems associated with this move and its consequences for the British trade.[64] Although experienced Belgian workmen and their managers moved to London, they were unable to manufacture a good record at the factory. After a large turnover in staff and industrial action the ventilation system was discovered to be hopelessly wrong and the site quite unsuited to the manufacturing process.[65] Edison blamed the labour force and used the opportunity to cut his European losses, ordering the closure of the plant and consolidation of manufacturing at the West Orange factory.[66] If Brussels was poorly placed to serve the needs of the time-sensitive popular British record market then West Orange was a disaster, and from that point on NPC became a marginal player.

The decline of NPC's trade was precipitous. In December 1907, after a successful year, British manager Thomas Graf reported, despite a one third price reduction, "our business in this country had a decided downward tendency."[67] In the midst of recession the situation worsened, causing Frank L. Dyer, Edison's attorney and new president of the US parent, to visit London. In August 1909 he told Edison, "Undoubtedly, we are doing 90% of the cylinder business in this country; in fact all of the cylinder lines are now out, with the exception of the Edison Bell . . . who does very little."[68] The bewildered American executives could neither explain nor understand the rapid changes occurring in British and European markets. After all they were used to operating within the American manufacturer's oligopoly, whose purpose was to exclude competition and distort the market. The collapse of the British and European market in cylinder products stood in marked contrast to the buoyant situation in America where, according to data in the 1910 United States census of manufacturing, a total of 27 million records had been manufactured of which 18.6 million were cylinders and only 8.4 million discs.[69] The following year Dyer expressed his despair at the state of Edison's British phonograph business, "Are we not foolish in allowing the profits on the films to be eaten up by the losses on the phonograph? I am getting to the point of view that so far as the phonograph is concerned, it is hopeless in Europe and that we had better realise that fact before continuing for an indefinite period in the business."[70] Manager Thomas Graf responded, "Generally speaking, the cylinder business is bad, and although I have hesitated so long to own it to myself, I have come around to the view that with the present means at least a large business cannot be expected."[71] Graf pleaded with Dyer for a disc record to restore the fortunes of the ailing phonograph trade.[72] Unfortunately, when a disc finally appeared it failed to conform to the industry standard zigzag cut. In 1911 Thomas Graf's successor Paul Cromelin wrote to Dyer asking for an attachment that would allow this new record to be played on a standard gramophone. Although Dyer agreed with the sentiment Edison refused to consider the notion, as Dyer wearily observed, "It is difficult to always reconcile Mr Edison's views with principles of commercial expediency."[73] During the first nine months of 1911 NPC's British phonograph sales made a net loss of £2,684, whilst the film and kinetoscope business made a profit of £11,000.[74] In 1912, as if to signal the abandonment of the phonograph as the primary product, the name of the venture was changed to Thomas A. Edison Ltd. In 1914 Edison announced the closure of his European phonograph business. In the future if factors wanted his phonograph products they had to order them directly from West Orange; the war effectively ended the trade.[75]

This review of the NPC business illustrates how in the space of two short years a major player dominating its sector was unable to control critical organic change within the market. The inability of NPC to control or even delay change led directly to its being marginalised and eventually withdrawing from the field. Many of the problems NPC experienced were the result of a lack of continuity and the fickleness of Thomas Edison himself. However the business on both sides of the Atlantic confronted many of the same difficulties faced by The Gramophone Company. These included the control of branch managers in overseas locations, getting the right kind of machines from a US-based manufacturer and the inability of US-based businessmen to understand the complexities of the British and broader European record industry. This latter problem proved crucial, especially when the British market began to restructure along single format lines.

★   ★   ★

The early dominance of the cylinder record and phonograph in Britain was based on a fiercely competitive domestic manufacturing and selling base, increasingly bolstered by imports of continental European and American machines. However by 1909 everything had changed. For after that date, as

NPC's manager ruefully observed, "We are practically the only people who sell cylinder machines."[76] This sudden and largely unpredicted collapse was a function of a number of coinciding factors, including the abandonment of the cylinder market by German and Swiss manufacturers, who switched to the easier to manufacture and equally cheap disc records and machines. In the teeth of a recession there was an overcrowded market caused by over-production, which precipitated a collapse of the price structure. Added to this the price of disc records also fell, which eliminated any price advantage the cylinder records may have enjoyed. There was also a cultural dimension to all this, with the failure of manufacturers of cylinder records to respond to the developing musical tastes of their customers. To all this must be added the relative fragility and two-minute time limitation of the cylinder record before 1908, and finally the internecine warfare between Edison Bell and NPC.

NOTES

Billy Williams (born Richard Banks, 1878–1915) was an Australian-born music hall performer and the recording artist who made "Lets have a song upon the phonograph" famous. He sang this and any other song for those record companies willing to pay him a flat fee and freely adapted the song to reflect the name of whatever company he happened to be working for and the technology it employed. So the song appeared as "Lets have a song upon the Gramophone" or even "Graphophone." This broad-minded approach to business reflected the rough and tumble of the early British record industry.

1. "Trade Topics," *Talking Machine News* 6, no. 7 (2 November 1908): 1.
2. The British Bell-Tainter master patent for cutting sound signals into wax tablets expired in 1900, freeing up much of the industry and permitting Columbia to trade in Britain.
3. E. H. Phelps Browne and Margaret H. Browne, *A Century of Pay: The Course of Pay and Production in France, Germany, Sweden, the United Kingdom and the United States, 1860–1960* (London: Macmillan, 1968). According to this work, by 1913 annual wages in Britain averaged £57, compared to £19 in Italy.
4. Cyril Ehrlich, *The Piano: A History* (London: Dent, 1976), 86.
5. J. Van Allen Shields, "Some Considerations of the Bill as It Affects Mechanical Reproduction of Music" (copyright file, EMI).
6. J. Van Allen Shields, "Joint Trade Memorandum" (copyright file, EMI).
7. This figure is computed partly from the 13 million estimated disc record sales in 1913, together with German import figures and data compiled from Alfred Clark's 1912 "Lindström Amalgamation Report" (discussed in chapter 4). A 1916 "Memorandum to the Board of Trade" (discussed in chapter 8) suggests that annual prewar machine imports from Germany, America, Switzerland and other sources amounted to 350,000 units. This figure took no account of German and Swiss clockwork motors used in the domestic manufacture of machines or imports from sources such as France. With these additional units, the figure is nearer the estimate of 500,000.

8. See R. B. Mitchell, "Number of Houses at Census–UK 1851–1951," in *Abstract of British Historical Statistics* (Cambridge: Cambridge University Press, 1962), 239.

9. There is a compelling parallel between the pre-1914 take-up of talking machines and the later growth of radio and television. Plotting market penetration of radio and television is possible because of the British licensing system. In 1926, when The British Broadcasting Corporation received its charter, there were 2.17 million receiving licences and 9 million households (just over 25 per cent therefore had radio). By the outbreak of war in 1939, there were 9 million licences and 10.9 million households (more than 80 per cent market penetration). Post-1945 television developments were slower. In 1950 there were 343,000 television licences and 14.2 million households (less than 2.5 per cent). By 1955 (the year commercial television began) this figure had risen to 4.5 million, more than one in three. Thus, the growth of talking machine ownership finds a closer parallel with the growth of television in the early 1950s than with radio in the late 1920s and 1930s. Data compiled from Mitchell, "Number of Houses at Census," *Statistics*: 239; Asa Briggs, *The History of Broadcasting in the United Kingdom* (London: Oxford University Press, 1961–1979): "The Golden Age of Wireless," 9; "The War of Words," appendix B, Table 1, "Number of Sound-TV Licences 1947–1955 and of Sound Licences 1922–1930," "Sound and Vision."

10. William Edgar Gilmore to Thomas Edison, 27 August 1903 (phonograph co-foreign, Edison National Historic Site).

11. John Schermerhorn to William Edgar Gilmore, 22 December 1905 (document files, 1905, phonograph manufacturing, Edison National Historic Site).

12. "Monthly Epitomes to the Board of The Gramophone Company," May 1907 (board papers, EMI).

13. "Monthly Epitomes."

14. Frank L. Dyer to Thomas Edison, 10 August 1909 (document files, 1909, phonograph-foreign-England, Edison National Historic Site).

15. Schermerhorn to William Edgar Gilmore, 23 February 1906 (document files, 1906, phonograph manufacturing, Edison National Historic Site).

16. For an account of the pre-1914 British film industry and its audiences, see Rachael Low, "The Industry and the Public," *The History of the British Film Industry, 1906–1914* (London: Allen & Unwin, 1949).

17. "Telephone Directory of UK Talking Machine Companies," *Talking Machine News* 5, no. 10 (March 1907): 82.

18. See glossary for an explanation of the terms used to describe talking machines.

19. William Edgar Gilmore to Schermerhorn, 24 October 1906 (record manufacturing division, box 16, Gilmore, Dyer, Wilson correspondence, 1906, Edison National Historic Site).

20. See Frank Andrews, *Sterling Records* (Bournemouth, UK: Bayly, 1975): 3–4.

21. William Edgar Gilmore to Thomas Edison, 27 August 1903 (phonograph co-foreign, Edison National Historic Site).

22. For NPC manufacturing costs, see the monthly reports by E. J. Reihl (record manufacturing division, box 16, Gilmore, Dyer, Wilson correspondence, 1905, Edison National Historic Site).

23. Schermerhorn to William Edgar Gilmore, 29 September 1906 (record manufacturing division, box 16, Gilmore, Dyer, Wilson correspondence, 1906–1910, Edison National Historic Site).

24. "Trade Circulars" (record manufacturing division, box 16, Gilmore, Dyer, Wilson correspondence 1905, Edison National Historic Site).

25. J. H. White to William Edgar Gilmore, 2 June 1905 (document files, 1905, phonograph-sales, January-June, Edison National Historic Site).

26. Thomas Graf to Frank L. Dyer (document files, 1908, phonograph-manufacturing, Edison National Historic Site).

27. George Croydon (later Lord Marks of Woolwich) Marks (1858–1938) was Edison's British patent agent and, between 1903 and 1915, a director of NPC. A founding partner of Marks and Clerk patent agents, Marks was an engineer, businessman and politician—first a Liberal, then a Labour MP. Unique in the British record industry, Marks was in turn a founding director of NPC, then of The Columbia Graphophone Company Ltd 1917 to 1931 and Electric and Musical Industries Ltd between 1931 and 1938. See Michael R. Lane, *Baron Marks of Woolwich* (London: Quiller, 1986), though this work is unreliable with regard to the record industry aspect of Mark's career.

28. Marks to William Edgar Gilmore, 19 December 1906 (document files, 1906, phonograph-NPC-foreign-legal, Edison National Historic Site).

29. This assertion is noted in the evidence of Columbia's James van Allen Shields to the 1909 *Law on Copyright Committee*, Cmd. 4976 (London: HMSO, 1909).

30. William Edgar Gilmore to Schermerhorn, 22 April 1904 (record manufacturing division, box 15, Gilmore, Dyer, Wilson correspondence, March-May 1904, Edison National Historic Site).

31. See company registration file, The Russell Hunting Record Company Ltd, BT31/82918 (The National Archive, Kew).

32. Born in New York, Louis (later Sir Louis) Sterling (1879–1958) settled in Britain in 1903 and found employment with The Gramophone Company Ltd, creating the British Zonophone catalogue. A brilliant salesman and entrepreneur, he formed his first venture in 1904 with Russell Hunting. After the failure of this business in 1908, he established The Rena Manufacturing Company, which he sold to the British branch of Columbia in 1909. He then became Columbia general manager and, subsequently, European manager. In 1917 Sterling became managing director of The Columbia Graphophone Company Ltd and in 1923, with the US parent in bankruptcy, organised a management buyout of the British business. In 1925 he bought the parent, beginning an extensive acquisition policy. In 1931 his Columbia conglomerate merged with The Gramophone Company to form Electric and Musical Industries Ltd (EMI), and Sterling became managing director. He resigned in 1939 after a serious disagreement with Alfred Clark, EMI's chairman, with whom he enjoyed poor personal relations. His extensive European and American business dealings brought him into close contact with bankers and financiers, and he was a founding director of S. G. Warburg. His philanthropy and help to Jewish refugees fleeing Nazi Germany formed an important component of his socialist "equalitarian" philosophy. He was knighted in 1937 (the first honour for the industry) and endowed the Sterling Library at London University. Sterling was the second of the two industrial giants of British sound recording and electronics. See Louis Sterling and Columbia files (EMI). Also *Who Was Who*, 1960; Peter Martland, *Since Records Began* (London: Batsford, 1997), 104; and Martland, "Sir Louis Sterling" in *Oxford Dictionary of National Biography: From the Earliest Times to the Year 2000*, ed. H. C. G. Matthew and Brian Harrison (Oxford: Oxford University Press, 2005).

33. Andrews, *Sterling Records*, 4–5.

34. Andrews, *Sterling Records*, 9.

35. Schermerhorn to William Edgar Gilmore, 22 September 1906 (record manufacturing division, box 16 Gilmore, Dyer, Wilson correspondence, 1906, Edison National Historic Site).

36. Thomas Graf to William Edgar Gilmore, 19 December 1907 (document files, 1907. phonograph-manufacturing, Edison National Historic Site).

37. "Monthly Epitomes to the Board of The Gramophone Company," June 1908 (board papers, EMI). Thomas Graf to Frank L. Dyer, 19 November 1908 (document files, 1908, phonograph manufacturing, Edison National Historic Site).

38. *Talking Machine World* 6, no. 8 (August 1909), reported Sterling and Hunting Ltd transferring its exclusive British and Australian selling rights (including Odeon and Fonotipia) to music wholesalers Barnett Samuel and Sons Ltd.

39. See company registration files, BT31/7861 (The National Archive, Kew). Details of the Edison Bell business are listed in the *Stock-Exchange Yearbook* for the years 1898 to 1909. There are also individual entries for each of the Edison Bell businesses in the *Registry of Defunct and Other Companies Removed From the Stock Exchange Official Year Book 1968* (London, 1968), 172. See also Frank Andrews, *Edison Phonograph the British Connection* (Rugby: City of London Phonograph and Gramophone Society, 1986)

40. James White to William Edgar Gilmore (phonograph-manufacturing files, Edison National Historic Site).

41. Data compiled from Edison Bell, *Stock Exchange Yearbook*, 1900–1909. See also "A. E. Squire to William Edgar Gilmore," 29 June 1904 (phonograph-legal files, Edison National Historic Site); *Talking Machine News* 2, no. 3 (July 1904): 107; and *Talking Machine News* 3, no. 1 (May 1905): 25.

42. *Talking Machine New* 4, no. 9 (February 1907): 797.

43. See *Talking Machine World* 3, nos. 8 and 9 (August 1906 and September 1908).

44. How Edison Bell obtained phonographs from Germany and Switzerland is discussed in chapter 2.

45. "Schermerhorn to William Edgar Gilmore," 29 September 1909 (record manufacturing division, box 16, Gilmore, Dyer, Wilson correspondence, January-April 1906, Edison National Historic Site).

46. William Edgar Gilmore to Schermerhorn, 11 October 1906 (record manufacturing, box 16, Gilmore, Dyer, Wilson correspondence, September-December 1906, Edison National Historic Site).

47. For further details, see Andrews, *Edison*, 40–48. See also "Edisonia Ltd Auction Particulars," 24 March 1909 (document files, 1909, phonograph-Edison notes, Edison National Historic Site).

48. Graf to Dyer, 26 May 1909 (phonograph-legal files, Edison National Historic Site).

49. Marks to Dyer, 19 May 1909 (document files, 1909, phonograph-legal, Edison National Historic Site). The first Edison Bell disc was released in 1908 initially employing a Pathé-type vertical or hill-and-dale cut before adopting the emerging standard zigzag format. Unfortunately, this venture was short-lived, as the business went into liquidation. I am grateful to Frank Andrews for highlighting this important point.

50. The formation of The Winner Record Company was in keeping with the still rough-and-tumble of the times. Initially, the records were sold without a firm statement of price, and J. E. Hough Ltd was not even acknowledged as proprietors of the business. The business was at first described as "The Winner Syndicate" and its address as c/o *The Phono' Trader's* of-

fices in the City of London. The venture was incorporated as a private company four months after it commenced trading. I am grateful to Frank Andrews for this additional information.

51. See Karlo Adrian and Arthur Badrock, *Edison Bell Winner Record* (Bournemouth, UK: Bayly, 1989), especially the introduction by Frank Andrews, "The History of the Variously Labelled Winner Labels as Sold in Britain 1912–1935." See sales data, *Talking Machine World* 16, no. 11 (November 1919): 188. See also chapter 8.

52. See Companies House, file 73,188, "National Phonograph Company Ltd." In 1902 J. Lewis Young and Ernest Sinclair, who had no connection with the US business, registered a business called National Phonograph Company Ltd. This was a preemptive move to tie up the business name before Edison could form a British company. They were quickly eliminated. and the 1902 return shows George Croydon Marks in charge. He reconstituted it with a share capital of £5,000, raised to £50,000 in 1908.

53. Attachment to James White to William Edgar Gilmore, 26 October 1903 (phonograph-manufacturing files, Edison National Historic Site).

54. White to William Edgar Gilmore, 28 October 1903 (phonograph-manufacturing files, Edison National Historic Site).

55. "The National Phonograph Co," *Talking Machine News* 1, no. 6 (October 1903): 127.

56. See Alfred F. Wagner, *Recollections of Thomas A. Edison* (London: City of London Phonograph and Gramophone Society, 1991). Wagner joined NPC in 1904, was appointed manager in 1913 and remained with the company until his retirement in 1949. His memoirs provide a vivid insight into the pre-1914 record and talking machine trade. See also William Hayes's undated typescript memoir of National Phonograph Co Ltd (phonograph recording, Europe files, Edison National Historic Site), reproduced in *Antique Phonograph Monthly* 2, no. 9 (November 1974).

57. William Edgar Gilmore to Thomas Edison, 27 August 1903 (phonograph co-foreign, Edison National Historic Site).

58. See letters: Marks to William Edgar Gilmore, 12 December 1903; William Edgar Gilmore to White, 22 December 1903; White to William Edgar Gilmore, 26 January 1904; Marks to William Edgar Gilmore, 30 January 1904 (document files, 1903–1904, phonograph manufacturing, Edison National Historic Site).

59. For more on this, see chapters 5 and 6.

60. For an assessment of Edison's business methods, see chapter 1, and Andre Millard, *Edison and the Business of Innovation* (Baltimore: Johns Hopkins University Press, 1990).

61. For an account of the prior and subsequent career of pioneer filmmaker James White. see Kemp R. Niver and Bebe Bergsten, "James H. White: Primitive American Film-maker," in *Performing Arts Annual 1988* (Washington, DC: Library of Congress, 1988), 74–96.

62. Wagner, *Recollections*.

63. White to William Edgar Gilmore, 10 June 1905 (record manufacturing division, box 15, Gilmore, Dyer, Wilson correspondence, January-June 1905, Edison National Historic Site).

64. See chapter 2, Wagner, *Recollections*, and correspondence (phonograph-foreign, April-July 1908, Edison National Historic Site).

65. Marks to William Edgar Gilmore, 24 April 1908 (record manufacturing division, box 16, Gilmore, Dyer, Wilson correspondence, 1908, Edison National Historic Site).

66. Dyer to Reihl, 22 July 1908 (record manufacturing division, box 16, Gilmore, Dyer, Wilson correspondence, 1908, Edison National Historic Site).

67. Graf to William Edgar Gilmore, 19 December 1907 (document files, 1907, phonograph manufacturing, July–December, Edison National Historic Site).

68. Dyer to Thomas Edison, 10 August 1909 (document files, 1909, phonograph-foreign, England, Edison National Historic Site).

69. See also the *US Census of Manufacturing 1910,* "Manufacturing" (Washington, DC: GPO, 1910), vol. 10.

70. Dyer to Graf, 13 October 1910 (document files, 1910, phonograph manufacturing, Edison National Historic Site).

71. Graf to Dyer, 14 November 1910 (document files, 1910, phonograph manufacturing, Edison National Historic Site).

72. Graf to Dyer, 14 November 1910 (document files, 1910, phonograph manufacturing, Edison National Historic Site).

73. Dyer to Paul Cromelin, 28 July 1911 (document files 1911, phonograph manufacturing, Edison National Historic Site).

74. National Phonograph Company Ltd balance sheet at 30 September 1911 (document files, 1911, phonograph manufacturing, Edison National Historic Site).

75. For more on this move, see the editorial "What's the Matter With Edison," *Talking Machine News* 13, no. 2 (June 1915).

76. Graf to Dyer, 17 December 1909 (document files, 1910, phonograph manufacturing, January–June, Edison National Historic Site).

4

THE RISE AND RISE OF THE DISC RECORD TRADE: 1903–1914

"Land of Hope and Glory"

> The remarkable prominence of disc goods came rather as a surprise to the English visitors, who had . . . always been accustomed to regard this class as one of secondary importance. . . . When one considers the great influence the German trade has always had on the talking machine markets of the world, it looks almost as if the cylinder type of machines and records is eventually to be superseded by the rival genus.
>
> —News report on The Leipzig Spring Trade Fair,[1] April 1905

Previous chapters show how the cylinder format dominated in Britain during the early years of the twentieth century and just how one-sided this battle of technologies was; with cylinder records and phonographs massively outselling their disc equivalents. This was the case not just in Britain but also on the European continent and in the Americas. However, it did not last, and after 1903, in Britain and Europe where free markets prevailed but not in the United States where they did not, the Berliner Johnson zig-zag cut disc record moved from the margins to become the industry standard. Just as the previous chapter illustrated the rise and fall of the cylinder record by use of relevant case studies this one examines the experiences of several early-twentieth-century disc record companies. There are though some differences. In reviewing Pathé Frères and The Columbia Phonograph Company General, reference is made to their previous manufacture of cylinder records before turning to their exploitation of disc technology. Also, the experience of The Gramophone Company, the British market leader, is considered separately in chapters 5 and 6.

★   ★   ★

To recap, a British market for disc records and Gramophones began when American salesman William Barry Owen came to London in 1897 as the representative of inventor Emile Berliner. He started a trade in American manufactured discs and Gramophones and eventually found capitalists to invest in a British and European venture, styling it "The Gramophone Company." The business was a success attracting competitors into the field, but because of the premium cost of Gramophone goods it was not until after 1903 that the trade broke out of its mainly middle class niche. There-after, it developed mass markets, cutting into the existing cylinder trade and attracted new consumers. However, as described in the previous chapter, this late development left mass market formation firmly in the hands of the cylinder trade. Also after 1903 a critical industrial reformation began within the British and wider European industry that led to the abandonment of the cylinder and the adoption (with the notable exception of Pathé) of the Berliner Johnson zigzag cut disc as an industry standard. Also during this period the British and European record and talking machine industry en-tered a period of integration and consolidation.

Events surrounding this format conflict can be plotted quite easily, especially by reviewing trade journals and surviving business papers. For example, in October 1905 the US trade journal *Talking Machine World* reported 1904 domestic German record sales at six million, which even then were roughly evenly divided between cylinders and discs.[2] In contrast, Sydney Dixon (the British branch manager of The Gramophone Company) reported two months later, "In Great Britain the phonograph trade is gi-gantic, the disc trade is very small."[3] That said, even in Britain things were changing, and fast. This transition can be seen in trade journal reports of the Leipzig Spring Trade Fair or Frühlingsmesse. Before the First World War trade fairs, such as the one held in the German city of Leipzig, provided both shop window and neutral meeting ground for European manufactur-ers, traders and trade press. Manufacturers took stalls to display their latest goods for the coming selling season, and everyone could view the competi-tion's new products. The April 1905 quotation at the head of this chapter says it all. As did the report of the same fair in the American trade journal *Talking Machine World*, which noted,

> My general impression of the Messe was that the disc machine is the talking machine of the future, at least until someone invents something better with which to replace it. The majority of the exhibits represented low priced goods, both in machines and records. This is a field which larger and older manufacturers of disc apparatus have never tried.

The same correspondent reported the appearance of: "a large number of new disc records: Homophon, Beka, Favorite, Auto-record, Lyrophon, National Phonogram and Kalliope."[4] Many of these and other German-sourced record labels soon appeared in Britain.[5] The following year confirmation of the fatal marginality of the cylinder record in the broader European market was seen at the Leipzig Trade Fair as the *Talking Machine News* reporter wrote, "National Phonograph Company are the only firm exhibiting cylinders and phonographs."[6]

Underpinning this dramatic change was a rational and commercial logic, for German and Swiss manufacturers unencumbered by patents (unlike those in the United States) abandoned the complex cylinder phonograph in favour of more easily made and cheaper to make disc models. They also saw in disc records a more durable product that played longer, was easier to store, and was also easier and cheaper to manufacture. In these circumstances the transition was rapid, but for those manufacturers who stuck with the cylinder (like Edison Bell and National Phonograph Co Ltd) it proved deadly, especially once the disc gained ground in Britain (the wealthiest consumer market in Europe) during the 1907–1908 recession. In these perilous economic circumstances there was a general collapse in trade, which proved fatal for many poorly capitalised British cylinder record companies, lacking sufficient reserves to survive the storm. In contrast the disc record companies, particularly those in Germany, had long term finance from the industrial banks and survived. 1908 was the year of crisis for the cylinder business, as Sydney Dixon reported, "The whole trade, both factors and dealers are shaken with the sudden changes and collapses which have taken place. . . . The cylinder trade has gone to pieces altogether. Columbia and Edison Bell are unsalable—in fact I hear of the records of both companies being offered at 2d each. Further than all this the collapse of the Odeon Co has also affected trade."[7]

This crisis year was the subject of a *Talking Machine News* editorial: "One by one the unstable firms have dropped out. . . . They have not all died in the odour of sanctity. In an industry like this, still in the throes of development, this is always so. Time . . . is the great winnowing machine inexorably sifting the wheat from the chaff. We have seen a great deal of the sifting process going on in the last 19 months."[8] In the end most of the manufacturers who survived were those producing disc records and machines. In September 1908 Sydney Dixon reported the changing nature of the volume disc market to The Gramophone Company board:

> We now have five competing 10-inch discs single-sided at 2/6d. These
> are the Discaphone, the Russell, the Royal, and the Clarion; the Odeon

move against Zonophone has resulted in putting out the Jumbo record, viz: the 10-inch double sided at 3/-. They have some very excellent bands, and of course have the use of all the artists bound up to the Odeon. The Odeon . . . are now bringing out . . . a double-sided at 4/-. The Columbia have kept to 3/- for their double sided, 10", and 2/- for their single sided 10-inch. With the exception of a few good sellers they get now and again, their trade, however, lies entirely in machines, where they do very well indeed.[9]

In 1912 the British correspondent of *Talking Machine World* commented on the wholly different marketing situation to that in the United States: "[There are in Britain] nearly forty labels to choose from [with prices] ranging from 30s to 1s.6d. Almost every week a new record appears on the market—usually 1s.6d. To Americans this is strange with only six records. There are few, if any, patent restrictions in force here, while on your side in the talking machine trade at any rate, seems to be hedged around by patent monopolies and commercial policies not to be tolerated this side of the pond."[10] Nonetheless British dealers were badly affected by this organic change, which forced them to adapt or lose custom. In a January 1909 *Talking Machine World* editorial, the situation was summed up thus, "The disc record, especially the double sided variety, is outstripping in popular favour the cylinder record, which succeeding years show is more proportionately on the wane than ever. Nine cases out of ten the disc secures new buyers."[11]

★ ★ ★

To understand the key developments in the British disc record and gamophone trade during the years leading up to the outbreak of war in 1914 it is essential to grasp the central role played by German manufacturers. They were highly successful in penetrating the British market, particularly at the volume end of the trade. By 1914, largely because of this penetration there had developed a very large and important trade in cheap discs and gramophones. Most British manufacturers hated it but were forced to match the prices of this new competition. The extent of this penetration is demonstrated in the import data cited in table 4.1.

Although derived from incomplete data, table 4.1 demonstrates the steep prewar curve of German penetration. The trajectory clearly pushed ahead of market growth, suggesting consumers were also replacing cheap cylinder records and phonographs with equally cheap (if not cheaper) discs and gramophones. This table also shows the depth of the 1907–1908 recession and its impact on domestic consumption, with the value of record

Table 4.1. German Record and Machine Exports to Britain, 1907–1913

Year	Records Value		Records Quantity	Machines Value	
1907	£154,700	[$773,500]	NA	£105,100	[$525,500]
1908	£103,000	[$515,000]	NA	£63,000	[$315,000]
1909	NA		NA	NA	
1910	NA		1,800,000	NA	
1911	£272,500	[$1,362,500]	2,836,000	£242,500	[$1,212,500]
1912	£236,000	[$1,180,000]	3,027,000	£211,000	[$1,055,000]
1913	NA		4,202,000	NA	

Source: Series compiled from news reports in *Talking Machine News*, 1908–1913.

imports falling by £51,700 or around one third and machine imports by £42,100 falling again by around a third. In quantitative terms the years 1910 to 1913 are telling, with imports of German records more than doubling. It is worth noting that these figures exclude records pressed in Britain for German businesses. An assessment of the 1913 record sales in Britain shows the extent of German penetration. That year around 12 million records were sold; therefore German imports accounted for about one third of the total market, a remarkable achievement in so short a time.[12] To this figure must be added the one third market share held by the British branch of The Gramophone Company Ltd[13] and the balance by other British manufacturers like Columbia and Edison Bell, together with a host of often transient British minnows and other importers such as Pathé. To this must be added those British-pressed records for German businesses.

The prewar dominance of German gramophone manufacturers is also shown in table 4.1. In 1907, for example, exports to Britain were valued at £105,100; by 1912 that had doubled to £211,000. Germany was not the only continental manufacturer in this market, nor was the trade confined to complete machines. For example, in 1912, the Swiss engineering concern Thorens exported £75,000 worth of clockwork motors for use in British manufactured gramophones. The degree of penetration is further highlighted by comparing the 1912 machine turnover of the British branch of The Gramophone Company with German import figures. The former was £108,242 compared with the latter £211,000. As German prices were up to 80 per cent cheaper, the extent of German and Swiss domination of the British talking machine trade must have been phenomenal.

★   ★   ★

The first challenge to The Gramophone Company's British disc monopoly came in November 1899 when American-manufactured Zonophones and records appeared.[14] In 1901 American businessman and importer Frederick Marion Prescott formed the Berlin-based International Zonophone GmbH, which developed a manufacturing and marketing strategy similar to that of The Gramophone Company with branches across Europe, Russia and South America. Using the Berliner-Johnson zigzag cut recording process he created a first rate multifaceted Zonophone catalogue. Prescott also had access to US and other recordings. Initially, he obtained records and machines from the United States, but in 1901 opened manufacturing facilities in Berlin. To assist the venture, Prescott hired three Berliner-trained recording and matrix making engineers, Daniel Smoot, Edward Pancoast and Raymond Glötzner.[15] With these key personnel Prescott established a Zonophone recording studio in Berlin and his recording engineers travelled Europe making high-quality disc records for the British and European markets and he sold Zonophones as "an improved gramophone."[16]

As no International Zonophone GmbH business papers survive, it is impossible to locate basic details such as revenue, unit sales and market share. Nor is it possible to establish the role played by Zonophone in developing the disc sector of the British market. International Zonophone GmbH was a multinational business and created an international structure complete with subcompanies. It also appointed selling agents in various countries. In Britain the first agents were the musical box manufacturer and retailer Nicole Frères and later the London business of the French firm Ch. and J. Ullmann (with whom Prescott had further relations—see below); though contemporary Edison Bell and Columbia catalogues also carry Zonophone advertisements.

Throughout its existence Zonophone was an important advertiser, particularly in its key German market. This aggressive marketing was noted in a 1901 letter forwarded to The Gramophone Company's London office by its Australian manager, in which he quotes from correspondence sent from New York by Prescott to an Australian wholesaler full of knocking copy:

> You will find the records which we make very much superior to those of The Gramophone Co of London, they may not be superior in title or the assortment may not be so large but as far as the musical quality and the naturalness of the voice is concerned, and the quietness and freeness of hissing, our records are away ahead of theirs.
>
> The Manager of The Gramophone Co of London, came over here last month [to New York], and he told me our records were much superior in tone to their own, and he wanted to know how we made them that way, but of course we would not tell him.[17]

Zonophone records were made in three sizes, 7, 9 and 10 inches with a sound signal printed on one side. The first British-made recordings appeared in late 1901 or early 1902 and, by May 1903, a catalogue of 5,000 recordings was claimed. The British catalogue contained the traditional musical fare found on most early records, predominantly brass and military band arrangements and popular British songs, many recorded by local and nationally known names. Like Columbia and The Gramophone Company, Zonophone had a celebrity catalogue of premium priced recordings by some of the greatest performing artist's active at the time. These included a series, made in April 1903, by the Italian tenor Enrico Caruso.[18] As a consequence, Prescott became an important player in the disc sector of the market and a serious competitor to The Gramophone Company. It did not last long, and in June 1903 The Gramophone Company deployed its economic muscle to buy International Zonophone GmbH from Prescott and his associates. After the takeover the Berlin Zonophone recording studio was closed as were the disc and instrument factories. Thereafter, The Gramophone Company used Zonophone as a cheap record label to acquire market share and as a vehicle to break into mass markets; it also used the marquee on cheaper machines. And what happened to Prescott? He promptly established a new disc record venture, International Talking Machine Company GmbH (for more on this see below). He took with him many of his Zonophone employees, including, critically, the recording and matrix engineers.

Frederick Marion Prescott was a remarkable albeit somewhat shady businessman, whether selling in the United States, or into Britain, continental Europe or the British Empire. His business methods were not without critics, and by 1903 he was something of a leftover from the freewheeling pioneering days. William Gilmore, president of National Phonograph Company Inc, clearly had strong views and after meeting his fellow American in Europe in 1903 wrote to the inventor, "He is still as crooked as a ram's horn."[19]

★ ★ ★

The French movie pioneers Pathé Frères entered the sound recording industry in 1898 as a cylinder record and phonograph manufacturer and was, by 1901, trading as La Compagnie Générale des Phonographes, Cinématographes et Appareils de Précision Société Anonyme.[20] Although it supplied the French market there was also a clandestine patent busting British trade in its products. Furthermore until 1902 the business supplied

Columbia Phonograph Company General and Edisonia Ltd with cylinder blanks. In that year the end of the Edison Bell monopoly allowed a British venture to legally commence. In the same year French wholesaler Soury et Cie, who were Compagnie Générales' Parisian sales outlet, became British concessionaires for Pathé Frères products and formed Pathé Frères (London) Ltd with a nominal capital of £10,000.[21] For the French manufacturer this was advantageous; lacking the capital to start the British business it was able to make risk-free profits by simply filling orders for products. By 1903 the international trade in the range of Pathé Frères goods was such that the business had become a large multinational concern, with a capital base of £250,000 and employed more than 3,000 people in its film and sound recording divisions.[22]

Pathé Frères (London) Ltd created a marketing and distribution network under the management of experienced trader Tim Jellings Blow. It also created a British record catalogue and a London recording studio opened with composer Colin McAlpine as musical director. In 1905 a Glasgow studio opened. This enabled recordings of ephemeral popular music to be made quickly and British-based performers no longer had to make the journey to Paris, though record and machine manufacture took place at the Pathé Frères Chatou factory near Paris.[23] Pathé Frères (London) Ltd produced an impressive record catalogue, featuring several top-of-the-range military bands and performers like tenor Ben Davies and contralto Louise Kirkby Lunn, together with music hall artists Ada Reeve, Harry Lauder, Marie Lloyd and Vesta Tilley.[24] The catalogue also contained listings from the French, German, Italian and other Pathé Frères catalogues. Furthermore, the French parent did a deal with the Anglo Italian Commerce Company, gaining access to the 1903 series of cylinder recordings made by the young Italian tenor Enrico Caruso. The 1903 Pathé Frères British catalogue advertised thirteen types of cylinder phonograph including one aptly named the "John Bull" which retailed at £2.12s.6d. Others sold from £1.7s.6d up to £30.00, though most sold for less than £3.00. The most popular phonograph was the "Coq." It was a clone of the Columbia "Eagle" Graphophone retailing at £2.10s.0d (the equivalent of $12.50) and therefore cost $2.50 more than an Eagle in the US.[25]

Unfortunately Pathé Frères (London) Ltd was not a well managed concern and evidence suggests it never made a profit. The price of its products as shown in catalogues was purely nominal and throughout its existence the firm engaged in secret discounts and under-the-counter deals for cash payment.[26] In 1904, Pathé Frères (London) Ltd was so cash-strapped it had to move to cheaper premises and take out a £12,000 mortgage. And this was a time when the industry was booming. Its difficulties were such that in June 1905 Pathé Frères (London) Ltd was liquidated and another company formed with the same name and trading on the same basis as its predecessor.[27] In 1905 this venture took out a further mortgage, this time for £4,000 and yet another mortgage for £3,900 in 1906.[28] Also at this time, and in order to generate cash, the retail price of Pathé Frères records was cut, though the failure to maintain a coherent price structure made this a purely nominal move. It was not just bad financial management; the varied quality of Pathé phonographs and poor quality control of record manufacture caused constant dissatisfaction among wholesalers, retailers and customers alike. Frankly, Pathé Frères did not enjoy a good reputation in Britain, and with good reason.[29]

In 1906 Pathé Frères (London) Ltd was liquidated and the Compagnie Générale des Phonographes, Cinématographes et Appareils de Précision Société Anonyme ended the relationship with British concessionaire Soury et Cie and at the same time purchased the assets of the British venture. Thereafter, until 1911, the French manufacturer traded on its own account as Pathé Frères London, an unregistered arm of a foreign business.[30] These moves gave the impression (at least to the British trade and those artists its predecessors in business had under contract) that nothing had changed. The new business even took over the former premises at Lamb's Conduit in central London. In 1911 Pathé Frères Pathéphone Ltd was created to undertake the British trade. It was a private company with a nominal share capital of £400 and the size of the capital reflected the size and marginality of the business.[31]

This decision to trade in its own right was made because Compagnie Générale planned to abandon the cylinder record and phonograph and move to discs. The Pathé disc applied a curious Gallic logic to the problem of sound recording, with recordings starting at the centre of the disc and finishing at the edge. It also employed the hill-and-dale cut of cylinder records rather than the zigzag cut of the Berliner-Johnson record.[32] Pathé records were made in metric sizes 21 cm or 8.5 inches retailing at 1s.6d, 25 cm or 10-inch retailing at 3s, 27 cm or 11.75-inch retailing at 4s, 29 cm or 12-inch, 35 cm or 14-inch, and a 50 cm or 20-inch diameter record which revolved at speeds up to 120 revolutions per minute.[33] Pathé Frères designed special machines (called Pathéphones) retailing from £2.5s.0d to £12.12s.0d, on which to play these records. They also sold adaptors which permitted them to be played on conventional gramophones.[34]

These prewar years saw a continuance of the pioneering disdain for honest business methods, and Pathé Frères provides a good example. The company's attitude towards the contracted recording artists it inherited was breathtakingly cavalier. In fact the new venture repudiated all Pathé Frères (London) Ltd artist contracts, specifically the annual fee clauses. This did not prevent them using this valuable back catalogue and, in 1909, hired Russell Hunting as transfer engineer to exploit it. Hunting created an ingenious mechanical process (possibly using an old Columbia duplicating machine) to transfer the very best cylinder recordings from the old Pathé and Sterling record catalogues on to the new Pathé discs. Among these were two made in 1906 for Sterling by Irish tenor John McCormack and others by Harry Lauder as a contracted Pathé Frères (London) Ltd artist. Although the Hunting transfers were of outstanding quality there was, of course, no recompense for the artists and, to cover its tracks, Hunting excluded the spoken announcement made at the start of each original record, which included the company name.[35] Whatever the shenanigans, the impact on Pathé Frères accounts is easy to see. In 1912 the parent company published trade press advertisements showing annual turnover for the three previous years. If these figures are to be believed, they show a cumulative turnover on its international record and talking machine business of almost £500,000.[36]

Although Pathé Frères enjoyed success in France and Russia it remained marginal in Britain, where the zigzag cut disc was the industry standard.[37] With the onset of war in 1914 the British trade in these non-standard products practically ended although the brand continued into the 1920s, but with the standard zigzag cut. In October 1928 Pathé Frères was acquired by Louis Sterling's Columbia Graphophone Company Ltd and in 1931 the brand became a part of EMI; making it the oldest continuous label in the EMI stable.

★   ★   ★

The Columbia Phonograph Company General began its continental European trade in 1897 and opened its British operation in May 1900. It traded as an unregistered subsidiary of a foreign business until 1917, when it was incorporated as The Columbia Graphophone Company Ltd.[38] The 1900 move to Britain and its lucrative consumer markets provided the business with an opportunity for commercial success. In an optimistic June 1903 *Talking Machine News* interview Columbia manager Frank Dorian claimed the venture was flourishing. To support this there appeared a somewhat fanciful drawing of the company's warehouse with a tagline suggesting it had a capacity of 300,000 cylinder and disc records.

Dorian is quoted as saying sales of Columbia cylinders made by the new moulding process were in the region of "some hundreds of thousands per month" and its 108 page catalogue listed over 5,000 recordings.[39] All this suggested a venture able to navigate and prosper in the burgeoning British market, but the reality was quite different.

Until 1901 all Columbia recordings were derived from the US parent and in that year Charles Butler Gregory, an experienced young American Columbia sound engineer, came to London where he opened a recording studio and created a British catalogue of cylinder records and, after the introduction of Columbia discs in 1902, a catalogue of disc records. Like his colleague Fred Gaisberg (the pair had worked together in the early 1890s), Charles Gregory remained in London for the rest of his life and made many notable recordings, eventually becoming manager of EMI's Abbey Road studios. Alas, unlike Gaisberg, he never wrote memoirs, so little is known of his early years in London.[40] The rate of recording was such that as early as 1903 (as Dorian asserted in his *Talking Machine News* interview) Columbia was manufacturing "50,000 records a month all made by British artists and for the British market." Columbia records, both discs and cylinders, were manufactured in the United States and exported to Britain until 1905 when Columbia opened a pressing factory at Earlsfield in Surrey, near London. The European business had pressing facilities in St Petersburg, Paris and Berlin, but this was largely to avoid paying import tariffs. The British Columbia catalogue was supplemented by European and US derived recordings. As Columbia was engaged in both the cylinder and disc business, Gregory was master of both arts. His British recordings included the standard repertoire, that is to say pages of military and brass band music together with seriocomic songs and ballads. However, like The Gramophone Company and International Zonophone, Columbia created a premium priced celebrity catalogue, with recordings taken in Europe and the United States by Columbia's chief engineer Frank Capps. Among the celebrities he recorded were the American soprano Lilian Nordica, tenor Alessandro Bonci and soprano Emmy Destinn. Furthermore, in 1911, the British branch of Columbia scored a singular coup over The Gramophone Company by signing the great contralto Clara (later Dame Clara) Butt. Columbia also produced the first recordings by the then rising soprano Mary Garden and other important British and European musicians. The business was also innovative, signing up star British conductors Sir Henry Wood and Thomas (later Sir Thomas) Beecham both of whom made their first orchestral recordings in the cramped and uncongenial conditions of the pre-1914 Columbia recording studios.[41]

Like most other early record companies few business papers survive for the pre-1914 period, making an assessment of the venture difficult. For example, there are no production runs nor sales or financial statements on either side of the Atlantic and, therefore, excessive reliance has to be placed on comments in the trade press and the observations of competitors. Whichever way this business is assessed, it is clear that during this period Columbia was a peripheral player much affected by the financial travails of its American parent. Evidence of instability is seen in several well-documented attempts to engage in under-the-counter price-cutting deals, which became a byword among the trade.[42] Furthermore, compelling evidence on both sides of the Atlantic suggests Columbia, in order to get trade and ready cash, arranged price fixing deals with its competitors and then by offering extended credit and other incentives secretly undercut them with wholesalers and retailers. This general instability had a major impact on the development of Columbia and damaged its reputation as a manufacturer and trader.[43]

In November 1906, Sydney Dixon reported, "Columbia owing to US troubles have withdrawn all their travellers off the road and their recording experts and salesmen are applying for jobs."[44] Further evidence of Columbia's decline was noted in a March 1908 letter from NPC's managing director in London to West Orange. He said, "Factors [wholesalers] have reported to me that they [Columbia] have given up in this country their branch retail houses in Manchester, Cardiff, Glasgow etc. Today their Oxford Street premises have been offered to me by a house agent."[45]

In 1909 Columbia abandoned the cylinder trade, retaining its disc record catalogue and US manufactured machines. In the aftermath of the 1907 to 1908 recession, which saw its American parent go into administration, British branch manager Frank Dorian quit his post and returned to the United States to help relaunch the business. It was in these unpromising circumstances that Louis Sterling, former head of The Russell Hunting Record Company Ltd, saved the British and European Columbia business from extinction. After the 1908 collapse of The Russell Hunting Record Company Ltd, Sterling formed The Rena Record Company as a disc record concern and, rather than create his own catalogue, placed large pressing orders with Columbia's London factory. The deal was simple enough. Rena records were sourced from Columbia's catalogue and preexisting disc matrix stock, using cover names on the records, and retailing at prices below the regular Columbia list. His success at selling Rena records persuaded Columbia to buy The Rena Record Company and thereafter, till the outbreak of the First World War, Columbia records were sold as

Columbia-Rena records. Sterling came with the Rena acquisition and became general manager. Columbia's finances were so bad that, as Sterling's surviving contract indicates, he was paid nothing but a sales commission, up to a maximum of £2,000. He successfully reorganised the selling side of the enterprise and in the first year earned his full commission.[46]

The transformation in the fortunes of this industry sick man is revealed in a 1911 report by Gramophone Company managing director Alfred Clark who knew of Sterling's skills as a salesman, though he enjoyed poor personal relations with him. He noted, "Columbia is dead throughout the continent, but is quite alive at the present time in England, and although they are not serious competitors yet, they should not be overlooked in this country."[47] It was not just in the field of records, for by the eve of war Columbia had a catalogue of twenty US manufactured machines (sold as "Disc Graphophones" or "Grafonolas"), capable of rivalling Gramophone Company machines. These retailed at prices ranging between £2.12.6d and £12.10s, with top-of-the-range bespoke models selling at up to £105.[48] Clark was correct to be on the lookout for this new competition for, under the leadership of Louis Sterling, it was the start of the rise and rise of the Columbia juggernaut.

★   ★   ★

The early-twentieth-century record industry was not just about businesses like Edison Bell or Columbia, it included several important firms who made metal matrices and pressed records for firms without their own facilities. Perhaps the most important was The Crystalate Manufacturing Company Ltd of Tonbridge, Kent.[49] Formed in 1901, its origins were in the late-nineteenth-century American-venture The George Burt Company of Milburn, New Jersey. George Henry Burt manufactured a shellac-based plastic composition, which was used to press Berliner and Zonophone disc records. In order to break into the disc record business, Edward Easton and the Columbia interests in the United States acquired The George Burt Company and The Globe Record Company, its disc record-making arm manufacturing Climax records. The Crystalate Manufacturing Company Ltd in Britain was therefore a licencee of Burt technology; the firm also made pool and billiard balls, bottle stoppers and other plastic products.[50] As a jobbing matrix maker and record manufacturer Crystalate was the first venture to press disc records in Britain. It serviced the needs of a variety of usually small, often transient, record companies, though it also pressed records for Frederick Marion Prescott concerns, first International Zonophone GmbH and then International Talking Machine GmbH with its Odeon and Jumbo labels. It did not emerge as a record company in its own right until the 1920s.[51]

Burt had strong connections with The Nicole Frères Record Company Ltd, which had the distinction of being the earliest disc record company failure.[52] The business was a spin-off of Nicole Frères Ltd, a Swiss musical box manufacturer with a branch in Geneva; though when it was registered in August 1897 the business was controlled by German interests.[53] In October 1899 Nicole Frères Ltd commenced a trade in phonographs and gramophones and became British agents for International Zonophone GmbH. By 1902 the musical box and ancillary products had been pushed to the side, with records and talking machines the main focus of the business.[54] Supply problems with Crystalate caused Nicole Frères, with the assistance of George Burt, to develop pressing facilities in anticipation of the growing Zonophone trade. Unfortunately, Zonophone was acquired by The Gramophone Company in 1903 leaving Nicole Frères in serious difficulties. It had pressing facilities but no product and had either to accept huge losses or get into the disc record business. The latter was the only option. Using a process invented by Burt, Nicole Frères manufactured an unbreakable record consisting of a compressed cardboard core coated with a film of celluloid. The firm also used its links to Prescott, who sent recording engineer Daniel Smoot to London where he made the first Nicole Frères recordings and trained in-house engineer Rudolf Eckhardt in the process.

In July 1903 The Nicole Frères Record Company Ltd was formed with a capital of £10,000 to acquire the recording business of Nicole Frères Ltd. Among the directors were George Burt and Rudolf Eckhardt. To develop a European trade Eckhardt went to Germany and was succeeded by American Steve Porter; that is until 1904 when he went to India to create a local catalogue.[55] Nicole Frères then appointed Arthur H. Brooks as head of the recording department. Brooks also undertook European recording tours and captured the art of several members of the San Carlo Opera Company on the 10-inch Nicole Master Record series, which sold for 5s twice the price of regular 10-inch Nicole Frères discs.[56] In October 1905 Nicole Frères issued double-sided 7- and 10-inch discs known as the Duplex, though these were mainly couplings of back catalogue. The first release of 141 seven-inch British Nicole Frères records retailing at 1s appeared in the Autumn of 1903, in time for the lucrative Christmas trade. At the time its 7-inch record was the cheapest disc record on the British market. The 10-inch record appeared in March 1904 selling at 2s.6d. It was a seemingly prosperous new company operating in a rising market with a

British record catalogue running to 24 pages in 1905. It contained many military and brass band records and popular singers like Peter Dawson.[57] An international trade quickly developed and the British catalogue was joined by those for the French, German, Norwegian, Swedish and Indian markets. The imperial trade was also a primary market and agents were appointed for South Africa. In addition to the 7- and 10-inch records, The Nicole Frères Record Company Ltd marketed a range of own-brand but German-manufactured machines retailing at between £2.2s and £3.17s.6d.[58]

With catalogues of recorded music supplemented by monthly releases, a line of machines, a national and international marketing and distribution system and operating in a rising market, what went wrong? The primary cause was the failure of the original venture Nicole Frères Ltd, whose core nonrecord business collapsed. However, like many early record industry failures, it was down to a weak capital structure. Nicole Frères Ltd had created a record company with a mere £10,000 capital. It clearly had little by way of cash because in Sept 1903 it raised two £1,000 debentures (bonds) and increased the nominal capital first to £15,000 and then, in 1905, to £30,000. The latter was an attempt to raise cash so as to pay off the debentures, but it proved unsuccessful and there were further debentures issues to provide ready cash. Given its debt levels, the profit of £3,600 for the selling year 1904–1905 was insufficient to meet its overall liabilities. Overtures were made to The Gramophone Company for a takeover, but these came to nothing. When The Gramophone Company reduced the price of its 7-inch record to match the Nicole Frères product, it was the end of the road. In March 1906, at a time when the record and machine trade (especially the disc sector) was booming, the company chairman and chief creditor put the business into receivership for failing to repay debenture holders (of which he was one of the largest). The business was sold off and its assets liquidated.

What happened thereafter reflected the prewar disc record boom. Between 1904 and the collapse of 1906 Jack Watson Hawd was one of the largest Nicole Frères Record Company Ltd shareholders and he was also a director. A former Gramophone Company executive, in June 1906 Hawd formed The Disc Record Company Ltd of Stockport with a nominal capital of £5,000. Like Crystalate this business and its successors were matrix makers and pressing contractors. The Disc Record Company Ltd acquired the plant, machinery and stock of The Nicole Frères Record Company Ltd for £2,500 and with George Burt as factory manager (having abandoned the cardboard and celluloid mix in favour of the standard shellac-based mix) began marketing records. Thereafter, down to the outbreak of war in

1914, Jack Watson Hawd, The Disc Record Company Ltd and its successors exploited Nicole Frères metal matrices. In this booming market, there
were innumerable customers and the metals were recycled for many often
small short-lived cheap labels with names like Britannic, Burlington, The
Leader, The Conqueror, Sovereign Records and Universal Records. They
were also used to press records used by the so-called tally-man system. A
tally-man was a door-to-door commission salesman who signed up customers to buy a record each week for a certain number of weeks with a
talking machine thrown into the deal. It was a pretty shady operation, and
that probably summed up Jack Watson Hawd, clearly another fly-by-night
pioneer of the record and machine industry who was able to hang in at the
bottom of the market until the war changed everything.

★   ★   ★

The rapid growth of the continental European disc record manufacturing
base was noted in a 1906 report from the Leipzig trade fair, from where
the correspondent of *Talking Machine News* observed: "The manufacturers
of discs and disc machines are about equally divided. Excepting the Gramophone and the Odeon, practically no other firm is represented which builds
and manufacturers its own discs and machines. The rest of the manufacturers either manufacture records alone, or if they handle machines they
buy them elsewhere, or else they manufacture machines and buy records
elsewhere."[59] It was therefore to serve the burgeoning British and European
markets that these largely German ventures were established. Of these the
largest and most dynamic was Carl Lindström AG. In a 1912 report Alfred
Clark, managing director of The Gramophone Company Ltd,[60] explained
the business started in 1904 when the businessmen Max Strauss and Otto
Heinemann,[61] who had traded in cinematographs and films, "drifted into
the record and player business." They met Carl Lindström, a Swedish-
born but German-based mechanic and inventor. With a small workshop
and staff he repaired machines for The Columbia Phonograph Company
General and manufactured disc machines using the name "Parlophon."
Strauss and Heinemann placed orders for Parlophons, but discovered he
lacked sufficient capital to meet their needs. In 1904 they formed the Carl
Lindström ACT to acquire the business, with the eponymous mechanic
remaining as technical manager. Heinemann and Strauss were financed by
the Bank fur Handel und Industrie and the business created an impressive
disc machine manufacturing capacity. When it became a public company
in June 1908 Carl Lindström had 700 employees, which had increased to

1,800 worldwide by 1913; that same year it produced 500,000 gamophones for domestic and export markets (including Britain).[62]

Although the Carl Lindström factories were churning out machines at a rate of knots, they were mainly but not exclusively at the cheap, volume end of the market. The quality simply did not compare to the expensive models manufactured for The Gramophone Company by The Victor Talking Machine Company. In his 1912 report, Alfred Clark noted these differences and of the markets in which the two firms traded: "But as the great bulk of Lindström's business is in the very cheap type, it may be taken that the two companies divide between them the two classes of machine trade." Clark also commented on the differences in quality and manufacturing:

> The class of goods sold by Lindström companies is very low. The Lindström machines are not good in any sense of the word. The sound-boxes only give a fairly good result; the general workmanship throughout is bad but of course this is due to the extremely low prices at which they are manufactured.
>
> The cabinets are of the cheapest quality and the very best that they had to show me would never have been accepted by any of our customers. They do not seem to appreciate the need of good cabinet work.[63]

Although the data are incomplete, the figures in table 4.2 indicate a six fold increase in turnover between 1908 and 1911. It also shows how the business conserved capital assets (it had a reserve of M629,750 or £31,487 or $157,435) by revealing only small net profit used to pay dividend, mainly to its banking shareholder.

Table 4.2.   Carl Lindström AG: Group Turnover and Net Profit, 1908–1911

Year	Gross Turnover		Dividends
1908	£104,000	[M2,080,000 or $520,000]	NA
1909	£161,400	[M3,228,000 or $807,000]	£23,030 [M460,600 or $115,151]
1910	£260,800	[M5,216,000 or $1,304,000]	£26,230 [M524,600 or $131,150]
1911	£660,000	[M13,200,000 or $3,300,000]	£35,100 [M702,000 or $175,500]

Source: Series compiled from news reports in *Talking Machine News*, 1908–1913. Before the First World War the exchange rate was 20 German marks to the British pound or 6.25 German marks to the US dollar. Exchange rate data derived from Alan S. Milward and S. B. Saul, *The Development of the Economies of Continental Europe: 1850–1914* (London: Allen & Unwin, 1977).

During these prewar years, and in stark contrast to the way the British trade was organised, Carl Lindström engaged in aggressive bank-driven vertical and horizontal integration of the German gramophone and record manufacturing industries, and suppliers of record-making material. The outcome of all this was the creation of a large and important multinational holding company operating on a worldwide basis, more than capable of competing with The Gramophone Company in Britain or any other market. An examination of these acquisitions shows how important the Carl Lindström business became by 1914. In August 1910 it acquired Beka AG from its founders Bumb and Koenig of Berlin. Beka had been an international success. For example *Talking Machine News* reported in June 1908 that Beka records had achieved "tremendous success in India over the past two years." The report claimed the Beka Indian record catalogue contained one thousand titles and this competition had compelled The Gramophone Company's Indian branch to reduce its prices by one third.[64] Furthermore, in April 1909, with the industry emerging from recession, the price of British Beka records was reduced to 2s.6d for 10-inch and 5s for 12-inch, a move that started a major price war in the volume end of the market.[65] In September 1911 *Talking Machine News* reported another acquisition: "Carl Lindström takes over Fonotipia Ltd." Societa Italiana di Fonotipia, Milano was an Italian venture formed in 1905 by the Italian music publisher Titto Ricordi, Harry Higgins manager of the Royal Opera House, Covent Garden and banker Baron Frederick Derlanger. By exploiting Ricordi's huge musical copyright portfolio, it sought to tie up the finest operatic and instrumental music and use that monopoly to control the record market. This aspect of the venture failed miserably, though Fonotipia remains a magical name and continues to provide record collectors with a rich vein of early historic recordings.[66] The Milan venture used Odeon engineers to make records, which were pressed at the International Talking Machine Gmbh factory in Berlin. In April 1906 the Italian business became a branch of Fonotipia Ltd, a British registered company.[67] Although the business created a catalogue of stellar names, it was badly managed, sales were poor and the firm languished until it was acquired by the Lindström group. The same *Talking Machine News* report went on to chronicle the businesses acquired by the combine: "within recent memory this firm has absorbed . . . Beka Records Ltd, Franz Poppel and now Fonotipia Co. Ltd (London) which controls the output of Odeon, Jumbo and Fonotipia from International Talking Machine GmbH."[68] By the time of its acquisition by Carl Lindström AG, International Talking Machine GmbH was an important player in the British record market with the midpriced Odeon and cheaper Jumbo labels; Odeon maintained its position with an excellent catalogue of records (see below).

International Talking Machine GmbH had been formed in 1903 by American businessman Frederick Prescott in partnership with French music industry entrepreneurs and gained financial support from the German industrial banks. Odeon was the first record to incorporate the then novel feature of a recording sound on both sides of the disc. Odeon discs were manufactured in metric sizes: 19-cm 7½-inch known as the standard which sold for 2s.6d, 27-cm 10¾-inch concert selling at 5s.0d and a 30-cm 12-inch opera which retailed at 8s.6d. There were a small number of band and operatic records on a 37-cm 13½-inch grand opera single-sided at 10s.0d. The Odeon record label successfully sold in Britain and across continental Europe, demonstrating the potential of this new mass market in midpriced records. To develop the market Odeon created a catalogue of British recordings, opening a recording studio at 14 Hamsell Street, London, under the direction of experienced sound engineers Daniel Smoot (until 1906), ex-Nicole Frères engineer Arthur H. Brooks, Oscar Preuss and later William Ditcham.[69] The 1906 British Odeon catalogue, which ran to 78 pages, reveals an impressive list of records, to which monthly releases were added. According to this source the link with The Russell Hunting Record Company Ltd and Sterling and Hunting Ltd (who were British agents) was not confined to marketing. Many artists appearing on Sterling cylinder records also appeared on Odeon discs.[70] To confirm the link, the 1906 catalogue states, "All the new 'Odeon' records, which are being made by Messrs Sterling and Hunting Ltd, will be accompanied by that perfect combination known as the 'Sterling Orchestra.'" Substantial international classical celebrities recorded as Odeon artists; including Emmy Destinn, Jan Kubelik, John McCormack and Mario Sammarco. It was not all plain sailing, and during the 1908 recession the International Talking Machine GmbH British business, which was managed by Sterling and Hunting Ltd, went spectacularly bust. Thereafter, to 1913, marketing what eventually became the British Carl Lindström AG stable records and machines was handled by wholesalers Barnett Samuel and Sons. In 1911 Frederick Prescott sold International Talking Machine GmbH to Carl Lindström AG. Carl Lindström AG used Fonotipia Ltd as the vehicle to acquire the business and with it came the ubiquitous Frederick Prescott. This all changed in 1913 when Carl Lindström (London) Ltd was formed, with a nominal share capital of £1,000. Its purpose was to secure its growing British asset base and position the venture to acquire an even larger market share. To this end, a British record manufacturing facility opened in Hertford, to the north of London. It was managed by Swiss-born manager Otto Rühl from 77 City Road, London; that is until the coming of war in 1914. In 1916 the concern was seized and sold off as an enemy-controlled company.[71]

In terms of British market penetration during the prewar years The Carl Lindström AG conglomerate was by far the most successful foreign venture trading in records and talking machines, whether as an exporter of German manufactured goods or British manufactured pressings of German master records.[72] Its British record labels included: Beka Grand, Beka Meister, Jumbo, Decapo, Favorite, Odeon and Fonotipia. Furthermore, in its earliest days, Carl Lindström AG launched the Parlophon record label in Germany, which remains one of the oldest labels in the world.[73] In 1911 total Carl Lindström AG British record sales (both imports and those pressed in Britain) amounted to more than £70,122 compared to Gramophone Company British sales of £189,595. However, as Lindström's records were selling at the same or much cheaper prices than most Gramophone Company records, they could have sold very similar quantities.[74]

The size, importance and ambition of Carl Lindström AG were such that in 1911 it proposed an amalgamation with The Gramophone Company and The Victor Talking Machine Company. The board of The Gramophone Company took the approach seriously and sent managing director Alfred Clark to Germany to assess the Carl Lindström AG venture and the potential of this deal. His report provides a remarkable insight into the business. Although the deal never came to fruition, it pointed the way forward to this industry's 1920s mergers movement.[75] In April 1912, following the failure of the proposed merger, Carl Lindström AG continued its bank-funded policy of acquiring new businesses, this time the Automaten Sprechmachinesfabrik, "Phoenix," J. Wolzen and A. Winter of Dresden which, in a rapidly rising market, provided additional machine and component making capacity for the international trade. It cost M2,000,000 [£100,000 or $500,000]. In October 1913 the combine merged with another large German venture Grunbaum and Thomas, whose overseas manufacturing plants stretched from Russia to Britain. By the outbreak of war in 1914 Carl Lindström AG was the largest German record company and, with markets across Europe, Asia, India and the Far East and into South America, a major world player in this field of commerce.

The reaction of the British trade to German market penetration with cheap machines and records was swift and intemperate. To compete with this flood, British manufacturers were forced to produce equally low cost records. (As far as machines were concerned most of the rest, apart from those imported by Columbia and Gramophone Company components which were both American-sourced and those Pathé Frères imports from France, were of either Swiss or German manufacture, or constructed in Britain from parts derived from those countries. This meant lower profits and increased costs.) Some record manufacturers like Columbia and The Gramophone Company could mine extensive back catalogues, while the pressing agents like Crystalate used its own substantial holding of metal matrices. Such was The Gramophone Company's power that, in 1913, it created the 1s.1d Cinch record, entirely from back catalogue.[76] Columbia matched this with its own Phoenix label. Unfortunately, J. E. Hough Ltd, a relatively new disc manufacturer, had only a small back catalogue of disc records it could recycle. That firm, led by its blustering eponymous manager, launched a counterattack in the trade press and elsewhere characterising the German cheap record trade and those big record companies who matched their products as "wreckers" of the British trade undermining the price structure which would ultimately destroy the industry.[77] Despite all the hyperbole consumers loved it. As discussed in chapter 3, cheap machines and records expanded the market dramatically to the point that by the start of the First World War recorded music had become an essential part of domestic leisure activity, especially in the homes of the skilled and semiskilled working classes.

★ ★ ★

By the outbreak of the First World War in 1914 cheap gramophones and records had expanded the market dramatically and these products had become an essential part of domestic leisure activity, especially in the homes of the skilled and semiskilled working classes. Although the trade had initially begun as an arm of American enterprises it had, by 1914, become international. Also by that date the two principal ventures in the British market, Carl Lindström AG and The Gramophone Company, were owned and located in Europe rather than America. Within no more than a decade the British industry had become an established feature in the growing leisure, cultural and communications revolution. A market-led business, it had grown by being alert to competition, technological innovations and low cost manufacturing. It had succeeded in developing sophisticated marketing and opportunities to cut the pricing structure, together with a dynamic manufacturing base. The future seemed assured; that is until the events of August 1914 intervened.

NOTES

Composed in 1901 by Sir Edward Elgar, the music for "Land of Hope and Glory" is taken from his *Pomp and Circumstance Military Marches* (Number 1), which was performed at the coronation of King Edward VII. The words were added later by A. C. Benson, for the coronation of King George V in 1911. "Land of Hope and Glory" was recorded that same year by contralto Clara (later Dame Clara) Butt (HMV 03239), accompanied by the band of the Coldstream Guards, conducted by Captain J. Mackenzie-Rogan (Clara Butt went on to record it many times for Columbia). First as a piece of music and later as a song and then a record, "Land of Hope and Glory" was a tremendous success. Given the destruction experienced by the British in two world wars, pre-1914 Edwardian Britain took on an idyllic quality for which this song provided the perfect musical backdrop. Today it has become an alternative British national anthem.

1. "Leipzig Trade Fair," *Talking Machine News* 2, no. 12 (April 1905): 540.

2. *Talking Machine World* 2, no. 10 (October 1905).

3. "Monthly Epitomes to the Board of The Gramophone Company," December 1905 (board papers, EMI).

4. "The Great Leipzig Fair," *Talking Machine World* 1, no. 5 (May 1905): 1.

5. In a 1906 *Talking Machine World* interview, Prescott claimed that "there are approximately twenty disc manufacturers operating in Germany, the majority small and not well capitalised." He was clearly unaware of the role played by the industrial banks in providing finance and pushing forward with integration.

6. "From Our Correspondent," *Talking Machine News* 3, no. 11 (March 1906): 59.

7. "Monthly Epitomes to the Board of The Gramophone Company," June 1908 (board papers, EMI). It is worth noting that at this time, the Odeon dealership was held by Sterling and Hunting, whose cylinder record business had just gone bust bringing with it the collapse of this subsidiary trade.

8. "Trade Topics," *Talking Machine News* 8, no. 7 (November 1908): 370.

9. Sydney W. Dixon to Calvin G. Child, 22 September 1908 (Victor files, 1908, EMI).

10. "European Editorial," *Talking Machine World* 8, no. 12 (December 1912): 36.

11. "European Editorial," *Talking Machine World* 5, no. 1 (January 1909).

12. Cited in "Foreign News," *Talking Machine News* 10, no. 5 (September 1913): 16.

13. For more on this figure, see chapter 6.

14. For an account of the origins and ownership of International Zonophone GmbH, see chapters 2 and 3 together with *The Zonophone Record: A Discography*, ed. Ernie Bayly and Michael Kinnear (Victoria, Australia: Kinnear, 2001), from which much of the detail for this section has been drawn.

15. See Sooy, "Memoir of My Career at Victor Talking Machine Company," http://www.davidsarnoff.org) and Bayly and Kinnear, *The Zonophone*.

16. See F. W. Wortman to William Barry Owen, 25 April 1900, in which he remarked, "Can't you stop this Mr Prescott from calling his nasty machine an improved gramophone" (Zonophone papers, EMI).

17. Cited in Bohanna to William Barry Owen, 9 July 1901 (Zonophone papers, EMI). I am grateful to Frank Andrews for pointing out this correspondence, which included copies of trade press advertisements.

18. The seven Caruso Zonophone recordings were made on 19 April 1903 by The Anglo-Italian Commerce Company in Milan but published by International Zonophone GmbH. For more information on these historic recordings, see John R. Bolig, *Caruso Records a History and Discography* (Denver, COL: Mainspring Press, 2002), 5–7.

19. William Edgar Gilmore to Thomas Edison, 27 August 1903 (phonograph co-foreign, Edison National Historic Site).

20. French patent law is discussed in chapter 1. Its working clauses permitted Pathé Frères to enter the market and become pioneers of the recording and movie industries. They manufactured phonographs and cylinder records and were one of the most important early filmmakers.

21. See company registration file, Pathé Frères (London) Ltd, BT31/72856 (The National Archive, Kew).

22. "Interview With Jellings Blow Manager of Pathé Frères," *Talking Machines News* 1, no. 3 (July 1903).

23. The system of recording adopted by Pathé Frères sound engineers was unique. They used large-diameter cylinders approximately 9 inches in length, capable of recording up to sixteen two-minute duration records. These were subsequently transferred on to standard-size cylinders, which were then made into moulds for mass production.

24. Because of the complex structure of the venture, these British-made recordings were owned by Pathé Frères London Ltd, which was in turn a subsidiary of Soury et Cie. When, in 1906, its concession with Compagnie Générale lapsed, the latter acquired all the British recordings, trademarks and other assets (see below).

25. Data from Pathé Frères (London) Ltd, *Catalogue of Phonographs Cylinders and Accessories*, 1903. See also flysheet for "The Perfecta" Phonograph, circa 1903 (author's collection).

26. There are numerous references to this practice in The Gramophone Company epitomes and various letters from NPC Ltd to West Orange. See also chapter 3.

27. See company registration file, Pathé Frères (London) Ltd, BT31/8244 (The National Archive, Kew). The capital was 160,000 £1 shares, of which 100,000 were fully paid up.

28. For more on these financial dealings, see company registration file, Pathé Frères (London) Ltd, BT31/8244 (The National Archive, Kew).

29. For more details, see Gramophone epitomes and NPC Ltd correspondence.

30. For winding up particulars, see company registration file, Pathé Frères (London) Ltd, BT31/8244 (The National Archive, Kew).

31. For more on the creation of this venture, see *Talking Machine News* 9, no. 11 (April 1911): 42.

32. Pathé was not the first to manufacture vertical-cut records. Neophone Disc Phonograph Records, System Dr. Michaelis, were on sale between 1904 and 1907 (the last releases as System White; James White had previously been founding head of National Phonograph Co Ltd).

33. For an example of an early Pathé disc catalogue, see *Pathé Standard 10-In Double-Sided Discs 1915–1916* (reprint of the City of London Phonograph and Gramophone Society, n.d.).

34. "The Pathephone" list of cabinets and machines, Pathé Frères, London, circa 1906 (my collection).

35. It was a good move on Hunting's part. After working as a Pathé Frères transfer and recording engineer, Hunting returned to the United States, where, based in New York, he worked for the US arm of Pathé Frères until his retirement.

36. Cited in *Talking Machine News* 10, no. 2 (June 1912): 144.

37. *Hillandale News* (October 1989 to February 1990): 258–63, 289–95 and 320–26.

38. For more on this, see chapter 8. See also Columbia files (EMI) and "Columbia Graphophone Company Ltd," Companies House, file 145,983. For an early account of the British branch of Columbia, see "Columbia Phonograph Co, Genl," *The Phono Trader and Recorder* 1, no. 8 (December 1905): 182–88.

39. "The Columbia Phonograph Co Gnl," *Talking Machine News* 1, no. 2 (June 1903): 25–28.

40. See also "Typescript Note by Charles Gregory" (8 November 1944): "Fifty Years of Recording," *The Voice* (spring 1945); F. W. Gaisberg, "Charlie Gregory's Fifty Years of Talking Machines," typescript, n.d.; F. W. Gaisberg, "A Tribute to Charles Butler Gregory a Pioneer of Recording," *The Voice* (spring 1946); Herbert C. Ridout, "An Appreciation of Charles B. Gregory," *The Gramophone* 24, no. 10 (March 1946) (all in Charles B. Gregory file, EMI).

41. See *Columbia Catalogue Celebrity Series* (reprint, City of London Phonograph and Gramophone Society, n.d.). For more on the recordings of this and other record companies before the outbreak of war in 1914, see chapter 7.

42. For evidence in support of this, see chapter 2.

43. See, for example, Alfred Clark to William Barry Owen, 29 May 1902 (Columbia files, EMI).

44. "Monthly Epitomes to the Board of The Gramophone Company," November 1907 (board papers, EMI).

45. Thomas Graf to William Edgar Gilmore, 23 March 1908 (document files, 1908, phonograph-Columbia, Edison National Historic Site).

46. See Columbia and Louis Sterling files (EMI). Also Thomas Graf to Frank L. Dyer, 11 October 1910 (document files, 1910, phonograph manufacturing, Edison National Historic Site). Evidently, NPC Ltd was trying to entice Sterling from his job at Columbia to take over its London business.

47. Alfred Clark, "Report on the Lindström Amalgamation," January 1912 (Lindström papers, EMI).

48. See *Columbia Graphophone and Grafonolas Season 1913–1914* (reprint, City of London Phonograph and Gramophone Society, 1980).

49. The venture was formed in October 1900 as G. H. Burt & Company Ltd, though it was sold in August 1901 for £9,000 to the newly formed Crystalate Manufacturing Company Ltd with Burt a director of the new concern, a major shareholder and the beneficiary of the purchase price. See company registration file "Crystalate Manufacturing Co Ltd," BT31/71040 (The National Archive, Kew), and Michael Kinnear, *Nicole Record* (Victoria, Australia: Kinnear), 11–12. See also Frank Andrews, "The History of the Crystalate Companies in the Record Industry 1901–1937," *Hillandale News*, nos. 134–136 (October and December 1983 and February 1984).

50. See "Catalogue of Burt Composition Pool and Billiard Balls," n.d. (photocopy in the possession of the author). This lists Columbia head Edward D. Easton as Burt company president. See also, letter, Joseph Sanders to Roland Gellatt, 1 October 1953: "You asked me where I obtained the information for making record material. I made a search and found in a notebook that it was Milburn. I believe in New Jersey. Mr Burt had been pressing some records for us and arranged to show me the manufacturing and pressing of the material" (Robert Sanders Collection, Recorded Sound Division, LC).

51. For more on this, see chapter 9.

52. The introduction to Kinnear, *Nicole Record*, provides the key information used in this section on this interesting but complex early disc record company.

53. For more on this business, see company registration file, BT31/54615 (The National Archive, Kew).

54. For more on the position held by Nicole Frères in the emerging British disc record market, see Frank Andrews, "The Under Twenty-Fives," *The Hillandale News*, no. 161 (April 1988).

55. Stephen Carl Porter (1862–1936) was an American recording artist, engineer and associate of Russell Hunting. He recorded for Berliner with, among others, the Hayden Quartet. He came to London in 1902 to make records for The New Century Cylinder Record and was hired in the spring of 1903 by Nicole Frères as both recording engineer and performer. He worked for Nicole Frères until 1904, then went to India creating the Nicole Frères Indian record catalogue. He returned to the United States in 1906, where he spent the rest of his career. See Kinnear, *Nicole Record*, 14–21. See also, Alan Sutton, "Steve Porter, Global Entrepreneur," http://www.mainstreampress.com/porter.

56. See Arthur H. Brooks, in Peter Martland, *Since Records Began* (London: Batsford, 1997), 119, and Arthur H. Brooks and Perceval Graves, "Round the Recording Studios," *The Gramophone* 5, no. 1 (May 1928): 487–90.

57. See "Nicole Record Catalogue Season 1905–1906" reprint, *The Talking Machine Review* (Bournemouth, England), n.d.

58. These machines were rebadged Zonophones, and very few were sold as they were already obsolete by 1905. They had been disposed of by The Gramophone Company as unsaleable. I am grateful to Christopher Proudfoot for pointing this out.

59. "The Leipzig Fair," *Talking Machine News* 3, no. 11 (March 1906): 59.

60. See Alfred Clark, "Report of the Lindström Amalgamation." Much of the information in this section is derived from this report (Lindström papers, EMI).

61. German-born Otto Heinemann (1876–1965) was a founder of Carl Lindström AG and an important industry consolidator. He relocated to the US during the First World War and became an American citizen. He created the Otto Heinemann Phonograph Corporation in New York in 1916, publishing Okeh records: he later renamed the business The General Phonograph Corporation, which he sold to Columbia in 1926.

62. Data derived from *Talking Machine World* 8, no. 1 (May 1912): 27.

63. Clark, "Lindström Amalgamation."

64. See "Notes on India," *Talking Machine News* 6, no. 2 (June 1908): 148. For an account of the Beka recording expedition to India and the Far East, 1905–1906, see "The Great "Beka" Expedition 1905–06" (translated and adapted by John Want from Heinrich Bumb), in *Der Phonographische Zeitschrift*, 1906, http://www.recordingpioneers.com/docs/The-Great-BEKA-Expedition-1905-6.pdf.

65. See *Talking Machine News* 6, no. 12 (April 1909): 37. The effects of this price reduction were dramatic, with *Talking Machine News* 7, no. 8 (January 1910): 305, reporting turnover for November and December 1909 three times greater than the previous year.

66. In 1907 the Berne Convention on copyright acted to prevent record companies like Fonotipia tying up musical copyrights. In fact, all pre-1914 copyright legislation (including the Copyright Act of 1911) established the novel concept of the compulsory licence. Under its provisions, a composer could refuse permission to have his work recorded, but if he gave permission to one record company, he could not refuse others. Although a new concept at the time, the compulsory licence remains an important principle of mechanical copyright down to the present.

67. For details regarding this venture, see company registration papers, BT31/88504 (The National Archive, Kew).

68. *Talking Machine News* 9, no. 4 (August 1911): 206. The September 1911 edition reported that Lindström had bought the major portion of Fonotipia shares from the London banker Baron d'Erlanger for 3 million German marks [£150,000].

69. For more on Oscar Preuss, see Martland, *Since Records Began*, 119. William Ditcham later became head of recording for The Crystalate Manufacturing Co Ltd.

70. For more on the somewhat esoteric distinctions between "exclusive" artists for both cylinder and disc recordings, see chapter 7.

71. See company registration file, Carl Lindström (London) Ltd, BT 31/127948 (The National Archive, Kew). For an account of its travails during the First World War, see chapter 8, and its postwar experiences, see chapter 9.

72. Until 1913, records for the British market released on International Talking Machine GmbH labels were manufactured by The Crystalate Manufacturing Co Ltd.

73. It created Parlophone's distinctive £ trademark (originally superimposed on a horn gramophone), which stood for the L in Lindström and not the British currency: the label did not appear in Britain until the early 1920s, although the trademark was familiar on Lindström gramophone motors in Britain before 1914.

74. Clark, "Lindström Amalgamation."

75. For more on the Carl Lindström business, see chapter 5.

76. For more on this label, see chapter 5.

77. "The Wreckers," *Talking Machine News* 8, no. 6 (October 1913): 305. Unfortunately, the German trade realised what was about to hit them, and all the British German-owned labels introduced records marketed at 1s.0d, undercutting the British cheap records by 1d. These included Arrow, Lyceum, The Stars, Kalliope, Philharmonic and Operaphone. I am grateful to Frank Andrews for providing this additional information.

5

THE GRAMOPHONE
COMPANY LTD: 1903–1914

"Yip-I-addy-I-ay!"

In fifteen years from now talking machine men will point to
the time when the Victor and Gramophone Co held practical
control of all the great artists and say what a great thing they
had and did not know it.

—Eldridge Johnson, President of
The Victor Talking Machine Company,[1] 1910

Of all the British record companies active in the decade or so before
the outbreak of war in 1914 only The Gramophone Company Ltd
has left behind business and other papers in any quantity. Today this pre-
cious archive is cared for by The EMI Music Trust and provides historians
with a remarkable and detailed window not just of this business but also the
broader industry. As a result the sources used in this chapter and the next
have been drawn largely from The EMI Music Archive. Because of the
position held by The Gramophone Company Ltd both as British market
leader and a major international player an understanding of its activities is
of critical importance to this history. This chapter therefore provides an
explanation of how this venture achieved and maintained its position, while
the next examines the British branch during this decade.

★ ★ ★

Chapter 2 examined the fortunes of The Gramophone Company from its
formation in 1897 until 1903, when its founding managing director William Barry Owen left to raise chickens in Vineyard Haven, Massachusetts.
During his tenure The Gramophone Company earned substantial profit,
derived largely from its initial competitive advantage and among the bequests

Owen left his successor Theodore Birnbaum were cash reserves in excess of £400,000, an international marketing and distribution network, important record making and manufacturing facilities and the all-important Victor contract.[2] As if to round off the pioneering period, company chairman Trevor Williams concluded an optimistic annual report in 1902 with the remark that the venture "was a thoroughly sound commercial enterprise."[3] The company's achievements to that point certainly justify this assessment, though subsequent events suggest the remark was misplaced.

Central to the initial success of The Gramophone Company was the personal relationship between Owen and Williams, cemented by their large shareholdings. With strong vested interests they resolved problems on a personal level, often without recourse to the board. This relationship ended not just because of Owen's departure, but because of dramatic changes within the firm and in the market for the company's shares. The management structure Owen employed was based on two strategically placed administrative units sited at nodal hubs of the business, London and Berlin. Management and coordination responsibilities were divided between Owen in London and Birnbaum in Berlin, both of whom were also board members and substantial shareholders. Down to Owen's departure, this model successfully addressed the needs of a small multinational marketing organisation. The size of the business meant they were able to deal personally with the manufacturers of its products and at the same time meet the demands of the selling organisation. The flattened structure also resolved many problems experienced by multinational enterprises in the age before modern communications. For instance large British multinational contemporaries like arms manufacturer Vickers, rubber giant Dunlop, textile producer Courtaulds and pharmaceutical manufacturer Glaxo required much more elaborate mechanisms to control their foreign subsidiaries. As business historian Geoffrey Jones suggests, they relied on crisis management: "The usual form of parent control over foreign subsidiaries came when a director or official from Britain was dispatched on an investigation or special mission."[4] By contrast, The Gramophone Company's structure had great strengths and, until 1903, did not require these mechanisms.

The Owen model may have worked until 1903, but Birnbaum needed an organisation more suited to the long-term aims of a business operating in a fiercely competitive international market. He adopted a new London-based structure that differed with the original in three ways. First, it had a centralised executive headquarters. Second, power was concentrated on the managing director and third a British branch was created to manage the domestic sales organisation.[5] Previously, Birnbaum had been coequal to Owen with a seat on the board, whereas under the new arrangement his replacement in Berlin had no seat on the board and was his subordinate. This didn't work and, as Birnbaum found to his cost, based in London he was unable to manage the central European and Russian branches. Furthermore, the company was overly dependent on profit from these branches, which amounted to 60 per cent of total profits in 1906. This left the business dangerously exposed and when a cost control crisis emerged during the 1907–1908 recession, it precipitated the collapse of the Russian branch, the disintegration of group profit, and finally ended his managing directorship.

Furthermore, because of its size and operational requirements, the organisation Owen created does not fit easily into business historian Alfred Chandler's model of a multidepartmental structure, which has a central executive controlling and overseeing manufacturing and branch activities.[6] On the other hand, Birnbaum's new arrangements, with an executive headquarters and a single chief executive (and once local factories began manufacturing for branches, the appearance of multidivisional activity and organisation), clearly do fit the Chandler model. Although Chandler argued that Britain was slow to adopt this model, Birnbaum's organisation shows such a structure clearly existed, which makes The Gramophone Company a British management pioneer. This structure was Theodore Birnbaum's great contribution to the company, and was retained after he left in 1909. While it proved a long-term success serious weaknesses remained, not least its overreliance on profit from foreign branches. By 1914 non-British sales contributed more than 60 per cent to the overall turnover and profit. In contrast, foreign branches of contemporary multinationals like Vickers, Dunlop, Courtaulds and Glaxo contributed little to overall turnover and profit; instead the bulk of profit was derived from strong domestic markets with easily managed British-based manufacturing and selling organisations.[7]

Although the structure concentrated power and responsibility in Birnbaum's hands, he sought to balance that by creating an organisation capable of improving the flow of information on which he could base decisions. To this end Birnbaum created a centralised headquarters structure, with functionalised departments and a line and staff organisation. In creating this he followed well-established principles of business management. Alfred Chandler described the mid-nineteenth-century American origins of this important organisational development: "This line and staff concept, by which the managers on the line of authority were responsible for ordering men involved with the basic functions of the enterprise, and other functional managers (the staff executives) were responsible for setting standards was first enunciated in American business . . . in . . . 1857."[8] In The Gramophone Company's structure, head office monitored and coordinated the work of selling branches and manufacturing facilities and provided an interface with the Victor Company. Head office collected profits from foreign branches and serviced the organisational needs of the managing director, the board and shareholders. In these circumstances, Birnbaum's creation of an executive headquarters and the post-1909 changes adopted by his successors proved crucial to steering the business in the prewar international markets.

In order to compete effectively, The Gramophone Company management needed precise, accurate and up-to-date information. Therefore, if the company was to prosper, it was essential to engage professional staff to gather such knowledge. Frank H. Knight's classic study of the firm highlighted the need for such specialist knowledge within organisations: "The fact of uncertainty means that people have to forecast future wants. Therefore you get a special class springing up who direct the activities of others whom they give guaranteed wages."[9] The first evidence of the new organisational model comes in a 1904 letter from Birnbaum to Alfred Clark in Paris:

> I had a long conference with Williams last night on general business matters, and I have suggested that in addition to the regular board meetings, a committee of managers should be formed to meet bi-monthly, or monthly if necessary, to discuss all questions relating to the business policy of the company. The deliberations of this committee would be probably confined to the questions of prices, types, trade conditions, and general suggestions concerning the commercial policy of the Company.[10]

These committees testify to Birnbaum's development of a strong head office organisation complete with professional assistance.

After Birnbaum's departure, an executive committee was formed to strengthen further the head office organisation and the position of the managing director. His successor, Alfred Clark, viewed its function as being "to give all important matters the combined experience of the staff so that all subjects which come before it for its decision can be considered from every possible point of view."[11] The executive committee had the power to act in the absence of the managing director, and its minutes reveal a body of managers dealing with bread and butter issues: either by deciding policy themselves or preparing policy submissions for the board. By pulling professional staff to the centre, this organisational model delineated between line and headquarters staff. By 1909 this division was complete, with The Gramophone Company employing a patent agent, lawyer, accountants and an engineer.[12]

These important developments indicate an implicit need to economise in transaction costs. Such savings were essential if the company was to maintain its position in the market. Furthermore, by employing specialists rather than purchasing their services in the market the firm was able to oversee their activities and thereby hope to affect significant control over costs. Such economies in transaction costs and their relation to the growth of businesses have been noted in the literature on the firm. The economist Oliver Williamson observed, "The modern corporation is mainly to be understood as the product of a series of organizational innovations that have had the purpose and effect of economizing transaction costs."[13] Insofar as The Gramophone Company saved money and time by internalising functions rather than dealing in the market place, it could, of course, develop, as suggested by R. H. Coase in his classic work on the theory of the firm, "to determine the size of the firm, we have to consider the marketing costs (that is, the costs of the price mechanism, and the cost of organising of different entrepreneurs) and then we can determine how many products will be produced by each firm and how much of each it will produce."[14] On the other hand, not all specialist functions were carried out in-house, nor were all markets for professional services internalised. This applied, for example, to legal and accounting services, which often remain outside corporate organisations. In the case of The Gramophone Company it was singularly well advised from its earliest days by two established figures from London's financial district, John Broad, a solicitor and Colin Cooper of accountants Cooper and Cooper. Colin Cooper was an important figure active in the affairs of the company, for instance he acted as mediator in the attempted merger negotiations between The Gramophone Company and Victor Talking Machine Company. Furthermore he was, during the First World War, instrumental in resolving a major conflict between Alfred Clark and the board and in its subsequent reconstruction.[15] In 1919 he joined the board, and the following year joined the Victor board; John Broad became a director of The Gramophone Company in 1929. Furthermore Cooper's firm acted as company auditors, maintaining an accountancy team on permanent circuit around the selling and manufacturing branches. This mixture of internal and external professional support might at first sight seem to be a wasteful addition to transaction costs. However, Broad and Cooper proved themselves indispensable to the organisation and played significant roles in its development.

These innovations were intended to cope with dramatic changes taking place within the company and the international record industry during the decade under review. As Coase has argued, "all changes which improve managerial technique will tend to increase the size of the firm." Between 1909 and 1914 Alfred Clark created the conditions he hoped would enable the business to grow.[16] He did this by rationalising the organisation to gain overall control of product from manufacture to retail sale. It was his bad luck that the war broke out before his plans reached maturity. The boom he anticipated did not occur until the 1920s.

The ability to exercise control of foreign branches was crucial to a business whose domestic market accounted for only 40 per cent of turn-over. In fact various mechanisms were designed to retain control of manufacturing, selling and finances. Unfortunately, these failed during Birnbaum's time with catastrophic consequences. The difficulties were there to see. In November 1908, Birnbaum wrote, "One of the most difficult questions with which we are faced today is the expense of handling our goods."[17] To control expenses a series of controls and mechanisms existed, including allocations of budgets for advertising and printed matter, recording budgets, twice yearly audits, the forwarding of monthly sales, stock and banking statements and the lure of performance bonuses. Up to 1907 this systemic control worked, however, between 1907 and 1909 it collapsed because of corruption in the Russian business, increased competition and a failure to control costs. The consequences of this collapse were devastating for the company's profits and for Birnbaum personally.[18]

In 1909, his health shattered, Birnbaum was forced to resign to be succeeded by Alfred Clark, the former French branch manager, and Sydney Dixon, the British branch manager. Initially, they formed a joint managing directorate, but in 1912 Clark became sole managing director and Dixon sales director with a seat on the board. During their joint tenure Clark and Dixon divided their responsibilities, with Dixon managing the Russian and central European sales branches and supervising the British branch, whilst Clark supervised the French and Italian businesses together with relations with Victor. Furthermore Clark, the dominant member of the duo, managed and developed the functions of the executive head office. Clark's entry in *The Dictionary of Business Biography* asserts he was "autocratic . . . and . . . widely responsible for setting up a structure of committees which proved unwieldy."[19] This assessment, which is an accurate reflection of Clark's performance during the interwar years, fails to take into account his management in the prewar years. At this time he saw how a complex multinational enterprise needed to be managed, and was also aware of the organic changes taking place within the company and the need for professional advice. In 1913, he wrote of this issue to Eldridge Johnson:

Our Company is fast becoming a manufacturing concern and we have no old organisation upon which to draw for men who could form competent aids [*sic*] to a head. We will have great difficulty in surrounding ourselves with intelligent men who can discuss problems which may arise in Committee on a footing of equality with the other members of the Committee. I think that we are alive to the dangers of not getting the organization we want, and in fact have been for some time.[20]

The joint managing directorate was a partial reversion to the Owen model and it worked. From its 1908–1909 low of £58,803 profit in 1909–1910 was restored to £155,628. The transaction-cost economies were significant and achieved by Clark's restructuring of the organisation, centralising power and control through his enhanced committee structure and developing the company's existing internal market. From its outset, the business operated a rudimentary internal market with the factory manufacturing and selling product to head office, which in turn sold it on to the sales branches. Within that system factories and head office were not the prime profit generating components; if they broke even or made a small loss the company was satisfied. This internal market did not maximise profits at each stage, rather it relied on the final outturn. Clark abandoned final outturn, replacing it with a system more closely mimicking competitive markets, which forced all components of the business, sales, manufacturing and head office, to maximise profit. Such a system helped identify potential transaction-cost economies and more generally, by exposing weaknesses within the company, provided Clark with an essential tool enabling the business to prepare for and adapt to growth. Figures 5.1 and 5.2 illustrate the changes wrought by Clark's development of the internal market.

Figure 5.1.   The Gramophone Company Ltd: Components of Profit, 1905–1906

Sales
Manufacturing
Head office

Source: Data compiled from annual report June 1906 and report on accounts, 1911–1912 (board and meetings file, EMI).

By delivering key intelligence concerning all aspects of the business, the internal market helped Clark identify and control costly functions, so that resource allocation could be made on the basis of known returns

Figure 5.2.   The Gramophone Company Ltd: Components of Profit, 1911–1912

■ Sales
■ Manufacturing
☐ Head office

and long-term assessments of local markets. Clark sought to develop the internal market further by transferring charges, such as record royalty payments to artists and patent expenses (which had previously been borne by head office) to the selling branches. These moves, together with the creation of an internal capital market (discussed below), gave the branches a carefully controlled autonomy and cost-based incentives to remain profit-generating components of the business. An internal capital market was also created so as to identify and encourage the more or less profitable elements within the business. F. J. Wyatt, head of accounts, wrote in 1912, "Beginning as at July 1st last . . . interest computed at the rate of 5% per annum has been charged to all Branches with the exception of Hanover."[21] By internalising costs which would otherwise have been ignored, Clark's structure made for a more rational allocation of funds and activities. It enabled head office to impose a discipline on branches, which involved savings in internal transaction costs as the business had less need for continuous oversight. As this implies, the internal capital market provided essential information concerning rates of return on capital invested in both branches and manufacturing facilities. In this way branches were given a powerful incentive to become more efficient. For example, in the years immediately prior to the outbreak of war the German branch, which enjoyed poor growth rates, received little fresh investment. By contrast, the British and overseas imperial branches with buoyant growth rates and local manufacturing advantages gained most.

By 1914 these changes had enabled Clark to create a sophisticated and effective headquarters organisation; figures 5.1 and 5. 2 show how head office benefited. By imposing charges on the manufacturing and sales branches, it creamed off a portion of branch profit at an earlier stage than previously possible. Although this reduced branch net profits, it had the effect of stabilising overall profit and brought the selling branches under closer head office supervision. Clark also extended the practice of monthly financial returns, and by these and other means tightened his grip over the factories and head office. Writing to Dixon in December 1909, Clark remarked on the new controls, "I think you know that schemes have been devised for getting monthly balance sheets of all factories and the Head Office, so that with those of the Branches, we will have complete figures, and so far they are working admirably."[22]

The strengthening of control over profit base, together with the consolidation of power in the hands of Clark and head office was only a part of this reorganisation. The role of branch managers was substantially altered and subject to Clark's scrutiny. Before the days of modern communications, branch managers in multinational enterprises exercised almost plenipotentiary powers. They had to be trusted to make operational judgments and manage large budgets; Clark changed all this. After 1911, branch managers became part of the head office organisation and became part of the head office payroll. Budgets were allocated by head office as a fixed percentage of branch turnovers.[23] These changes in branch management created a relationship of dependency and control. This peaked in 1914 when Clark called the company's first branch managers conference in London; whether this move was borrowed from US business practice remains a matter of speculation. All branch managers attended, even the one from India. Although no conference report survives Clark referred to it in a letter to Johnson in which he described visits to the new factories at Hayes and products in development. Clark observed, the managers "were brought into closer touch with the methods of the Head Office and the requirements of the new factories and were brought face to face with the changes that have taken place in the manner of doing business from here during the last few years. On the other hand those at Head Office were able to judge and compare the value of the different Branch Managers."[24]

These radical changes gave Clark a personal and organisational control Owen, Birnbaum and most other British corporate contemporaries never had, and this was extended to the company record factories. In 1904, record manufacturing was concentrated at two factories in Hanover and Riga (serving Russia). By the outbreak of war, there were factories in India, France, Spain, Austria-Hungary and at Hayes, Middlesex. This expansion resulted in the declining importance of the Hanover plant, and with it the influence of Joseph Berliner. After Owen's departure and more so after Birnbaum left, Joseph Berliner became a marginal, somewhat eccentric figure. He attended board meetings, but was clearly not at one with the changes taking place in the company. He particularly resented Clark treating him as an employee; as a 1910 board minute noted, "Mr Berliner to accept the position of salaried servant of the Company under the direction of the Management."[25] In 1914, Clark forced Joseph

Berliner to give up the management of the Hanover factory, which was prevented only by the outbreak of war.[26]

In 1907 The Gramophone Company opened a record factory at Hayes near London. Although a state-of-the-art facility, it was within two years making annual losses of £17,000, as outgoing managing director Theodore Birnbaum confessed, "the erection of the factory at Hayes on its present scale must be regarded as a mistake."[27] Whether this loss was due to inefficiency or a precipitous reduction in retail prices, or even the forced development of uncompetitive manufacturing facilities at five other European locations, remains something of a mystery. Whatever the cause, cost control was high on the agenda of the new regime and by 1914 Clark had rationalised manufacturing, bringing factories under the control of the head office manufacturing committee. He also hired Canadian-born engineer, Wilburn N. Dennison, formerly factory manager at the Victor plant.[28] He designed and built a gramophone factory at Hayes, which cost the company £110,000 and was closely associated with Clark in the manufacturing reorganisation.[29] Thus, by 1914, Clark had remade The Gramophone Company's management, organisation and structure and his strategy was paying dividends. Profit had been restored and the internal profit-centres identified. Furthermore, by building a gramophone factory he hoped to control all elements in the business throughout the vast gramophone empire, including product from raw material to point of sale. From this juncture, Clark could be justified in looking forward to a period of sustained growth. However, international events dictated otherwise.

★   ★   ★

In the years before 1914 the relationship between The Gramophone Company and Victor underwent a dramatic change, with Victor emerging as the dominant force. The failure to merge the businesses and the departure of Owen saw relations between the Victor and Gramophone Companies governed by a series of agreements concluded over the period 1901 to 1919. These were based on the joint ownership of patents and trademarks, the worldwide division of trading territories and the licencing deal to share each other's recordings. The first agreement established the basis of future commercial dealings.[30] It was a manufacturing contract with record licencing royalty arrangements. It created a jointly funded research laboratory in Camden and a price fixing deal. It also vested ownership of the "His Master's Voice" (HMV) picture and other trademarks with each company. This agreement bound The Gramophone Company to purchase 50 per cent of Johnson's machine output for ten years. A second agreement in 1904 was limited to three years.[31] It restated the 1901 manufacturing and other clauses and, reflecting the growing importance of the records as diffusers of high culture, clarified the record licencing agreement.[32] Although The Gramophone Company had pioneered a Celebrity record catalogue in 1902, by the third agreement in 1907 the initiative had passed to Victor, who had recognised the importance of controlling the world's greatest performing artists. In a move that prefigured Hollywood's own dash for talent by at least a decade, Victor signed on long-term royalty-based contracts the cream of the Metropolitan Opera and the finest virtuoso performers active at the time. In August 1910, Johnson wrote to Alfred Clark, "We must not only control more artists but we must sell more records of those we do control."[33] The 1907 agreement further clarified and consolidated relations between the two and set out detailed sales territory boundaries, with Victor taking the Americas, the Far East and certain other areas and The Gramophone Company the rest of the world.[34]

Despite these businesslike agreements, following Owen's departure Johnson became increasingly alienated from his British partner. This is illustrated by his attitude towards the Zonophone record. The Gramophone Company acquired this business in 1903 and used the brand to meet competition and break into the emerging mass markets in disc records. Johnson dismissed the Zonophone venture as not providing sufficient profit to warrant its use, despite its use to fight the competition in exactly the way Johnson had previously suggested.[35] Johnson also opposed Birnbaum who wanted to establish gramophone-manufacturing facilities in Europe, arguing:

> Concentration of manufacturing is the modern invention for lowering the cost of production. . . . I do not think that it will be possible to make any arrangements whereby the same grade of goods can be manufactured in Germany or any other country at the same cost. . . . You will never be able to divide your manufacturing to any advantage as far as economy in cost of production is concerned, or in the maintenance of a certain quality. You can never get the same grade of goods without our co-operation.[36]

The relative success of the Gramophone and Victor Companies can be judged by their differing pre-1914 growth rates. These indicate spectacular early growth for the British venture then, after 1911, Victor overtook on all fronts: see figures 5.3 and 5.4. However, these impressive growth rates need to be placed in perspective. Victor enjoyed the benefits of a single

Figure 5.3.   Victor-Gramophone Turnover, 1901–1913

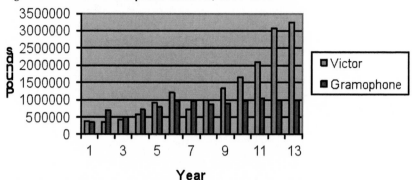

Source: Compiled from an abstract of Victor data for the period 1902 to 1916 (file 63, Johnson papers, Johnson Victrola Museum). Gramophone data developed from half-yearly reports, notes on accounts and yearly comparative results, 1908–1909 to 1912–1913 (board papers, EMI).

Figure 5.4.   Victor-Gramophone Profit, 1901–1913

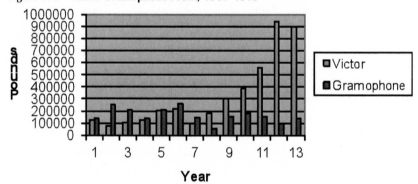

Source: See source note for figure 5.3.

integrated continental market, protected from foreign imports by high tariffs and with the monopolistic patent pool able to exclude domestic competition. In sharp contrast, The Gramophone Company operated in a multiplicity of patent-free, tariff-protected markets and faced stiff, effective competition. To meet these conditions (especially across the many European national tariff barriers), The Gramophone Company was forced to divert capital resources to build uneconomic local record pressing and gramophone assembly plants. Furthermore, to compete in fragmented European markets with widely differing linguistic and cultural tastes, The Gramophone Company had to accept lower profit margins and higher selling costs. Unit sales data provide further evidence of the performance gap between the two companies (see table 5.1).

Table 5.1. The Gramophone Company Ltd and The Victor Talking Machine Company: Unit Sales, 1901–1913

	Gramophone		Victor	
Year	Records	Gramophones	Records	Victrola
1901–1902	2,750,178	12,589[a]	256,908	42,110
1902–1903	5,414,269	19,828	1,696,296	40,601
1903–1904	3,908,889	71,453	1,966,036	47,074
1904–1905	3,859,656	64,713	2,595,011	65,591
1905–1906	4,675,417	66,478	3,565,679	82,589
1906–1907	6,144,467	74,288	7,051,775	107,432
1907–1908	6,285,752	66,178	5,248,147	50,732
1908–1909	6,045,109	58,368	4,639,463	68,231
1909–1910	7,310,473	58,173	5,988,004	94,666
1910–1911	7,993,508	68,739	6,205,929	124,927
1911–1912	7,906,925	64,607	9,150,374	206,798
1912–1913	7,059,822	67,949	11,086,489	251,909

Source: Gramophone data compiled from half-yearly reports and yearly comparative results (board papers, EMI). Victor data compiled from Aldridge, *The Victor Talking Machine Co.*, app. 4, 109, and Sherman, *The Paper Dog*, 43.

[a]Six months only.

Other factors help explain this divergence. One important comparative is pre-1914 US per capita income data. This shows Johnson's market was of a significantly higher order to that of his European counterparts. In 1900 US per capita income was $445 compared to $285 in Britain, which enjoyed the highest per capita income in Europe. In 1913, the figures stood at $590 and $315.[37] As Victor's customers tended to be urban and therefore more likely to be employed in manufacturing, US per capita income of that sector provides a more accurate yardstick of the incomes enjoyed by potential Victor customers.[38] Between 1905 and 1909 these were $880 compared to a British average of $450.[39] Not only were Victor's trading conditions wholly different to those of its European partner, the price of its talking machines reflected the fact that they were made by US workers paid American wage rates. Dependent on Victor components, The Gramophone Company was unable to compete with cheaper German and Swiss machines. The remarkable Victor growth rates suggest Johnson's American customers had sufficient surplus wealth to purchase luxury goods such as records and talking machines. This growth also suggests that these were increasingly accepted in the homes of affluent educated middle-class Americans. This aspect was highlighted in a National Phonograph Company trade intelligence report which claimed, "The Victor Company is now catering to the educated people of the country, who are fond of music, and are willing to pay for the best, and there is no other talking machine company or phonograph company, who have the class of records to put out that will stand the test the same as the Victor Company have and are putting out."[40]

★   ★   ★

The prewar Gramophone Company board contained up to three executive directors and four nonexecutives, including the chairman. One of these, Edgar Storey (a member of the original partnership), retired in 1906 and died soon after.[41] He was replaced by former cabinet minister Walter (later Lord) Long MP, then in the political wilderness.[42] The other nonexecutive directors were chairman Trevor Williams and his two brothers-in-law Romer Williams and Ernest (later Sir Ernest) de la Rue.[43] On formation Trevor Williams and his wife held about 150,000 or 30 per cent of the ordinary shares, making them the largest shareholders. However, according to Alfred Clark, by 1916 their shareholding was around 40,000 or 8 per cent of the equity.[44] During the early years Williams and other original Gramophone Company shareholders made a financial killing, selling shares when the price was high. According to the *Directory of Directors*, Williams held directorships in other new technology ventures. He was a founding director of Roneo Ltd, manufacturers of office equipment and duplicating machines and The British Mutoscope and Biograph Ltd and he speculated in that black hole of British capital, overseas mining companies.[45] The Gramophone Company articles of association provided for £2,500 payable in annual fees to nonexecutive directors. These fees were divided among three directors, each receiving £500 and the chairman £1,000. In the pre-1914 period, despite the profitability of the business these were never increased, suggesting the nonexecutive directors relied on dividend income rather than fees.

With a board made up of largely nonexecutive directors, day-to-day knowledge of the business and constructive oversight of the managing director must have been at best slight or at worst a dead hand. However, the nonexecutive directors did handle one aspect of the company's finances. On two occasions the company was forced to borrow money from its bankers to cover short-term liquidity difficulties. On both occasions negotiations were handled by nonexecutive directors. Trevor Williams's lack of financial knowledge was highlighted in a letter written in 1909 from the London head of recording William Gaisberg to his brother Fred, "Things are still very uncertain as to management, there is only one thing everyone now realises and that is the condition of the business. You remember the speech Mr Trevor Williams made at the last public meeting? I have since found out he would never have made such a good speech if he had fully realised the condition of the business."[46]

On formation three of the seven directors were executives, though the German-based Theodore Birnbaum and Joseph Berliner were unable to attend many meetings, which allowed nonexecutives to dominate. With the departure of Owen, the number of executive directors was reduced to two. It was never suggested that a senior manager, for instance Wilburn Dennison, who was head of manufacturing between 1912 and 1917, should join.[47] The management style of the Victor and Gramophone Companies could not have been more different and resulted in much misunderstanding. The Victor board was composed entirely of executive directors who doubled as departmental heads. As president and chief executive Johnson appeared uneasy managing the detail of the enterprise and withdrew from day-to-day management in 1907 after a serious depressive illness, though he retained the post of president. At this time (and in contrast to The Gramophone Company) Johnson restructured Victor's management to provide an effective organization, creating an executive committee to manage what had become a complex multidivisional enterprise.

In both ventures board members were also substantial shareholders. The key difference lay in the knowledge of the business and management. Johnson argued The Gramophone Company board was too conservative and content to make high dividend payments and claimed it did not know what was going on in the business. The extensive private and personal correspondence between Clark and Johnson, who constantly contrasted the quality of Victor's wholly executive board with that of The Gramophone Company, reveal their feelings for the nonexecutive component of the board. As late as 1916 Johnson was complaining that "The Gramophone Company needs a board of directors who understand the business. Your directors will never learn the business in a thousand years. No doubt they are substantial men, but they don't get in sufficient daily contact with the business to learn it."[48] He was right, and boardroom tensions came to a head during the First World War.[49]

After Owen's resignation, problems of personality were also apparent. His successor, Theodore Birnbaum, was British. He had established much of the continental European operation and managed the highly profitable central European and Russian branches. To him, based in Berlin, the United States and Johnson must have seemed a long way from his daily business. To make matters worse, Johnson could not stand him. In December 1902 he wrote to Owen, "I am quite sure he is prejudiced against us as manufacturers."[50] In another letter dated 24 December 1903, containing little in the way of Christmas spirit, Johnson commented, "I don't mean to go into a letter of abuse of Mr Birnbaum to you. He may be a very good man and indispensable, although it is quite more than probable he will act as unfairly towards you as he has towards me if the opportunity ever comes or if it suits his purposes."[51] The basis for Johnson's hostility to Birnbaum has been lost. Possibly it was his management style or that Birnbaum, in fighting the competition, was pressing for the development of a European gramophone factory; or it may have been that he was Jewish. Whatever the reason, in 1908, Johnson got his revenge. During the 1907 to 1908 recession, The Gramophone Company came close to bankruptcy. The causes of the crisis were numerous and are discussed above and in chapter 6. One reason was the failure of Victor to manufacture a talking machine capable of competing with Swiss and German machines on price. In November 1907, Birnbaum wrote to Johnson, "The cry of our Branches for a cheap machine becomes more and more insistent."[52] Unfortunately, due to the recession, Gramophone sales slowed and selling difficulties together with the difficulties in Russia turned problems into crisis. This forced Birnbaum to cancel orders from Camden. In the end it took a visit from an angry Johnson, who was not a director, to spur the British board into making decisions. During a tense meeting Birnbaum was forced to resign and was succeeded by Dixon and Clark, an American and coinventor with Johnson of the improved sound box.[53] Clark's first letter to Johnson as managing director expressed the change in position in stark terms, "There is one thing you may be sure of, and that is that the new management starts in with a feeling of absolute friendship for the American Company, and that this will at least assure all matters being handled in a perfectly fair spirit."[54] Alfred Clark usually addressed his letters to "Mr Johnson" and Johnson usually replied "Dear Clark." For Clark this was the beginning of a thirty-six-year period as a Gramophone Company and later EMI executive. Throughout this period the keystone of his policy was a commitment to the American link, with Victor providing the leadership. This respect was not always appreciated by Johnson, as he observed in a 1927 letter describing Clark's character as "utterly and hopelessly selfish."[55] Indeed, Alfred Clark's dramatic 1946 resignation as president of EMI occurred at an angry board meeting, during which he flung his papers across the table, stormed out and never returned. This fit of temper was motivated by the adoption of policies that led, in the mid-1950s, to the severing of the RCA Victor-EMI record licencing agreement.[56]

Furthermore it took the collapse of profit to persuade the board, at Clark's insistence, to allow him to reform the organisation. After Clark became managing director, as can be seen in minutes and reports, the board became increasingly marginalised from day-to-day and strategic management. After February 1910, information concerning payments to the US, cash balances and details of investments disappear. Furthermore, the half-yearly financial reports, which had often amounted to eighty pages of detailed analysis, were replaced by an abstract of ten pages or less. Clark, by starving his board of financial data, accumulated power himself. He became the only person who knew what was going on and this caused friction within the board. However, as the nonexecutive directors were incapable of running the business themselves, they had little option but to accept the Clark reorganisation. The marginalisation of the board, the role of its nonexecutive members and its relations with its managing director stored up problems for the future and reached a crisis during the First World War.

The important manufacturing agreement which tied The Gramophone Company to expensive American-made machine components proved the most significant weakness, providing another insight into this intercompany relationship. During negotiations that led to the 1907 agreement, the board never raised the issue of a European gramophone factory and Johnson failed to appreciate the necessity of creating one. As late as February 1916 he was writing in typically robust terms, "The first fatal mistake The Gramophone Company made was to try to beat the Germans at the cheap machine trade. Birnbaum started this and he might as well have tried to catch a skunk with his bare hands."[57] In 1908 Johnson highlighted what he believed to be Birnbaum's and the board's most serious error, how to restructure prices after the end of initial competitive advantage. He wrote to Birnbaum, "You have created a business and left a fat margin of profit for your competitors continuously, although at the proper time you could have reduced your profit very well, which would have had the effect of tremendously stimulating your business and discouraging your competitors who at the time did not have sufficient volume of business to follow you with profit."[58] Recognising the weakness of The Gramophone Company's position in the European gramophone markets, Clark took two significant steps to strengthen it. The key move was a 1912 amendment to the 1907 agreement, releasing The Gramophone Company from its obligation not to engage in machine manufacture. That he persuaded Johnson of the necessity to build a manufacturing capacity at Hayes was a major coup, although Johnson must have known from his production figures that the percentage of machines being sent to London had slumped dramatically. In 1911 Alfred Clark wrote, "The Victor Co earned last year £315,000 nett profit, of which we contributed only £14,400. Therefore our manufacturing is really an unimportant part of the whole."[59] Johnson's correspondence with Clark on the subject reveals either a complete about-face in his thinking or a selective recollection of his earlier position. In 1911 he wrote, "I have felt for some time that some such move as this [the need to manufacture in Europe] would be ultimately necessary on your part on account of radical changes in your patent laws and also on account of tariff etc. . . . Your contract with the Victor Company was a very short cut to securing goods of high efficiency, but it was a weak policy nevertheless."[60] With Johnson's agreement and support,[61] Clark built a gramophone factory on the same site as the record pressing plant at Hayes Birnbaum developed in 1907; production was due to begin in August 1914, the same week as war broke out.

In 1912 The Gramophone Company's main European competitor Carl Lindström AG approached it with a merger proposition. This business was largely owned by German bankers, who also held between ten and fifteen per cent of Gramophone Company ordinary shares. The issue was complex as Lindström had international interests, including manufacturing plants and licensing agreements throughout the Americas and these transcended the boundaries of the Victor-Gramophone agreement. Initially Lindström proposed the merger of all three companies, but Johnson rejected this. Then a proposition to merge The Gramophone Company and Lindström proceeded, but was eventually vetoed by Johnson who threatened to commence trading in Europe if it went through. The best Clark could get was an agreement whereby Lindström acknowledged Gramophone Company machine patents and accepted licencing and royalty arrangements. That The Gramophone Company sacrificed its own self-interest on the altar of the Victor relationship reveals the extent of its weakness and the strength of its associate.

★   ★   ★

In the years immediately after 1903 The Gramophone Company experienced high growth rates which tailed off after 1907. Two available sets of data assess performance; one is in the form of unit sales and is set out in table 5.1. The other is financial data, setting out details of turnover, profit, fees, tax, dividend and reserves and is shown in table 5.2 below. Together these tables place in context the whole business for the years 1900–1914. It should be noted that there are no firm measures as to the size of the pre-1914 international record industry, therefore only the roughest estimate can be made. This suggests that, by 1913, and in a rising market, worldwide sales of seventy million records were achieved. Of these, thirty million

Table 5.2. The Gramophone Company Ltd: Financial Performance, 1900–1914

Year	Turnover	Net Profit	Fees, Taxes and Dividend	Retained Profit	Reserves
1900–1901	NA	£79,348 [$396,740]	£47,504 [$237,520]	£31,844 [$159,220]	£31,844 [$159,220]
1901–1902	£342,218 [$1,711,090]	£137,268 [$686,340]	£53,513 [$267,565]	£83,755 [$418,775]	£115,599 [$577,995]
1902–1903	£685,593 [$3,427,965]	£253,285 [$1,266,425]	£107,063 [$535,315]	£145,222 [$726,110]	£260,721 [$1,303,605]
1903–1904	£500,505 [$2,502,525]	£211,750 [$1,058,750]	£105,447 [$527,235]	£106,303 [$531,515]	£414,832 [$2,074,160]
1904–1905	£722,820 [$2,114,100]	£140,229 [$701,145]	£109,764 [$548,820]	£30,465 [$152,325]	£445,296 [$2,226,480]
1905–1906	£785,362 [$3,926,810]	£212,236 [$1,061,180]	£122,857 [$614,285]	£89,379 [$446,895]	£534,676 [$2,673,380]
1906–1907	£968,894 [$4,844,470]	£263,950 [$1,319,750]	£140,711 [$703,555]	£123,239 [$616,195]	£657,915 [$3,289,575]
1907–1908	£973,757 [$4,868,785]	£145,412 [$727,060]	£158,701 [$793,505]	–£13,289 [–$66,445]	£644,626 [$3,223,130]
1908–1909	£866,498 [$4,332,490]	£58,803 [$294,015]	£137,116 [$685,580]	–£78,313 [–$391,565]	£566,313 [$2,831,565]
1909–1910	£894,877 [$4,474,385]	£155,628 [$778,140]	£42,806 [$214,030]	£112,822 [$564,110]	£679,135 [$3,395,675]
1910–1911	£955,257 [$4,776,285]	£184,749 [$923,745]	£595,148 [$2,975,740]	–£410,399 [–$2,051,995]	£268,736 [$1,343,680]
1911–1912	£1,031,543 [$5,157,715]	£156,628 [$783,140]	£110,510 [$552,550]	£45,958 [$229,790]	£314,694 [$1,573,470]
1912–1913	£995,500 [$4,977,500]	£100,854 [$504,270]	£17,863 [$89,315]	–£17,009 [–$85,045]	£297,684 [$1,488,420]
1913–1914	£1,000,113 [$5,000,565]	£138,186 [$690,930]	£128,832 [$644,160]	£9,354 [$46,770]	£39,426 [$197,130]

Source: Profit is shown as it appears in the published balance sheet. A comparison with profit shown in the published and in-house reports indicates a difference of only a few thousand pounds, suggesting the in-house reports were made before the final closure of accounts. It also suggests that profit in the balance sheet represented real profit, or at least the profit base the company used to plan its business. "Reserves 1910–1911": £482,847 was deducted from reserves and transferred to patents, goodwill and trademarks, suggesting that the cash had already been invested in the business. "Reserves 1913–1914": £267,611 from earlier years was identified as a separate item on the balance sheet, in accordance with the 1913 debenture deed. Data compiled from annual reports and balance sheets, 1901 to 1914 (meetings file, EMI); managing directors' half yearly reports, 1904 to 1910 (board papers, EMI); notes on accounts, 1911 to 1913 (board papers, EMI).

Table 5.3. The Gramophone Company Ltd: Indexed Growth in Turnover and Profit, 1901–1914

Year	Turnover	Profit
1901–1902	100	100
1902–1903	200	184
1903–1904	146	154
1904–1905	211	102
1905–1906	229	151
1906–1907	283	192
1907–1908	284	106
1908–1909	253	43
1909–1910	261	113
1910–1911	279	135
1911–1912	301	114
1912–1913	291	73
1913–1914	292	101

were sold in Europe, including Russia. It is therefore possible that The Gramophone Company, with European record sales of seven million, held a quarter of the market. Furthermore, the growth in record sales suggests that the company maintained market share, combating competition and penetrating the mass markets both in Europe and beyond. Of course the most depressing element of table 5.1 is machine sales, which show an effective zero growth. As measures of performance unit sales are, by themselves, of limited value. They demonstrate the degree of commercial activity and portion of market share, but say nothing about profitability.

Table 5.2 illustrates how during this period The Gramophone Company experienced a three phase development: first initial competitive advantage, then the pressure of emerging competition and finally reconstruction and revival of profit. Perhaps the most startling features of table 5.2 are the figures for turnover and profit and the speed at which they grew during the first six years of trading; and the speed with which this growth ended. Revealed in the turnover figures is (as might be expected) a business in luxury products conforming to movements in the wider economy, with downturns in 1903–1904, 1908–1910, and 1912–1913. The use of indexed figures shows these developments more clearly.

Profit as shown in table 5.2 and in indexed form in table 5.3 reveals the extent of the initial competitive advantage. They also show the failure to control selling costs between 1907 and 1910, and during the period of reconstruction 1909–1914. Fortunately for its survival, early profits were not used to pay large and unsustainable dividends. On the contrary, significant cash reserves were created which financed long-term growth. Specifically these reserves financed extensive factory building in Britain, Europe, Russia and India. They also permitted profit equalisation on the two occasions when annual profits failed to cover minimum dividend payments. The allocation of profit to growth allowed the company to remain free of financial encumbrances until 1913, when a £300,000 debenture (bond issue) was raised to finance capital projects. Of the debenture, the chairman said in the 1913 annual report it was necessary because a financial crisis caused by the Balkans war had brought a downturn in trade and depressed the value of the company's then £100,000 investment portfolio; showing that reserves appearing in the balance sheets had been converted into capital investments.[62] Together with the decision to retain and allocate early profits to future developments the belated decision to manufacture gramophones in Britain must be the board's wisest and most farsighted decision during the whole of this period. Turnover figures were not published and therefore contemporary measurements of performance did not use return on capital.[63] Even so, it is surprising that such an important yardstick was not used in-house to plot trends within the business. Data derived from various sources has been used to estimate the return on capital, as shown in table 5.4.

Table 5.4.   The Gramophone Company Ltd: Percentage Return on Capital, 1900–1914

Year	Assets		Profit		Return
1900–1901	£81,032	[$405,160]	£74,570	[$372,850]	92.0%
1901–1902	£172,544	[$862,720]	£137,268	[$686,340]	79.5%
1902–1903	£412,477	[$2,062,385]	£253,285	[$1,266,425]	61.4%
1903–1904	£524,351	[$2,621,755]	£211,750	[$1,058,750]	40.4%
1904–1905	£554,653	[$2,773,265]	£140,229	[$701,145]	25.3%
1905–1906	£646,681	[$3,233,405]	£212,236	[$1,061,180]	32.8%
1906–1907	£772,567	[$3,862,835]	£263,950	[$1,319,750]	34.2%
1907–1908	£757,309	[$3,786,545]	£145,412	[$727,060]	19.2%
1908–1909	£675,671	[$3,378,355]	£58,803	[$294,015]	8.7%
1909–1910	£793,319	[$3,966,595]	£155,628	[$778,140]	19.6%
1910–1911	£868,736	[$4,343,680]	£184,749	[$923,745]	21.3%
1911–1912	£914,694	[$4,573,470]	£156,468	[$782,340]	17.1%
1912–1913	£887,684	[$4,438,420]	£100,854	[$504,270]	11.4%
1913–1914	£906,838	[$4,534,190]	£138,186	[$690,930]	15.2%

Source: Return on capital is calculated as profit divided by assets. Assets were assessed by computing the value of short-term book debt, land and buildings, plant and machinery, furniture and fittings, stock in trade, cash, investments and matrix account (the value of the copper matrices on which the sound records were engraved), as they appear in the balance sheets. These reflect depreciation applied at the time. Liabilities have also been deducted. Profit, with the exception of formation expenses in 1900–1901 accounts, is shown before deductions for dividend, director's fees and taxation. Profit was calculated by measures applied by the company accountants.

Table 5.5. The Gramophone Company Ltd: Net Profit as a Percentage of Turnover, 1901–1914

Year	Percentage
1901–1902	40.1%
1902–1903	36.9%
1903–1904	42.3%
1904–1905	19.4%
1905–1906	27.0%
1906–1907	27.2%
1907–1908	14.9%
1908–1909	6.8%
1909–1910	17.4%
1910–1911	19.3%
1911–1912	15.2%
1912–1913	10.1%
1913–1914	13.8%

Source: Derived from data in annual reports and reports on accounts (meetings file, EMI).

These figures show extraordinary returns even after the end of period of initial competitive advantage, and would be the envy of any modern company. In the 1960s, media tycoon Lord Thompson of Fleet described commercial television as "a licence to print money." It would seem, from these figures at any rate, that The Gramophone Company was capable of "printing money" as well as gramophone records! The main tools used internally to assess performance on a year-to-year basis were profit as a percentage of turnover, and year on year comparisons of notional profit. Net profit as a percentage of turnovers is shown in table 5.5.

These figures are less depressing than the failure of turnover and profit to grow. That said, the magnitude of profit during the period of competitive advantage is once again illustrated, although the figures also reveal that after its end profit as a percentage of turnover (with the exception of three recession years) never fell below an impressive 15 per cent. These figures reveal the biggest problem facing this company after 1907, its inability to grow significantly. It was a dangerous trend and despite the fact that compounded annual growth rates calculated from data in table 5.5 over the whole period, 1901 to 1914 was 10.6 per cent, between 1907 and 1914 the indexed figures in table 5.3 remain virtually unchanged. These figures heighten the importance of the cushion of retained profits, which hid the 1907–1909 crises from the outside world and provided both a breathing space to reorganise and most of the cash needed to carry it out. Perhaps Alfred Clark's greatest achievement was not only to recognise the problem, but also to find solutions and effect the necessary changes. Without this the business would have either failed, or been sold off cheaply.

Retained profit and reserves are among the figures cited in table 5.2. Of all the figures, these remain the most uncertain. The balance sheets make it clear that the sums reported are not accounted for by cash in hand, or cash held at the bank, or by the investment portfolio, which peaked at £150,000. These sums were evidently used to finance an extensive capital investment programme. In October 1909 a shrewd *Financial Times* analyst concluded his examination of the worst accounts the company ever published, "Though the large sum of £566,300 is carried forward, it has to be remembered that the bulk of it is being used in the business, the only cash and independent securities to offset it amounting to £145,700, or about 25 per cent of the total. Thus too much stress must not be put on this item, the worth of which must necessarily diminish with any depreciation in value of the Company's assets."[64] The published reports and accounts of The Gramophone Company were the subject of scrutiny and comment by competitors, the trade and the financial press.[65] In the good years the company was lavishly praised. Everyone loves a winner and the *Financial Times* of 9 October 1906 was no exception. In an analysis of the annual report it commented on the finances in the following terms:

> We find a position which, if not unique, is most extraordinary. It has no Debentures; its capital is £600,000, of which £100,000 consists of Five per cent Preference shares. In six years it has distributed dividends and bonuses on the ordinary shares aggregating 90 per cent; it has amassed a huge sum, not far short of half a million, as a "carry forward." It possesses £150,000 sunk in first class investment securities, and its net assets (irrespective of patents, trade marks, and goodwill) and those of foreign Companies and branches which it owns stood at the end of June at three-quarters of a million.[66]

Equally, no one loves a failure and in 1909 the same newspaper commented, "There has been something like a landslide in revenue, and trading profits are down just on 60%, and are less than a quarter what they were in 1906–07, the record year; they are indeed the smallest in the history of the undertaking."[67] The response to a crisis that could not be concealed (even by the company's ample reserves) provides a useful example of crisis management prior to 1914. Without turnover figures to judge performance, the financial press could only comment on changes in profit and assets. The chairman was therefore in a strong position to stress the short-term nature of the firm's poor performance and disguise the true nature of the problems it faced. In this way Trevor Williams attributed the disastrous 1907–1909 showing "to depressed trade conditions and competition in foreign branches, and particularly gross profit in Russian territory."[68] His shareholders were largely placated, receiving a dividend substantially paid for out of those same reserves so desperately needed for reconstruction.

★   ★   ★

The market's judgement of The Gramophone Company's performance can be assessed by the size of dividend payments and the quoted share price. By not revealing turnover and other critical data the company was able to conceal (at least for a time) the true nature of its position. The original 1900 allotment of Gramophone Company shares was analysed in chapter 2. This showed how all 500,000 ordinary £1 shares in the business were allotted pro rata to shareholders of the predecessor company. In addition, 80,000 of the 100,000 5 per cent cumulative £1 preference shares were sold, mainly to shareholders in the predecessor company. In 1904, the remaining 20,000 preference shares were allotted to Alfred Clark in exchange for his 25 per cent stake in Compagnie Française du Gramophone. Thus none of the original ordinary shareholders actually paid cash for their shares, their disbursement being a component in the sale of the old company. By 1903 a buoyant market in these shares had been created, and in 1904 they received a quotation on the London stock market. Although the high profitability must have attracted early investors, the sustained level of dividend was undoubtedly the major incentive. Table 5.6 sets out details of dividend payments together with the high and low prices of £1 Gramophone ordinary shares.

Table 5.6 shows how between 1901 and 1907 the original shareholders of the allotted £1 earned in excess of £500,000, with the asset base remaining well in excess of the share capital. By 1907, those original shareholders who held on to their shares had received dividends in excess of the share's nominal value and retained a valuable asset, for which they had made no payment. In sharp contrast, if The Gramophone Company £1 ordinary shares had been bought between 1906 and 1908, when their market price reached highs of between £3.10s and almost £4.00, the return per share relative to the highest values for the years 1909 to 1914 would have been as low as 2.4 per cent and no higher than 8.8 per cent. This information, when taken with the published results, depressed the market in its shares and undermined confidence in the company; which added to management problems at a time when it was engaged in a massive recon-

Table 5.6. The Gramophone Company Ltd: Ordinary Share Performance and Dividends, 1900–1914

Year	Dividend	Earnings per Share	Share High	Share Low	Per Cent Dividend of High
1900–1901	6%	1s.2d [6p or $0.30]	—	—	—
1901–1902	6%	1s.2d [6p or $0.30]	—	—	—
1902–1903	8%	1s.7d [8p or $0.40]	—	—	—
1903–1904	20%	4s [20p or $1]	30s [£1.50 or $7.50]	25s [£1.25 or $6.25]	13.3%
1904–1905	20%	4s [20p or $1]	28s.1d [£1.40 or $7]	23s.9d [£1.18 or $5.90]	14.2%
1905–1906	20%	4s [20p or $1]	57s.3d [£2.86 or $14.30]	26s.3d [£1.31 or $6.55]	7%
1906–1907	25%	5s [25p or $1.25]	79s.4d [£3.96 or $19.80]	55s [£2.75 or $13.75]	6.3%
1907–1908	30%	6s [30p or $1.50]	70s [£3.50 or $17.50]	34s.4d [£1.72 or $8.60]	8.6%
1908–1909	25%	5s [25p or $1.25]	44s.3d [£2.20 or $10.30]	18s.1d [£0.91 or $4.55]	11.4%
1909–1910	5%	1s [5p or $0.25]	41s.3d [£2.06 or $10.30]	19s.3d [£0.96 or $.80]	2.4%
1910–1911	10%	2s [10p or $0.50]	45s.6d [£2.27 or $11.35]	34s.6d [£1.72 or $8.60]	4.4%
1911–1912	20%	4s [20p or $1.00]	45s.6d [£2.27 or $11.35]	35s [£1.75 or $8.75]	8.8%
1912–1913	10%	2s [10p or $0.50]	37s [£1.85 or $9.20]	22s.3d [£1.11 or $4.55]	5.4%
1913–1914	10%	2s [10p or $0.50]	28s.9d [£1.44 or $7.20]	18s.9d [£0.94 or $4.70]	7%

Source: Dividend payments compiled from annual reports (meetings file, EMI). Data concerning share prices compiled from The Gramophone Company entries in the *Stock Exchange Yearbook*, 1903–1914.

struction. As major shareholders controlled the board maximum returns on shares was always a priority, something Eldridge Johnson continually bemoaned. This dominance explains the decision to maintain high dividend payments between 1907 and 1909, when the company was experiencing a near fatal crisis. Figure 5.5 plots movements in the share price.

The table 5.6 and figure 5.5 data shows how, in 1908, the value of Gramophone Company ordinary shares hit a low. Yet despite the downward movement in dividend payments after that date, the share price was relatively stable at about half of its former high; although it fell to just below

Figure 5.5. The Gramophone Company Ltd: Fluctuations in Share Prices, 1903–1914

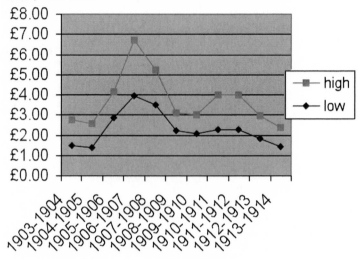

par during the financial crisis of 1913. Given the post-1907 problems this relative stability must be attributed to the strategy of keeping shareholders happy with large dividends. This required silence about the true nature of the company's underlying performance and an acceptance by shareholders, despite warnings by financial journalists, of the implied claim that the cash assets shown in the balance represented a liquidity amounting to a sum in excess of the total share capital. The dividend equalisation payments were necessary to maintain both the incomes of shareholders and the price of shares, sustaining confidence in the company during the period of reconstruction. However, it came at a price, for paying dividends that had not been earned reduced the asset base at a critical time when these needed boosting not reducing. The volatility in the price of The Gramophone Company's £1 ordinary shares during the decade prior to 1914 needs placing into perspective. The company was a pioneer of new technology and initially enjoyed important prime mover advantages, which were lost when a competitive market was formed. This is not an unfamiliar phenomenon, for example in the late 1920s there was the boom in the shares of radio manufacturers on both sides of the Atlantic and in more recent years, pioneers of new technology such as the computer, dot com and social networking industries. In all cases these new technology industries, during the period of market formation, experienced wild movements in their shares and in their performance.

★ ★ ★

Assessing the Victor-Gramophone relationship on the eve of war, with the British gramophone factory about to go into full production, it is evident that the period of dependency on Victor had ended. No longer based on manufacturing, the remaining features of the relationship rested on: the territorial division of the world, pricing, together with the patents and trademark agreements and crucially the record licencing arrangements. From the latter The Gramophone Company gained access to Victor's catalogue of records made by international celebrity artists. This factor, together with important new developments in American popular music, which included, after 1917, jazz and dance music, helped The Gramophone Company establish its reputation as an important diffuser of both high and popular culture. The very speed at which jazz crossed the Atlantic might be seen as a tribute to the Gramophone-Victor relationship.[69]

The Gramophone Company and Victor both derived benefits from their relationship and it is possible that during the various crises neither would have survived without the benefit of the other. However the relationship had inherent weaknesses. The failure to consolidate created uncertainties, and the longer the issue dragged on the more it became an irrelevant diversion. That said its greatest weakness was the failure to create machine manufacturing facilities in Europe. Johnson did not and could not know the nature of Europe's complex network of competitive markets. He had a single continental protected market to exploit from a single factory and a single distributive organisation, whereas The Gramophone Company was seriously weakened by its dependence on US instruments. Victor could not supply a cheap machine capable of competing in the volume markets of Europe and beyond.[70] The relationship was at its best when Johnson was dealing with those American executives employed by The Gramophone Company. The Birnbaum debacle leaves many unanswered questions as to the nature of Johnson's power over The Gramophone Company and his relationships with Alfred Clark and Trevor Williams. In the long term Clark is the key to understanding the Victor-Gramophone relationship. He altered the relationship from one of equals to senior and junior partners. In these circumstances, and so long as he mediated between The Gramophone Company board and Johnson, the relationship had the potential to work. Johnson regarded Clark as a trusted subordinate and in a 1916 comment that is remarkable even by the standards of frankness that characterised their relationship, Alfred Clark summed this up, "no-one more than myself has been convinced of the need for The Gramophone Co to follow the broad policy of the Victor Co and no-one has honestly strived so hard to adopt that policy."[71]

★ ★ ★

In the decade or so before the outbreak of the First World War in 1914, The Gramophone Company experienced something of a roller-coaster existence. It initially generated large profits, then huge and unsustainable losses and finally stable profits against a background of an effective nil growth in the business. But it is difficult to say if these sharp changes in fortune could have been avoided, and if so to allocate blame. Because the board exercised an early prudence, retaining a large portion of profit rather than paying them out in dividends, it can be seen as being farsighted. However, it can be criticised for wavering over the manufacture of machines in Europe. The board's hands-off approach towards day-to-day management, whether from ignorance or policy, meant they failed to see the managerial and financial dangers in 1908. It took an emergency visit from Eldridge Johnson to galvanise them into activity, even if that was only to get rid of their managing director. However, that action paved the way for the appointment as managing director of the man who dominated the company and the industry for almost forty years, Alfred Clark.

NOTES

The exuberant American hit "Yip-I-addy-I-ay!" by Will D. Cobb and John H. Flynn, featured in the 1909 musical *Our Miss Gibbs* at London's Gaiety Theatre, which starred Gertie Millar in the title role. The show ran for an impressive 636 performances: its 1910 Broadway run was a less-impressive fifty-seven performances. "Yip-I-addy-I-ay!" was one of the great pre-1914 pop songs and remained popular with British troops during the war. It was recorded in 1909 by the male star of the show, George Grossmith Jr. (HMV Black label 02219); he also recorded it for Jumbo records. Also in 1909, a version was released by Zonophone featuring Arthur Collins and Bryon G. Harlan from a Victor-derived matrix (Zono X-44128).

1. Eldridge Reeves Johnson to Alfred Clark, 20 August 1910 (Clark papers, Johnson Victrola Museum).
2. As indicated in chapter 2, Birnbaum was an experienced manager and merchant who had been in the gramophone business with Owen from the start.
3. Trevor Williams, "Chairman's Report," Annual Meeting of The Gramophone Company Ltd, 13 November 1902 (meetings file, EMI).
4. Geoffrey Jones, "Origins, Management and Performance," in *British Multinationals: Origins, Management and Performance*, ed. Geoffrey Jones (Aldershot, UK: Gower, 1987): 13.

5. For more on this, see chapter 6.

6. As described in Alfred D. Chandler's seminal work *The Visible Hand* (Cambridge, MA: Harvard University Press, 1977).

7. See "Total Turnover" in "Past History of the Entire Business," 1921 (statistics file, EMI).

8. Chandler, *The Visible Hand*, 106.

9. Frank H. Knight, *Risk Uncertainty and Profit* (New York: Houghton Mifflin, 1921), 270.

10. Theodore Birnbaum to Alfred Clark, 1 December 1904 (experts file, EMI).

11. Birnbaum to Clark.

12. For a breakdown of the personnel employed in the executive office in 1909, see Cooper and Cooper, "Report on Branches" (board papers, 1909, EMI). This reveals that executive salary costs, including Birnbaum's £4,000, totalled £13,078.

13. Oliver E. Williamson, "The Modern Corporation: Origins, Evolution, Attributes," *Journal of Economic Literature* (December 1981): 1537.

14. R. H. Coase, "The Nature of the Firm," in *The Firm the Market and the Law* (Chicago: University of Chicago Press, 1988), 53.

15. For details, see chapter 8.

16. Coase, "The Nature of the Firm," 46.

17. Theodore Birnbaum to Sydney W. Dixon, 6 November 1908 (advertising file, EMI).

18. For an account of foreign branches of The Gramophone Company, see Peter Martland, "A Business History of The Gramophone Company Ltd 1897–1918," unpublished PhD thesis, Cambridge University, 1993.

19. See "Alfred Corning Clark," in *Dictionary of Business Biography*, ed. David J. Jeremy and Christine Shawe (London: Butterworth, 1985), 1: 671–75; Peter Martland, "Alfred Clark," in *Oxford Dictionary of National Biography: From the Earliest Times to the Year 2000*, ed. H. C. G. Matthew and Brian Harrison (Oxford: Oxford University Press, 2005); and Martland, "Alfred Clark," in *Since Records Began* (London: Batsford, 1997), 24.

20. Alfred Clark to Eldridge Reeves Johnson, 21 February 1913 (Victor papers, EMI).

21. Wyatt to Alfred Clark, 5 March 1912 (accounts file, EMI).

22. Alfred Clark to Sydney W. Dixon, 3 December 1909 (Clark-Dixon correspondence, Alfred Clark papers, EMI).

23. For details of this change, see "Minutes," 16 September 1910 (board papers, EMI). For further details, see Alfred Clark to Sydney W. Dixon, 9 April 1910 (Clark-Dixon correspondence, Alfred Clark papers, EMI).

24. Alfred Clark to Eldridge Reeves Johnson, 22 June 1914 (Victor papers 1914, EMI).

25. "Minutes," 19 June 1910 (board papers, EMI).

26. For more details, see chapters 6 and 8.

27. "Remarks on the Accounts," Theodore Birnbaum to Edmund Trevor Lloyd Williams, 25 October 1909 (board papers, EMI).

28. Although Dennison was Canadian born, the passenger ship manifest for *SS Mauritania* outbound from Southampton 27 February 1919 states that he became a naturalised US citizen in 1915.

29. See also chapters 6 and 8 and "Minutes," 24 November 1914 (board papers, EMI).

30. "1901 agreement" (agreements file, Victor papers, EMI).

31. "1904 agreement" (agreements file, Victor papers, EMI).

32. This aspect of the business is examined in chapters 7 and 8.

33. Eldridge Reeves Johnson to Alfred Clark, 20 August 1910 (Clark papers, Johnson Victrola Museum).

34. "1907 Agreement" (agreements file, Victor papers, EMI).

35. Eldridge Reeves Johnson to Alfred Clark, 27 October 1909 (Victor papers, EMI).

36. Eldridge Reeves Johnson to The Gramophone Company, 29 December 1905 (Victor papers, EMI).

37. E. H. Phelps Browne and Margaret H. Browne, *A Century of Pay: The Course of Pay and Production in France, Germany, Sweden, the United Kingdom and the United States, 1860–1960* (London: Macmillan, 1968), Table 2.1.

38. According to an Edison trade intelligence report by J. F. McCoy, "Victor Co Report No 1" (phonograph file, 1909, Edison National Historic Site), Edison cylinders records dominated the poorer rural market, whilst Victor and Columbia discs competed in the wealthier urban markets. See also the evidence of F. L. Dyer, *Law on Copyright Committee 1909*, Cmd 4976 (London: HMSO, 1909): 161–64. "[Cylinder records] are sold very largely to people in the rural districts, though the disc machines are probably more largely used in the large cities."

39. Browne and Browne, *A Century of Pay*, Table 2.1.

40. McCoy, "Victor Report No 1" (phonograph file, 1909, Edison National Historic Site).

41. The role played by the board in the company's formation, and early development is examined in chapters 1 and 2. In 1916, his brother Herbert became a director (see chapter 8).

42. Walter Long's papers are held at the Wiltshire Record Office, but contain no reference to his pre-war business activities.

43. According to *The Directory of Directors*, de la Rue held no other directorships and appears to have been a retired gentleman of independent means. In contrast, Romer Williams was a businessman and lawyer with a number of directorships.

44. Alfred Clark to Eldridge Reeves Johnson, 31 January 1916 (Clark papers, Johnson Victrola Museum).

45. Until The Gramophone Company established an Indian business, the trade was handled by the Indian branch of The British Mutoscope and Biograph.

46. William C. Gaisberg to F. W. Gaisberg, February 1909 (experts letters file, EMI).

47. The reverse seems to have been the case. For instance, in 1907, Joseph Sanders, nephew of Emile Berliner and expert in the manufacture of records and the shellac-based material, was offered the post of manager at the Hayes record factory. His demand for a seat on the board was turned down on the grounds that it was not the policy of British public companies to allow company servants positions on its boards. Sanders refused to take the job, and The Gramophone Company lost the services of the world's expert in this field of manufacture. (See "Joseph Sanders Diaries" in the Robert Sanders Collection, Recorded Sound Division, Library of Congress.)

48. Eldridge Reeves Johnson to Alfred Clark, 23 February 1916 (Clark papers, Johnson Victrola Museum).

49. For more on these issues, see chapter 8. Johnson's 1916 correspondence with Clark is peppered with references to The Gramophone Company board and its inability to supervise management.

50. Eldridge Reeves Johnson to William Barry Owen, 1 December 1902 (Victor papers, EMI).

51. Eldridge Reeves Johnson to William Barry Owen, 24 December 1903 (Victor papers, EMI).

52. Theodore Birnbaum to Eldridge Reeves Johnson, 14 November 1907 (Victor papers, EMI).

53. The circumstances surrounding his appointment are curious. Clark had failed to develop the French branch and resigned in early 1908, though he remained in Europe as a director of the French company. The suspicion must remain that Johnson and Clark planned Birnbaum's downfall. Although nothing survives regarding this episode, the 1908 correspondence between Clark and Johnson reveals the breakdown in relations between Clark and Birnbaum. See Alfred Clark to Eldridge Reeves Johnson, 27 July 1908 (Clark papers, Johnson Victrola Museum). It also suggests that Johnson was biding his time over Birnbaum. See Eldridge Reeves Johnson to Alfred Clark, 5 October 1908 (Clark papers, Johnson Victrola Museum).

54. Alfred Clark to Eldridge Reeves Johnson, 2 January 1909 (Clark papers, Johnson Victrola Museum).

55. Eldridge Reeves Johnson to Edward E. Schumaker, 29 August 1927 (Schumaker file, Johnson Victrola Museum).

56. Information provided by Leonard Petts, former EMI archivist.

57. Eldridge Reeves Johnson to Alfred Clark, 23 February 1916 (Clark papers, Johnson Victrola Museum).

58. Eldridge Reeves Johnson to Theodore Birnbaum, 12 October 1908 (Victor papers, EMI).

59. Alfred Clark, "Report on Visit to America," 19 March 1911 (board papers, EMI).

60. Eldridge Reeves Johnson to Alfred Clark, 11 September 1911 (Victor papers, EMI).

61. Johnson sent the Victor chief engineer Wilburn E. Dennison with a five-year contract to oversee the construction and manage the new facility. Johnson's detailed memorandum to Dennison survives indicating a high degree of commitment to the project.

62. See chairman's annual report, 1913 (meetings file, EMI), and table 14.

63. A modern assessment of Gramophone Company performance has a number of advantages over contemporary efforts. For example, unlike modern accounts, turnover figures were considered a valuable trade secret and never made public. To assess overall performance of the business, the trade and financial press, shareholders and competitors were forced to rely on chairman's reports, statements of profit and variation in assets.

64. "The Gramophone Slump," *Financial Times* (26 October 1909).

65. For example, the Edison National Historic Site, West Orange, New Jersey, has a collection of newspaper cuttings and letters relating to The Gramophone Company from NPC Ltd commenting on its competitor's performance, dividend payments and share values.

66. "A Fine Gramophone Record," *Financial Times* (9 October 1906).

67. "The Gramophone Slump," *Financial Times* (26 October 1909).

68. "Chairman's Report," annual meeting of The Gramophone Company Ltd, 2 November 1909 (meetings file, EMI).

69. See also chapters 8 and 11.

70. From 1907, Victor supplied The Berliner Gramophone Company of Canada and exported to South America. These were seen as secondary markets, and prior to 1918 the South American market, which in many ways reflected the European experience, was not seriously exploited.

71. Alfred Clark to Eldridge Reeves Johnson, 20 March 1916 (Clark papers, Johnson Victrola Museum).

6

THE BRITISH BRANCH OF THE GRAMOPHONE COMPANY LTD: 1903–1914

"Now, the Moon Shines Bright on Pretty Red Wing"

Although our records were dearer than phonograph [cylinder] records, we gave on them the actual artists which mechanics and miners in [the industrial] districts had heard singing in the local Music Halls and Pantomimes and they could only hear them on the gramophone.

—Sydney Dixon, British branch manager,[1] 1905

The creation of the British branch of The Gramophone Company Ltd was part of Theodore Birnbaum's 1904 reorganisation. Contemporary documents refer to it as the "London sales branch" or even the "English branch," however, for the sake of consistency and accuracy it is described here as the British branch. Although The Gramophone Company Ltd was a British registered business the British branch was, in contrast to the French, Italian, German and many other branches, never organised as a separate selling company. Its creation must be seen as reflecting business needs rather than compliance with local company law.[2] This somewhat confusing situation is resolved by treating the British sales branch as though it were a subcompany.

In earlier chapters it was shown how records and machines to play them became a feature in many early-twentieth-century British homes, though, initially, the cylinder phonograph and not the disc gramophone dominated. During a 1903 British visit William E. Gilmore, president of Thomas Edison's National Phonograph Company Inc, noted this, "The disc business in Great Britain . . . is a very small percentage of the talking machine trade."[3] That same year Edward Easton, the head of Columbia Phonograph Company General, also visiting Britain noted the same phenomenon, "In the US, the disc record [is] undoubtedly [more popular] but that is because there are more disc than cylinder machines in existence. Our experience over here is quite contrary, why, for each disc we sell here, we sell three wax [cylinders]."[4] Supporting these views was Sydney Dixon, the manager of The Gramophone Company's British branch. He wrote in 1905, "In Great Britain the phonograph trade is gigantic and the disc trade is very small."[5] Yet within a few years the situation was reversed, with the cylinder record and phonograph pushed to the margins and the Berliner-Johnson zigzag cut disc record and Gramophone the industry standard. In 1908 the trade journal *Talking Machine News* noted this rapid change, observing, "The disc record has come to the front this season."[6] Furthermore, by the outbreak of the First World War in 1914, market penetration was such that possibly as many as 40 per cent of British households had some kind of talking machine (by then mainly disc gramophones) and annual sales of all kinds of records amounted to more than fourteen million.[7]

★ ★ ★

The success of the British branch in developing both a strong market for its products and driving its cylinder competitors from the field is demonstrated in table 6.1, which shows branch turnover and profits.

Table 6.1. The Gramophone Company Ltd, British Branch: Turnover and Profit, 1900–1914

Year	Turnover		Profit	
1900–1901	£47,955[a]	[$239,775]	£24,524	[$122,620]
1901–1902	£76,194	[$380,970]	£46,591	[$232,955]
1902–1903	£116,438	[$582,180]	£77,242	[$386,210]
1903–1904	£134,990	[$674,450]	£42,617[b]	[$213,085]
1904–1905	£124,220	[$621,100]	£27,301	[$136,505]
1905–1906	£157,986	[$789,930]	£37,344	[$186,720]
1906–1907	£270,040	[$1,350,200]	£61,433	[$307,165]
1907–1908	£242,735	[$1,213,675]	£53,788	[$268,940]
1908–1909	£247,076	[$1,235,380]	£42,480	[$212,400]
1909–1910	£256,291	[$1,281,455]	NA	
1910–1911	£296,837	[$1,484,185]	£26,213	[$131,065]
1911–1912	£277,871	[$1,389,355]	£40,781	[$203,905]
1912–1913	£282,702	[$1,413,510]	£27,613	[$138,065]
1913–1914	£313,237	[$1,566,185]	NA	

Source: Compiled from managing director's reports, 1902–1911; notes on accounts, 1911–1913, and "Future Prospects for the Entire Business," 1921. It has not been possible to obtain net profit figures for the year 1909–1910; however, gross profit derived from monthly epitomes stood at £101,254 (board papers and statistics files, EMI).

[a]Half year to December 1900.
[b]Half year to December 1903.

In sharp contrast to the experience of its continental European branches (see figures 6.1 and 6.2), table 6.1 shows an early slow growth for the British branch that accelerated after 1907, when it overtook the Russian branch as The Gramophone Company's most important single market. It should be remembered that after 1911 important changes in accountancy procedures deliberately depressed branch profits and focused profit on head office (these changes are explained in chapter 5). British branch turnover figures represented sales of a luxury product and provide an accurate mirror of the wider British economy. The three downturns in branch turnover, in the years 1903–1904, 1908–1909 and 1911–1912, parallel slowdowns in the broader economy. With the exception of these periods, the British branch enjoyed significant annual growth down to 1914. Comparative turnover and profit for the British and the other major European branches of the company before 1914 are found in figures 6.1 and 6.2.

Compared to the rest of Europe and Russia the slow early British growth was unusual and reflected the penetration and persistence of the cylinder format in the market. Edison never traded in Russia and, as a consequence, it was largely immune from the technology-based fragmentation experienced in Britain. Hence the ability of the Russian branch to exploit its prime user advantage. The growth of the British branch after 1907 was a function of a number of factors. First there was the collapse of the cylinder

Figure 6.1. The Gramophone Company Ltd: Branch Turnover, 1901–1914—Britain, France, Germany and Russia (in Pounds)

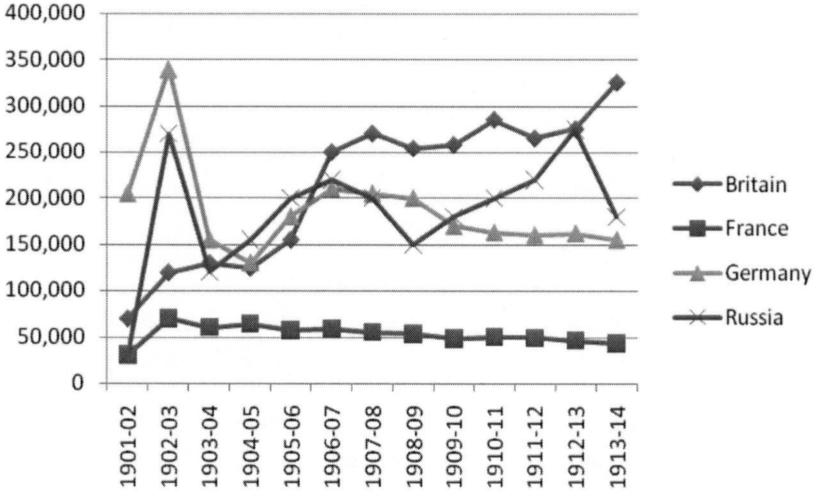

Source: Compiled from "Annual Reports" and "Notes on Accounts," 1911 to 1913 (meetings files and board papers, EMI).

Figure 6.2. The Gramophone Company Ltd: Branch Profit, 1901–1914—Britain, France, Germany and Russia (in Pounds)

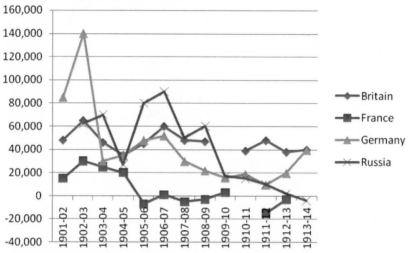

Source: See source note for figure 6.1.

business and growth in the number of disc manufacturers and retailers. Second, following on from the recession there were buoyant markets. Third, the branch used sophisticated marketing strategies. Fourth, the branch deployed a range of products as offensive and defensive record labels, and finally the strength of The Gramophone Company's international recording activities and access to the Victor recordings.

The beginnings of the British Gramophone trade were outlined in chapter 2 and in chapter 5 the development of the parent company was examined. Put succinctly, William Barry Owen found a disorderly market when he arrived in Britain, with The Edison Bell Phonograph Company Ltd maintaining its monopoly. Although his Gramophones and records found a ready market, Owen was attacked by Edison Bell for patent infringement and in an attempt to take over the market his US supplier cut supplies of disc records and later introduced Zonophone products into Britain. Overcoming these difficulties, Owen found venture capitalists to invest in his business. Furthermore, with the help of British businessman Theodore Birnbaum he created selling organisations in Britain and Europe, acquired record pressing facilities in Germany and created recording studios in Britain, continental Europe and Russia. From the start the British business was managed by a London-based marketing team, supported by a central office structure. In 1899, when Birnbaum left to manage the central European and Russian business, Owen assumed his former duties as British manager. However, the demands made on Owen as managing director and the amount of time he spent in the United States prevented him from personally cultivating the business. The latter point was particularly telling, as in his final years Owen spent a large portion of each year away from the office. As his then assistant Sydney Dixon noted, "Mr Owen is a good deal in America now, and in fact I have to run the show here four or five months of this year alone." In fact Dixon was hired in 1902 specifically to plug this gap.[8] Uniquely, the British business was serviced by the company head office. As noted in chapter 5, Theodore Birnbaum reorganised the business creating both a headquarters executive and a separate British selling branch headed by Dixon. Soon after, Dixon wrote about these changes to a colleague in the United States: "The English business is separated from the Administrative Office; there exists therefore the Gramophone and Type-writer Ltd, with Managing Director Theodore Birnbaum. . . . Then there is the English branch, of which I have been made Manager."[9]

When Dixon joined The Gramophone Company annual British turnover was £116,438, this had risen to £313,237 by 1914.[10] Much of this success can be attributed to Dixon's managerial skills, which he combined with a flair for business, salesmanship and a thorough knowledge of the advertising world, specifically mass circulation national newspapers and magazines. As British branch manager, Dixon had the same responsibilities as the other branch managers. These he spelt out to Birnbaum in a May 1904 letter, "As I understand the circumstances . . . the English business was to be placed upon the same basis as the other branches such as Paris, St Petersburg, Milan etc. A London Manager to be appointed who should while controlling his own staff, internal and economical arrangements, stock, and methods of conducting business in his territory, be personally answerable to the Board through the Managing Director for the result of his endeavour."[11] Dixon had other responsibilities. For example, he submitted monthly branch sales and trade intelligence reports to the board. These have survived in The EMI Group Archive and contain a wealth of detail together with monthly epitomes of sales for the period 1904 to 1914. Dixon also undertook commissions on behalf of the board, such as negotiating and arranging recording sessions for celebrity or other prestigious artists. A lesser man might have been fazed by this task, but Dixon was an energetic, educated, sophisticated individual, totally at ease in the frenetic world occupied by international performing artists.

★   ★   ★

In order for Sydney Dixon not just to create a successful British market in Gramophones and disc records but also place them on a par with the piano and other quality musical goods, he had to overcome a number of deep-seated problems and prejudices. For example, when he first joined the company in 1902 there was little in the British record catalogue representing anything like middle or high culture, though this changed that same year with the first catalogue of celebrity records made by some of the world's finest performing artists (see below). At that time the most successful recordings consisted of brass or military bands, cornet or banjo soloists or singers whose merit lay more in their recordable voices than in their art. Most established artists regarded the talking machine with contempt and many potential middle-class customers shunned it, believing it to be a vulgar instrument (for more on this point see chapter 7).[12] These same prejudices were encountered by the equally infant cinema, and for the same reasons. Both industries exploited new mechanical technologies and grew from the bottom up.

By 1914 Dixon had changed attitudes to the point that Gramophone Company dealerships were largely in the hands of piano retailers or other high-class music retailers, and no great performing artist dared refuse to make records. He also spotted and took advantage of a number of important developments. For instance, when in 1910 the business lost the proprietary right to the term Gramophone, he rebranded Gramophone Company products using the picture of "His Master's Voice." Thereafter, all the core records and Gramophones bore this image, and the label announced them as "His Master's Voice" records. From this point, Dixon "boomed" the HMV label as a sign of quality. He identified specific target groups and ran high-profile advertising campaigns in national newspapers and magazines, introducing his products to middle-class consumers aspiring to the good life. In these campaigns he sold HMV products by associating them with the domestic activities of the comfortable leisured middle and upper classes. In seeking acceptance HMV advertising promoted the records made by celebrity artists, together with the warrants awarded to the company by British and foreign royalty.

Retailing was another way to gain a foothold in these desirable markets and although before 1914 the British branch engaged in several such ventures they took the form of failed retail outlets with outstanding dealer debt. Dixon took them over, put in managers and after clearing the debt sold them on. The Regent Street shop was an exception. Although initially a debt-encumbered retail outlet, once Dixon's managers cleared the debt they continued to trade, providing the branch with a central London presence. This venture paved the way for extensive interwar retailing developments, which eventually became the HMV international record chain.

To aid this strategy Dixon came up with other initiatives; for example, the original Gramophone Company record line was a single series of Black label discs, initially just 7-inch, then after 1900 10-inch and after 1903 12-inch, all recorded on one side only. However, in 1902, The Gramophone Company began making Celebrity recordings of major international performing artists. Of this Owen said, "It has been the policy of your Company during the last year to very largely increase the number of [records made by] expensive and world-celebrated Artists, and in doing of this we have spent a very great deal of money. . . . The Gramophone Company has derived from this expenditure a standing that makes it far and away higher than any of its competitors."[13] Owen regarded Celebrity records as part of a new strategy to convince consumers that the company purveyed high-quality products. It was also risky, as National Phonograph president William Gilmore observed, "I know that the records that they are putting out of Calvé, Tamagno, Caruso and others are not finding a large sale in this country."[14] Celebrity records bore a distinctive red label and were initially sold at the premium price of 10s for 10-inch and 15s for 12-inch discs. Thereafter the price varied, reflecting differing contracts with these performers: for more information see chapters 7 and 11.[15] For example, by 1914, solos by the Italian tenor Enrico Caruso cost 8s for a 10-inch record and 12s.6d for a 12-inch record; though a recording released in 1908 of the sextette from Donizetti's opera *Lucia de Lammermoor* (HMV 054205) featuring the voice of Caruso with five other musical luminaries cost a staggering £1.10s.0d.[16]

In 1912, The Gramophone Company introduced a third HMV label, the Plum record. It was a midpriced 10- and 12-inch record, recorded on both sides. They retailed at 2s.6d for a 10-inch and 4s for a 12-inch record. The Plum label was designed to fill an important gap in the midprice market, but it went much further, to become one of the most enduring of all record labels. By the time it was discontinued in 1960 more than 5,000 ten-inch recordings had been released and more than 4,000 twelve-inch.[17] Pricing became an important part of The Gramophone Company's pre-1914 selling strategy. Before the Hayes record factory opened in 1907, Black label records were sold to retailers at 1s.6d for 7-inch, 3s.4d for 10-inch and 5s for 12-inch records; consumers paid 2s.6d, 5s and 7s.6d respectively. When the new factory opened the 7-inch record was discontinued and other prices reduced, with dealer prices of 2s.8d and 4s and retail prices of 4s and 6s. The unit sales chronicled in table 6.2 cover the period from the first full year of Dixon's management until 1914, and are an indicator to the breadth of his success.

Table 6.2.   The Gramophone Company Ltd, British Branch: Unit Sales, 1903–1914

Year	Records	Gramophones
1903–1904	598,200	NA
1904–1905	566,716	15,010
1905–1906	943,538	16,076
1906–1907	1,711,943	17,816
1907–1908	1,995,463	17,240
1908–1909	1,892,084	18,461
1909–1910	1,877,290	19,507
1910–1911	1,904,012	23,545
1911–1912	1,844,452	22,966
1912–1913	1,879,351	22,132
1913–1914	3,867,406	17,645

Source: Years are calculated using the company accounting year June to June. Compiled from "Epitomes 1904–1914" (board papers, EMI).

As discussed in chapter 5, growth in the instrument sector was lamentable, but even so the performance of the British branch compared favourably with its European counterparts. In Britain, where annual sales amounted to 500,000 units by 1914, The Gramophone Company held a market share of between 3 and 5 per cent. These were top-of-the-market machines, but nonetheless overall sales remained poor, especially given the position held by this venture in the trade. Unit sales of records conceal the fact that the bulk of British branch sales were not the expensive Celebrity, or Black, or Plum HMV records, but rather the cheaper Zonophone, Twin and Cinch brands. Table 6.3 breaks down record sales into their product range. As these figures show by the outbreak of war in 1914, despite the up-market profile and the advertising campaigns, The Gramophone Company was in fact a major producer of cheap records for the volume market. These competed with its main German rivals for the affections of the British public.[18]

Distribution of the HMV core products was based on principles worked out by Owen and Birnbaum in the earliest days of the trade. In contrast to its competitors, who sold through the wholesale network, The Gramophone Company sold its premium gramophone products through an exclusive dealer system, though the lesser brands were sold through the wholesale trade (see below). The dealer network varied in size; in 1907 it was around 2,000, however by 1913 it was 1,300 with weaker dealers eliminated and the trade focused on a single dealer per British town.[19]

Table 6.3.   The Gramophone Company Ltd, British Branch: Record Sales by Label, 1904–1914

Year	Celebrity	Black	Plum	Zonophone	Twin	Cinch	Total
1904–1905	14,895	409,406	—	142,415	—	—	566,716
1905–1906	35,144	410,687	—	497,707	—	—	943,538
1906–1907	26,939	445,114	—	1,239,890	—	—	1,711,943
1907–1908	64,671	435,633	—	1,495,159	—	—	1,995,463
1908–1909	41,756	436,959	—	1,152,955	260,414	—	1,892,084
1909–1910	55,706	387,825	—	869,850	563,909	—	1,877,290
1910–1911	46,355	408,711	—	565,182	883,764	—	1,904,012
1911–1912	37,355	404,232	—	1,402,865	—	—	1,844,452
1912–1913	34,040	242,270	189,616	1,413,425	—	—	1,879,351
1913–1914	35,587	349,628	159,558	755,924	—	2,566,709	3,867,406

Source: Compiled from "Epitomes 1904–1914" (board papers, EMI).

This strategy, while it may have had an impact on supply, enabled the branch to control products through to point of sale and ensured retail price maintenance. It was also in line with the strategy of marketing the Gramophone range of instruments and records as high-value low-volume premium products. In these circumstances, dealerships came to be concentrated in the hands of high-class music and piano retailers. Dixon wrote of this change in December 1906: "For the past eighteen months, it has been our strenuous endeavour to transfer gramophone business from the small dealer of the old days to the good piano warehouses."[20] Piano retailers oozed respectability and occupied premises in areas of town frequented by potential middle-class patrons.[21]

★ ★ ★

Although the trade in Dixon's HMV Black, Celebrity and later Plum label records fell into the hands of high-class retailers, the rest of the record industry (whether the cheaper Gramophone Company product range or the broader trade) traded largely with small general dealers, tobacconists, bicycle dealers and the like, who had little if any knowledge or appreciation of music. Furthermore, the quality of entertainment provided by cheaper records was designed for the musically uneducated, rather than the more sophisticated aspirational patrons Dixon was aiming for with his core product.[22] Therefore, his twin marketing strategy was to protect and develop his core products and at the same time break into the growing mass markets. Furthermore, he had to differentiate in the minds of would-be middle-class patrons his core gramophone products from the cylinder and emerging cheap disc competitors. This strategy began with the acquisition in 1903 of International Zonophone GmbH, which became a second-string cheap label aimed at the volume market. Single-sided Zonophone records initially retailed at 2s for a 7- and 4s for a 10-inch record; later reduced to 1s.6d and 3s. The new Zonophone team (among who was Louis Sterling) searched for appropriate records in the existing Black label catalogue (which had about 2,000 titles), together with the considerable back catalogue of deleted Gramophone Company records and from the existing Zonophone record catalogue. Appropriate music meant popular music, music hall songs by both well-known and unknown artists (who often provided cover versions), together with brass and military band records and religious and sacred music; musical genres that remained a favourite staple of the masses. Dixon wrote of this quest for appropriate records, "I have eliminated from the Gramophone [Black label] Catalogue certain records which, although

good ones, are practically out of date. These I have put on to the Zonophone."[23] To accomplish this without disclosing the origins of recordings,
the names of performers or bands were often changed. In this way five of
the recordings made by the Irish tenor John McCormack at his first ever
recording sessions in September 1904 appeared in the Zonophone catalogue under the cover name of "John O'Reilly."[24] Other performers, such
as the bass-baritone Peter Dawson, were also used under a variety of alternative names on the various cheap labels (see chapter 7).[25] Therefore the
Zonophone catalogue, when it emerged in 1904, provided the first known
example of a British record company exploiting "back catalogue."[26] This
distinction went beyond physical separation of musical genres to involve a
different method of distribution; the HMV label records and gramophones
sold via accredited dealerships, while the wholesale trade distributed the
cheaper Zonophone and later The Twin, Zonophone-Twin and Cinch records and the Zonophone instruments (see below) to around 8,000 traders.

In May 1907 Dixon described this trade and highlighted its well-established seasonality, "The Zonophone trade . . . is very largely handled by the
cycle trade, hardware trade and sports and games trades. The abnormally
fine weather at Easter led to the trades above mentioned to give up the
talking machine earlier than usual to get out their bicycles, their gardening
implements and their athletic appliances."[27] The volume trade was highly
regional and subject to local economic conditions. In February 1908, Dixon
wrote, "Trade in the second of our most profitable Zonophone territories,
Tyneside, including Northumberland and Durham, has been standing still
owing to the shipbuilding troubles. Our best territory of all Lancashire has
been hovering on the eve of a cotton strike, and the Lancashire operatives
have been shy of spending money."[28] When trade was good, the working
classes spent freely on Zonophone records and related products. Dixon told
the board, "There is during four months of the year an enormous so called
Saturday night trade in cylinder and cheap discs. It is a common occurrence
for a small talking machine dealer to sell one thousand records between 2
o'clock on Saturday afternoon and closing time."[29] In June 1908, during the
recession, Dixon commented: "In the North, Midlands and North Eastern
Counties we have suffered severely. It is in these strongholds of ours that
the shrinkage in wages and the bad trade has told heavily."[30]

The original purpose of the Zonophone record was to protect the core
gramophone labels, though it turned out to be a commercial success in its
own right. Although it was not designed to siphon off existing gramophone
customers, in the early days it was noted, "We have lost a certain amount
of business in Gramophone goods owing to the Zonophone, but there

can be no question that this trade would have been lost to us during this coming autumn owing to the cheaper discs."[31] Initially, artists who made records were seen and appreciated as novelties. However, just as early moviegoers wanted to know the names of performers they saw in films, the record buying public expressed a clear preference for specific artists and in doing so created the recording star.[32] Dixon gave his customers the stars they wanted and the competition quickly caught on, recruiting their own stable of known artists. Of this Dixon was forced to concede, "For the past few months these very same artists have sung for the 'Odeon,' for the 'Columbia,' the British 'Zonophone' and the 'Nicole,' all of whose records are considerably cheaper than our [records]."[33] In order to meet this competition, Zonophone engaged in vigorous advertising campaigns to push records of music hall artists and other popular performers and the ephemeral popular music of the day, such as the song "Red Wing" which gave this chapter its title. As Dixon observed, "Zonophone records are as to 90% made up of the topical song or march of the hour."[34] Central to Zonophone strategy was the ability to find and retain key recording artists. Highlighting this, James Goff, who managed the British branch between 1909 and 1912, wrote, "The future is more dominated by the Artist question than ever. We must never relax our predominance over other makes in the way of talent."[35] To achieve this Goff and Dixon maintained up-to-date record catalogues for each label, complete with monthly additions. This required a high quality musical and recording team based at the London studio, the prompt availability of finished records, a well-oiled distribution system and an effective trade intelligence network. In a 1908 report Dixon defined these different strands of the business, highlighting the success of his strategy: "We have goods with which to supply the best piano dealers and high class talking machine dealers in England, while with the Zono-phone we have created a disc business with a repertoire equal to National Phonograph Co and with this repertoire we have built up a business with factors who supply a class of dealer very different to the special gramophone dealers. . . . The Zonophone has become also a high class mark and is so considered by the talking machine dealer."[36]

In 1908 and again in 1913 the British branch of The Gramophone Company used its economic muscle and extensive back catalogue to domi-nate and mould the British record market, and at the same time protect its existing product range. It achieved this by creating two new labels, The Twin and The Cinch. Like the Zonophone they were marketed as anony-mous brands through the wholesale trade and bore no marks to connect them to The Gramophone Company. The Twin was a short-lived 10-inch label. It existed between 1908 and 1911 and retailed at 2s.6d and had a sound signal printed on both sides of the record. Its creation reflected the success of the Zonophone and its transformation from a defensive line into a core product. The rationale behind The Twin was simple; the branch wanted to maintain a 3s.6d single-faced Zonophone yet meet competition from companies publishing cheaper double-faced records. The intention was to hit the competition hard. In June 1908 Dixon was claiming, "The advent of The Twin double-disc at 2/6 has seriously upset the plans of Barnett Samuels with their treble lines of Fonotipia, Odeon and Jumbo. Further Hough Managing Director of the Edison Bell makes no secret of telling the trade that we have injured his chance of coming into the disc trade. So far the Twin record has not affected the Zonophone in any shape or form."[37] The Twin was marketed on a shoestring, with initial recording costs amounting to no more than £12.10s. As with the early Zonophone catalogue, records were mainly sourced from back catalogue and to control costs no factory stocks were maintained, with dealer debts amounted to no more than one month's trade. In June 1908 Dixon wrote to Birnbaum of his prelaunch preparations, "I have taken an office at 27s.6d a week and put some second hand furniture in it. . . . It only requires then a clerk, a stenographer and a boy."[38] The Twin unit sales data in table 6.3 reflects its success. However, by 1911, following cumulative sales of 1.7 million records, the label had served its purpose, the double-sided record had come to the fore and The Twin was merged as a revamped double-sided 2s.6d Zonophone known as The Zonophone-Twin record.[39]

In the fiercely competitive post-1908 disc record market prices fell significantly, especially in the cheaper volume sector. Such was the pressure and so overcrowded the market that, in 1913, the British branch marketed a product aimed at undercutting its competitors, especially the flood of cheap German records. This was a 10-inch The Cinch record, which retailed at 1s.1d and marketed using The Twin formula of back catalogue recordings and selling on a shoestring. It was, as the data in table 6.3 indicates, another successful though short-term expedient. The Cinch record harassed the competition, drove the weak from the field and forced leading competitors to follow suit. Almost immediately, Columbia introduced its Phoenix label at 1s.1d and J. E. Hough Ltd (manufacturers of the Edison Bell range of records) marketed a 1s.6d record. These records outraged many British manufacturers and traders, who saw them as a destabilising force at the bottom of the market and the trade press overflowed with their fulminations.[40]

★   ★   ★

Table 6.4 shows a breakdown of British branch Gramophone sales and indicate little growth during the period 1904 to 1914. Given that annual British sales of disc instruments post-1908 were 500,000, the 3 to 5 per cent market share indicated is pitiful.[41] Yet, compared with French and German sales, the British branch accounted for about one third of all Gramophone Company machine sales. The Gramophones (largely made by Victor) were an excellent product and enabled The Gramophone Company to dominate the low-volume high-value end of the market. However, the inability of Victor to supply a cheap machine capable of competing in the volume market remained an intractable problem. The Gramophone Company's British machine business was, like the record trade after 1904, divided into two, with the higher priced Gramophone range sold through the dealer network, and the Zonophone models through the wholesale trade. Table 6.4 breaks down unit sales between the two product groups.

Table 6.4 shows annual sales of Gramophones range averaging around 13,000. As there were around 1,300 dealerships this means annual average dealer sales of no more than ten machines or less than one per month; clearly these products were not major sellers. The failure to develop this sector is attributable to a variety of factors. First, Gramophones were only available through the dealership network and therefore had a clientele limited by both class and location. Second, there were only around 1,300 appointed dealers in 1913 and these thinly spread across the country, creating a supply problem denying some customers access to the product. Third, with prices ranging from £5 to £100 they were the domain of the

Table 6.4.   The Gramophone Company Ltd, British Branch: Machine Sales, 1904–1914

Year	Gramophone	Zonophone	Total
1904–1905	13,718	1,292	15,010
1905–1906	13,207	2,869	16,076
1906–1907	13,947	3,869	17,816
1907–1908	12,887	4,353	17,240
1908–1909	13,617	4,844	18,461
1909–1910	12,068	7,439	19,507
1910–1911	13,259	10,286	23,545
1911–1912	14,831	8,135	22,966
1912–1913	15,654	6,478	22,132
1913–1914	12,770	4,875	17,645

Source: Compiled from "Annual Reports," 1904–1911, and "Notes on Accounts," 1911–1913 (meeting files and board papers, EMI).

wealthy. Fourth, the goods were advertised in class-specific newspapers and magazines, leaving the mass of the population unaware of the product and finally, cheaper products were available.

The key problem was the inability of the British branch to break into the cheap end of the mass market. This was due to the poor quality of Zonophones supplied by the US Victor company. In November 1908, an exasperated Dixon reported, "The great trouble is with the machines. The whole trade is absolutely disgusted with Zonophone machines and it is very hard indeed to get any orders at all."[42] Not only did the Victor-built Zonophone fail to compete in terms of price, they were so shoddily designed that they were an embarrassment. Of them Dixon said, "We must consider ourselves absolutely beaten in the machine trade with factors. So terrible is our position affected by the distrust of Zonophone machines, that I seriously propose to cease selling Zonophones. . . . There is not a single factor in Great Britain who will handle a Zonophone machine if he can possibly avoid it. Our machines have become a bye-word in the trade."[43] The long-term solution was to develop British manufacturing capacity. Although the decision was taken in 1912 the timing was unfortunate, as the project came to fruition just as war was declared. In the meantime, so as to remain in the market, the British, European and the other overseas branches were forced to sell machines at a loss. In fact machine sales were subsidised by the profitable record side of the business.[44]

★   ★   ★

The most important weapon available to the British branch was mass advertising. This encompassed record and machine catalogues, advertising posters, newspaper and magazine advertising, stockrooms, the use of celebrity artists, royalty endorsements and the HMV trademark. The advertising budget, specifically in newspapers and magazines, proved Dixon's most flexible weapon, and no other record company executive had so big a budget or applied such skill in using it. By advertising in the right journals at the right time Dixon reached the markets he wanted to influence, and at the same time he dished the competition. Advertising budgets were allocated annually on a branch-by-branch basis, with the British marketing team receiving often more than double the allocation of other branches; it averaged about 10 per cent of turnover. The comparison of British and European turnover and profits in the decade before 1914 suggests that this was money well spent.

The advertising budget was in two parts. First, record and machine catalogues, monthly supplements, posters and other printed matter, and second, direct advertising in newspapers and magazines. Unfortunately, surviving sources do not break advertising expenditure into its components, though overall British branch figures for 1910 to 1911 survive and show how from an overall budget of £12,790 37 per cent (or 4.3 per cent of branch turnover) was spent on newspaper and magazine advertising.[45] In a 1924 work *The Inner Side of Advertising*, Cyril C. Freer gave near contemporary advice to manufacturers on the level of advertising necessary to boost sales of specific products. He claimed record and gramophone manufacturers needed to spend 5 per cent of turnover on advertising. This compares favourably with the 5 per cent recommended for tobacco manufacturers, 7 per cent for automobile manufacturers and 10 per cent for patent remedies.[46] Although The Gramophone Company's total advertising budget of £80,000 made the company a major international advertiser, the budget of the British branch was, in contrast, not in the big league. In 1891, for example, the advertising budget of Beecham's Proprietary Medicines was £120,000; while in 1897 the cigarette manufacturers W. D. and H. O. Wills spent £20,000 advertising their new brand "Diamond Queen" cigarettes just in the cities of Birmingham and Liverpool. The advertising budget of the Victor Talking Machine Company was, in comparison to its British affiliate, huge and in 1913 and 1914 it ranked fourth in a table of the largest US advertisers in national magazines.[47]

Dixon combined personal connections within the trade with skill and experience in the world of advertising. As a result, he proved a master of mass advertising. Recognizing from the start its importance as a key to extending sales, his pursuit of publicity before 1914 made The Gramophone Company and the "His Master's Voice" trademark amongst the country's most visible businesses. For example, the British branch regularly took space in the national press. It began its advertising year in September with weekly two-column-width advertisements on the front pages of the middle-class oriented *Daily Mail* and other national newspapers. The newspaper budget was spent with specific aims in mind, of which Dixon left numerous examples. In April 1904 he wrote, "I have spent £320 in an operatic page in the [*Daily*] *Telegraph* on the day the Covent Garden season commenced and in a front page advertisement in the *Daily Mail*."[48] Because the British market was so diverse, advertisements had to follow the reading habits of each target group, and advertisements in national newspapers were balanced by extensive coverage in the provincial press. In 1902, Dixon wrote, "We are advertising tomorrow in the *Birmingham Post, Manchester Courier, Liverpool Post, Yorkshire Post* and *Daily Mail*."[49] The costs were substantial; advertising on the front page of the *Daily Mail*, for example, could cost £200 per insertion.[50] A six months' agreement with Pearson's newspapers and magazines in 1903 cost almost £4,500.[51] Clearly, compared to the rest of the trade, the British branch had, as George Orwell put it, "the biggest stick to rattle in the swill bucket." The impact of mass advertising could be dramatic, as publicity agent Turner Morton wrote in 1905, "Two or three thousand pounds must be spent if a hit is to be made, twenty or thirty thousand if anything like a sensation is to be caused." If Morton's assessment is correct then Dixon got the results he wanted on the cheap.[52]

The advertising budget was used to great effect in pushing new products, particularly the records of celebrity artists. Of all the celebrities associated with The Gramophone Company, the best known was Australian soprano and socialite Nellie (later Dame Nellie) Melba. A shrewd businesswoman, Melba made her first records in 1904 and realised the importance of advertising her records from which she received large advances and royalties.[53] Melba even allowed her name to be associated with the most expensive Gramophone in the company's range and advertisements for her records were prominently featured in her concert programmes. Dixon wrote of her first records:

> 2,000 Melba records were sold at 14s each [to dealers]. The advertising appropriation for Melba records amounts to £1,066 for June. The net profit to the Company on the 2,000 records sold in England amounts to £725. Deducting the first heavy output on advertising, the loss for June is only £391. It is of course needless to point out all the Melba records mean to the business from an advertising point of view.[54]

Dixon used very similar arguments for the advertising budgets accompanying record releases by other celebrity artists. His utilitarian view of celebrity recordings reflected that of managing director Theodore Birnbaum who in 1904 told Johnson in America, "this class of business is very difficult to handle, and it is questionable whether it can be regarded from either side on any other basis than a high-class advertising scheme."[55]

Just as today's tabloid press sell newspapers on the strength of royal stories, so the British branch sold records on the back of the royal warrant granted by Queen Alexandra in 1907. Dixon waxed, "the effect on our trade of [Her Majesty] the Queen's appointment has been most beneficial in extending business to new channels."[56] Great artists like Melba might raise the acceptability of The Gramophone Company's products to the middle classes, but royal patronage was the ultimate seal of respectability. At a time when the crowned heads of Europe really meant something, British royalty were but the icing on the royal cake. By 1908, The Gramophone

Company could and did boast five Royal Warrants; apart from Queen Alexandra's, these were from the Khedive of Egypt, the King of Italy, the King and Queen of Spain and the Shah of Persia.

Advertising was also used to harry the competition. In 1907 Dixon reported, "We are top dog in Britain and this coming season have the opportunity of severely hammering and disheartening the Odeon, the Columbia and the other dozen odd disc manufacturers."[57] Dixon also used his advertising muscle to obtain information about competitor's plans: "Learning at the eleventh hour that the Odeon or Columbia are coming out with a big advertisement in a certain paper, or with a big new scheme. We immediately get out a half page or more on the same day in the same paper, and in a better position, or make a counter move against the scheme. This takes the heart out of the competition as the Columbia, the Odeon and other companies have time after time admitted to third parties."[58]

The British branch dominated the trade using a variety of means beyond advertising and product development, for example through the trade press. In the decade leading up to the outbreak of war in 1914 there were three major talking machine trade journals selling in the Britain. *Talking Machine News*, which began publication in 1903, was the most influential and enjoyed the largest circulation.[59] In 1911 The Gramophone Company secretly acquired control of this journal, to deny importers of cheap German machines and records access to its advertising columns.[60] Maintaining control of dealers and obtaining reliable trade intelligence was also used to good effect. Annual stockrooms held at the start of the autumn selling season were another way of meeting retailers and wholesalers, and placing new products before them. Held in all major cities, they brought manufacturers and retailers together to talk, inspect and buy. Unfortunately, few data survive concerning the size of trade with individual retailers. Those that do show Keith Prowse, the London music retailer and one of the oldest Gramophone Company dealers, bought £5,641 worth of goods in 1912, while Harrods' account for the same year stood at £9,373. Even fewer figures survive from the provincial trade, though in 1912 goods to the value of £5,520 were sold in Birmingham and £6,454 in Manchester.[61]

★   ★   ★

The British branch faced stiff competition from the broader musical trade, principally from the piano, player piano and musical box and sheet music publishers. The opening up of markets in some of these products occurred half a century or more before the appearance of recorded music, and they had by the start of the twentieth-century permeated middle-class society. Capitalising on this, the British branch of The Gramophone Company shrewdly sought dealerships among piano dealers. Cyril Ehrlich's history of the piano chronicles the development of that industry, and he found a similar lack of firm figures for the pre-1914 piano sales market. Instead, he estimated annual British sales of 75 to 100,000 pianos and player pianos in the three decades immediately before 1914.[62] This compares to estimates of up to 500,000 talking machines sold annually in Britain during the six years prior to 1914. Although Ehrlich did not suggest the record industry had a negative impact on the piano trade, an important contemporary source does argue that it affected the music business.

Music publishers, giving evidence to a 1909 Board of Trade committee considering the extension of copyright to records, argued that their trade had been reduced by record sales.[63] Edwin Goodman, a director of music publishers Chappell and Co, gave evidence citing sales of the musical score to Lionel Monckton's 1902 comedy *The Country Girl*. Between 1902 and 1904 he claimed his firm sold over 59,000 copies of this work, compared to sales of 37,000 (between 1905 and 1907) for the equally popular 1905 Franz Lehar operetta *The Merry Widow*. Goodwin ascribed the difference in the sales of these two to the malign influence of recordings.[64] Unfortunately, no music publisher was prepared to cite overall sheet music sales, while record industry representatives presented the committee with letters from dealers suggesting that records actually helped sales of sheet music.[65]

If the evidence that sales of records depressed sheet music sales remains contentious, the debate about its impact on the sale of musical boxes and like devices is conclusive; the record industry killed the trade. In a 1908 interview Alfred Imhof, of Imhof and Mukle, music dealers of Oxford Street, London, in reply to the question, "And do you think . . . that the talking machine has affected the sale of other instruments?" said, "Well, it has undoubtedly killed the musical box . . . sales of these instruments is practically nil."[66] The first bankruptcy of the disc trade was The Nicole Frères Record Company Ltd, a company descended from a long line of musical box manufacturers.[67] Although the argument that the record industry killed the musical box is persuasive, there is no substantive evidence to support the view that the record industry injured the trade in pianos, player pianos or even music publishing. From this it must be concluded that rather than taking over existing markets, the record industry tended to create new markets for its products.

★ ★ ★

By the outbreak of the First World War, the British branch of The Gramophone Company led the field in recording and selling records of international celebrities, and had to a significant extent developed and moulded
the volume market. With a total of thirteen million records sold annually
in Britain, the Company with sales of almost four million controlled about
30 per cent of the market, with significant representation at all levels. Although the gramophone portion of the business made an operating loss
and was therefore a charge against record profits the product was kept in
the public eye ready for when the new machine factory came on stream.
Compared to the European branches of The Gramophone Company, the
British performed in a remarkable and consistently successful manner, producing sustained growth in turnover and profit. This was due to different
trading conditions unique to the British market before 1914. Unlike the
European branches, the British branch never experienced early monopoly
trading conditions; rather, during market formation, it faced formidable
competition from the cylinder record and, as a result, took much longer to
establish its dominant position. In order to achieve this, the British branch
had to convince middle-class consumers that the gramophone and the disc
record were both an acceptable diffuser of musical culture and an indispensable item in the modern household. To overcome these not inconsiderable
hurdles it had to produce quality products capable of outgunning competitors and through advertising convince consumers that records and gramophones were essential features in the drawing rooms of the social elite. The
measure of this achievement is shown in the rapid growth of turnover and
profit after 1907. With the fruits of this success, the market swung deci-
sively in its direction, making The Gramophone Company's British branch
the business's engine of growth and profit; then came the war.

NOTES

Written and composed by Thurland Chattaway and Kerry Mills in 1907, "Red Wing"
was a success on both sides of the Atlantic. During the First World War, new more topical
words were added, and it became "When the Moon Shines Bright on Charlie Chaplin."
Both versions were recorded in Britain: the first, in 1908, by Ernest Pike (as Herbert Payne)
(Zonophone X-42751) and then, in 1915, by Stanley Kirkby (as Murray Johnson) (HMV
B550). In the United States today, it is regarded as either folk or bluegrass and, in Britain, a
successful war song. There have been other variants.

1. "Monthly Epitomes to the Board of The Gramophone Company," March 1905 (board papers, EMI).

2. The British branch was never organised as a separate subcompany, though its two-volume labels The Zonophone and The Twin were.

3. William Edgar Gilmore to Thomas Edison, 11 December 1903 (document files, 1903: phonograph-manufacturing-NPC, Edison National Historic Site).

4. "Edward Easton," *Talking Machine News* 1, no. 5 (September 1903): 83.

5. "Monthly Epitomes to the Board of The Gramophone Company," December 1905 (board papers, EMI).

6. "Editorial," *Talking Machine News* 5, no. 6 (October 1908).

7. For an explanation of this estimate, see chapter 4.

8. Sydney W. Dixon to Peter Bohanna, 4 December 1903 (Australian file, EMI).

9. Sydney W. Dixon to Calvin G. Child, 29 June 1904 (Victor papers, EMI).

10. Data compiled from "Annual Reports" and "Notes on Accounts," 1911–1913 (meetings file and board papers, EMI).

11. Sydney W. Dixon to Theodore Birnbaum, 5 May 1904 (Sydney Dixon papers, EMI).

12. Such attitudes persisted. In 1915, a judge hearing an application for changes to The Gramophone Company's articles of association to permit the manufacture of munitions expressed a hope "that the new product of the Company would not give any less pain than the former product." Annual meeting, November 1915 (meetings file, EMI).

13. "William Barry Owen Report 1902" (board papers, EMI).

14. William Edgar Gilmore to Thomas Edison, 11 December 1903 (document files 1903: phonograph-manufacturing-NPC, Edison National Historic Site).

15. The price structure of celebrity artist records can be found in The Gramophone Company record catalogues. See also *Celebrity Records by International Artists* (London: Gramophone Company Ltd 1914).

16. *Celebrity Records.*

17. For an account of this important British label, see Michael Smith and Frank Andrews, *The HMV Plum Label Catalogue* (London: Oakwood Press: 1974). See also Frank Andrews and Ernie Bayly, *Catalogue of HMV "B" Series Records* (Wells-Next-the-Sea, Norfolk: City of London Phonograph and Gramophone Society Ltd, 2000). The first work is a listing of all the 12-inch records and the second a listing of the 10-inch records.

18. For more on the German trade in Britain, see chapter 4.

19. "Monthly Epitomes to the Board of The Gramophone Company," February 1907 (board papers, EMI).

20. "Monthly Epitomes to the Board of The Gramophone Company," December 1906 (board papers, EMI).

21. A. L. Bowley in his estimates of early-twentieth-century British income distribution suggested 26.6 per cent of earnings exceeded £225 per annum. A. L. Bowley, *The Change in the Distribution of the National Income 1880–1913* (Oxford: Clarendon Press, 1920), 16–17. It was to these groups that Dixon instinctively turned as he created markets for his premium gramophone products.

22. For an assessment of these issues, see chapter 7.

23. "Monthly Epitomes to the Board of The Gramophone Company," August 1905 (board papers, EMI).

24. The five John O'Reilly records were "Believe Me, If All Those Endearing Young Charms" (X-42208), "The Minstrel Boy" (X-42209), "Hath Sorrow Thy Young Days Shaded" (X-42210), "Green Isle of Erin" (X-42310) and "Eileen Alannah" (X-42318). For further details of these recordings and a broader discussion of the numbering and other marks on Zonophone and other Gramophone Company records, see Frank Andrews and Ernie Bayly, *Numerical Listing of Zonophone Records* (Wells-Next-the-Sea, Norfolk: City of London Phonograph and Gramophone Society Ltd, 1999).

25. For a list of names and pseudonyms, see Sydney W. Dixon to Hanover Factory, 28 March 1907 (Australian branch file 1907, EMI).

26. For a complete listing and introduction to Zonophone records, see Andrews and Bayly, *Numerical Listing of Zonophone Records*.

27. "Monthly Epitomes to the Board of The Gramophone Company," May 1907 (board papers, EMI).

28. "Monthly Epitomes to the Board of The Gramophone Company," January 1908 (board papers, EMI).

29. "Monthly Epitomes to the Board of The Gramophone Company," January 1905 (board papers, EMI).

30. "Monthly Epitomes to the Board of The Gramophone Company," June 1908 (board papers, EMI).

31. "Monthly Epitomes to the Board of The Gramophone Company," October 1905 (board papers, EMI).

32. For a description of the pressures that brought about the star system in the film industry, see Rachael Low, *The History of the British Film 1906–1914* (London: Allen & Unwin, 1948), 2:124–28.

33. Low, *The History of the British Film*.

34. "Monthly Epitomes to the Board of The Gramophone Company," May 1906 (board papers, EMI).

35. "Monthly Epitomes to the Board of The Gramophone Company," April 1912 (board papers, EMI).

36. "Monthly Epitomes to the Board of The Gramophone Company," May 1908 (board papers, EMI).

37. "Twin Report: Epitomes," October 1908 (board papers, EMI).

38. Sydney W. Dixon to Theodore Birnbaum, 19 June 1908 (The Twin file, EMI).

39. The initial release of sixty-six British Zonophone-Twin titles was made up of couplings from previously available Zonophone single-sided discs. Furthermore, if each The Twin sale is counted as a double and the totals added to Zonophone sales for 1908, 1909 and 1910, then they are comparable to previous annual sales of single-sided Zonophone records. I am grateful to Frank Andrews for pointing out this important statistic.

40. For competitor reaction to The Cinch, see letter by J. E. Hough, "The Wreckers," *Talking Machine News* 10, no. 6 (October 1913): 305. See also Dixon's reports in "Epitomes," September 1913 to June 1914 (board papers, EMI). For an account and listing of The Cinch records, see Arthur Badrock and Frank Andrews, *The Cinch Record* (Wells-Next-the-Sea, Norfolk, City of London Phonograph and Gramophone Society Ltd, 2000).

41. See chapters 5 and 6 for an explanation of this failure.

42. "Monthly Epitomes to the Board of The Gramophone Company," November 1908 (board papers, EMI).

43. "Monthly Epitomes to the Board of The Gramophone Company," November 1908 (board papers, EMI).

44. See yearly comparative results, 1908 to 1909 and 1912 to 1913 (board papers, EMI).

45. "Annual Report 1910–1911" (meetings file, EMI).

46. Cyril C. Freer, *The Inner Side of Advertising* (London: Library Press, 1924), 205.

47. Cited in Daniel Pope, *The Making of Modern Advertising* (New York: Basic Books, 1983), 45, Table 2.5. See also, T. R. Nevett, *Advertising in Britain* (London: Heinemann, 1982), 71–74, and B. W. G. Alford, *W. D. and H. O. Wills* (London: Methuen, 1973), 127.

48. "Monthly Epitomes to the Board of The Gramophone Company," April 1904 (board papers, EMI).

49. Sydney W. Dixon to N. Rodkinson, 3 July 1902 (Russian papers, EMI).

50. For rates, see T. B. Browne, *The Advertisers' ABC* (London, 1900–1914); full front-page *Daily Telegraph* advertisements cost £200, whilst full-page insertions in *Punch* cost £60; for a full page facing the editorial in the *Illustrated London News*, £100, and in the *Strand Magazine*, £50.

51. See 1903 agreement between The Gramophone Company and Pearson's (Hunting and Dixon Advertising Agency file, legal files, EMI).

52. See Turner Morton, "The Art of Advertising," *Pearson's Magazine* (November 1905): 488–89.

53. For more on this, see chapter 7.

54. "Monthly Epitomes to the Board of The Gramophone Company," June 1904 (board papers, EMI).

55. "Theodore Birnbaum to Eldridge Reeves Johnson," 3 November 1904 (Victor papers, EMI).

56. "Monthly Epitomes to the Board of The Gramophone Company," March 1907 (board papers, EMI).

57. "Monthly Epitomes to the Board of The Gramophone Company," July 1907 (board papers, EMI).

58. "Monthly Epitomes to the Board of The Gramophone Company," July 1907 (board papers, EMI).

59. Although no circulation figures survive, in June 1907 *Talking Machine News* claimed 2,000 colonial and foreign subscribers and, in November 1920, a mailing list of 10,000.

60. See "Board Minutes," November 1911 (board papers, EMI).

61. "Monthly Epitomes to the Board of The Gramophone Company," April 1913 (board papers, EMI).

62. Cyril Ehrlich, *The Piano: A History* (London: Dent, 1976), 157.

63. *Law on Copyright Committee Report 1909*, Cmd 4976 (London: HMSO, 1909).

64. "Evidence of Mr E. Goodman," *Law on Copyright Committee 1909*, 215.

65. Cited in "Appendix of Evidence," *Law on Copyright Committee 1909*, 250–55.

66. "Prominent Dealers of Today," *Talking Machine News* 5, no. 9 (February 1908): 762–63.

67. For more on this business, see chapter 4. See also "Winding Up Resolution," *Talking Machine News* 3, no. 10 (March 1906): 155, and Michael Kinnear, *Nicole Record* (Victoria, Australia: Kinnear).

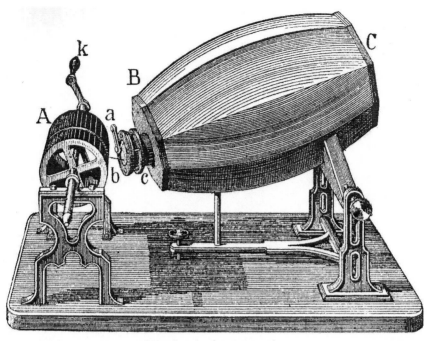

Leon Scott's phonautograph.

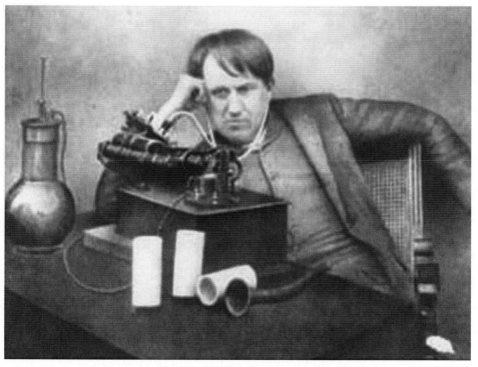

Thomas Edison listening to his perfected phonograph in 1888.

The first British demonstration of Edison's tinfoil phonograph by post office engineer W. H. Preece in February 1878.

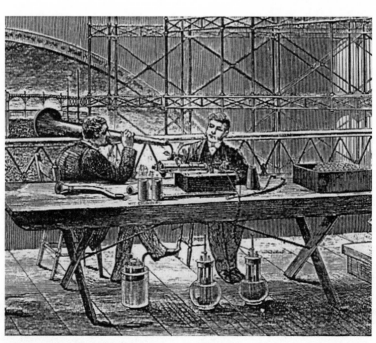

Edison's British agent Colonel George E. Gouraud and J. Lewis Young recording parts of the Handel Festival on a perfected phonograph at the Crystal Palace in July 1888.

Colonel Gouraud and his family making records at their London home, "Little Menlo," in 1888. J. Lewis Young is on the balcony taking the record.

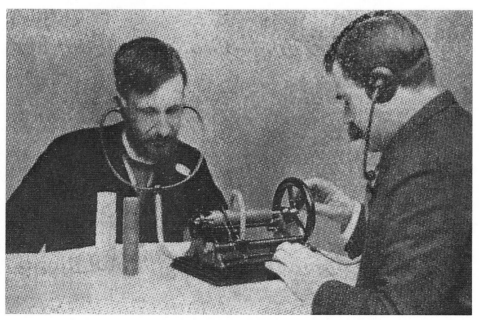

Inventor Charles Sumner Tainter listening to the Graphophone in 1887.

Engineer Henry Edmunds witnessed the first demonstrations of the tinfoil phonograph in 1877. He later became British licencee of Graphophone technology.

To make multiple copies of cylinder records in the absence of a duplicating process, artists during the 1890s had to pour their art into the horns of a cluster of machines.

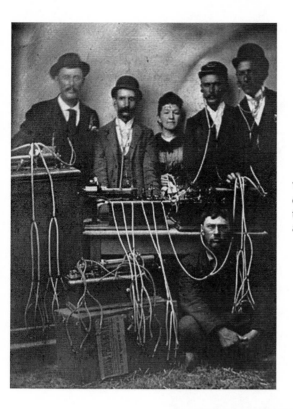

Very poor sound levels were achieved on early cylinder records and they had to be listened to via tubes resembling a physician's stethoscope.

Emile Berliner, inventor of the gramophone.

Founding president of the Victor Talking Machine Company, Eldridge Reeves Johnson was also an inventor, engineer and businessman.

William Barry Owen came to London in July 1897 as Berliner's agent. He became the founding head of The Gramophone Company Ltd.

NOTICE.

"GRAMOPHONES."

Edison-Bell Consolidated Phonograph Company,
LIMITED.

It having come to the knowledge of the EDISON-BELL CONSOLIDATED PHONOGRAPH COMPANY, LIMITED, that instruments known as GRAMOPHONES are being made in this country, and imported from the United States of America and elsewhere, and sold in this country in contravention of the Patent Rights owned by this Company, NOTICE IS HEREBY GIVEN that the Company has already COMMENCED PROCEEDINGS AGAINST PERSONS who are MAKING and IMPORTING and selling "GRAMOPHONES," and will take immediate proceedings against all other persons who may be infringing its Patent Rights. All persons owning, selling, or purchasing GRAMOPHONES are liable to be proceeded against for an injunction, damages, costs, and an order for delivery up of the infringing articles. The Company has no desire to treat innocent infringers in any harsh manner, and is prepared in cases where it is proved to its satisfaction that the machines have been innocently acquired to license the owner of the same to continue to use the machine on payment of a Royalty, and upon giving an undertaking to commit no further infringement.

All communications should be directed to the EDISON-BELL CONSOLIDATED PHONOGRAPH COMPANY, LIMITED, 39, Charing Cross Road, London, W.C., from whom may be obtained Price List and all information regarding the latest types of Phonographs.

In 1899 Edison Bell tried to see off competition from The Gramophone Company by starting an action for patent infringement. This newspaper advertisement was intended to frighten dealers into abandoning disc products; it failed.

Theodore Birnbaum was an early associate of William Barry Owen. He became manager of the Central European branches of The Gramophone Company Ltd and, in 1903, Owen's successor. He left the industry in 1908.

Alfred Clark came to Europe in 1899 as head of the French branch of The Gramophone Company. In 1908 he became managing director of the concern and chairman in 1930. In 1931 he became founding chairman of Electric and Musical Industries Ltd (EMI Ltd).

Francis Barraud RA painting a copy of "His Master's Voice," the work that made him famous and created one of the world's iconic trademarks.

Recording engineer William Sinkler Darby and Gramophone Company executive Theodore Birnbaum play with a "Nipper" lookalike in a still from a short advertising film.

In 1898 Fred Gaisberg created the first European disc recording studio in a basement of The Gramophone Company's offices in Maiden Lane, London.

Pressing disc records for The Gramophone Company in Germany around 1899.

The Gramophone Company's first ever meeting of all branch managers occurred in early 1914. It was intended to signal what Alfred Clark hoped would be a rapid expansion of the business; but the First World War intervened.

Washington, DC-born William Sinkler Darby was one of the best Berliner-trained recording engineers in the business. He worked for Berliner, The Gramophone Company and Brunswick.

The brothers Fred and Will Gaisberg were doyens of the recording studio. Fred recorded all the great artists active in the first half of the 20th century as either engineer or impresario.

Actor, businessman, journalist, recording artist and engineer Russell Hunting was a key industry pioneer on both sides of the Atlantic.

In the cramped conditions of the Columbia studio, conductor Sir Henry Wood and orchestra making records around 1914.

American businessman Frederick Marion Prescott was a British and European record industry pioneer. He organised International Zonophone GmbH and created International Talking Machine GmbH with its Odeon, Favorite and other labels.

The self-styled "father of the British trade," James Edward Hough was a patent infringer in the 1890s, then general manager of Edison Bell, which he subsequently bought out of bankruptcy as J. E. Hough Ltd.

National Phonograph Co. Ltd headquarters, Clerkenwell Road, London, 1903.

The New **Edison**
Bell "POPULAR"
Phonograph **RECORDS**

Made in London at the rate of

2,500,000
Per Annum.

LOUD, CLEAR, and DISTINCT.
Over 2,000 Selections.

1/- THE POPULAR PRICE, **1/-**
ONE SHILLING.
Sample Post Free 1s. 1d.

HEAR AT YOUR OWN HOME
GOOD SINGERS.
GOOD BANDS.
GOOD SOLOS,
AND GENERAL SELECTIONS.

They FIT ALL KINDS OF PHONOGRAPHS, Even the Cheapest.

Send for our Complete Catalogue, or Call and Hear them at
The EDISON BELL CONSOLIDATED PHONOGRAPH Co., Ld.,
39, Charing Cross-road, London, W.C. ;
20, Cheapside, E.C.; 61, High-st., Manchester; West Nile-st., Glasgow.
Or at our Agencies in every town in the Kingdom.

Opening shots in the trade war between Edison Bell and National Phonograph Co Ltd: Edison Bell *Daily Mail* front page advertisement 23 September 1903.

To Factors, Dealers, and Users
Phonographs, Records, and Accessories.

CAUTION!

THE ONLY GENUINE AND BONA-FIDE

EDISON

PHONOGRAPHS AND

EDISON RECORDS

have the following
Registered Trade Mark thereon:—

Thomas A Edison

The autograph signature of the inventor and
originator of the Phonograph.

WARNING!

Information concerning the selling of Records or Phonographs as
Edison Records or **Edison** Phonographs
which do not bear the above Registered Trade Mark, or as to any
misuse of the name "**Edison**," should be sent in confidence
to Mr. G. CROYDON MARKS, 18, Southampton-buildings,
Chancery-lane, London.

National Phonograph Co. Ltd responded in the same newspaper three days later.

Record industry entrepreneur Sterling was the British general manager of Columbia who bought up and integrated the post-1918 international record industry. He went on to become founding managing director of EMI Ltd. He was knighted in 1937.

GOD SAVE THE KING.

In recognition of the Peace just concluded, we announce the following special records. *Suitable for all Graphophones and Phonographs. Made in "P" and "G" styles only.*

London Military Band.

200604 **Field Call Galop,** introducing the Bugle Calls used in South Africa.

200605 **Patrol of the Boers,** introducing their National Hymn.

200606 **The Warriors' Return,** as played for the return of the troops from South Africa.

200607 **When the Boys Come Home Once More.** A welcome to the fighting heroes.

200442 **Rose, Shamrock and Thistle.** Sousa's Patrol founded on Melodies of the British Empire.

200596 **New Colonial March.**

200597 **Our Favourite Regiment March.**

200598 **Rule Britannia** and God Save the King.

Gilmore's Band.

1603 **God Save the King.** This record can be furnished in the XP (high speed, extra loud) variety. Price **2/-** each.

"P" Records 1/6 each. "G" Records 5/- each.

Postage extra—3d. each for "P" Records.
6d. each for "G" Records.

Columbia Phonograph Company Gen'l,

122, OXFORD STREET, LONDON, W.

1902 Columbia record supplement issued to mark the peace treaty ending the Anglo-Boer War.

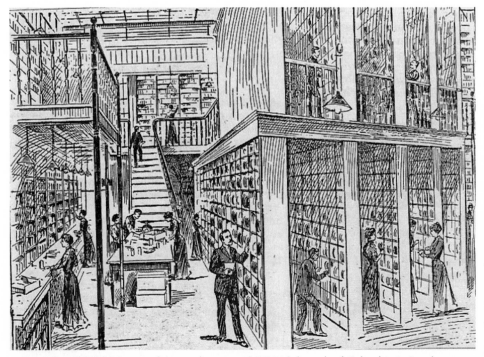

A fanciful 1903 image of the stockroom at the British branch of Columbia in London.

Barnett Samuel and Sons Ltd was a London-based wholesaler. This 1904 trade advertisement shows the range of talking machines and records it stocked.

Talking machines and records often had to compete with bicycles, sports and gardening equipment and household appliances in pre-1914 British shops.

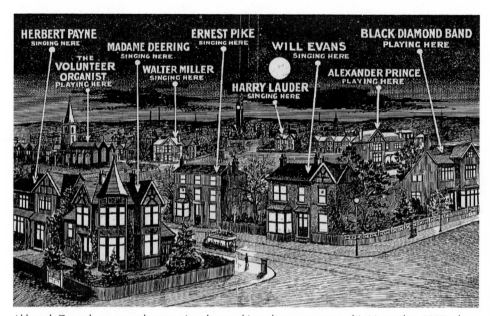

Although Zonophone records were aimed at working-class consumers, this November 1907 advertisement portrays them as staples in the homes of wealthy middle-class patrons.

The wartime ban on German goods provided opportunities for British manufacturers to enter the talking machine trade.

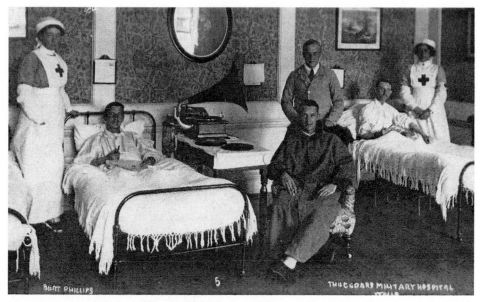

New wartime markets for talking machines and records opened up, with military hospitals providing many new consumers.

The great Victorian soprano Adelina Patti was one of the first established performers to make records.

Enrico Caruso was the greatest of all Italian tenors. He made his first recordings for Fred Gaisberg in 1902.

Another established performer, the great Australian diva Dame Nellie Melba, made her first records in 1904. They sold for £1.1s each and bore a unique mauve label and her signature in gold.

British contralto Dame Clara Butt was a mainstay of the Columbia record catalogue for decades.

John McCormack made his first records at age twenty in 1904 and went on to enjoy an unparalleled international career as an operatic tenor, recitalist and record star.

In 1917 the Original Dixieland Jazz Band became the first jazz ensemble to make records. They proved a sensation both in the United States and on a 1919 British tour, during which they made a series of recordings for Columbia.

Led by Debroy Somers, the Savoy Orpheans were best-selling HMV artists in the early to mid-1920s.

Impresario, musician and dance band leader Jack Hylton was the best-selling of all recording artists of the later 1920s, in fact until the Beatles in the 1960s.

Messages to the Boys and
Girls of the British Empire
FROM
THEIR MAJESTIES THE KING AND QUEEN
RECORDED AT BUCKINGHAM PALACE
(See page 1.)

"His Master's Voice"
RECORDS

Supplementary List
JUNE, 1923

Before the advent of radio the medium of records provided the king and queen with the only method of speaking directly to their British and Imperial subjects. They made their recording debut with a message to the children of the Empire made to mark Empire Day 1923.

Articistically creative and imaginative supplements were used to sell records in the 1920s.

Christmas has always been a peak-selling period for records, even in the depths of the Great Depression.

7

THE ART AND BUSINESS OF
RECORD MAKING: 1903–1914

"Down at the Old Bull and Bush"

To have to stand with one's face in close proximity to a couple of fierce and greedy looking horns and in a calm and cold blooded fashion to shout the most hilarious and mirthful song (or patter) in a voice more in keeping with a gentleman who sells coals, than a highly respectable and harmless humorist, is an experience of a quaint and unusual nature.

—W. H. Berry,[1] 1903

The gramophone of today, I find, is such an improved instrument for recording the human voice that my hitherto objection to allow the thousands who cannot hear me sing personally to listen to the reproduction of my voice through the instrumentality of your gramophone is now quite removed, and the records you have lately made for me I think are natural reproductions of my voice.

—Adelina Patti,[2] 1905

By the outbreak of war in August 1914 playing records had become established as a leisure activity in the home, with anything up to 40 per cent of British households owning some kind of talking machine and a collection of records. The industry underpinning all this was dominated by British and German manufacturers. These operated in rapidly rising markets, with 1913 sales standing at around thirteen million records and around half a million machines. Such was their reach that by 1914 this industry could claim to have created recorded culture as a new and important art form. It was a relatively cheap innovation and readily accessible by consumers via retail outlets in most British towns and cities. Furthermore, by 1914 record companies had

179

created substantial catalogues of recorded music made by all kinds of performing artists, which were added to with monthly supplements listing new releases. These ranged from the most up-to-date popular songs and melodies of the moment to the sounds of the greatest classically trained performers.

This chapter explores the art of record making as it developed in the years before 1914. For it was during this period that artists such as the Italian tenor Enrico Caruso, the Australian soprano Nellie Melba and Polish pianist Ignacy Jan Paderewski made substantial royalty-based fortunes from the worldwide sale of their records. In the case of Caruso, annual earnings by the end of the war included guaranteed yearly advances of $100,000, plus royalty payments.[3] Furthermore, the records they made spread their art throughout the world, giving record companies a new and important role in the growing popularisation and diffusion of the performing arts.

★   ★   ★

From its earliest days there had been speculation on the utility of sound recording as a vehicle for preserving and spreading musical culture and the art of performing artists. For example, during the course of his 1888 Franklin Institute address *The gramophone: etching the human voice*, inventor Emile Berliner asserted, "Prominent singers, speakers, or performers, may derive an income from royalties on the sale of their phonautograms, and valuable plates may be printed and registered to protect against unauthorised publication. Collections of phonautograms may become very valuable, and whole evenings will be spent at home going through a long list of interesting performances."[4] Although Emile Berliner had a vision as to the future utility of his invention it did not reach fruition for some time, because until the late 1890s the technology remained primitive and no serious performer was prepared to make records. Yet by 1914 the situation was transformed, with few performing artists, great or otherwise, ignoring the blandishments of the recording horn. This was due to important developments in disc recording achieved by the American engineer, inventor and record manufacturer Eldridge Johnson and others.[5] Johnson's work, especially the adoption of wax as the recording medium, dramatically improved the sound quality. It also permitted disc size to increase from 7 to 10 inches in 1900 and to 12 inches in 1903, the impact of which was to increase the maximum playing time to four and a half minutes. This remained the industry standard until the 1940s, when developments in magnetic tape and long-playing records were introduced.[6] To meet this rigid time limit, longer musical scores were either cut to this length or broken into four-and-a-half minute blocks and recorded as multidisc sets. This irksome limitation made little difference to a ballad, song, aria, short musical piece or comic song, which could usually be fitted on a single 10- or 12-inch disc. However, the ambitions of some record companies went beyond this and several made multidisc recordings of relatively complete works of symphonic music and operas. These recordings reveal not just the highly restricted sound quality but also cuts and mutilations to the original score.[7]

★　★　★

From the earliest days record companies enticed performing artists into their primitive studios to pour something of their art on to records. However, due to the inherent limitations of the mechanical recording process, particularly the frequency range and dynamics, large parts of the musical repertoire remained either unrecorded or at best very inadequately recorded. For example, in order to make the bass section audible on orchestral records, the lower strings were often replaced with trombones and tubas. Although this compromise brought orchestral records into the catalogue, they sounded rather like augmented brass or military bands. It proved easier to record individual instruments and before 1914 virtuoso violinists and pianists like Fritz Kreisler and Ignacy Jan Paderewski made successful recordings, which vied with the world's top singers for the attentions of those with the wealth to invest in this type of record. Although the art developed within fairly narrow parameters, record catalogues were filled with records of singers, brass and military bands, and certain solo instruments such as banjos, cornets, xylophones and bells because they recorded well and appealed to consumers. In these circumstances record companies offered a surprisingly wide range of music.

Curiously, although several British and American record companies maintained research facilities, recording technology changed very little between 1903 and 1914 and few major in-house innovations were noted. Such research as existed centred on widening the range and dynamics of the mechanical recording process, lengthening the duration of records and recording studios developments. David Bicknell, who started his record industry career in the mid-1920s as an assistant to Fred Gaisberg, claimed that acceptable recordings of orchestral music only entered record catalogues after 1910, and were the result of empirical work with recording equipment and the placing of instruments in the studio.[8]

Mechanical recording required major concessions from performers. For instance, in the absence of volume control, singers had to draw back from the recording horn on high notes and move closer on low notes. The pioneer recording artist Peter Dawson[9] described how he first encountered this strange world during a 1903 Edison Bell voice test and of a run-in he had with the ubiquitous American recording engineer Russell Hunting:

> I shall never forget my first sight of the little funnel which I had to stand in front of, and sing into, and the shock of feeling a hand on my shoulder during the singing of my song, which pushed me closer or farther away from the funnel as the song proceeded. . . . I was quite satisfied. But whatever I thought, the recording chief, an American named Russell Hunting, thought otherwise. His verdict . . . was, "His voice is too powerful, and that makes it very difficult to record." Fortunately his word was not the final one.

Dawson soon got used to recording studio conditions and became one of the most recorded singers active in the first half of the twentieth century. He also described the mechanical process of recording: "In those days one of the most important secrets of making a good evenly balanced record was the weaving in and out from the mouth of the funnel. You had to think ahead of your tone emission to know when to move forward and when to move away."[10]

Recording required artists to think in a quite different way, as comic singer W. H. Berry noted, "such things as gestures and facial contortions are of course useless. They are completely wasted on the unimpressionable trumpet, although, of course they may be employed for the amusement of the presiding genius, who is 'taking' the record, or even for the benefit of the pianist."[11] Pianist Gerald Moore also left an account of the process, writing of his first recording session in 1921 at The Gramophone Company's studios:

> The recording room was set in the uttermost interior of the building, completely shut off from daylight and outside noise. It was purely utilitarian. . . . The walls . . . were of unpolished deal, the floor of hardwood and, in the absence of any absorbent sound, my footsteps thundered on the bare boards. . . . I ran my fingers over the keys of the pianoforte and was appalled at the metallic harshness of its tone. . . . This brittle sound was not to be attributed entirely to the acoustics of the chamber, for I found . . . that the piano . . . had been rendered as percussive as possible by filing down the felts on the hammers.[12]

Making records in those prewar days was also remembered by British recording engineer Arthur Clarke, who began his career at The Gramophone Company in 1908:

We used to resort to many devices for obtaining satisfactory records. All the artists had to huddle round the horn and Stroh violins [which had a horn in place of the belly] were used in symphony orchestras because they projected the sound better than ordinary instruments. Besides having rehearsals for timing the length of the pieces, we also had to rehearse a series of contortions and gymnastics in order that the artists should be in front of the horn at the proper time. Sometimes artists were very zealous in trying to get unusual effects in the records. When a Guards Band was making some records one morning the bright young lieutenant who was conducting them thought he would provide a novel effect by firing a blank from his revolver down the horn. The effect was certainly unusual, for it blew my best recording diaphragm to bits.[13]

In the cramped conditions of recording studios, engineers and musical directors needed all the skills they could muster to keep often nervous artists calm, as noted in a 1904 interview with the Gaisberg brothers:

Many artists who are perfectly at their ease on the concert platform seem to lose their accustomed confidence before the recording horn. No doubt they realise that the tiniest little fault will be permanently registered and reproduced before the mighty audience of the talking machine public not of today but of days to come. With the great artist the slightest mistake in breathing or phrasing, although not noticeable to the untrained ear, will entail the repetition of the song until perfection be attained, and the "master" accepted.[14]

Enticing great performers into the recording studio was only the start; once there studio professionals had to obtain the best results. To some, like Fred Gaisberg, recording was regarded as akin to taking a photograph, providing a snapshot of a performer's art.[15] The Victor musical director Emilio de Gogorza's account of the first recordings made by the French bass Pol Plançon is illuminating. He was described as being very nervous, repeating over and over, "At my age this is not dignified and I am certain my voice will not record." At the conclusion of what de Gogorza described as a recording *séance*, the singer vowed he would never record again, but he did. Listening to his records for the first time Plançon asserted that it was not his voice and that some mistake had been made, though he later admitted without irony, "Yes, it is my execution, for no one could do what that record shows but myself."[16]

Even at its best the mechanical process of recording had limitations, as music critic and writer J. B. Steane has written,

The loss [of tone, intonation and artistic freedom] was greater than any gain, however for a voice remarkable for its purity of tone, as Melba's was, would be reduced to something pipelike when the harmonics were cut. Tenors generally came off best; the characteristic tenor's sound is bright-edged, and the voice is well in the middle of the gramophone's frequency range.[17]

Gaisberg summed up these limitations, "The top frequencies were triple high C, 2,088 vibrations per second [Hertz], and the low remained at E, 164 vibrations per second [Hertz]. Voices and instruments, especially stringed instruments, were confined rigidly within these boundaries."[18]

For the most important performing artists their early-twentieth-century change in attitude towards record making was influenced by two quite different though equally critical reasons. One was the offer of potentially lucrative royalty-based contracts, complete with substantial advances and the possibility of long-term annuity incomes. Another was the appeal to artistic vanity, as through their records artists could gain not only worldwide fame but also, for the first time in history, a form of artistic immortality.

The transition from disdain and dismissal to acceptance was not easy. Gaisberg recalled that in the years immediately after his arrival in Britain in 1898, "Our recorded repertoire consisted only of ballads, comic songs, and band records. When we approached the greatest artists, they just laughed at us and replied that the gramophone was just a toy."[19] To overcome this hostility, record companies used the improved recording technology and employed musical directors. These were usually well established and trusted musical figures; today they would be known as artist and repertoire managers. The Gramophone Company's first musical director was the composer, conductor and accompanist Landon (later Sir Landon) Ronald.[20] An admiring Gaisberg wrote of him, "In Landon Ronald we saw the agent who could bring us into contact with those unapproachable."[21] In his memoirs, Landon Ronald saw his primary task as overcoming "the tremendous prejudice that existed in the minds of all artists against what was considered by them an outrage on their art."[22] Although Landon Ronald was the best-known music director he was by no means the only one. Columbia employed the composer Albert W. Ketèlbey, who often doubled as house conductor for recordings ranging from operatic arias to popular tunes and for his own compositions.

Despite these appeals established performers initially resisted the blandishments of record companies, but the rising generation had fewer reservations. Among these was the Italian tenor Enrico Caruso, who began his stunning recording career in 1902 with a series of records made in Italy for The Gramophone Company.[23] Writing three years after the singer's death

in 1921, the writer and adventurer Compton (later Sir Compton) Mackenzie, said of him, "If you are anxious to test the measure of Caruso's vitality,
consider what he meant to the gramophone. He made it what it is. He im-
pressed his personality through the medium of his recorded voice on kings
and peasants."[24] These comments fit neatly in with another aspect of that
first Caruso recording session, the role of records as chronicler of the performing arts. As it turned out, the 1902 Italian recording tour undertaken
by the Gaisberg brothers took on a Janus-like quality when they not only
recorded Caruso, the voice that looked forward into the twentieth century,
but also a voice representing what was by then a virtually dead tradition,
that of the castrati as personified by Alessandro Moreschi, the director of
the Sistine choir in the Vatican.

Because of the central position held by Enrico Caruso in the early record industry and in the wider artistic world during the first two decades of
the twentieth century, his attitude to the 240 recordings he made between
1902 and 1920, which music historian J. B. Steane described as: "the richest
legacy we have from those early days of the gramophone," is of great importance.[25] Although Caruso never wrote of his recordings, a biography by
his son contains an account of a 1919 Caruso recording session he witnessed
at The Victor Talking Machine Company studios at Camden, New Jersey:

> I was surprised that he was no more apprehensive than any clerk or
> plumber on his way to work. . . . When he did [talk], it was obvious that
> he was not trying to spare his voice. . . . Father recorded multiple takes of
> a group of Italian songs. . . . The sound that filled the studio was a marvel.
> . . . The volume and beauty of his voice were overwhelming. . . . It struck
> me that Father was not merely delivering a tune but was living each song.
> His face was animated, and he acted out the words as he would on the
> concert stage, so that I not only heard but I also *saw* the song.[26]

From this we can reasonably deduce that Caruso gave his full art to
record making, though that commitment needs perspective. When that session took place Caruso was the highest paid recording artist in the world,
with an annual guaranteed advance of $100,000, plus 10 per cent of retail
sales.[27] In addition to the artist, these recordings benefited the Victor and
Gramophone Companies. That said, as late as 1907 Eldridge Johnson could
write, "Signor Caruso believes that he is even of greater importance than
he really is. This is quite a common failing, of course, with all artists, but
where the artist is really of such great importance as Caruso, it makes the
matter somewhat difficult to handle."[28]

The extraordinary success of Caruso persuaded more established artists to make records and their commercial and artistic success provided The

Gramophone Company, the pre-1914 British market leader in this field, with the key to middle-class acceptance and respectability. The strategy also affected the artists, who began to see their records not just as a means of making money, but as a new and important way of communicating with their public; as the quote from the great Victorian soprano Adelina Patti at the start of this chapter shows. Furthermore, recording Patti was not just good advertising copy, she was paid an advance of £1,000 and received 4s per record sold. Within three years her records sold an impressive 10,403 copies in Britain alone. Overall the investment and dividends were hugely profitable for all concerned for, like the records made by the Italian tenor Francesco Tamagno in 1904, Patti's records sold at the premium price of £1.[29] It took just a few years for artists and record companies to recognise the manifold benefits of Celebrity records. On the one hand, artists gained new audiences and saw their art spread throughout the world, while on the other record companies gained kudos from the association, which was used to great effect in advertising. This can be best illustrated by the case of Sir Edward Elgar, who made his first records as a conductor of his own works in 1914. As Gaisberg observed, "Elgar's association with my company before 1925 was chiefly decorative, his name carrying the prestige of England's greatest composer."[30]

The unit sales and financial return on Celebrity records was slight. In the years 1908 to 1913 they averaged no more than 3 per cent of total Gramophone Company record sales.[31] In 1904 the managing director of The Gramophone Company, Theodore Birnbaum, wrote, "Although I consider that Celebrity Records are indispensable for advertising purposes, as a profit maker the percentage of celebrity sales is so small, compared with the aggregate sales, that the price at which they are sold is quite a minor consideration, provided, of course, that they are not sold at a loss." Notwithstanding his jaundiced view, Birnbaum used family connections to gain the services of such artists. His father-in-law was Sir George Lewis, the lawyer to King Edward VII, the head of a major civil and criminal practice legal and advisor of many great performers The Gramophone Company wished to record. It was, for example, through the agency of Lewis that The Gramophone Company made the records of his client Adelina Patti. Furthermore, these same family connections resulted in the first recordings of Sir George Henschel, the Anglo-German singer and conductor, as Birnbaum wrote in 1906, "Through my Mother-in-law, I learn that George Henschel, who is a very intimate friend of the family, is very anxious to make a few records for private use."[32]

Artists from the world of popular culture had fewer misgivings about record making, and all major companies competed for popular performers singing their current hits. As Sydney Dixon, British branch manager of The Gramophone Company, informed his head office in 1904, "The big sale of our records comes when they are brought out [*sic*], and the majority of records, except those by very celebrity artists, do not reach [sales of] more than 1,000, which is probably the life of the shell [the metal matrix]."[33] Nonetheless salesman Dixon told dealers in a 1905 circular, "Have you tried our Harry Lauder and Florrie Forde Records? They are enormous sellers here; in fact, the biggest sellers we have among comic records."[34] Unlike Celebrity label artists, who usually received royalty-based exclusive contracts, popular performers were usually paid session fees amounting to as little as £5.5s.0d or £10.10s.0d per record, and held on a nonexclusive basis. In 1904 Dixon had an annual budget of just £2,500 to pay for talent.[35]

Among the most popular prewar entertainers was the Scot, Harry (later Sir Harry) Lauder. He recalled his earliest experiences with recording in his memoirs, "It was no unusual thing for me to go to the recording office and make half a dozen records in a day for a pound a time or six songs for a fiver."[36] Bitter experience taught him to be suspicious of music hall managers and others he made contracts with. As a consequence he had a negative attitude towards record making, due to the meagre fees generated by the long-term contracts he signed before becoming internationally famous. Certainly they were meagre when compared to fees earned by classically trained performers.[37] To make matters worse one of his early contracts was with the British branch of Pathé Frères. In 1905 Pathé Frères's British manager Jellings Blow noted: "The conviction grows on me more that the future depends on the supply of artistic reproductions by vocalists of unquestioned repute as opposed to records by indifferently qualified artists."[38] That may have been the sentiment, but within a year Pathé Frères abandoned its existing British business only to start trading in its own right as a disc manufacturer. By this means it repudiated the contracts of Lauder and all other artists. The new business reissued Lauder's old recordings, which had been transferred from cylinder to its new discs.[39] In 1907, Lauder signed a five-year cylinder record contract with National Phonograph Company Ltd. The contract stipulated Lauder visit its London recording studio six times, for an annual fee of £500. A supplementary agreement made in 1909 to cover making four-minute Amberol cylinder recordings increased his annual fee to £600.[40]

Lauder was clearly a difficult artist to deal with, as Alfred Wagner, British manager of National Phonograph Company Ltd, recalled:

> As I saw him then in our Recording Rooms he was a short squat figure with an expressionless face and wearing glasses with the thickest lenses I had ever seen. He was shabbily dressed but arrived in a Rolls Royce car although the chauffeur—his own brother—wore no collar or tie.
>
> Lauder was not altogether popular with our recording staff. He insisted on singing only one verse and chorus of each song but this did not fill the two minute record of those days, he would bend close to the recording needle to watch the cut and when his song was ended, leaving still a space uncut on the record, he would repeat "Och aye-mind I'm tellin' ye" many times until the space was filled.
>
> To ensure the co-operation of the "boys" of the recording staff he would promise to take care of them and before he left he would redeem his promise by presenting each one with a picture postcard of his photograph complete with autograph![41]

In 1904, the twenty-year-old Irish tenor John McCormack had a similar experience with his first Gramophone Company contract, which stipulated the making of twenty-five records at a rate of £1.1s.0d per song, plus a bonus of a Gramophone and two-dozen records.[42]

If making records were not enough of an ordeal for artists, another awaited in the form of the recording committee. All record companies had these committees which listened to and assessed new records (including test records by new artists) and passed them for release or rejected them. They also made decisions about release dates and signing new artists. These committees were made up of recording engineers, musical directors, sales and marketing personnel and sometimes senior management. The National Phonograph Company Ltd serial of recording committee minutes has survived and provides fascinating insights into the process. For example, the twenty-first meeting held on 4 April 1906 records that twelve two-minute cylinder records of comic ditties, songs, ballads and band records were heard. Each selection is listed and commented upon. For example:

3. *The Playwright* Will Edwards—passed for June supplement. A very humorous record, and was thought to be the very thing to have a big sale.
9. *Processional March from Henry VIII*, National Military Band—passed for June supplement. This selection was quite a hit with the Committee, and the Recording Department were well complimented on the Record.

Artist trials and test records were heard and brutally dealt with:

Alf Hurley, Irish Comedian, excellent brogue. Trial date.
Archie Anderson, baritone, fair. Thrown out.
Avondale Quartette, rotten. Thrown out.
David's Mixed Quartette, worse than Avondale. Thrown out.
Rooney, Irish tenor, no good. Thrown out.
Miss Clough, contralto, charming voice but would not make a good
    record.[43]

It was in these circumstances, with great speed (and despite technical restrictions) that the art of sound recording developed, so much so, that by the outbreak of the First World War practically all the great and popular performing artists active in Europe and the United States had committed their art to records. This acceptance is a testimony to men like Landon Ronald, Albert W. Ketèlbey, Fred Gaisberg and other studio professionals.

★   ★   ★

The important question of performers' attitudes towards their pre-1914 records can only be partly answered by reference to contemporary accounts, memoirs and other sources. Curious but noteworthy is the fact that, aside from Harry Lauder and Peter Dawson's valuable insights into the industry's prewar days, few artists ever bothered to leave behind impressions of their own recordings or record making experiences.[44] This omission, interesting in itself, might simply be a reflection of the ambivalence artists may have felt towards them. Alternatively it might reflect the fact that for most, record making was peripheral to their main artistic life, just a way of making money.

Those artists who bothered to talk about record making in their memoirs often dismissed it with a humorous story. Nellie Melba's memoirs provide a good example of this though, no matter how unintentionally, she concluded her remarks with a perceptive insight into the power of records,

One of the most curious features which the gramophone brought into my life was a succession of marriage proposals from people who had heard my records, but who had never even seen me. There was something almost uncanny in the idea of some man in the remote prairies sitting down in front of a little instrument, listening to the echo of my voice, feeling that he had found his ideal woman and writing to tell her so.[45]

In sharp contrast the comic singer W. H. Berry said of his records, "It was not until the Autumn of 1901 that I commenced singing into the Graphophones of the Columbia Phonograph Co. I need hardly say I have never regretted my debut as a record maker, as, not only does it keep a singer in constant practice, but also the wide circulation of his efforts is an excellent advertisement for a professional man."[46]

By 1914, the record industry provided some performing artists with a new and, for a few, lucrative ways of making a living, though these earnings were generated within a novel framework. Data held at the EMI Group Archive and the Edison National Historic Site indicates the development of new contractual forms. It was, for example, with the exception of stars like Harry Lauder, the practice of Edison's American recording studios to hire artists as cheaply as possible and on a sessional basis. However, conditions in Britain were quite different to those in America, as William E. Gilmore, the president of National Phonograph Company Inc, told Edison in a 1904 letter from London, "It is going to cost a great deal of money for artists as they are paid a great deal higher price here than with us."[47] Again, fees and annual retainers seem to have been the rule; The National Phonograph Company Ltd apparently never entered into a royalty-based contract with an artist.

After 1903 the British record industry quickly moved towards a system of exclusive contracts with well-known artists. In June 1905, James H. White, the London manager of National Phonograph Company Ltd told Gilmore:

> Columbia, Edison Bell and Pathé make a business of contracting [well-known] artists and we frequently receive letters from the trade reminding us of the fact that while we charge 1s 6d for our records we do not offer as high class of talent as some of the manufacturers whose records retail at 1s. . . . There is no doubt that there is a great demand for songs by popular music hall people and concert artists, and in a territory like Great Britain popular artists are known throughout the length and breadth of the land.[48]

Initially, rather in the manner of modern tabloid and broadsheet newspapers from the same ownership stable, contracts had a technology-specific definition of the term "exclusive." As the cylinder and disc trades were quite separate, artists could enjoy two mutually compatible exclusive contracts, one with a cylinder and the other with a disc company. For example, by 1907, Harry Lauder had two contracts, one with NPC exclusive for cylinder records and the other with The Gramophone Company exclusive for discs. Although these two exclusive contracts benefited Lauder, they caused headaches for the American affiliates of the British companies who had made these contracts. Frankly, this esoteric definition of the word "exclusive" was lost on them and during Lauder's 1909 tour of America National Phonograph Company Inc and Victor advertised Lauder's records as being exclusive. The result was an acrimonious correspondence involving both British companies and ended with the publication of clarifying notices in the American trade press. This unique correspondence also provides fascinating insights into the problems of drawing up international contracts in the days before instant communications.[49]

British record companies often paid nonroyalty artists retaining fees for "exclusivity," with an additional fee for each song recorded. Although a new source of income, such a system meant artists whose records enjoyed great popularity failed to get a fair share of the profits. One of these was the Australian-born music hall performer Florrie Forde (the stage name of Flora Barnett). Sydney Dixon of The Gramophone Company often cited her records as being amongst his company's British best sellers. During the period 1904 to 1913 she had several fee-based cylinder record contracts as well as a disc contract with The Gramophone Company. Her Sterling record contract generated "Down at the Old Bull and Bush," the song that gave this chapter its title. Her Gramophone Company contract stipulated an annual fee of £30, which had risen to £40 by 1913. In addition she received further fees of between £2.12s.6d and £3.12s.6d per recording made. In total, over the decade 1904 to 1913, these arrangements netted her a mere £1,133. Regrettably, as she was not a royalty artist there is no way of quantifying her record sales.[50] Another Australian-born music hall performer was Billy Williams (the stage name of Richard Banks), popularly known as "the man in the velvet suit." Between 1906 and his death in 1915 he was a prolific nonexclusive recording artist. He went from studio to studio around London making records of his latest hit songs for cash payments. His professionalism was such that he required little by way of rehearsal. As such he was very popular figure with recording engineers and musical accompanists alike. Despite the many versions of popular songs he made for different companies, he remained a prize artist whose records were aimed at the growing mass markets and his records continued to sell years after his untimely passing.[51]

In those prewar days, record companies recognised the advantage of employing singers with good recordable voices as session artists. One of these was Peter Dawson for whom, in those preradio days, record making provided a more important source of income than either concerts or other public performances.[52] He wrote of a period in 1912 when "we made several of the operas, and worked regularly for about ten weeks. I must have averaged 30 guineas [£31.10.0d] a week."[53] His services were so valuable that The Gramophone Company made him an exclusive fee-based contract performer. As Dawson was both a regular session artist and a classically trained singer his fees were higher than those of Florrie Ford. His prewar Gramophone Company contract shows he received £3.3s.0d for solos, and £1.1.0d for ensemble recordings. In 1912 this was increased to £5.5s.0d for solos, £4.4s.0d for duets and £3.3s.0d for ensembles. He also enjoyed the higher annual retaining fee of £100. Between 1910 and 1912, Dawson earned nearly £900 from his recording activities and during the five years 1913 to 1918, which included the war years, enjoyed total earnings in excess of £1,800.[54]

The difficulty of comparing fees and incomes between recording artists and those engaged in various similar professions is compounded by the fact that, with the exception of a few individuals whose income was generated solely from making gramophone records, most recording artists enjoyed a career and income from public performances. That said it has been possible to collate some data of parallel fees and incomes. Compared to the fees Peter Dawson, the highest-paid nonroyalty artist cited, the data in table 7.1 suggests recording fees provided performers with a good income, placing them on a par with many other medium-ranked entertainment professionals and for a few on a par with medical practitioners.

In 1898, soon after the first London disc-recording studio opened, Gramophone Company founder William Barry Owen made the first known royalty-based contract with Albert Chevalier, a leading British music hall performer. For ten songs he received an advance of £15 a song and a royalty payment of 1s per dozen records sold "payable till 10 years after his death."[55] After 1901, the select group of Gramophone Company Celebrity

Table 7.1.   Fees and Incomes of Comparable Professionals: Circa 1911

Orchestral fees per week: Leader £1.15s.0d, first violin and flute £1.13s.0d, cornet £1.11s.6d.

Singers at a concert or function outside London: £1.1s.0d to £3.3s.0d, musical sketch at piano £1.10s.6d to £5.5s.0d, plus expenses.

At-home or a reception at a London Society home: "popular turn" £10.10s.0d to £52.10s.0d.

Professional footballer: £2 to £3 per week in England and up to £6 in Scotland.

Songwriter: £2.10s.0d per thousand copies of sheet music sold for 6d and £5 per thousand sold for 1s each.

Popular writer: Copyright royalties averaging £250 per work.

Serial writers: £1.1s.0d per thousand words.

Medical practitioner: up to £1,000 per annum.

Source: Data compiled from George Edgar, ed., *Careers for Men, Women and Children* (London: Newnes, 1911–1912).

artist's received advances and royalties that provided a new relatively secure and very lucrative source of income. The first Celebrity records were made by The Gramophone Company in Russia during 1901 and 1902.[56] However, after 1907, The Victor Talking Machine Company increasingly dominated this market, though the British company had access to them via its licencing agreement.[57] Victor had an aggressive policy of signing topflight international performing artists active in the United States to the point that, by 1914, few great performers were missing from its (and The Gramophone Company's) international Celebrity catalogue.

The making of Celebrity records in Britain was dominated by The Gramophone Company, though Zonophone and Fonotipia were also important players. They were joined in 1904 by The Columbia Phonograph Company General who created their own US and European Celebrity catalogue. Like the existing Celebrity catalogues, those made by Columbia did not enjoy great sales, though they provided excellent advertising copy.[58] As part of his post-1910 reconstruction of the British Columbia business, sales director Louis Sterling secured the services of the Victorian singer Sir Charles Santley and the conductors Sir Henry Wood and Sir Thomas Beecham to his roster of exclusive celebrity artists. In 1914, Sterling scored a major coup in tempting the celebrated contralto Clara (later Dame Clara) Butt, away from The Gramophone Company. Thereafter till her death in 1936, Clara Butt remained a Columbia artist and her records graced its Celebrity catalogue.

Columbia, Victor and The Gramophone Company engaged in a fierce competition to sweep up great classical performers. This had the positive effect of ensuring the appearance of new artists and the latest music in celebrity listings. From its founding in 1904 the Italian record company Societa Italiana di Fonotipia, Milano with its Fonotipia label had an impressive celebrity list (which was distributed by Columbia in the US), although sales were poor, largely due to bad management. By 1914, following an important consolidation of much of the European record industry, Fonotipia and many other record labels had become part of the Carl Lindström AG group. Odeon was another of its labels, and it too had a celebrity catalogue under the Royalty label. Among those on its list were operatic singers Emmy Destinn, Frieda Hempel, Leo Slezak and Lilli Lehmann, supplemented by the recycling of the pre-1910 series of recordings made by John McCormack for International Talking Machine GmBH. In addition, this catalogue boasted pages of military and brass band extracts from the great operas together with an almost complete Act III of Richard Wagner's opera *Lohengrin* with Emmy Destinn and Rudolf Berger; this was spread across five double-sided records.[59]

Table 7.2 sets out Gramophone Company unit sales and royalties for the years 1906 to 1913 by five top Celebrity artists, all of whom were singers. Listing Gramophone Company royalty payments for sales across its territory, this table takes no account of payments made by the Victor Company for sales in the Americas. Taking Caruso as an example, his enormous popularity across the Americas, together with the higher incomes in the USA and Canada, suggests his Gramophone Company earnings could have accounted for as little as one-third of his total record earnings. If this is correct, then in the years before 1914 Caruso had an annual income from his records of about $100,000, easily making him the best paid recording artist at the time.

It is a matter of regret that British sales and royalty data for the decade after 1913 have not survived (though see also chapter 9). Thus table 7.2 presents a tantalising glimpse of the developing celebrity record star system. The contrast between record sales and royalty earnings is quite striking. Table 7.3 analyses the five artists' individual contracts and places earnings and perceived worth as individual artists into perspective.

Enrico Caruso's British earnings and contracts reflect the power of that unique artist. In contrast to unit sales of other celebrity artists those of Caruso and McCormack grew steadily (see table 7.2). In fact between 1907 and 1912 sales of Caruso's records doubled and between 1910 and 1913 McCormack's nearly doubled. This was due to various factors. First, to maintain a high profile and maximise earnings potential Caruso and McCormack made regular visits to the recording studio. As a result fresh releases of their records appeared each month. In contrast, the contracts of most other celebrity artists stipulated the making of blocks of records every few years. Second, the profiles of both artists were raised by their use in record advertisements. Third, compared to other artists both tenors recorded extremely well. Finally, both had become famous as operatic and concert performers and regularly made extensive international tours and therefore had a strong fan base.[60] The latter point and connection to record sales was noted in a 1904 letter from The Gramophone Company's German branch. Commenting on Caruso's German debut, it quoted a local newspaper, "Caruso who has become famous in other countries through his voice and his art and whose name has become a household word in Germany; through the Gramophone."[61] In a 1910 letter from The Gramophone Company's Italian agent there was further support, this time for McCormack sales, "It is hardly possible to believe that they [his records] are not sung by an Italian artist. . . . I consider his records to be fine first class stuff which will no doubt be much appreciated by the Italian public."[62]

Table 7.2. The Gramophone Company Ltd: Selection of Celebrity Singers, Non-American Record Unit Sales and Royalties Earned, 1906–1913

Year	1906	1907	1908	1909	1910	1911	1912	1913
Enrico Caruso								
Unit sales	11,450[a]	27,950	36,438	34,221	51,028	61,696	59,701	51,592
Royalties	£1,311	£3,300	£4,124	£3,957	£5,450	£6,331	£7,085	£6,099
	$6,555	$16,540	$20,620	$19,785	$27,250	$31,655	$35,425	$30,495
Feodore Chaliapine								
Unit sales	—	4,495	11,361	10,330	11,023	14,863	11,909	7,592
Royalties	—	£990	£2,244	£1,895	£1,638	£2,746	£2,142	£759
		$4,950	$11,220	$9,475	$8,190	$13,730	$10,710	$3,795
John McCormack								
Unit sales	—	—	—	—	11,863	15,367	16,396	19,847
Royalties	—	—	—	—	£586	£401	£346	£436
	—	—	—	—	$2,930	$2,005	$1,730	$2,180
Nellie Melba[a]								
Unit sales	30,772	22,508	18,481	15,215	11,713	11,324	7,029	8,111
Royalties	£6,060	£3,786	£2,302	£1,899	£1,821	£1,830	£1,110	£1,013
	$30,300	$18,930	$11,510	$9,495	$9,105	$9,150	$5,550	$5,065
Luisa Tetrazzini								
Unit sales	—	—	25,242	11,037	7,228	7,382	6,778	5,509
Royalties	—	—	£6,038	£3,404	£3,333	£2,611	£725	£268
	—	—	$30,190	$17,020	$16,665	$13,055	$3,625	$1,340

Source: Data compiled from royalty sheets and artists files, EMI.

[a]Enrico Caruso's 1906 data half year only. Between 1902 and 1906, Caruso made 36 records for The Gramophone Company and Victor, for which he received flat fee payments. Unfortunately firm unit sales data for these recordings have not survived. There is, however, some evidence of pre-1906 unit sales in the EMI Caruso artist file, which cites a total of 46,727 Caruso records being pressed at the Hanover record factory between July 1903 and June 1905. The premium price of Melba's records was reduced in 1907 to bring them into line with other celebrity artists.

Table 7.3. The Gramophone Company Ltd: Celebrity Artist Contracts, 1906–1913

Date	Company	Term	Advance	Royalty	Number of Records
Enrico Caruso					
1904	Victor	5 years	$10,000 [£2,000]	None	10 records
1906	Victor	5 years	$2,000 [£400] per record	50¢ 12" 25¢ 10"	25 min
1909	Victor	25 years	$4,000 [£800] per record	as 1906	10 per year
Feodore Chaliapine					
1907	Gramophone	5 year	$3,000 [$15,000]	4s [20p $1]	15 records
1911	Gramophone	Unspecified	£1,500 [$7,500]	4s [20p $1] Russian 2s [10p $0.50] foreign	10 records
John McCormack					
1910	Victor	5 years	$500 [£100] opera	30¢ 12", 20¢ 10"	40 records
1912	Gramophone	3 years	$300 [£60] ballad	15¢ 12", 10¢ 10"	
1913	Victor	25 years	$500 [£100] flat fee for ensembles as above	10% retail Solos 5% retail Trios 3.3% Quartets 2%	
Nellie Melba					
1904	Gramophone	Unspecified	None	5s [25p $1.25] 12" 3s [15p $0.75] 10"	15 records
1907	Victor	Unspecified	£1,000 [$5,000]	1907 reduced to 3s [15p $0.75] Vic 4s [20p $1] 12" 3s [15p $0.75] 10" Victor 50¢ [10p] Gramo 2s.6d [12.5p $0.62]	
Luisa Tetrazzini					
1907	Gramophone	3 years	$2,000 [£400] per record	4s [20p $1] first 1,000 then 1s.7d [8p $0.20]	12 records
1910	Gramophone	Unspecified	£1,000 [$5,000]	2s [10p $0.25]	12 records
1914	Gram-Victor	5 years	£6,000 [$30,000]	2s [10p $0.25]	

Source: Between 1918 and 1925, these artists signed new contracts in the following terms: Caruso, 1919–1934 (Victor); 40 records over 10 years with a guarantee of $100,000 [£20,000] per annum and a royalty of 10 per cent of retail selling price payable in perpetuity. Chaliapine, 1921–1924 (Gramophone); £1,500 [$7,500] advance for six records and a royalty of 10 per cent of the retail selling price and continued so long as artist remained exclusive; royalties to heirs and executors. 1923–1929 (Gramophone): Guarantee £3,000 [$15,000] per annum with a royalty of 10 per cent of retail selling price. McCormack, 1919–1938 (Victor); 90 records to 1938 with an advance of $1,500 [£300] per record making the total advance $135,000 [£27,000] and a royalty of 10 per cent Victor list price, with duets etc 10¢ 10" and 15¢ 12". Melba, 1919–1924 (Gramophone); advance of £5,000 [$25,000] payable at £1,000 [$5,000] per annum and 10 per cent of retail-selling price. Tetrazzini, 1919–1922 (Gramophone); advance £945 [$4,725] over three years, with a royalty of 10 per cent of the retail selling price (artist files). Tetrazzini, 1922–1926 (Gramophone): advance £1,000 [£5,000] payable over three years and a royalty of 10 per cent of the retail-selling price (artist files, EMI).

In 1911 The Gramophone Company British branch manager Sydney Dixon wrote to Victor about his tactics in selling this kind of record, "In going through figures we find it surprising how the advent of a new list with fresh titles increases the sales of the general celebrity list." He continued: "We find the greatest of all is for a big singer to appear in person in a given district where sales have been slack. For instance two years ago we hardly sold any Caruso records in Germany. Last year, during the three days he was singing in Munich, our big dealer there averaged 1500 records a day, and again in Hamburg they reached 1200 a day."[63]

Although Caruso was rewarded handsomely for his records, this review reveals that McCormack was not. Neither Gramophone nor Victor considered McCormack to be Caruso's equal, a fact reflected in their contracts. Unlike Caruso, whose records were all Celebrity, McCormack's ballads and other songs were placed on a special and cheaper intermediate label. Only his operatic arias and duets with the Austrian violinist Fritz Kreisler were sold as Celebrity records.[64] Table 7.3 also reveals that McCormack received lower advances or, after 1913, no advances and smaller royalties. In 1904, before receiving musical training in Italy, he had recorded for The Gramophone Company, National Phonograph Company and Edison Bell. When he returned to London in 1906, he obtained a recording contract with International Talking Machine GmbH and appeared on its Odeon label. He was spotted by Victor in 1909 during his first tour of the United States, and they bought out his existing record contract for $10,000 and signed him on an exclusive contract. The Gramophone Company was suspicious of these moves and did not see him as being any more than a domestic British artist.[65] The disparity with Caruso on advances and royalties evidently annoyed McCormack, and in a 1914 letter to his American manager he gave vent to his feelings:

> I am very glad indeed that you sent a letter to Mr Child [Victor's recording manager], because if you remember I told you that he said Caruso and Farrar took no advance Royalty well Caruso told me on the boat that he gets $50,000 a year advance that he has 50 cents on large records and 25 on small records. Contrast that with my 15 cents on large and 10 cents on small. Of course I have no one to blame but myself as I made that contract voluntarily. . . . I am writing to Mr Child this mail and will tell him a few things.[66]

It would appear that Caruso was in the habit of upsetting fellow artists on the subject of record royalties. Harry Lauder relates how "once I discussed the matter [of royalties] with my old friend Caruso and the figures he gave me made me so ill that I suddenly changed the conversation."[67]

The Gramophone Company made repeated efforts to tempt the soprano Nellie Melba into the recording studio. Her position as the leading singer in Britain (and in much of Europe and America) gave her a unique standing way beyond her value as a performer. As Gramophone Company managing director Theodore Birnbaum told Sydney Dixon, "if we can secure Melba we shall have done something far beyond what we have up to now achieved."[68] In the end Melba made records, but on her terms and these were demanding. They included a special mauve coloured "Melba" label, a 4s per record royalty and the selling price of £1.1s. However, in the end, the means employed by Birnbaum and Dixon to engage Melba proved costly and dangerous. In a highly confidential 1907 letter to Victor, Birnbaum explained how he bribed Melba's then lover, the Australian writer Haddon Chambers, to persuade her to make records. In return Chambers received "for obtaining articles and press notices in regard to Madame Melba's gramophone records" a £500 advance and a 1 shilling royalty per record sold. In 1907 he forced Birnbaum into a final payoff, the staggering sum of £3,750.[69] Melba's first records sold well, in the four years after 1904 sales totalled 31,333, earning Melba £7,833.[70]

Apart from singers, only one other group of celebrity artists enjoyed substantial royalty-based contracts; the top virtuosi pianists and violinists. Of all pianists active in the two decades immediately prior to 1914, Ignacy Jan Paderewski was the most successful. His 1911 four-year thirty-record contract with The Gramophone Company provided for a £2,000 advance and a 2s per record sold. Between 1911 and 1913 his records enjoyed world sales (including Victor sales) of almost 48,000, earning the artist nearly £5,000. By contrast, in 1909, the British-based pianist Mark Hambourg signed a three-year contract with The Gramophone Company. It contained no advance and the royalty was 10 per cent of the retail-selling price of the much cheaper Black label HMV records; later his records appeared on the HMV Plum label. In all 4,100 Mark Hambourg records were sold between 1909 and 1912, the vast majority in Britain and the British Empire. From these sales Mark Hambourg earned £115, a fraction of Paderewski's royalty earnings.[71]

Before 1914, two virtuosi violinists Fritz Kreisler and Jan Kubelik were dominant in international terms. In 1910, Kreisler signed a five-year contract with Victor and in 1911 Kubelik signed a five-year joint contract with Victor and The Gramophone Company. Under the term of his contract, Kubelik made sixty records for which he received £1,000 advance and an 11% royalty on the retail price. In contrast Kreisler made only thirty records, for which he received a $250 advance on each record, plus a royalty of 10 per cent on the retail price; for records made with other artists he received 5 per cent. Between 1911 and 1913 almost 50,000 copies of Kubelik's records were sold in The Gramophone Company's territory, earning the artist just under £2,000. During the same period, just over 25,000 of Kreisler's records were sold, earning him just over £800. Clearly, unless you were Paderewski, then to make serious money from gramophone records, you had to be a singer and preferably Caruso or Melba.

The figures in table 7.2 reflect only a portion of Celebrity artist's income, and it is therefore difficult to make comparisons with other top artists and performers, though such comparisons are intriguing. The infant moving picture industry paid large sums to entice known celebrity actors into film studios. For example, in 1909 filmmaker William G. Barker "paid Sir Herbert Tree £1,000 for one day at my studio at Ealing."[72] Art historian Jeremy Maas suggests the incomes of the highest paid painters in late Victorian Britain "might be anything from £5,000 to £15,000 a year. Outstandingly successful painters like Sir John Everett Millais and Sir Edwin Landseer commanded earnings of £30,000 to £40,000 a year."[73] Between 1910 and 1913 the rising artist William Orpen enjoyed an income of between £5,000 and £8,000 per year.[74] In contrast, the best paid man of letters in the early twentieth century was Arnold Bennett who earned, in the years between 1912 and 1914, around £16,000 per year.[75]

★　★　★

The creation and development of the international record industry in the early twentieth century coincided with advances in transport. This included the completion of a worldwide steam transport system with transcontinental railway routes criss-crossing the Americas, Europe, Russia, The Middle East and beyond. These linked into timetabled transoceanic passenger steamships creating global transport networks linking continents and major population centres. This allowed performing artists to undertake the first world tours. The opportunity this revolution provided to operatic singers was highlighted by music historian John Rosselli. Using Buenos Aires as a model, he remarked, "From 1873 to 1925 . . . two ambitious competing [operatic] seasons remained the norm [in Europe], often they were combined with further short seasons along the southern circuit."[76] Citing examples of Celebrity recording artists who regularly toured the South American circuit, Rosselli said: "The great baritone Tita Ruffo recalled that for 18 years he never experienced a summer."[77]

There are other examples; for instance, in his biography of Enrico Caruso, the tenor's son relates the adventures his father and mother, the singer Ada Giachetti, experienced during their various and separate tours of South America.[78] International touring was not restricted to South America and in 1911 Melba and McCormack toured Australia together; McCormack undertook his first solo world tour in 1913. In 1907 Harry Lauder began making annual tours of North America and the rest of the English-speaking world.[79] This creation of a world stage on which top artists could perform developed rapidly before the First World War, with important consequences for record companies and performers alike. It became possible to boost the sale of visiting artists' records before their arrival at a distant location, and those who attended their performances were encouraged to purchase records in the knowledge that they were unlikely to hear them live for several years. These opportunities created new patterns of buying and the formation of new relationships between the performer and public.

★   ★   ★

Thus in the few short years before the outbreak of war in 1914, this new medium created a dynamic new art form. It was, however, limited and for many one of marginal utility. Until the mid 1920s, when the electric microphone opened up the possibility of realistic recordings of the orchestral repertoire, the art was forced to develop along relatively narrow lines. It was also during this period that some artists with the good fortune to possess recordable voices found a new source of income. It also established the Celebrity record as an important new symbol of high art. The usefulness of this first flowering was not confined to the pre-1914 generation of artists and record users. For these early recordings have given subsequent generations, for the first time in history, a window from which they can listen and learn about the art of performance, especially singing, as it sounded to a previous generation.

The utility of records has never rested on their ability to educate. For most people the enduring strength remains its capacity to entertain and provide a bridge between performer and listener. In certain circumstances records can also act as a spur to the memory, recalling past experiences, people and places, especially after the First World War as people recalled the idealised "long Edwardian summer" that ended so brutally in 1914. Sir Compton Mackenzie characterised these personal, and for some highly emotional needs, when he wrote: "There are three things in this life that seem to store up the warmth of dead summers-pot-pourri and wine and the records of a great singer."

NOTES

"Down at the Old Bull and Bush" was an adaptation of the 1903 American drinking song "Under the Anheuser Bush," by Harry von Tilzer and Andrew B. Sterling. The British lyrics were written by the American record industry pioneer and recording engineer Russell Hunting and Percy Krone for the music hall artist Florrie Forde, who made it her own. In September 1905, she recorded it for Sterling records (Sterling 161), the employer of Russell Hunting.

1. W. H. Berry, comic singer, "How I Sing to Make Records," *Talking Machine News* 1, no. 1 (May 1903): 3.
2. Sydney Wentworth Dixon, "How Great Artists First Made Records," *The Voice* 4, no. 6 (11 June 1921): 6–7.
3. For more on the recording career of this remarkable artist, see below and chapter 11.
4. For an account of this event, see chapter 1.
5. This issue is discussed in chapter 1.
6. There were several early-twentieth-century attempts to extend the playing time of records, but they were either technically or commercially unsuccessful. Long-playing records were not successfully introduced until late-1940s developments in microgroove technology and vinyl plastics.
7. For further discussion of this point, see chapter 11.
8. David Bicknell, "The Gramophone," in *New Grove Dictionary of Music and Musicians*, ed. Stanley Sadie (London: Macmillan,1980), 7:620–24.
9. Peter Dawson (1882–1961) enjoyed a unique recording career. He made his first records for Edison Bell using the cylinder format and his last for EMI in 1955 in stereo. In his memoirs *Fifty Years of Song* (London: Hutchinson, 1951), he claimed to have made a total of 3,700 records. See also Peter Martland, *Since Records Began* (London: Batsford, 1997), 53.
10. For more on this, see chapter 11. See also, Dawson, *Fifty Years of Song*, 31, 35. During 1990 and 1991, the author interviewed Kathleen Darby (daughter of recording engineer William Sinkler Darby) and Gwendolyne McCormack-Pyke (daughter of tenor John McCormack), now both deceased, who both made recordings as children in about 1916. They recalled the pulling into and pushing away from the recording horn as an important feature of the process.
11. Berry, "How I Sing," 3.
12. Gerald Moore, *Am I Too Loud?* (London: H. Hamilton, 1962), 59.
13. Arthur Clarke, "Twenty-Five Years of Gramophone Recording," *The Talking Machine and Wireless Trade News* 30, no. 1 (1933): 70.
14. "Some Famous Recording Rooms," *The Sound Wave and Talking Machine Record* 1, no. 5 (May 1907): 72–78.
15. For more on this issue, see chapter 11.
16. Emilio de Gogorza, "Tenors and Basses of the Past," *Opera News* (29 November 1937): 4–7.
17. J. B. Steane, *The Grand Tradition* (London: Duckworth, 1978), 7.
18. F. W. Gaisberg, *Music on Record*, 81.
19. Gaisberg, *Music on Record*, 42.
20. Born Landon Ronald Russell (1873–1938), Sir Landon Ronald was a British conductor, composer of ballads and other works. He also coached and accompanied many great singers active before 1914, including Nellie Melba and Adelina Patti. In addition to

his activities as The Gramophone Company musical director, Landon Ronald was, between 1910 and 1938, principal of the Guildhall School of Music and a music critic. His *Who's Who* entry details his career, which in record industry terms was crowned, in 1930, by a directorship of The Gramophone Company. In 1931 he became a founding director of Electric and Musical Industries Ltd. Unique among the directors of The Gramophone Company, he wrote two volumes of memoirs, in which he wrote of his experiences with the company: *Variations on a Personal Theme* (London: Hodder, 1922) and *Myself and Others* (London: Sampson Low, 1931).

21. Gaisberg, *Music on Record*, 42.

22. Ronald, *Variations*, 97.

23. See Peter Martland, "Caruso's First Recordings: Myth and Reality," *ARSC Journal* 25, no. 2 (1994): 193–200. See also letters and telegrams (Enrico Caruso, artist file, EMI) and F. W. Gaisberg, "Notes From My Diary," *The Gramophone* 21, no. 9 (January 1944).

24. Compton Mackenzie, *My Record of Music* (London: Hutchinson, 1955), 32–33.

25. Steane, *The Grand Tradition*, 46.

26. Enrico Caruso Jr. and Andrew Farkas, *Enrico Caruso: My Father and My Family* (Portland, OR: Amadeus, 1990): 286–87.

27. For more on Caruso's record sales in The Gramophone Company's territory and his earnings, see below and chapter 9. The definitive account of the Caruso recordings is to be found in John R. Bolig, *Caruso Records: A History and Discography* (Denver, CO: Mainspring Press, 2002). See also Caruso and Farkas, *Enrico Caruso*, 419, and Michael W. Sherman, *The Paper Dog* (New York: APM Press, 1987), 43.

28. Eldridge Reeves Johnson to Theodore Birnbaum, 17 July 1907 (Victor papers, EMI).

29. For details of Patti's contract, see Patti, artist file (EMI). Calculations of sales taken from board minutes (board papers, EMI).

30. Gaisberg, *Music on Record*, 233.

31. Data compiled from yearly comparative results, 1908–1909 to 1912–1913 (board papers, EMI). See also table 20.

32. Theodore Birnbaum to Calvin G. Child, 13 April 1904 (Victor papers, EMI). See also John Juxon, *Lewis and Lewis* (London: Collins, 1983), and Sir George Henschel, artist file (EMI). Also, 1988 conversations with Theodore Birnbaum's son, the late Sir Anthony Burney OBE.

33. Sydney W. Dixon to head office, 25 November 1904 (statistics file, EMI).

34. Cited in Sydney W. Dixon to Calvin G. Child, 29 March 1905 (Victor papers, EMI).

35. Theodore Birnbaum to British branch, 18 May 1904 (statistics file, EMI).

36. Sir Harry Lauder, *Roamin' in the Gloamin'* (London: E. P., 1928), 128.

37. For details of Lauder's pre-1914 dealings with both The Gramophone Company Ltd and National Phonograph Company Ltd, see Harry Lauder, artist file (EMI) and record manufacturing division (box 12, Harry Lauder, Edison National Historic Site).

38. "The Coming Winter Season," *Talking Machine News* 3, no. 4 (September 1905).

39. For more on this point, see chapter 5.

40. Harry Lauder contracts April 10, 1907, and May 13, 1909 (record manufacturing division, box 12, Harry Lauder, Edison National Historic Site).

41. A. F. Wagner, *Recollections* (London: City of London Phonograph and Gramophone Society, 1991), 7.

42. See record agreement, September 1904 (John McCormack, artist file, EMI).

43. Extracts from "Minutes of 21st Committee Meeting Held at the British Recording Rooms," 4 April 1906 (music room collection, Edison National Historic Site).

44. One of the most prolific recording artists of the pre-1914 period was John Mackenzie-Rogan, director of music of the band of the Coldstream Guards. Curiously, his memoirs, *Fifty Years of Army Music* (London: Methuen, 1926), make no mention of his extensive recording career.

45. Dame Nellie Melba, *Melodies and Memories* (London: T. Butterworth, 1925, 1980, reprint cited), 176.

46. Berry, "How I Sing," *Talking Machine News* 1, no. 1 (May 1903): 3.

47. William Edgar Gilmore to Thomas Edison, 27 May 1904 (document files, 1904, phonograph-manufacturing, Edison National Historic Site).

48. White to William Edgar Gilmore, 2 June 1905 (document file, 1905, phonograph-sales, January–June, Edison National Historic Site).

49. See Lauder, artist files (Edison National Historic Site and EMI).

50. See Florrie Forde's contracts (legal files, EMI).

51. For more on this important early recording artist, see Frank Andrews and Ernie Bayly, *Billy Williams* (Bournemouth, 1982). See also "The Death of Billy Williams," *Sound Wave* 9, no. 4 (April 1915).

52. Dawson, *Fifty Years of Song*, 30.

53. Dawson, *Fifty Years of Song*, 127.

54. See Peter Dawson's contracts and royalty sheets (Peter Dawson, artist file, EMI).

55. See Albert Chevalier, artist file (EMI).

56. See Peter Martland, "A Business History of The Gramophone Company Ltd: 1897–1918," unpublished Cambridge University PhD thesis, 1993.

57. This is discussed in chapter 5.

58. For an example of the advertising, see "Exclusive Columbia, Bonci the World's Greatest Tenor," *Talking Machine World* 5, no. 7 (1909): 42–43.

59. For more on the rise of Carl Lindström AG, see chapter 5. See also Odeon, record catalogue, 1914 (author's collection).

60. The careers of these two remarkable tenors have been chronicled in numerous works published during their lifetime and since. Both wives wrote biographies: Dorothy Caruso, *Enrico Caruso: His Life and Death* (London: Laurie, 1945) and Lily McCormack, *I Hear You Calling Me* (London: Allen, 1950). Three more rigorous works assess Caruso's and McCormack's lives and careers: Michael Scott, *The Great Caruso* (London: Hamilton, 1988); Caruso and Farkas, *Enrico Caruso*; and Gordon T. Ledbetter, *The Great Irish Tenor* (London: Duckworth, 1977).

61. DGAG to Theodore Birnbaum, 12 October 1904 (Caruso, artist file, EMI).

62. Alfredo Bossi to Sydney W. Dixon, 11 June 1910 (McCormack, artist file, EMI).

63. Sydney W. Dixon to Louis Geissler, 19 September 1911 (Caruso, artist file, EMI).

64. See 1909–1910 correspondence (McCormack, artist file, EMI).

65. See Victor Gramophone correspondence, 1909 (McCormack, artist file, EMI).

66. John McCormack to Charles Wagner, 2 June 1914, John McCormack papers, Heinemann Collection (Music Division, Library of Congress).

67. Lauder, *Roamin' in the Gloamin'*, 128.

68. Theodore Birnbaum to Sydney W. Dixon, 15 February 1904 (Melba, artist file, EMI).

69. Theodore Birnbaum to Child, 6 March 1907 (Melba, artist file, EMI).

70. See royalty sheets (Melba, artist file, EMI).

71. See royalty sheets (Mark Hambourg, artist file, EMI.

72. William George Barker, "Before 1910: Kinematograph Experiences," *Proceedings of the British Kinematograph Society* 38 (1936): 14. Tree appeared as Wolsey in Barker's film *Henry VIII*.

73. Jeremy Maas, *The Victorian Art World in Photographs* (London: Barry & Jenkins, 1984), 13.

74. Bruce Arnold, *Orpen: Mirror to an Age* (London: Cape, 1981), 432.

75. Frank Swinnerton, ed., *Arnold Bennett: The Journals* (Harmondsworth: Penguin, 1971), 358, 368–69.

76. John Rosselli, "The Opera Business and the Italian Immigrant Community in Latin America 1820–1930: The Example of Buenos Aires," *Past and Present* 127 (1990): 155–81.

77. Tita Ruffo, *La mia parabola* (Milan, Italy, 1937).

78. Caruso and Farkas, *Enrico Caruso*, chap. 3.

79. For accounts of these various tours, see Melba, *Melodies and Memories*; McCormack, *I Hear You Calling Me*; and Lauder, *Roamin' in the Gloamin'*.

8

THE BRITISH RECORD INDUSTRY DURING THE FIRST WORLD WAR: 1914–1918

"Till the Boys Come Home"

> Whenever I hear the sound of a gramophone after this war, it
> will all come back to me.
>
> —News report,[1] 1918

The First World War was the first general war between the great European powers for one hundred years, in fact since the defeat of Napoleon Bonaparte in 1815. However the world in 1914 was wholly different to 1815. For during the intervening century Europe with its empires and trading systems increasingly dominated the world. As a consequence, the continent prospered and its population increased. It also became increasingly industrialised and urbanised, with highly developed and sophisticated consumer markets underpinned by mature financial institutions. These in turn supported both European and transglobal trading networks. Formed towards the end of that century of relative peace, the British talking machine industry entered these markets and joined the trading networks. This wholly novel industry proved highly successful, creating manufacturing and marketing facilities and new opportunities for performing artists, composers and others. The international record industry defined new forms of intellectual property, created new kinds of domestic entertainment and revolutionised the way art and culture was spread. Trading in luxury products, this industry epitomised the wealth, prosperity and consumer aspirations of a Europe at peace. Unfortunately this liberal progress did not last and the war brought its pan-European trade grinding to a halt. It remained frozen for more than four years as national governments poured treasure into the war and their armies tore the fabric of Europe and its peoples to shreds.

This chapter examines how the British record industry traversed these difficult years and the impact of the war on its development.

★   ★   ★

In common with everyone else in Europe record industry executives were taken by surprise at the speed and suddenness of the war crisis. As Gramophone Company chairman Trevor Williams noted, "When the war burst upon us . . . we, with the rest of civilisation, were quite unprepared for such a contingency."[2] That said, the previous year managing director Alfred Clark, who was disturbed at the deteriorating international situation, had discussed with the manager of the French branch "the possible impact of a war between Germany and France."[3]

The shock of the declaration of war caused consumers to panic and they stopped buying luxury goods like records and gramophones. This happened not just in Britain; in fact the whole European continent experienced this collapse. Describing the situation Alfred Clark said, "There was . . . an immediate cessation of all buying. The public decided to save rather than spend."[4] This crisis affected not just British record companies but also foreign companies trading in Britain. A week after war was declared Alfred Clark wrote to Eldridge Johnson in the United States, "There is no business, and it would be foolish to attempt to do any."[5] The crisis was critical, with wholesalers refusing to place orders, arguing that retailers would not carry stock. As a consequence there were industry-wide wage cuts and redundancies. In an editorial the British trade journal *Sound Wave* appealed for calm: "In the present grave crisis the *Sound Wave* wishes to point out to the trade the folly of giving way to panic. That the trade will suffer, and suffer severely, from the war is, unfortunately, certain. But manufacturers, factors, and dealers will only increase the difficulty by proclaiming that the war will kill the trade for the season."[6]

James Hough the pugnacious manager of J. E. Hough Ltd, manufacturers of The Winner records, climbed on the patriotic bandwagon and solved his redundancy problems by posting the following at the London factory:

> All unmarried men in our employ who answer the description of men required by Lord Kitchener [secretary of state for war] are hereby given notice that their employment at these works will terminate at the end of this current week. Each man joining the national forces will receive a bonus of £2.2s.0d, and his employment guaranteed to him on his return.

Any person entitled to exceptional treatment should lay his case before the undersigned. (J. E. Hough, managing director)[7]

By November 1914 fourteen former employees had joined the armed forces.[8] In fact J. E. Hough Ltd had a successful war manufacturing war *matériel*, and by its end employed hundreds more workers than in 1914.[9]

Eschewing the general panic Louis Sterling, European manager of The Columbia Phonograph Company, seized the initiative and released a series of war record supplements on the Regal label. This supplement contained both new popular war songs and recycled patriotic recordings from the back catalogue. Throwing his weight behind the initiative, Sterling persuaded wholesalers and dealers to take the records and engaged in a massive advertising campaign to sell them. The move succeeded and was quickly copied by competitors.[10] Noting this revival, *Talking Machine News* observed, "There is . . . a very big demand for patriotic songs and selections."[11] Demand was not simply a British phenomenon, as Clark noted, "In Berlin, St Petersburg and London . . . there is a brisk little trade in special new patriotic records, but of course the total of this turnover is but a drop in the bucket."[12] In common with some other record companies (most prominently J. E. Hough Ltd), Sterling paid a one penny royalty per Regal war record sold to the Prince of Wales National Relief Fund (a charity formed on the outbreak of war to aid war-related distress). By January 1915, J. E. Hough Ltd had paid £1,000 to the fund with respect of The Winner record sales and by April sales of Regal records had raised £1,500.[13] A penny per record suggests sales of 240,000 The Winner and 360,000 of Regal war records. Monthly release data indicates they made up a significant proportion of new recordings into the spring of 1915.[14]

The only surviving record sales data for this period is shown at figure 8.1. It reveals the extent of the collapse as it compared Gramophone Company British branch unit sales for 1913–1914 with those for 1914–1915. This data, when taken with evidence from the trade press, suggests that by the end of 1914 sales staged an across-the-board recovery, though lacking industry-wide figures makes the strength of this recovery impossible to gauge. Worldwide sales of The Gramophone Company (but excluding Austria, Germany and Scandinavia), suggests there was significant post-1915 growth and is illustrated in table 8.1.

Although record sales data in table 8.1 indicate significant gains during the period 1915 to 1919, these mask the loss of the German, Austro-Hungarian and Russian markets. Compared to 1912–1913, when total

Figure 8.1.   The Gramophone Company Ltd, British Branch: Monthly Unit Sales of Records, 1913–1914 and 1914–1915

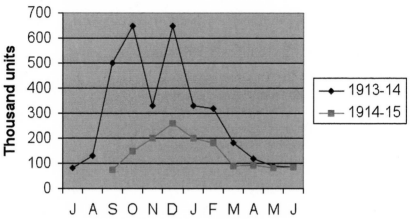

Source: Compiled from monthly epitomes, 1913–1914 and 1914–1915 (board papers, EMI). No figures survive for July 1914, and figures of –1100 (returned records) were recorded for August 1914.

Gramophone Company unit sales (including Germany, Austria-Hungary, Italy and Russia) amounted to seven million records, the 1919–1920 sales were around one million records less.[15] Assessing these sales and reviewing the British branch of The Gramophone Company in May 1915, Clark told Eldridge Johnson, "The gramophone business in the UK keeps up splendidly. . . . On the continent things are generally speaking as bad as they could be."[16]

The post-1914 recovery was mainly due to the gap in the market created by the banning of German imports of records and machines, though there was clearly some growth in demand especially from the armed forces. Before 1914, German manufacturers supplied around a third of the Brit-

Table 8.1.   The Gramophone Company Ltd: Worldwide Unit Sales Immediately before and during the First World War but Excluding Sales in Germany, Austria-Hungary, Russia, Belgium and Italy

Year	Records	Gramophones
1913–1914	4,145,213	29,571
1914–1915	1,877,806	16,438
1915–1916	4,125,205	25,002
1916–1917	4,298,754	10,936
1917–1918	4,790,083	7,428
1918–1919	5,868,840	4,468

Source: Compiled from monthly epitomes and "Past History" (board papers and statistics file, EMI).

ish record and more than half the machine market.[17] Quantifying this has proved problematic, made worse by the difficulty in defining German goods. As shown in chapter 4, not all goods of German origin were imported. For example, the German manufacturer Carl Lindström AG served its British markets from a factory in Hertford, to the north of London. The confusion was such that early in the war some of its labels claimed British nationality. For instance, in October 1914, The Beka Record Company wrote, "All [our] records are British made through and through in a British factory, at Hertford, by British labour."[18] Although German imports ceased, the British Lindström factory continued to manufacture records (including the Beka, Coliseum, Favorite, Jumbo and Scala labels) under the control of government-appointed trustees. In 1915 Carl Lindström (London) Ltd and Fonotipia Ltd were liquidated and The Hertford Record Company Ltd formed to acquire the assets, which were purchased by Columbia for £24,000. It has not been possible to quantify wartime sales from the Lindström record business or output from its British factory.[19] The exclusion of enemy imports provided British manufacturers with a golden opportunity and therefore the wartime increase in sales of British records was in part due to improved market share rather than increased market size. Table 8.2 details unit sales of The Gramophone Company's British branch between 1913–1914 and 1917–1918.

Table 8.2 shows unit sales of records and machines in the final prewar selling year, then the collapse during 1914–1915, together with the upturn and growth from 1915–1916. The figures do confirm Clark's assertion of supply problems with gramophones during the final war years. Table 8.2 also shows how, after the withdrawal of the cheap mass-market Cinch record in 1915, consumers continued to purchase the more expensive labels. Paradoxically, gains in unit sales were achieved against a background of high import duties imposed in 1915 on machines and parts like Swiss-made

Table 8.2.   The Gramophone Company Ltd, British Branch: Unit Sales, 1913–1918

Year	Records, All Labels	Celebrity Records	Gramophones
1913–1914	3,340,053	35,590	20,040
1914–1915	1,362,531	17,432	11,623
1915–1916	3,458,158	28,516	20,151
1916–1917	3,471,653	31,145	7,864
1917–1918	3,918,786	45,316	4,693
1918–1919	4,916,935	70,421	3,058

Source: Compiled from monthly epitomes, 1913 to 1919 (board papers, EMI). Sales of celebrity records in 1918–1919 grew because of significant price reductions and the general demand for records and gramophones at the end of the war.

clockwork motors, together with inflation-driven price rises. Wartime inflation was a major problem. Not only did wages together with transport and distribution costs rise with or even ahead of inflation, prices of commodities like shellac (the most important ingredient in record manufacture) went through the roof. In the immediate prewar years a hundredweight of top grade Indian shellac cost around £4 by 1918 it was more than £24.[20] Although prices increased in the later war years and beyond, they failed to keep pace with this kind of inflation. In 1918, for example, the cost of the midpriced HMV Plum label records rose by 6d to 3s.6d for 10-inch and 5s.6d for 12-inch. Indeed, by the end of the war, record companies compromised quality for price by reducing the proportion of shellac in their records, which resulted in a much poorer quality product. All this suggests that if there were supply side problems in dealing with war-generated demand for records, they were overcome.

The exclusion of German goods and withdrawal of cheap British labels like The Cinch clearly stabilised the market, making it more profitable, and with the stimulus of war-related demand the whole of the trade benefited.[21] J. E. Hough Ltd had entered the volume disc market in 1912 with its 1s.6d The Winner record. As table 8.3 shows unit sales for this label (the only run of data to survive apart from those of The Gramophone Company) indicate rising sales across these years but there were problems. For instance, the war disrupted links with transatlantic licencors, particularly during 1917 and 1918 and both Columbia and Gramophone Company catalogues and monthly supplements for this period show a marked decline in American-sourced recordings. That said, throughout the conflict leading British record companies maintained regular monthly releases of new records from their own studios, albeit in truncated form.

Table 8.3.   The Winner Record: Sales during the First World War, 1914–1918

Year	Records Sold
1913	700,000
1914	900,000
1915	1,200,000
1916	1,800,000
1917	2,100,000
1918	1,900,000

Source: The figure for 1919 was 2.6 million—hence, the headline "Eleven Million Winners Sold" in *Talking Machine World* 15, no. 11 (November 1919): 188.

substantial stocks of machines destined for sale by continental branches during the ensuing winter selling season, which never happened. That stock insulated The Gramophone Company from shortages in its now crucial British market. As Clark noted, "the stock [of gramophones] lying in Hayes was sufficient for the purely English trade for a long time to come." As this ran down fresh supplies were obtained from Victor in the United States, though the imposition of import regulations later in the war ended this trade.[30] As a result, Clark advised Johnson in March 1917, "Our machine trade is practically nil."[31] The manufacture of machines for the British market was severely disrupted but never entirely ceased, though the effects of increasing government restrictions, especially tariffs and import quotas, forced the broader industry to react. In 1915 a music industry committee (which included the record industry) was formed to lobby government. It was successful, and in May 1916 regulations were relaxed permitting the monthly import of 124 tons of musical instruments, including gramophones and clockwork motors. In the event during the last year of the war this concession was steadily reduced and by February 1918 it was down to fifty tons.[32] Prominent among wartime gramophones was the Decca portable, introduced on the very eve of war in August 1914 by the long-established musical instrument firm Barnett Samuel and Sons, as part of their existing "Dulcephone" range. The Decca helped create important markets, particularly with the armed forces. The Decca portable was easy to carry and large numbers found their way to the trenches of France and Flanders.[33]

The availability of Decca and other British-assembled machines, together with some imports, enabled the trade to survive the war, though by its end gramophone sales were perhaps as few as 50,000, a fraction of prewar levels. The end of the war saw the emergence of a new British light engineering industry, manufacturing gramophone sound boxes and motors. This fundamentally changed the industry, which was no longer dependent on imports. In these circumstances, the postwar years saw British manufacturers dominating the gramophone trade, protected from cheap German imports by the continuance of wartime tariffs. The industry was further helped by the maintenance of a trade ban against Germany until 1925.[34]

★   ★   ★

The war separated The Columbia Phonograph Company and The Gramophone Company from their German and Austrian branches, and Carl Lindström (London) Ltd from its German parent. Columbia was less affected, with the ownership and management of selling branches in belligerent states either transferred directly to the United States or run down to wait for better days. However, The Gramophone Company paid an unusually high price for the war, losing not just its central European branches but also the Russian branch. In 1917, the German state confiscated and sold Deutsche Grammophon and the British government seized and sold the British assets of Carl Lindström. Deutsche Grammophon had been pivotal in the early years of the business and a prewar manufacturing centre for several European branches. In many parts of Europe it was the registered owner of the "His Master's Voice" (HMV) trademark, the holding company of its European patents and the shares in other subsidiaries (including the Austrian, Danish and Swedish branches).[35] The Russian branch suffered the fate of all foreign businesses when, in 1918, it fell into the hands of the Bolshevik regime and was completely lost.[36] In this respect The Gramophone Company was unlucky, as business historian Geoffrey Jones has written, "The Gramophone Company was harder hit than other British firms by the war. While Dunlop's German subsidiary was also sequestered during the war . . . its former German management remained in contact with the British company during the hostilities and facilitated the reacquisition of the German company after 1918."[37]

To continue trading, those branches in neutral and allied Europe previously supplied by Germany needed fresh manufacturing and distribution networks. Equally worrying was the fate of the 50,000 original copper matrices stored at the Hanover plant. Of these Clark said:

> As early as 1909 plans had been prepared to transfer the bulk of the record pressing from Hanover to Hayes and when war broke out they were well advanced . . . but the transfer of the tens of thousands of copper matrices which had accumulated over a period of 15 years could not be made quickly without great dislocation to the continuity of the general business. . . . Hanover was still pressing for a number of foreign countries and in addition had the original matrices for all the International [Celebrity] Red Label artists.[38]

In 1915, Joseph Berliner, one of the German directors and former board member, contacted London through the sales branch in neutral Holland. Throughout the war the Dutch acted as a vital conduit between the two and overall a total of fourteen such contacts were recorded in the board minutes.[39] Berliner claimed the German government threatened to seize the copper matrices for recycling into munitions. To prevent this, he suggested sending an equivalent amount of copper to the Dutch branch to be exchanged for the matrices in Germany.[40] The matter was referred to the British government, who refused permission. In the event, very few matrices were seized.[41] In 1917, when news of the impending sale of its German assets reached London, Clark again tried and failed to secure the matrices, this time through the agency of Victor.[42] It took until 1922 to get possession of the matrices and then only after protracted litigation and prevarication on the part of the new owners of the German business.[43]

★　★　★

In order to keep The Gramophone Company solvent during the war years, Clark and factory manager Wilburn Dennison negotiated munitions contracts with the British, Russian and Belgian governments. As a result it became a manufacturer of ammunition boxes, cartridge cases, primers, fuses, aircraft parts and charger clips. By the end of the war these contracts had generated revenue exceeding £6 million.[44] This work was vital to the allied war effort and key to the survival of the business. As Clark told Johnson in 1916: "The policy of temporarily manufacturing other things than talking machines . . . was . . . the only one which would have saved our Company from bankruptcy."[45] Clark and Dennison were a formidable team, and the contracts they negotiated transformed the company's prospects. The factories proved easy to adapt and the munitions contracts saw employment increase from 1,141 at the start of the war to more than 4,000 by its end.[46] Stretching the factories' capacity meant large capital investments in plant and equipment, which saw the liquidation of cash reserves and investments. Furthermore, in September 1915, the venture became "controlled" under the terms of the Munitions of War Act 1915.[47] "Controlled" companies were engaged in substantial war-related work and subject to government regulation concerning labour, wages and conditions, prices, dividends, management and profit.[48] One way to retain profit was to write off capital costs in a single year. The Company used this and other accounting procedures to offset such costs against tax liabilities. Of this Clark told Johnson, "What I think will interest you specially is to know that the enormous new plant put in here since the machine Factory was constructed will, by next June, be written down, that the whole plant new and old will stand at less than the old peacetime plant would have stood now if there had been no war and it had not been added to."[49] Dennison used his contacts in the United States to subcontract a £500,000 Russian fuse contract. This alone generated a profit of £150,000. Other war related opportunities presented themselves. For example, by November 1914, demand for metal outstripped supply and The Gramophone Company in common with other contractors was unable to meet its obligations. To solve this problem, Dennison and Clark persuaded the board to create a metal purchasing agency, which developed into a profitable sideline. They bought stock in the United States and sold the surplus to other manufacturers.[50] It proved so successful that by the end of the wars it had generated revenue amounting to £767,874.[51]

The Gramophone Company clearly owed its wartime survival to Clark and Dennison. Yet despite his evident importance, Dennison was never invited to join the board. This curious omission was a part of a long-standing difficulty between management and nonexecutive directors. Under the pressure of war this difficulty erupted into a crisis during 1916 and led to an attempt by the nonexecutive board to dismiss Clark. In the spring of 1916, all the British Gramophone Company factories were working to capacity producing records and, in the buildup to the battle of the Somme, unprecedented quantities of war *matériel*. The crisis that arose at this crucial time could have engulfed the business and put the supply of munitions at risk. The background lay in Clark's prewar reorganisation of the business and strategy for growth, which concentrated control in his hands and marginalised nonexecutive board members. This had caused severe though containable strains.[52] Matters came to a head after the declaration of war, which brought significant changes in the board and in the fortunes of the company.

In 1914, nonexecutive board members were chairman Trevor Williams, together with Romer Williams, Ernest de la Rue and Walter Long MP (who left in 1915 to join the government). There were three executive directors, managing director Alfred Clark, sales director Sydney Dixon, who left for military service in 1914, and European factory manager Joseph Berliner, who was removed as a director because of his German citizenship. By early 1915 all that remained were Clark and the three nonexecutives, who were all retired and represented investors. In fact none had managerial experience or knowledge of day-to-day management. In a highly partial letter to Johnson, Clark described the situation thus: "[Trevor] Williams has actually visited the works on an average of just over three times a month since the outbreak of war." He described his fellow directors in the following terms: "de la Rue is 64 and very old for his age and Romer Williams is older. . . . Both have long since retired from business."[53]

During the first year of the war no dividends had been paid, reducing nonexecutive director incomes to a proportion of the £2,500 paid in fees, which had been increased substantially in 1915.[54] Clark, who along with other staff had accepted a 50 per cent salary cut at the start of the war, reacted angrily to the increase.[55] Evidence of this reliance on fees and dividends is strengthened by comments made by Clark to Johnson, "Trevor Williams has been hard hit by the war. His only fortune . . . is about 30,000 of our $5 shares, plus 10,000 belonging to Mrs Williams—which are paying no dividends."[56] According to Clark, a dispute arose in early 1916 between himself and Dennison and the nonexecutive directors over payments for their metal purchasing agency work. This was, if Clark is to be believed, part of a plot by the nonexecutives to take over the management of the company. Dennison was unhappy with the situation and the indifference of nonexecutives to the intense pressure under which he and Clark worked and told Clark he would leave the company as soon as his contract expired. Clark told Johnson: "I have heard members of our Board more than once say that many large works here are run by men who receive not more than $2,500 a year and that it is sheer waste to pay Dennison a higher salary."[57] The dispute became a crisis in February 1916 when Trevor Williams attempted to redefine the powers of the managing director, insisting that matters of day-to-day management be subject to his veto. Clark claimed Williams submitted this strategy to legal counsel, who told him he could not undermine the powers of the managing director.[58] Rejecting these moves, Clark confronted the board.[59] On 23 February, he cabled Johnson, "Board has terminated my employment taking effect March 31."[60] Between February and April 1916, Clark took on and beat the nonexecutive directors. Explaining the course of events to Johnson, Clark told of other forces working to resolve the impasse.[61]

> Mr Colin Cooper and Mr Broad have both informed Mr Williams he has made a serious mistake. Our bankers have told Mr Williams they are not prepared to finance the Company if Mr Williams is to be manager. . . . They could not . . . have that confidence if the business were to be managed by a retired lawyer. Mr Cooper and Mr Broad have seen Mr Herbert Storey [a major shareholder and the brother of Edgar Storey, one of the partners in the original 1898 gramophone venture] and other influential shareholders and it has resulted in my agreeing to come back on the following conditions.
>
> (a) The Board to be reorganised.
> (b) The Chairman to have no special powers other than is customary in England.
> (c) That the question of my remuneration be settled.

Clark referred to a suggestion Johnson had been pressing for years, "As regards (a) I told them that if the Company was to increase and prosper they should select their Board from their staff. This they said was impossible in England in the case of a public company with 3,000 shareholders."[62]

On 19 April 1916, Clark told Johnson of a settlement worked out along the lines he proposed. The nonexecutive directors had been totally defeated. Trevor Williams, according to Clark, "had to have the Riot Act read over him before he consented to the settlement."[63] Included was provision for two new nonexecutive board members, major shareholder Herbert Storey and Alexander Ormrod, a stockbroker who had raised the 1913 debenture and was a debenture trustee.[64] Both were experienced businessmen who had the confidence of Clark, the bankers and settlement brokers John Broad, the company lawyer, and Colin Cooper, the company accountant.[65] These dramatic events loosened the grip of the old nonexecutive directors and injected much needed new blood into the board. Clark wrote enthusiastically of the new regime, "Things seem to be shaping satisfactorily. We held two Board meetings—the second of which was held at Hayes, this being the first one here since the early days of the war and the atmosphere seems to have cleared and to be settling on to a good commercial basis."[66]

There was something inevitable about the 1916 crisis. Once the non-executive directors faced Clark across the board table without the mediating force of other directors there was going to be some kind of confrontation. That Clark emerged unscathed suggests his position had reached a peak; he had laid low the founding chairman and lived to tell the tale. There was a price. For although Clark remained in post Wilburn Dennison did not. According to Clark, early in 1917, the Ministry of Munitions requested his release and he never returned to Gramophone Company employment.

★   ★   ★

The Gramophone Company's wartime experience contrasted with the prewar period in a number of ways. First, the prewar period was one of relative price stability whereas the war brought unprecedented inflation. Second, during the war The Gramophone Company's traditional European and Russian markets were either disrupted or lost. Third, during the war the company diversified into the manufacture of war *matériel* and became "controlled." Fourth, whereas before the war the overseas trade dominated, by 1919 it accounted for only 40 per cent of turnover.[67] Table 8.4 sets out turnover and profit from both the gramophone and munitions business.

Table 8.4 charts The Gramophone Company's wartime financial recovery. A comparison of the 1913–1914 turnover and profit figures with those for 1917–1918 (the last full year of the war) shows the final prewar turnover figure at £1 million compared to 1917–1918 approximately £3.2

Table 8.4.   The Gramophone Company Ltd: Components of Turnover and Profit, 1914–1919

Year	Turnover: Records and Gramophones	Turnover: Munitions etc.		Total Profit
1913–1914	£1,000,113 [$5,000,565]	—		£138,186 [$690,930]
1914–1915	£450,862 [$2,254,310]	£212,500	[$1,062,500]	£16,772 [$83,860]
1915–1916	£638,040 [$3,190,200]	£749,500	[$3,747,500]	£181,100 [$905,500]
1916–1917	£669,703 [$3,348,515]	£1,595,590	[$7,977,950]	£163,314 [$816,570]
1917–1918	£648,456 [$3,242,280]	£2,585,988	[$12,929,940]	£218,749 [$1,093,745]
1918–1919	£876,196 [$4,380,980]	£1,078,501	[$5,392,505]	£145,397 [$726,985]

Source: Compiled from "Past History of the Company," 1921 (statistics file, EMI); AC, "Further Notes on the First World War," 1919 (First World War papers, EMI); and annual reports (meetings file, EMI).

million. Prices more than doubled during the war so a doubling of turnover might have been expected rather than the tripling achieved.[68] On the other hand, the controlled profit for 1917–1918 failed to keep pace with either turnover or inflation. It was nonetheless substantial compared to the earlier war years; controlled profit was limited to an average for the last two pre-war years plus 20 per cent. The average profit for those years was £120,000 with the 20 per cent added the limit was £144,000.[69] Profits conformed to this formula, with an additional £150,000 earned from the Russian fuse order. During a period of high inflation and controlled profits, the dividends on ordinary shares during the two final years of the war, as set out in table 8.5, were in real terms only respectively 25 per cent and 50 per cent of the 1913–1914 levels.[70]

Table 8.5 shows the impact of nil dividend payments on the 1915 share price. When it recommenced the following year the value of the ordinary shares rose. Other factors, including the growth in the asset base (as shown in table 8.6) may also have helped the share price. Inevitably, the 5 per cent preference shares suffered the fate of all fixed interest investments during periods of high inflation. Share prices suffered from forces other than nil dividends, for example, inflation, the loss of continental markets and controlled profits. There were also external factors. For instance, to help pay for the war the British government borrowed large sums and offered bonds at attractive rates, which diverted investment capital away from shares in public companies.

Table 8.5.   The Gramophone Company Ltd: Dividends and Shares Price, 1913–1919

		Ordinary Shares		Preference Shares	
Year	Dividend	High	Low	High	Low
1913–1914	10%	£1.85 [$9.25]	£1.12 [$5.60]	£1.00 [$5]	£0.81 [$4.05]
1914–1915	Nil	£1.44 [$7.20]	£0.93 [$4.80]	£0.85 [$4.25]	£0.76 [$3.80]
1915–1916	10%	£1.50 [$7.50]	£0.85 [$4.25]	£0.75 [$3.75]	£0.74 [$3.70]
1916–1917	10%	£1.57 [$7.85]	£1.07 [$5.35]	£0.76 [$3.80]	£0.68 [$3.40]
1917–1918	15%	£2.06 [$10.30]	£1.26 [$6.30]	£0.83 [$4.15]	£0.77 [$3.85]
1918–1919	15%	£2.25 [$11.25]	£1.31 [$6.55]	£0.95 [$4.15]	£0.77 [$3.60]

Source: Compiled from The Gramophone Company's entry in *The Stock Exchange Yearbook, 1913–20,* and "Prices of Gramophone Shares" (merger file, EMI).

The vagaries of wartime accounting procedures, due to Ministry of Munitions controls, creative write-downs, inflation and the loss of assets make an assessment of its wartime assets difficult. Table 8.6 sets out the figures declared in the balance sheets.

The figures in table 8.6 show the investment portfolio had been liquidated in 1916 to pay for capital investment. They also indicate the creation of a war contingency fund, as a hedge against an uncertain trading future, and a dividend equalisation fund to maintain shareholder confidence

Table 8.6. The Gramophone Company Ltd: Assets, 1913–1919

Year	Investments	Carried Forward	Assets	War Contingency	Dividend Equalisation
1913– 1914	£195,701 [$978,505]	£39,426 [$197,130]	£906,838 [$4,534,190]	£42,380 [$211,900]	—
1914– 1915	£164,437 [$822,185]	£14,248 [$71,240]	£891,461 [$4,457,305]	£42,380 [$211,900]	—
1915– 1916	£104,190 [$529,950]	£29,146 [$145,730]	NA	£108,689 [$543,445]	£50,000 [$250,000]
1916– 1917	—	£72,590 [$362,950]	£1,148,539 [$5,742,695]	£174,999 [$874,995]	£50,000 [$250,000]
1917– 1918	—	£163,804 [$819,020]	£1,120,126 [$5,600,630]	£174,999 [$874,995]	—
1918– 1919	—	£155,799 [$778,995]	£1,169,663 [$5,848,315]	£174,999 [$874,995]	—

Source: Compiled from annual reports (meetings file, EMI).

in difficult times. These also reveal the extent of forward planning.[71] By 1918, the business had written off £129,008 of assets in enemy countries, including the Russian assets, which were partly charged against the war contingency fund and possibly against excess profits taxation.[72] Two other changes suggest an asset write-down and the watering of stock to satisfy shareholders. Accounts for the financial year 1917–1918 show patents, goodwill and trademarks, formerly valued at £482,847, written down to £1.[73] By these devices The Gramophone Company had by the end of the war cleared its balance sheet of unrealistic encumbrances. This review of assets also reveals just how small cash reserves were. It also highlights the immediate postwar problem, specifically how to raise capital to restore its continental and overseas business, and plan for growth in the circumstances of potentially disorderly markets.[74]

★   ★   ★

In *The Great War and the British People* historian J. M. Winter examined British wartime living standards and explained the apparent paradox of increased consumption against a background of rising inflation: "for a substantial part of the working class population, standards of living were not only maintained but rose relative to the pre-war period." This, he argued, occurred because of rent controls, overtime pay, piece-rate payments, the eradication of unemployment, smaller families and material benefits of social policies such as the opening of industrial canteens. In addition there was the enforcement of closing hours on pubs, as well as the payment of government separation allowances to support the families of servicemen.[75] In their contemporary comments both Louis Sterling and Alfred Clark appear to support the assertion that "for many poorly-paid occupational groups, wage increases kept pace with or outstripped prices."[76] In 1916 Louis Sterling made an acute observation identifying these rapid social changes: "This . . . prosperity . . . may be attributed to a number of causes, chief of which is the fact that the working classes of Britain are earning more money . . . and spending freely. Less money is being spent for beverages [beer] and similar forms of 'amusement' and more is being spent on the brightening of the home. The working men are buying better furniture for their homes, together with talking machines and pianos."[77] Sterling's opinion was supported by Clark, who wrote to Johnson in 1917 that "the demand for machines and records is very great. Curiously enough this demand is for the higher priced types and therefore in no way due to the exclusion of cheap German competition we had in pre-war days."[78] Clark seems to overlook both the greater wealth and rising expectations of his working-class customers. That they were prepared to pay for higher-priced better quality goods does not necessarily mean they would have continued buying cheaper German goods had there been no war. In addition to the new consumers, demand was generated by hospitals, military camps, canteens and of course by soldiers in the trenches; static warfare meant front line and reserve soldiers were able to introduce some features of domesticity, like records and gramophones, into their lives. In the end, the evidence points to a domestic consumer boom fuelled mainly by high inflation-proof wages paid to civilian war-workers: evidently the gramophone did keep the home fires burning.

Although increased disposable income may have caused some wartime growth, other factors need to be considered. Due to the peculiar circumstances of the war it is possible that records and machines were no longer considered luxury products, becoming sufficiently essential for price increases to make little or no impact. Another possibility is income elasticity. With traditional entertainments, such as pubs, music halls and other places of public entertainment curtailed or closed, wage surpluses may have been spent on recorded music. Similarly, it could have been price elasticity. During the war the cost of entertainments like beer and tobacco, music halls and cinemas, football and horse racing and admission prices to other places of entertainment increased by a combination of inflation and additional taxes to the point where they may no longer have been affordable. In these circumstances, home-based entertainment was made more attractive. Evidence pointing to this can be found in the reaction to the government's 1916 entertainment tax levied on ticket sales in theatres and cinemas. A 1918 article in *The Era Annual* entitled "The entertainment tax" highlighted falling attendances at places of public entertainment which was due, it argued, entirely to the new tax. According to this article, the impact of this tax on takings was profound: "on average the takings of theatres, music halls, and cinemas in the United Kingdom had dropped over 23 per cent since October 1, the date of the new tax rate."[79] Again, it is possible that income may also have been spent on records and gramophones instead.

★   ★   ★

Perhaps the largest single market for records and gramophones were the British armies fighting in France, Flanders and elsewhere. This group made up the largest captive consumer market in the English-speaking world. A profile of these armies suggests the reason; they were all male (and prewar record buyers tended to be male) with an average age of between eighteen and twenty-five, an age group traditionally with the most disposable income. They were of an age and stage of emotional development which saw them at their most romantic and a group who were either unmarried or recently married. With this profile it is perhaps unsurprising to learn that these soldiers followed the traditions of past armies with few inhibitions about singing together as they marched, or at concert parties in rest areas, or indeed elsewhere on the Western Front or other theatres of war. Writing in 1930 John Brophy and Eric Partridge suggested that in addition to the straightforward rendition of songs these soldiers did what soldiers have done down the ages, taken popular and other songs and changed the words to poke fun at their superiors and to meet their own often quite explicit needs, sexual and otherwise.[80] However, in order for these parodies to be successful and gain the kind of diffusion suggested by Brophy and Partridge, soldiers had to be familiar with the original words and melodies. This would have been relatively easy with songs they had known before the war, but possibly less so with the songs written during the war. That they learned melodies and lyrics so quickly suggests there were good lines of communications back to Britain, the source of new songs.

Unfortunately there is no means of calculating the number of records and machines finding their way to the battlefields of the First World War. It is reasonable to suggest that given the circumstances of trench warfare significant numbers of portable gramophones, like the Decca, appeared along the Western Front, other fronts and on naval vessels. There is a considerable body of evidence in memoirs and other contemporary sources testifying to this in the British sector of the Western Front and elsewhere. For example, in the September 1918 edition of *The Voice* (The Gramophone Company's in-house magazine), an article by J. B. Goodliffe extracted from the *Daily Mail* noted:

> Nearly every mess has its gramophone. You hear them in the most unlikely places. As one goes up to the trench at night and passes the last battered house where the road ends and the communication trench begins, a crack in the mud-plastered wall reveals a candle on a biscuit tin and two or three wearily lit faces listening to the strains of the latest revue. And somehow the witching rhythm of a waltz refrain bringing memories of happier days in London has a strangely heartening effect on the laden men stumbling on the cracked trench boards.[81]

Probably the best account of a gramophone and records in the trenches comes from the pen of writer and broadcaster Christopher Stone.

In a 1923 article published in *The Gramophone* he described his wartime experiences with a Decca, albeit from the perspective of a frontline officer. He said, "The Decca arrived with half-a-dozen records while the battalion was in reserve billets at Bouzencourt, near Albert, in January 1917, and from that moment life in the headquarters mess was altered." Portability was its key attraction. As Stone observed, "Strange homes that old Decca has had, up and down the villages of France in ruined houses, in huts, in tents, in transport lines. Only once, I think, did it get as far forward as the support line and that was in the Dyke Valley, in front of Courcellete. . . . It was always waiting for us, with our kit and baths and pyjamas, to welcome us back to a semblance of a civilised life." He went on to describe how his battalion was broken up in early 1918: "And somehow or other the Decca, by a process of elimination, followed my fortunes. . . . A magnificent artillery ammunition box was fitted up and painted for it . . . and in this the barely portable hero of a thousand nights made the advance through Belgium into Germany, and had the privilege of playing *Where My Caravan has Rested* in the parlour of a house in Duren. This was to enjoy the sweets of victory, but not without a sadness, a desiderium."[82]

Another way gramophones and records arrived in the field was by gifts from British record companies, who regularly sent supplies of records, machines and needles to the armed forces. These were often mentioned in *Talking Machine News*, *The Sound Wave* and even in the American *Talking Machine World*. For example, in October 1914, J. E. Hough Ltd sent 12,000 records and 60,000 needles to the Royal Navy. In July 1915 *Talking Machine World* reported the same firm sending 48,000 records to British troops fighting in France, in August it sent 24,000 records and several hundred gramophones to British soldiers and sailors and in October 500 boxes each containing 24 records and 400 needles.[83] And, in December 1916, a further 100,000 records and several hundred thousand needles were despatched to the front.[84] Other evidence suggests record companies, war charities and individuals made gifts of records, machines and accessories not just to service personnel but also to institutions like the YMCA. It is easy to see how popular such gifts might be to sailors and those in YMCA huts behind the lines, but the postwar writings of veterans like Christopher Stone and others suggest that at least by the closing phase of the war the presence of portable gramophones, like the Decca, and records among soldiers' kit had become a commonplace in the fighting areas. Whether this presence in the many theatres of war was evidence of domestic life transferred to wartime life remains a matter of debate.

★ ★ ★

The speed with which new songs became popular and spread amongst the troops is also a factor suggesting gramophones and records were readily available. Wartime musical tastes, as revealed by the kinds of record manufactured, reflected not only divisions within the nation, but also different stages of the conflict. Noting this, Sterling wrote in April 1918:

> There exists in England today a tremendous demand for straight popular songs and there is also a notable increase in the call for good music. I refer particularly to high-class ballads and the many fine string and orchestral selections. We are shipping many thousands of records per month to the boys at the front, and the orders for these records almost invariably call for 50% of popular music, and the remainder good standard selections and operatic numbers. The demand for the so-called patriotic popular number has practically passed into oblivion, the boys at the front calling for the straight popular selections.[85]

As Sterling suggested, demand for patriotic records had quickly dissipated and was replaced in the affections of the British armed forces abroad and war workers at home by well-known popular songs and ballads. Traditionally, ballads have articulated the feelings of ordinary people in extraordinary situations. For generations, themes of love, parting and death have provided the standard fare of British songs and ballads and the simple stories they tell are the poetry of the masses. Paul Fussell argued in *The Great War and Modern Memory* that the First World War provided a distinct break with the past. He suggested British writers and others embraced new forms of literary expression, particularly irony, as they attempted to find meanings capable of encompassing the indescribable experiences of the world's first total war. Countering this J. M. Winter, in his book *Sites of Memory Sites of Mourning*, argues that soldiers and civilians tried to cling to the familiar as well as to the new in their attempts to accommodate their varying experiences.[86] Although not explicit, Paul Fussell in his examination of the themes used by war poets, and by implication writers of popular ballads, does not argue with this. As an example, Fussell highlighted the use of the rose, especially red roses. This was an important literary metaphor for Britain itself and the garden, that quintessential statement of the British nation. Furthermore roses have long featured in literature not just as potent symbols of love, but also of war, parting, pain and death. As if to highlight this, the myriad commonwealth war cemeteries scattered across northern France and Flanders are landscaped to remind visitors of rose gardens.[87]

There are many examples of the rose metaphor being used in popular wartime songs, the most poignant being "Roses of Picardy" by Frederic E. Weatherly and Haydn Wood. It was composed in 1916 and recorded late in the war. By setting the song in Picardy, the site of the murderous battle of the Somme, the emotions were heightened and given an immediacy and poignancy. For many the simple words of "Roses of Picardy" summed up the feelings of young men and women parted by war, perhaps forever. The song first appeared in all the major British record catalogues during 1918 and its retention for decades after suggests it too touched a chord with soldiers and civilians alike.

In the circumstances of the world's first total war young British soldiers and sailors experienced unbelievable stresses. The final body count was horrendous with 750,000 British service personnel dead and overall casualties at more than 3,000,000; a full 50 per cent of all those who served. It is perhaps not too surprising that servicemen turned for support and escapist relief to romantic ballads like "Roses of Picardy" and made them best sellers. It formed part of the desperate need for escapist diversions, which combined with nostalgia for home and the certainties of prewar life. There was a need to seek out tangible reminders of those days and of the loved ones from whom one was parted, playing records was clearly a response to those needs and more.

These British and American songs and ballads were sourced partly from music publishers, but also from London's West End theatres with their inexhaustible supply of musicals and revues. These often had the additional attraction of a star associated with a particular hit song. They provided many of the most enduring wartime songs and ballads; some were so successful that they outlasted the shows. By 1915 there was strong demand for records of these hits and Louis Sterling hired an impresario to sign up performers to make original cast recordings.[88] As a consequence, many important recordings were made from musicals like the 1914 *Business as Usual* starring Violet Lorraine, Vivian Foster and Harry Tate, then top stars of the musical stage and music hall. Harry Tate recorded "Fortifying the Home Front" (Columbia, 504), of which Christopher Stone wrote, "We all knew the Harry Tate by heart, except for one phrase which to this very day has baffled me."[89] It also provided two songs by Violet Loraine: "Three cheers for little Belgium" (Columbia, 2488) and "When we've wound up the watch on the Rhine" (Columbia 2484), a duet with Ambrose Thorn.

Possibly the greatest British wartime hit came from the 1916 show *The Bing Boys are Here*. Performed at the Alhambra Theatre, London, it featured the slow and heavily romantic "If you were the only girl in the world" sung by two improbable star-struck lovers, music hall entertainers George Robey and Violet Lorraine. This song struck a powerful chord with British service personnel, though by 1916 George Robey was well into middle age and Violet Lorraine was beyond the first bloom of youth; but that didn't seem to matter. Their stage performance and subsequent recording (Columbia, L1035) became a treasured experience for many servicemen and was probably the most important recording of the war and has remained an evergreen love song into modern times. Of this Christopher Stone said, "We had George Robey quips on the tips of our tongues always . . . and we wore out Violet Loraine with our adoration."[90] Clearly, the combination of a hit song coupled to well-known artists turned records into a unique link to life back at home. In 1917 *The Bing Boys Are Here* was followed by *The Bing Girls Are There* and in 1918 *The Bing Boys on Broadway*. The 1917 show produced another slow romantic hit "Let the great big world keep turning," recorded first by Violet Loraine (HMV 03552) and later by Jose Collins. In contrast, the 1918 show failed to produce a single hit, but it did point the way songs for the captive armed forces market was going. As the name implied *The Bing Boys on Broadway* was set in New York and all the songs were American or US related, for example, "Hello, New York" and "Indian rag."[91]

This preoccupation with America is not as strange as it might seem. For most British service personnel it was an unknown world far away from war and war-related experiences, but that was the point and American-related lyrics proved a key component of successful songs and ballads in the second half of the war. This was highlighted in a 1916 list of Columbia's seven best-selling records, published in *Talking Machine News*. These included three versions of "Down home in Tennessee," "Kentucky home," "If you were the only girl in the world," "Pack up your troubles," "There's a long long trail," "My mother's rosary," "Every little while" and "The broken doll," two of which had American themes. Not all these songs survived the war but several did, suggesting record companies had touched at least some of the right notes.[92] In February 1917, a second list derived from more general sources appeared in *Talking Machine News*.[93] In addition to many of the records cited earlier, the new list included: "It's a long long way to my home in Kentucky," "Are you from Dixie?" and "When you wore a tulip." A study of the lyrics of these songs reveals a curious paradox, for although the titles suggest faraway places like Kentucky and Dixie the lyrics are no more than typical messages of love and parting. The attraction of these songs to young soldiers and sailors from places like Barking, Bradford, Bolton and Bristol suggests they were used to create and occupy a fantasy world, a conjured space in Kentucky, Tennessee or Dixie. The soldiers who engaged in this understandable fantasy had no notion of the reality of life in these places. But that was the point. They were intended to be as far away as possible from their experience of wartime life on the Western Front or elsewhere.

These songs and the records they spawned were not always appreciated, as testified in a June 1918 letter by Philip Gillespie Bainbridge, then serving on the Western Front, to his former Cambridge University tutor Edward Dent: "It is almost comical to hear from anyone whose interest in music extends beyond those depressing songs about various of the United States—I sometimes wish some of their admirers *would* go to Utah or wherever it might be and be done with it."[94] Bainbridge was killed soon after writing these words.

In his 1933 memoirs, Christopher Stone suggested the First World War made records and gramophones popular with musically sophisticated and educated men. Before the war these people, he argued, regarded records as incapable of reproducing musical performances. However, during the war, especially during long periods of inactivity and boredom, there occurred a reappraisal of their potential for transmitting musical culture.[95] There is certainly some evidence to support this. For example, the Yorkshire-born Cambridge educated writer J. B. Priestley bought his first gramophone in 1919, having been converted to the instrument during the course of his war service.[96] Wartime correspondence supports Stone's assertion. For instance, in early 1916, composer Arthur (later Sir Arthur) Bliss, a future Master of the Queen's Musick, wrote from the Western Front to Edward Dent, "I have suddenly found solace in the gramophone, Kennard [his brother who was killed later in 1916] who I believe has ordered all Berlioz for that touching instrument says they sound divine."[97] Soon after, Kennard Bliss wrote to Dent about this new love affair: "[*Western Front*] 6 February 1916. My other item of news is a gramophone and *Prince Igor* Overture, Hector's [Berlioz] Hungarian Dances, *Carmen* Selections, and Light things [Rhapsody] in G and D and a mass of ragtime and revue selections. Hector's piece is played by Landon Ronald and his men appallingly, but better than nothing to my mind."[98]

Soldiers on leave in London saw musical shows and bought records, which they brought back to their unit; where they often became not simply an adjunct to life on active service but an important part of it. In a 1918 letter to his wife, Christopher Stone confided, "We are sitting in the mess with the gramophone playing a selection from *Zig-Zag* [then a hit London musical revue], quite a domestic pleasure: but every crevice of every entrance is blanketed and has been for two hours as we are being bombarded with gas shells this evening."[99] Such was the power of this image that EMI Music Ltd recreated it in tableau form as part of its 1997 centenary exhibition. The most popular British war songs remained in record catalogues decades after it ended, and were regularly rerecorded years after their original success. The most important recordings not only transcended the war, they became anchors identifying that period of history not just for the veterans but also for modern day society.[100]

Wartime sales data of individual records have not survived, making it impossible to gauge in quantitative terms the popularity of the wartime ballads, though tracking the use of this kind of music by record companies does provide some clues. By 1914 recordings of the latest songs and ballads were made as soon as the sheet music became available and, wherever possible, the artist associated with it. If sales were good musical adaptations were created for recordings by orchestras or brass or military bands. A review of the wartime releases by four of the most important 10-inch popular record labels, J. E. Hough Ltd The Winner, the Columbia own-brand and Regal and The Gramophone Company's HMV Plum, show all these things happened to the most popular of wartime songs and ballads. For example, "Till the boys come home" was published in the spring of 1915 and by early 1916 all four labels had produced recordings: The Winner label released its first in June 1915. By the end of the war a total of ten recording were released on these labels, six vocal and the remaining four brass or military band adaptations. The ballad "There's a long long trail" first appeared in 1916 when four recordings were published and of these two were orchestral versions. "Roses of Picardy" was published in the summer of 1917 and by the end of the war there were three recordings, one of which was an orchestral arrangement.[101] In the circumstances of the final year of this conflict it remains something of an achievement that most record companies published new recordings, despite the absence of many experienced recording stars and shortages of all kinds of raw material. (To make matters worse, in October 1917, Columbia's record factory was completely destroyed by fire.) Taken together this all suggests songs and ballads hit the consciousness of not just the civilian population, but also that massive captive market in France and Flanders.

★   ★   ★

One important feature of this chapter has been the story of how men like Christopher Stone began a wartime love affair with recorded music. For

Stone and many other veterans of that war, the sounds of particular pieces of music stimulated wartime memories in the most acute fashion. In March 1917, he wrote movingly to his wife, "The gramophone is playing John Walsh's favourite song 'Son of Mine' which he hummed very un-harmoniously most of his last evening in our mess. It seems rather tragic going away from that part of the world where he and so many of our best friends are buried. But from all accounts we are going back to where we buried many of [our] earlier friends. We shall see."[102] With these experiences, it is perhaps unsurprising that in 1923 Christopher Stone joined his brother-in-law, the writer and adventurer Compton Mackenzie, in establishing *The Gramophone* as a London-based monthly journal dedicated to both reviewing new records and pressing record companies to make quality recordings of classical and popular music. *The Gramophone* readership Stone and Mackenzie aimed at were those educated, musically sophisticated male veterans of the First World War. They succeeded in this, creating a stable readership of 5,000. The success of this magazine was quite extraordinary, and it continues to flourish long after the passing of the founders and its original readership. However, for that generation (and for so many others), their love affair with recorded music started with the First World War. It was a peculiarly British love affair forged in wartime and it succeeded long term in transforming the gramophone from a domestic entertainment for the working classes into an instrument capable of providing high art and culture.[103]

NOTES

"Keep the Home Fire's Burning" (also known as "Till the Boys Come Home") was composed by Ivor Novello, with lyrics by Lena Guillbert Ford (an American poet killed during a 1916 air raid over London). The song epitomised the stoicism of wartime Britain, striking a chord with both the men on active service and the civilians on the home front. It became one of the greatest of all war songs.

1. J. B. Goodliffe, "Gramophones," *Daily Mail*, article reprinted in *The Voice* 8 (September 1918): 12.
2. "Chairman's Report," annual meeting, 24 September 1914 (meetings file, EMI).
3. Alfred Clark to Adolph Reich, 29 August 1911 (French papers, EMI).
4. Alfred Clark, "His Master's Voice: A Record" (EMI), 149
5. Alfred Clark to Eldridge Reeves Johnson, 10 August 1914 (Clark papers, Johnson Victrola Museum).
6. "Editorial," *Sound Wave* 8, no. 16 (1 September 1914).
7. "A Clarion Call to the Trade," *Sound Wave* 8, no. 17 (1 October 1914).

8. *Talking Machine News* 12, no. 7 (November 1914): 272.

9. *The Story of Edison Bell: J. E. Hough Ltd* (London: Hough, 1924).

10. For further details, see Peter Martland, *Since Records Began* (London: Batsford, 1997), 108–9. See also Martland, "Sir Louis Sterling," in *Oxford Dictionary of National Biography: From the Earliest Times to the Year 2000*, ed. H. C. G. Matthew and Brian Harrison (Oxford: Oxford University Press, 2005).

11. "Editorial," *Talking Machine News* 12, no. 6 (October 1914).

12. Alfred Clark to Eldridge Reeves Johnson, 1 September 1914 (Clark papers, Johnson Victrola Museum).

13. See advertisements in *Talking Machine News* 12, nos. 6–12 (October 1914–April 1915).

14. For listings of these patriotic records, see Karlo Adrian and Arthur Badrock, *Edison Bell Winner Records* (Bournemouth, UK: Bayly, 1989); Sydney Carter, *Blue Amberol Cylinders* (Bournemouth, UK: Talking Machine Review, 1977): 102–3; Frank Andrews, *Columbia 10-Inch Records* (Rugby: City of London Phonograph and Gramophone Society, 1985); Frank Andrews and Arthur Badrock, *The Complete Regal Catalogue* (Malvern, Worcestershire: City of London Phonograph and Gramophone Society, 1991), 50–62. See also, Brian Rust, *Gramophone Records of the First World War* (London: David and Charles, 1974).

15. For prewar unit sales data, see chapter 5.

16. Alfred Clark to Eldridge Reeves Johnson, 27 May 1915 (Clark papers, Johnson Victrola Museum).

17. For further details of German penetration, see chapter 4.

18. *Sound Wave* 13, no. 17 (1 October 1914): 650.

19. As Italy was a wartime ally, the Italian-registered Fonotipia venture remained in business and its Swiss-born London manager Otto Ruhl in post. I am grateful to Frank Andrews for clarifying the complex situation regarding these businesses.

20. See chapters 10 and 11. "Shellac Costs," *Talking Machine News* 17, no. 4 (August 1919): 256.

21. Frank Andrews and Arthur Badrock, *The Cinch Record (September 1913–January 1916)* (Wells-Next-the-Sea, Norfolk: City of London Phonograph and Gramophone Society Ltd, 2000), 10.

22. "Some American Impressions: A Chat With Louis Sterling," *Talking Machine News* 12, no. 10 (February 1915): 164–65.

23. Correspondence, April 1917 (Columbia Graphophone Co Ltd, formation papers, EMI).

24. "Conditions in the Talking Machine Industry in England," *Talking Machine World* 14, no. 4 (April 1918): 55.

25. "Editorial," *Talking Machine News* 14, no. 6 (September 1916).

26. Clark, "A Record," 153.

27. See chapters 4 and 6 for an explanation of this figure.

28. See "Day of the Portable Gramophone," *Talking Machine World* 12, no. 11 (November 1916): 107.

29. A copy of the memorandum is contained in "The Question of the Hour: The Prohibition of Imports," *Talking Machine News* 13, no. 12 (April 1916): 56–59. The ban on imports has curious antecedents. A 1915 Foreign Office file indicates French concern that sensitive intelligence might be transmitted via gramophone records. In a somewhat comic correspondence that included the farcical suggestion that all records would have to be played by officials before being imported or exported, the Board of Trade confessed that it knew nothing of

the industry and agreed to the ban. Although The Gramophone Company, then a major munitions manufacturer and government contractor, was the major exporter of records, it appears that no one thought it necessary to consult it about the problem. See Foreign Office, file FO382 468 (The National Archive, Kew).

30. Alfred Clark, "Notes in Regard to The Gramophone Company's Activities in the Great War," October 1915 (First World War papers, EMI).

31. Alfred Clark to Eldridge Reeves Johnson, 24 March 1917 (Clark papers, Johnson Victrola Museum).

32. For an account of the negotiations, see "Association of Gramophone and Musical Instrument Dealers Formed," *Talking Machine World* 14, no. 6 (June 1918): 99–100.

33. Decca portables were made from Swiss components (the earlier Dulcephone range was largely German in origin), although there is evidence for some British-made copies of the normal Swiss sound box. I am grateful to Christopher Proudfoot for pointing this out. See Edgar Samuel, "Decca Days: The Career of Wilfred Sampson, 1886–1958," *Journal of Jewish History* 30 (1989): 235–74, and David J. Jeremy and Christine Shawe, eds., "Frank Samuel," *Dictionary of Business Biography* (London: Butterworth, 1984), 5:37–41.

34. For more on these postwar developments, see chapters 10 and 11.

35. For accounts of the company's wartime attempts to recover these assets, see minutes, 15 August and November 1917 and 13 February 1918 (board papers, EMI).

36. The loss of the Russian branch is beyond this present work. For more, see Peter Martland, "A Business History of The Gramophone Company: 1897–1918," unpublished Cambridge University PhD thesis, 1993.

37. Geoffrey Jones, "The Gramophone Company: An Anglo-American Multinational, 1898–1931," *Business History Review*, 59 (spring 1985): 91.

38. Clark, "A Record," 152.

39. For an account of these contacts, see Alfred Clark, "Report," 3 September 1919 (board papers, EMI).

40. "Minutes," 16 March and 15 June 1915 (board papers, EMI).

41. "Minutes," 6 July 1915 (board papers, EMI).

42. Alfred Clark to Victor, 23 March 1917 (Clark papers, Johnson Victrola Museum).

43. Although the matrices were returned to The Gramophone Company in 1922, many original metals of often important early recordings were retained in Germany, where they remain in the archives of successor businesses.

44. For quantitative details of output and earnings, see Alfred Clark, "Further Notes," 1919 (First World War papers, EMI). This figure does not include profit on a Russian fuse contract subcontracted to an American manufacturer. The firm produced 5,500,000 cartridge cases, 4,000,000 fuses, 19,200,000 primers, 127,000,000 cartridge cases, 2,000 wings and ailerons (for aircraft) and 500,000 ammunition boxes. Data cited from *The Voice* 13 (October 1919): 14.

45. Alfred Clark to Eldridge Reeves Johnson, 20 March 1916 (Clark papers, Johnson Victrola Museum).

46. Clark, "Further Notes," 1919.

47. Cited in "Chairman's report," annual meeting, 10 November 1915 (meetings file, EMI).

48. For a history of the Ministry of Munitions and its powers to control companies, see R. J. Q. Adams, *Arms and the Wizard* (London: Cassell, 1978).

49. Alfred Clark to Eldridge Reeves Johnson, 21 November 1917 (Clark papers, Johnson Victrola Museum).

50. Alfred Clark, "Report Concerning the Formation of the Metal Agency," 3 December 1915 (Clark papers, Johnson Victrola Museum).

51. "Report on Finance and Outside Contract Work," November 1918 (board papers, EMI).

52. The reasons for these strains are discussed in chapter 5.

53. Alfred Clark to Eldridge Reeves Johnson, 31 January 1915 (Clark papers, Johnson Victrola Museum).

54. See "Chairman's Report," annual meeting, 5 December 1917 (meetings file, EMI).

55. Regrettably, the only surviving evidence concerning this important incident is in the highly partial correspondence between Clark and Johnson.

56. Alfred Clark to Eldridge Reeves Johnson, 31 January 1916 (Clark papers, Johnson Victrola Museum).

57. Alfred Clark to Eldridge Reeves Johnson, 31 January 1916 (Clark papers, Johnson Victrola Museum).

58. Alfred Clark, untitled note, March 1916 (Clark papers, Johnson Victrola Museum).

59. See "Minutes," 22 February 1916 (board papers, EMI).

60. Alfred Clark to Eldridge Reeves Johnson, 23 February 1916 (Clark papers, Johnson Victrola Museum).

61. Alfred Clark to Eldridge Reeves Johnson, 28 February 1916 (Clark papers, Johnson Victrola Museum).

62. Alfred Clark to Eldridge Reeves Johnson, 20 March 1916 (Clark papers, Johnson Victrola Museum).

63. Alfred Clark to Eldridge Reeves Johnson, 19 April 1916 (Clark papers, Johnson Victrola Museum).

64. According to Clark, none of the new directors were friends of Williams. Alfred Clark to Eldridge Reeves Johnson, 19 April 1916 (Clark papers, Johnson Victrola Museum). According to the *Directory of Directors, 1916*, Alexander Ormrod was a director of numerous public companies.

65. For details of the settlement, see John Broad, "Conditional Agreement," April 1916 (board papers EMI).

66. Alfred Clark to Eldridge Reeves Johnson, 15 June 1916 (Clark papers, Johnson Victrola Museum).

67. The wealth of financial data on which chapter 5 was based ends in 1913. To assess wartime performance, reliance has to be placed on annual reports, entries in *The Stock Exchange Yearbook*, Alfred Clark's "Notes on the War," "Future Prospects for the Entire Business" and "Past History of the Company." None of these sources provide the detail of the prewar "notes on accounts" and "annual reports to the board."

68. British retail price index in 1914 = 100, 1915 = 123, 1916 = 146, 1917 = 176, 1918 = 203, 1919 = 215 and 1920 = 249, cited in B. R. Mitchell, *Abstract of British Historic Statistics* (Cambridge: Cambridge University Press, 1962), 478.

69. See "Chairman's Report," annual meeting, 10 November 1915 (meetings file, EMI).

70. Until 1914 the US dollar-pound sterling exchange rate was $4.85, though most businesses used $5.00. By 1918 this had slipped to $4.20 to the pound. This work uses the same exchange rate as contemporary businessmen, and so in this chapter it is the prewar rate of $5.00.

71. See "Chairman's Report," annual meeting, 13 November 1918 (meetings file, EMI).

72. Balance sheet 30 June 1918 and "Chairman's Report" (meetings file, EMI).

73. In the 1918–1919 accounts £250,000 of undistributed profit from 1912, frozen under the terms of the 1913 debenture, is shown as capitalised, converted into fully paid-up shares and distributed to shareholders. This indicates that the money had already been spent on capital developments.

74. For more on this issue, see chapter 10.

75. J. M. Winter, *The Great War and the British People* (Basingstoke: Macmillan, 1985), 213.

76. Winter, *The Great War*, 213.

77. "London Columbia Manager Here," *Talking Machine World* 12, no. 1 (January 1916): 31.

78. Alfred Clark to Eldridge Reeves Johnson, 24 March 1917 (Clark papers, Johnson Victrola Museum).

79. *The Era Annual 1918* (London, 1918), 33.

80. John Brophy and Eric Partridge, *Songs and Slang of the British Soldiers: 1914–1918* (London: Partridge, 1930). References to this can be found in war novels, including Robert Graves, *Goodbye to All That* (London: Cape, 1929) and Siegfried Sassoon *Memoirs of an Infantry Officer* (London: Faber & Faber, 1931).

81. J. B. Goodliffe, "Gramophones," *The Voice* 8 (September 1918): 12.

82. Christopher Stone, "A Decca Romance," *The Gramophone* 1, no. 2 (1923): 56.

83. Data derived from *Talking Machine News* 12, no. 6 (October 1914): 244, and 13, no. 4 (August 1915).

84. "From Our European Correspondent," *Talking Machine World* 11, no. 7 (July 1915), and no. 10 (October 1915). *Talking Machine News* 14, no. 8 (December 1916): 331.

85. "Conditions in the Talking Machine Industry in England," *Talking Machine World* 14, no. 4 (April 1918): 55.

86. Paul Fussell, *The Great War and Modern Memory* (London: Oxford University Press1975). J. M. Winter, *Sites of Memory Sites of Mourning* (Cambridge: Cambridge University Press, 1995).

87. Fussell, *The Great War*, 243–54.

88. For a listing of shows and recordings derived from them, see Robert Seeley and Rex Bunnett, *London Musical Shows on Record: 1889–1989* (Harrow, UK: General Gramophone, 1989).

89. Stone, "A Decca Romance."

90. Stone, "A Decca Romance."

91. See Seeley and Bunnett, *London Musical Shows on Record*.

92. "Which Are the Best Sellers?" *Talking Machine News* 14, no. 6 (October 1916): 247.

93. "Songs Without Singers," *Talking Machine News* 14, no. 9 (February 1917): 398.

94. Philip Gillespie Bainbridge to E. J. Dent, add. MS/7973/B7 (Manuscript Division, Cambridge University Library).

95. Christopher Stone, *Christopher Stone Speaking* (London: E. Mathews & Marot, 1933).

96. J. B. Priestley, *The Edwardians* (London: Heinemann, 1970), 133.

97. Arthur Bliss to E. J. Dent, 15 January 1916, add. ms. 7973/B/29 (Manuscript Division, Cambridge University Library).

98. Kennard Bliss to E. J. Dent, 6 February 1916, add. ms. 7973/B29 (Manuscript Division, Cambridge University Library).

99. Eds. G. D. Sheffield and G. I. S. Inglis *From Vimy Ridge to the Rhine: Great War Letters of Christopher Stone* (Marlborough, Wilts: Crowood, 1989): 117. Staged at the London Hip-

podrome in 1917, *Zig-Zag* was a musical revue starring the ubiquitous George Robey and Shirley Kellogg. The record referred to by Stone was either Columbia 667 or HMV C782. A collection of the hits from the show were recorded by Columbia and released in a twelve record album (Columbia L1222–23 and L1137–46). See *Columbia record catalogue 1918–19*, copy in the collection of the present author.

100. For more on this important point, see Dan Todman, *The Great War Myth and Memory* (London: Hambledon, 2005).

101. Data derived from Adrian and Badrock, *Edison Bell Winner Records*; Badrock and Andrews, *Regal Catalogue*; Andrews, *Columbia 10-Inch Records*; Frank Andrews and Ernie Bayly, *Catalogue of HMV "B" Series Records* (Wells-Next-the-Sea, Norfolk: City of London Phonograph and Gramophone Society Ltd, 2000).

102. Sheffield and Inglis, *From Vimy Ridge to the Rhine*, 88.

103. For more about the early years of *The Gramophone*, see chapter 9.

9

THE BRITISH RECORD INDUSTRY: 1918–1931

"I'm Forever Blowing Bubbles, Pretty Bubbles in the Air"

The talking machine industry is entitled to first place among the music industries as the retail turnover of this section is to-day larger than any other section and that is so because those responsible for the development have not only given the public what it wanted in music but were enterprising enough to keep a little ahead of the public mind.

—Louis Sterling,[1] 1926

At precisely 11 o'clock on the morning of 11 November 1918 the guns along the Western Front fell silent, signalling not just the end of four terrible years of war but also the defeat of Germany and its allies. In the weeks and months that followed the belligerents confronted the cost of war, which included ten million dead and countless millions wounded. The conflict had emptied treasuries, leaving once powerful currencies hopelessly debased and worthless. Adding to this chaos and confusion, the war ended with the European continent awash with bloody revolutions, famine and disease. In the face of such violence and volatility, the stable prewar world with its optimistic values and belief in progress had vanished. In these difficult and uncertain circumstances the British picked up the threads of life, including commercial life. In sectors like the talking machine industry this meant learning to navigate the treacherous waters of a new difficult-to-understand world, complete with unprecedented levels of first inflation then deflation in unpredictable roller coaster domestic and international economies. In the decade or so after the war the industry (like everyone else) experienced an initial domestic consumer boom then, in 1921 and 1922, economic collapse. Thereafter, till the onset of the Great Depression in 1929, it boomed, becoming a British industrial success story. During these same years the industry made the transition from light mechanical to electrical engineering at the cutting edge of audio and related technologies. It is against this extraordinary background that the present and two following chapters are set.

★   ★   ★

As far as the British record industry was concerned much had changed since 1914. For instance, by the end of the war the zigzag cut disc record was firmly established as the industry standard.[2] And, although the overall size of the wartime British market had not grown to any significant degree, it had attracted many musically sophisticated people and those who remained consumers forced record companies to take their musical needs seriously (see chapter 11). Furthermore, the 1920s saw a remarkable rise in sales of dance music records, the popular music of the time, which provided the industry with its main engine of growth. There were other changes too, for instance in 1915 the old policy of free trade was largely abandoned and tariffs introduced to raise revenue and curb consumer spending. These protectionist policies continued after the war with imported records, gramophones and electrical goods subject to a 33⅓ per cent tariff, which were critical in preventing German manufacturers regaining their pre-1914 dominance. There were also important changes to the United States record industry which had implications for the British industry. Central to this was the 1921 landmark judgement "Victor Talking Machine Company v The Starr Piano Company," which ended the patent-based oligopoly created by Edison, Columbia and Victor. As a result a free competitive market emerged based on the industry standard zigzag disc, causing a fundamental reorientation of the industry. In these circumstances record companies like Gennett, Emerson, Vocalion, Aeolian, Brunswick, Okeh and a host of others could use the standard zigzag disc format, which they used to create important new catalogues of jazz, dance and other forms of American popular music, which were often licenced to British companies.[3]

The 1920s saw dynamic change within the British industry as both sectors experienced significant downward pressures on prices and the impact of technical innovations, especially after the introduction of electrical recording in 1925.[4] There was also continued growth in the portable machine market, aided by the extension of hire purchase and other cheap credit schemes; though for record companies and retailers records remained a valuable cash product. And, just as the immediate prewar period was characterised by numerous cheap record labels, the postwar years saw the appearance of many equally cheap records. The effect of all this was to make records and machines more affordable and readily available to a much larger proportion of the population.

Before the war few talking machines were manufactured in Britain and during the war imports of machines and components were severely curtailed. Filling this gap, a new wartime British light engineering industry began making clockwork motors and other parts. After the war, firms like The Garrard Engineering and Manufacturing Company Ltd in Swindon manufactured springs, clockwork motors and sound boxes for the industry. This venture was formed in 1915 by royal jeweller Garrard and Company (reformed as a war contractor manufacturing delicate precision instruments), its motors were incorporated into machines manufactured by Decca, Columbia and many others. Garrard were not alone, with ventures like Collaro Ltd of Barking in Essex manufacturing a range of clockwork motors, spares and other equipment. These businesses were successful and during the late 1920s and early 1930s made the transition into electrical engineering, manufacturing gramophones, radiograms (combined radio and electrically powered gramophones) and other kinds of domestic and commercial audio equipment, and both survived into the modern era. Many existing light engineering firms moved into this line of business, for example J. Stead and Company Ltd of Sheffield made the "Vulcan" brand mainsprings for the trade and (see below) steel needles. There were also many new often small workshop-based manufacturers centred not just in traditional metal working centres like Birmingham and Sheffield but in and around London. These made or assembled the sound boxes used for playing records, together with clockwork motors and other metal components. Furthermore, despite the tariffs on machine imports the Swiss firm Thorens successfully reentered the postwar British market and found ready orders for its well-made goods. Thorens was joined by the long established German-Swiss sound box manufacturer Goldring, whose interwar success in the British market caused it to move production to Britain in 1933. These too made the transition into audio electronics and survived into the modern era.[5] One of the most important postwar manufacturers was the London-based musical instrument and record wholesaler Barnett Samuel and Sons Ltd. Under its Decca brand name, Barnett Samuel and Sons Ltd developed a range of relatively inexpensive portable machines.[6] Their popularity grew after the war and this demand was in turn fed by a range of relatively cheap and easily stored gramophones. Although The Columbia Graphophone Company and The Gramophone Company pushed their high-end-of-the-market products, sales were dominated by their range of portable machines.[7]

By the 1920s talking machines came in many shapes and forms. In addition to portables there were table and floor standing gramophones known as cabinet and consul models, which largely replaced the classic prewar design with its exposed "morning glory" horn and workings. These new machines had the horn folded under the mechanism and were encased in a wooden cabinet. Although the mechanism was largely standardised, the new designs made significant concessions to modern domestic furniture. The wooden cabinets were made from timbres ranging from cheap plywood and pine to expensive bespoke models constructed by cabinetmakers from rare woods and veneers. The first electrical gramophones were offered for sale in the late 1920s, and soon after radiograms appeared. Initially, these cost anything from £105 to £315 and were aimed at the super rich. Thus, by the early 1920s, a wide array of British manufactured mechanical machines were on offer to the public and most towns had a record shop and a machine repair depot well stocked with spare parts, often run by a war veteran.

The mild steel needles used to play the records were another vital component of the record industry. Until the introduction of vinyl plastic long playing microgroove records (which were played with a permanent jewel stylus) after the Second World War, records were played with disposable steel needles that were replaced after each playing. During the 1920s a wide range of needle types were available, there were even chromium plated needles that could, it was claimed, be used to play up to twenty records; but these were very expensive. Soft, medium and loud tone needles were on offer and there were even thorn and triangular fibre needles which reduced wear and avoided deposits of metal in the record groove. Rather than manufacture their own needles, record companies bought in but marketed them under their own brands. The Midland firm of W. R. Steel (Reddich) Ltd was an early postwar manufacturer, but the largest was J. Stead and Company Ltd of Sheffield (makers of "Vulcan" main springs and other components) who marketed its own range of "Songster" needles in distinctive boxes. Whatever the type, tens of millions of needles were sold annually, usually in brightly coloured metal boxes containing 100 needles; one brand even used a pyramid shaped tin. As a result of all this activity ownership of records and gramophones spread rapidly across the country and by 1931 nearly two-thirds of households owned a machine and some records, but less than a third had a radio and few were connected to mains electricity.[8]

Before 1914 the British government maintained a hands-off attitude towards its manufacturing base. The war changed all this and postwar governments pursued interventionist policies. To assist this process they conducted a number of production censuses, which provide invaluable data for the decade or so after the end of the war. The baseline data is a 1918 record and machine industry estimate of annual worth of around £600,000.[9] Table 9.1 has been developed from this data, providing a critical snapshot of the record and machine industry during the 1920s and early 1930s.

Table 9.1 shows how within five years of the war's end the total value of the trade had grown from £600,000 to £2,298,000. The 1930 figures shows why this was a 1920s glamour industry, with total value up to nearly £8 million more than 70 million records pressed and nearly 800,000 machines manufactured for domestic and export use. In sharp contrast the 1934 figures show the cruel depredations of the Great Depression and speak for themselves. Census data also included export figures which are set out in table 9.2.

Table 9.2 shows the 1920s export boom in British records and machines, with few imports and little sign of returning German manufacturers. Like table 9.1, the figures also show the devastation caused by the Great Depression. Looking beyond the censuses, other evidence supports the notion of an industry-wide boom. For example, a 1931 *Talking Machine News* article entitled "A Go-Ahead Industry," the Association of Gramophone and Musical Instrument Manufacturers and Wholesale Dealers claimed British exports for 1929 totalled 456,000 machines and 15,000,000 records.[10] The previous year a *Merchandising Survey of Great Britain* was published, with a volume devoted to the record and machine industry. Its figures concur with those cited in table 9.2, which also reveals pre-1930 record import data. In 1927, even with a 33⅓ per cent tariff, imports of records amounted to 110,556, in 1928 the figure was 147,228 and in 1929 226,800. Almost three quarters of these imports were sourced from the United States. As total British record sales in these years were between 50 and 60 million, these imports were negligible. Imports of machines tell the same story and never exceed 30,000 annually. There were significant imports of components, including clockwork motors amounting to £231,839 in 1927, £301,060 in 1928 and £233,056 in 1929; more than 90 per cent of which came from Germany or Switzerland. The few machines imported from the United States were top-of-the-range models, with an average wholesale value of £8, compared to the value of around 10 shillings for a Germany machine. Imports of clockwork motors and other components fed into the large British machine trade, making it difficult to gauge just what constituted a British manufactured machine.[11]

Right from its earliest beginnings the British record and machine industry attracted businessmen and others who mistakenly believed that they

Table 9.1. United Kingdom Census of Production 1924 and 1930 and *Report on Import Duties*, 1934: Record Industry Data

Year	Records		Machines			Total Value
	Units	Value	Units	Value	Parts, Value	
1924	22,238000	£992,000 [$4,960,000]	279,500	£907,000 [$4,535,0000]	£399,000 [$1,995,000]	£2,298,000 [$11,490,000]
1930	71,652,000	£4,399,000 [$21,995,000]	785,159	£2,720,000 [$13,600,000]	£824,000 [$4,120,000]	£7,943,000 [$39,715,000]
1934	29,700,000	£1,308,000[a] [$5,397,400]	112,667	£340,000 [$1,377,000]	NA	£1,648,000 [$6,674,400]

[a]In the midst of the financial crisis of 1931, Britain abandoned the gold standard and with it a fixed exchange rate. As a consequence, the value of the pound sterling fell from $4.85 to $4.05. This figure reflects that change.

Table 9.2.   United Kingdom Censuses of Production, 1924, 1930, and *Report on Inport Duties*, 1934: Records and Machines, Imports, Exports and Domestic Consumption Figures

Year	Records	Machines
1924		
Production	22,380,000	279,500
Exported	6,924,000	87,500
Imported	72,000	64,500
UK use	15,528,000	256,522
1930		
Production	71,652,000	789,000
Exported	12,732,000	307,550
Imported	324,000	41,218
UK use	59,244,000	523,168
1934		
Production	29,700,000	112,667
Exported	5,364,000	83,988
Imported	60,000	3,677
UK use	24,396,000	32,356

Source: The data used in these tables are derived from "Musical Instrument Trade," *Third Census of Production Final Report, 1924* (London: HMSO, 1924), 397–400; "Musical Instrument Trade," *Fourth Census of Production Final Report (Part IV), 1930* (London: HMSO 1930), 249–59; and "Musical Instrument Trade," *Report on Import Duties Act (1934)* (London: HMSO, 1934), 321–23.

could easily and quickly make lots of money. Many of these ventures were undercapitalised and their managers failed to understand the complexities of the market. Inevitably they fell by the wayside, though a few grew to become medium-sized businesses. Unfortunately, the business and other papers relating to these companies have not survived. However they did leave behind sufficient footprints to provide important insights into the vibrant business environment that made up the early interwar record and machine trade. The years 1927 to 1929 saw an extraordinary London stock market bubble in record company floatations; it really was a case of "pretty bubbles in the air." This frenzy was based on the remarkable success of two long-established record manufacturers, The Columbia Graphophone Company and The Gramophone Company. During the course of this so-called gramophone boom more than twenty new record and machine manufacturing concerns were formed. Some like Decca took over existing businesses (in Decca's case Barnett Samuel and Sons Ltd), whilst others were new ventures, like The Duophone and Unbreakable Record Company Ltd, formed to exploit new processes and inventions like the unbreakable record.[12] These new entrants, like those in the immediate prewar period, looked mainly to the cheap end of the market, producing records at prices as low as 9d and machines as cheap as £1.1.0d. According to the *Merchandising Survey,* around £3,500,000 was invested in new concerns.

This massively over optimistic assessment of the market ensured that even if the London stock market had not crashed in 1929, very few of these ventures would have made money.[13] As The Gramophone Company executive James Muir observed in 1928, "So far none of the records of the recent floatations have reached the market: I am wondering if some of them ever will."[14] Another indicator supporting this opinion can be found in *The Music Seller Reference Book 1928–1929.* This volume covers the peak of the "gramophone boom" and lists just sixteen record manufacturers, and of these a number are affiliated via ownership, licencing or pressing agreements. By the onset of the Great Depression in 1929 there were perhaps as few as twelve manufacturers and by 1938 the figure was down to two. Of those the only survivor from the 1920s entrants was Decca.[15] The tables and survey shows how shares in the record and machine industry peaked in 1929, a pattern of activity reflective of that other twentieth-century software bubble, the dot com boom of the late 1990s. And, just as that bubble burst in 2000, by early 1930 shares in record and machine business proved "pretty bubbles in the air" that burst under the bitter gale of the Great Depression. It wasn't just the economic collapse, by 1930 radio had emerged to rival records at the heart of domestic leisure activities and talking pictures provided another distraction. Whatever the reasons, the industry collapsed and it took until 1959 to regain 1929 volumes and values.

★   ★   ★

In the years after the war the British record and machine industry was dominated by two ventures, The Gramophone Company Ltd and The Columbia Graphophone Company Ltd. Although the experiences of these businesses form the core of this chapter and the next, to suggest they *were* the record and machine industry is to ignore the vital contribution made by many small and medium sized manufacturers whose contribution did much to ensure there was growth and success. It would be impossible to examine the fortunes of every business engaged in record and machine manufacture in these years, indeed many were transient and several never traded at all. The following is a sample and gives at least an indication of commercial activity during this remarkable decade or so.

At the end of the First World War, J. E. Hough Ltd was a private company with no trade in its shares. It was the successor in business to The Edison Bell Consolidated Phonograph Company Ltd and manufactured both records and machines. J. E. Hough Ltd survived the war with a combination of government contracts and good recordings. In 1918 it boasted a catalogue containing 4,000 titles.[16] In his memoirs the recording engineer Joseph Batten, who came to the firm after war service and later became its musical director, wrote of this end-of-war catalogue, "Until 1920 they had been one of the foremost manufacturers of popular records, selling many hundreds of thousands of Winner records; their catalogues of brass band music, light orchestral pieces, music hall celebrities and sentimental songs appealing to the unsophisticated." All this changed during the 1920s, as Joseph Batten and others helped make recordings for the newly reintroduced Edison Bell Velvet Face Records. These included recordings of classical music by figures such as conductors Dr (later Sir) Adrian Boult, Sir Hamilton Harty, Sir Dan Godfrey and Eugène (later Sir Eugène) Goossens. Batten was proud of his achievements, especially to have recorded the great oratorio *The Dream of Gerontius* by Sir Edward Elgar; the first ever recording (albeit in abridged form) of this massive work.[17] In 1927 Joseph Batten left and was succeeded by former music hall entertainer and accompanist George Ison who, together with studio manager and pioneer recording engineer Harry Hudson, made up an experienced team making excellent records. By 1930, Edison Bell claimed its various record catalogues contained more than 3,000 titles.[18] J. E. Hough Ltd were also British licencees to several US record companies, including Gennett, Emerson, Federal and Paramount, publishing a range of jazz, dance and other popular American music from these sources. The firm had always made a good living as a matrix maker and pressing contractor for small record companies lacking their own manufacturing facilities. It even leased matrices for use on other labels, usually following the convention of using cover names for its own performers.

At the head of the business was James Edward Hough, a bluff and formidable survivor. Already seventy years old when the war ended, Hough, who styled himself "father of the British trade," remained in the driving seat until his death in 1925.[19] In 1918 J. E. Hough Ltd, like many British companies, desperately needed fresh capital to affect a postwar relaunch. The following year it increased the nominal capital from £10,000 to £100,000 and in 1921 to £150,000. Given the state of capital markets in these years, the finance came from Hough, his family and friends rather than the City of London.[20] Building on wartime developments in radio, Hough also manufactured electrical components and later radios, transforming the business from light mechanical into an electrical engineering venture. In addition to Hough's London-based factory, the firm acquired manufacturing facilities in Huntingdon, to the north of London, which cost £12,500. These investments paid off with record sales during the financial year 1925–1926, one million up on the previous year. The relatively cheap Edison Bell records and machines brought many new consumers into the market; though Hough's death in 1925 proved a watershed for the business that bore his name.[21] In May 1926 the venture was renamed Edison Bell Ltd, and with assets of £167,961 it had ambitious expansionary plans. To this end the capital was increased to £300,000, made up of 150,000 7½ per cent £1.00 preference shares and 150,000 £1.00 ordinary shares. These were sold at a stock market floatation. Some financial data from this period has survived.

During the years to 1926 the privately owned J. E. Hough Ltd had no public trade in its shares. However, as table 9.3 shows, the dividend payments for these years suggest that prior to taking it to market the owners (largely the Hough family) stripped the available capital out of the business. In the boom years 1926 to 1928 the positive effects of the "gramophone bubble" can be seen in the price of its shares. Although this might suggest the company experienced reasonable returns, this was not the case, as table 9.3 shows. Even in the good years, Edison Bell's earnings failed to cover dividend payments on its ordinary shares. It also shows the company drawing on preference capital to make up the shortfall; in 1927–1928 £3,350 and 1928–1929 £400. Table 9.3 also illustrates the fate of Edison Bell shares

Table 9.3.   J. E. Hough/Edison Bell Ltd: Share Price, Profits and Dividends Paid, 1921–1931

Year	Share Price		Profit	Dividend Paid on Ordinary Shares
	Ordinary	*Preference*		
1921–1922	—	—	—	5% + 140% bonus
1922–1923	—	—	—	10%
1923–1924	—	—	—	7½%
1924–1925	—	—	—	7½%
1925–1926	—	—	—	10% + 25% bonus
1926–1927	£1.50 [$7.50]	£0.93 [$4.65]	£32,100 [$160,500]	8% [£12,000]
1927–1928	£1.62 [$8.10]	£0.94 [$4.70]	£15,400 [$77,000]	12½% [£18,750]
1928–1929	£1.15 [$5.75]	£0.77 [$3.85]	£15,400 [$77,000]	10% [£15,000]
1929–1930	£0.57 [$2.85]	£0.62 [$3.10]	£28,100 [$140,500]	NIL
1930–1931	£0.15 [$0.75]	£0.23 [$1.15]	NA	NIL

Source: Data from The Edison Bell Ltd entries in *The Stock Exchange Yearbook*, 1927 to 1934.

and is an indicator of the speed and ferocity of the Great Depression and its impact on the industry.[22]

In September 1926 Edison Bell released its first electrical recordings using an in-house process developed by Paul Gustavus Adolphus Helmut Voigt, a brilliant electrical engineer who joined the firm in 1922.[23] This recording system meant Edison Bell, unlike many other record companies, avoided paying costly royalties to patent holders like Western Electric. The Voigt process records were released on the existing 2s 10-inch The Winner and Velvet Face records, together with its new 3s and 4s.6d 10- and 12-inch Electron label; by its final releases in 1931 the Electron catalogue comprised nearly 370 recordings. That was not all, Edison Bell also entered the late-1920s cut-price market with the 1s.6d 8-inch Radio label, which utilised a narrower record cut enabling playing times as long as regular 10-inch records.[24]

In 1928, at the height of the stock market bubble, Edison Bell Ltd formed Edison Bell (International) Ltd to operate as its overseas arm. This company managed relations with European, specifically Italy, Yugoslavia and also its US licencors. It formed part of a plan to transform the business into a worldwide enterprise. Edison Bell (International) Ltd had a share capital of £300,000 of which £225,000 was made up of £1 preference shares. However, in a telling move, they were issued at the heavily discounted rate of 14s.3d. In September 1931, despite across the range price reductions, Edison Bell and Edison Bell (International) Ltd posted accounts showing losses of around £91,000 and within months both were in administration. The British and international business continued for a while, but it was the end of the road for the oldest British record company. In January 1933 an order was granted to wind up the ventures and although the receiver sought buyers there was no interest. Edison Bell and Edison Bell (International) disappeared leaving a total deficiency of £370,000. It was a sad end to this pioneering business.[25]

★ ★ ★

By 1918 The Crystalate Manufacturing Company Ltd was a well established matrix maker and contract pressing agent for record companies lacking their own manufacturing facilities.[26] All this changed in the postwar period when, starting in 1923, Crystalate became licencee of the American label Banner Records. It later became licencee for American Record Company (ARC), which claimed half of the US low-priced record market amounting to around thirty million records a year. The links were strong as Crystalate owned a one-third interest in ARC and Brunswick and had subsidiaries in France and Germany. After 1922 there were other changes. In that year Crystalate began pressing and marketing the 10-inch Imperial record for The Sound Recording Company Ltd. Imperial records retailed for 2s.6d (reduced to 1s.6d in 1927 and 1s.3d in 1931) and offered dance and other kinds of popular music.[27] Three years later Crystalate acquired the Imperial label, and with London recording studios managed by William Ditcham, the label had its fair share of good dance bands. They scored a coup when in 1931 one of the top British dance bandleaders, Jack Payne, signed a contract with them. However, by that stage of the Great Depression, many leading names had been dropped by the major record companies and top talent could be picked up at bargain prices.[28] Although Imperial was a relatively small label, it survived the worst of the Great Depression and continued to release fresh recordings until 1934. Crystalate products were varied, but mainly took the form of cheap records retailing at 6d. One was the 7-inch Victory, which appeared in 1928 and was succeeded in 1931 by the 8-inch Eclipse; this in turn was replaced in 1935 by the Crown record. Other records included children's label Kiddyphone, which were released in three sizes and Little Marvels. All these were manufactured for and sold through retail multiple F. W. Woolworth. Releases of the Crystalate's 7- and 8-inch range of records continued till 1937.[29]

Like Edison Bell, Crystalate was a medium-sized business. In order to expand it formed The Crystalate Gramophone Record Manufacturing Co Ltd in 1928, which went to a stock market floatation. The capital consisted of 200,000 8 per cent preference and 150,000 £1 ordinary shares. As table 9.4 shows Crystalate paid unrealistically high dividends in order to maintain its share price. In contrast to Edison Bell they were paid out of earned profit, though the level of dividends left the firm dangerously short of ready cash.

The diverse nature of its product range enabled Crystalate to survive the Great Depression. Its strength lay in the fact that, in contrast to most

Table 9.4.   Crystalate Gramophone Record Manufacturing Company Ltd: Profit Earned and Dividend Paid, 1929–1931

Year	Net Profit	Ordinary Share Dividend	Retained Profit
1929	£88,900 [$444,500]	41⅔% £62,500 [$312,500]	£18,900 [$94,500]
1930	£55,700 [$278,500]	33⅓% £40,000 [$200,000]	£8,800 [$44,000]
1931	£76,270 [$381,350]	NA	NA

Source: Data from Crystalate Gramophone Record Manufacturing Company Ltd entry, *Stock Exchange Yearbook*, 1928–1931; *Talking Machine News* 29, no. 1 (May 1931): 115; and *Merchandising Survey*, 7–11.

record manufacturers, it was never (partly or wholly) dependent on the record business. In March 1937, the Crystalate record business was sold to Decca for £150,000 and 400,000 Decca shares; in changed corporate form this firm existed into the modern era.

★   ★   ★

After the 1921 United States judgement in the case of "Victor Talking Machine Company v Starr Piano Company" a free market emerged and with it many new record companies. These either entered the British market as manufacturers or licenced British record companies to press their recordings.[30] One was The Brunswick-Balke-Collender Company, manufacturers of billiards equipment and records. In 1922 The Chappell Piano Company Ltd became its British licencees (Chappells were already the concessionaire for the Cliftophone gramophone) distributing discs derived from American masters. Initially, these were sold as Brunswick Cliftophone then Brunswick records.[31] This ended in 1926 when The British Brunswick Ltd was formed, with a share capital of £120,000 made up of 100,000 £1 preference shares and 200,000 ordinary 1s shares. The directors included pioneer recording engineer William Sinkler Darby and his father-in-law businessman George Roberts.[32] At first the catalogue consisted of American-derived records, supplemented from 1927 with British recordings; British Brunswick was also licencee of the German Polydor label and had access to the American Brunswick and Vocalion catalogues. Also in 1927 the American parent introduced the "Panatrope," the first all electric radiogram, which went on sale in Britain the following year. British Brunswick was never a success and in 1928 it was acquired by The Duophone and Unbreakable Record Company Ltd. The following year Duophone was itself bought by Decca (see below). In 1931 the US Brunswick record business was sold on to filmmaker Warner Brothers, who in turn sold it to American Record Company (ARC), whose British licencees were Decca. One of Brunswick's stable of artists was Bing Crosby, whose records were a mainstay of the shattered remnants of the record industry on both sides of the Atlantic for much of the 1930s.[33]

★   ★   ★

Formed in 1907, The Aeolian Company Ltd retailed player pianos as the British branch of the American parent and, after 1915, its product range expanded to include Vocalion gramophones. In 1920 the first British

Aeolian Vocalion records were released. These were made by a subsidiary The Universal Music Company Ltd[34] at a studio in the West End of London and pressed by Universal at its Hayes, Middlesex plant; subsequent releases were also from this source and the US parent. In 1922 Aeolian launched the Aco label, with records using British and US Aeolian masters and recordings licenced from Gennett. The Universal plant had a matrix making capacity and a sixteen press manufacturing facility.[35] This was an excess capacity, but enabled Aeolian to develop a matrix making and pressing contract business for record companies without manufacturing facilities.[36] In 1924, following the Brunswick purchase of the US parent, The Vocalion Gramophone Company Ltd was formed with a capital of £250,000 in 10s shares. Its purpose was to take over the Aeolian record and machine business, together with the subsidiary Universal Music Company Ltd. Results failed to match expectations; at one point The Gramophone Company Ltd was offered the business for £50,000 but turned it down.[37] In 1925 Vocalion acquired The Aeolian Company Ltd and it was for a while another glamour stock; in 1927 its 10s shares peaked at £1.14.6d.[38]

In 1927 Vocalion went into the mass market, dropping the Vocalion, Aeolian and Aco labels and launching its smaller and much cheaper Broadcast records, aimed at largely working-class consumers who regularly purchased cheap dance records. Broadcast records were released in three sizes, 6-inch retailing at 6d, an 8-inch Broadcast Junior retailing at 1s.6d (increased to 9 inches in 1931), which were sold to wholesalers at 8s per dozen. In 1929 a 2s 10-inch record was marketed as the Broadcast Super Twelve Dance Record and in 1931 the Broadcast Super Twelve appeared. With a narrower than standard record groove, Broadcast claimed its 8- and 10-inch records had the same playing time as conventional 10- and 12-inch records. The range proved highly successfully and in its first two years the business increased sales by 25 per cent. The 8-inch Broadcast record provoked a fast and furious row within the industry, reminiscent to the prewar interindustry spat over The Gramophone Company Cinch and Columbia Phoenix labels, which had been launched to outflank cheap German imports. So bitter was this 1920s row that for a time wholesalers and retailers refused to take Broadcast or similar cheap products, which had very slim margins. Vocalion got around the boycott (though it further inflamed the trade) by selling Broadcast records in a variety of nontraditional retail outlets, including cycle and toy shops and railway station bookstalls.[39] In the end, this market proved irresistible and others quickly entered. In 1928 Edison Bell Ltd issued the 8-inch 1s.3d Radio and Cystalate had its own stable of smaller sized cheap labels it manufactured for F. W. Woolworth and others. Unfortunately, as a survey of Vocalion finances shows, the business operated on perilous margins, though it had a capital base roughly comparable to that of Edison Bell.

Table 9.5 reveals The Vocalion Gramophone Company Ltd, like Edison Bell, made insufficient profit to pay the high dividends deemed essential to maintain the value of its shares. In the case of Vocalion, and unlike Edison Bell who milked capital to pay dividends, it supplemented the shortfall by using profit derived from other sources within the business. Undercapitalised and using assets to pay dividends Vocalion, like other record companies in the sector, saw its customer base melt away after 1929. In 1932 The Vocalion Gramophone Company Ltd was in liquidation and its assets were acquired by The Crystalate Gramophone Record Manufacturing Company Ltd.

Table 9.5. Vocalion Gramophone Company Ltd: Profit Earned and Dividends Paid, 1926–1931

Year	Net Profit		Dividend	Retained Profit	Share Price
1926	£14,700	[$73,500]	10% £10,000 [$50,000]	£4,700 [$23,500]	43p [$2.15]
1927	–£1,300	[–$6,500]	Nil	Nil	£1.73 [$8.65]
1928	£66,900	[$334,500]	40% £76,800 [$384,000]	Nil	NA
1929	£81,800	[$409,000]	40% £80,000 [$400,000]	Nil	NA
1930	£44,576	[$222,880]	Nil	Nil	NA
1931	£22,065	[$110,325]	Nil	Nil	NA

Source: Data from The Vocalion Gramophone Company Ltd entry, *Stock Exchange Year Book*, 1926–1930; *Talking Machine News* 29, no. 4 (August 1931): 250; and *Merchandising Survey*, 10–11.

★   ★   ★

By the end of the war Barnett Samuel and Sons Ltd had a well-established position as a record wholesaler and machine manufacturer. The business had been in the trade since the turn-of-the-century and was, at various times, agents for German businesses such as International Talking Machine GmbH with its Odeon, Jumbo, Favorite and other labels. The coming of the war transformed the business, setting Barnett Samuel and Sons Ltd on a fresh course. Seeing a gap in the market, it designed and patented a portable machine called the Decca[40] and after the war, sales soared. Unfortunately financial details do not appear to have survived, but the following gives some indication as to how sales went. In 1914 total turnover stood at £60,000 and by 1928 it was £419,000. Of all the Barnett Samuel and Sons products the Decca portable was the most popular. By 1925 home sales stood at £119,000 and by 1928 this had risen to £190,000. In 1925 exports accounted for £82,000 and by 1928 they were £166,000.

By any reading, the company accounts looked good.[41] However, by 1928, it was evident that market saturation would soon be reached. Furthermore, the rapid take-up of radio meant if it were to stay ahead the firm would have to move into the new medium and transform itself from a mechanical to electrical engineering concern. To enter this new market also required large capital investment, the acquisition of expensive technical know-how and licences to access patents. With this in mind, in 1928, the owners of Barnett Samuel and Sons Ltd (it was still a private family-owned company) decided to sell the business. Seeking to realise the value of the main business, they broke the firm into its component parts. The machine manufacturing division and the name Decca were sold for £400,000 to venture capital business British Equity Investment Company Ltd. Later that year British Equity took the venture to a stock market floatation, with the 370,000 10 shilling ordinary shares offered at the premium price of £1.4s.10d each, raising £458,000. Critically, the stockbroking firm handling the floatation was E. R. Lewis and Co, and at its head was the man who became Decca's guiding light for the next fifty years, Edward (later Sir Edward) Lewis. In his memoir *No CIC*[42] Lewis highlighted what he saw as the strange position the business was in. Here was a highly successful machine manufacturer that did not make records. He thought this analogous to a manufacturer of shaving equipment not making razor blades. He was quite right, but soon after Lewis introduced records Decca, as Barnett Samuel family member Edgar Samuel pointed out, came very close to insolvency.[43]

Trading as The Decca Gramophone Company Ltd, the venture soon found itself in difficulties. In 1929 Edward Lewis pressed for the move into record manufacture, but the directors refused. He then created The Malden Holding Company Ltd and bought the ailing Duophone and Unbreakable Record Company Ltd, which controlled British Brunswick. With this purchase came a manufacturing plant and a sales organisation. Lewis and the syndicate next bought out The Decca Gramophone Company Ltd with its established name, manufacturing facilities and trading network. In February 1929 a fresh Decca issue of £1,222,094 was floated and was massively oversubscribed. Soon after the issue, the old Decca Gramophone Company Ltd was bought and Lewis issued the first Decca records in July.[44] The founding of the business could not have been more ill-timed, and within months it was all but overwhelmed by the Great Depression. The sale of Decca records and machines collapsed into an apparently unstoppable downward spiral. Lewis reacted by cutting prices, but this did not work. The situation became desperate, with his bankers at one point threatening to foreclosure on loans and at another an unpaid bill caused the telephone to be disconnected. Lewis rose to the challenge. He ousted the old company chairman and senior management figures, becoming *de facto* managing director. He then made further reductions in retail prices, undercutting those charged by his great rival; the new EMI conglomerate. He even went on a nationwide tour to assess Decca's performance in retail markets. Lewis also poached several important artists from EMI, including leading entertainer Gertrude Lawrence and the long-standing HMV best-selling bandleader Jack Hylton.[45] Other initiatives included licencing deals with American Brunswick with its extensive catalogue of popular music with artists that included Bing Crosby and Al Jolson. There was also, from 1932, a licencing deal with the German Deutsche Grammophon export label Polydor, which gave Decca access to a major European classical record catalogue.[46] Decca survived the Great Depression because of Lewis's consummate business skill and determination, which he combined with a network of family and associates willing to support him. That said, Decca was not in a position to pay dividends until 1945. This was in itself a test of the loyalty of those investors who had participated in the original 1929 venture. It is unfortunate that Decca's experience of this turbulent period falls outside the time frame of this book, but it remains nonetheless a story that needs to be told.

★　★　★

The British government maintained its wartime trading ban with Germany until 1925. However, despite its efforts, trading through third parties made it impossible to exclude German records. Once trading links were reestablished they flourished until the Great Depression, though Germany never regained its pre-1914 dominance. Even before the ban was lifted, it was possible to obtain German-sourced records in Britain. For example, in 1924, the former German branch of The Gramophone Company licenced British agents to distribute their catalogue using the Polydor label. Before the war the largest German exporter of records to Britain was Carl Lindström AG. By 1914 its stable of labels included Beka, Coliseum, Jumbo, Favorite, Fonotipia, Scala and Odeon. These had become well known and profitable lines, with record catalogue's containing important British and internationally known figures from the worlds of classical and popular music. Although Carl Lindström's British assets were seized during the war and later sold to Columbia, German-sourced Parlophone recordings appeared in Britain as early as 1922. To achieve this, Carl Lindström AG created a Dutch subsidiary NV Transoceanic Trading (as a wartime neutral Holland proved an excellent conduit for embargoed goods) to hold its foreign assets and manage the overseas trade. NV Transoceanic Trading sent Carl Lindström metal matrices to Britain, where they were used to press Parlophone records. In August 1923 a small British venture was formed called The Parlophone Company Ltd, which purchased the old Carl Lindström record-pressing factory in Hertford from Columbia. As part of the deal, Columbia retained possession and agreed to press up to 200,000 Parlophone records monthly using Columbia's "New Process" record mixture. That year German national Paul Offenbacher was appointed Parlophone general manager, he engaged British recording engineer Oscar Preuss, who had previously worked for Carl Lindström. Preuss later became Parlophone artist and repertoire manager, a post he retained till his retirement in 1955.[47] A flourishing trade was soon generated but, alas, no Parlophone sales or financial data appear to have survived.[48]

In 1925 Columbia pulled off a remarkable coup when it acquired for £367,500 the worldwide Carl Lindström AG organisation, including NV Transoceanic Trading and The Parlophone Company Ltd. Sterling reorganised the British Parlophone business and thereafter, till the formation of EMI Ltd 1931, a combined Parlophone Odeon label remained an important feature of Columbia's British trade. Its catalogues were rich and varied and included many US-sourced jazz recordings, but it was best known for its recordings of central Europe's finest musicians; though by the 1930s new releases were dominated by the great Austrian-born tenor Richard Tauber.[49]

★ ★ ★

During the 1920s The Columbia Graphophone Company Ltd was the most successful British record company. Under the leadership of Louis Sterling the venture became a dominant and innovative business, which integrated much of the international record industry. Such was its power that in 1931 Columbia was one of the two components of the depression-led merger that was Electric and Musical Industries Ltd (EMI), the other being The Gramophone Company Ltd. The Columbia Graphophone Company Ltd and its predecessors in business had traded in Britain since 1900, having begun a continental European trade three years earlier. It later developed record making and manufacturing facilities in London and had, by 1914, created a good market for its products.[50] Unfortunately, due to a chronically weak capital structure and bad management, Columbia in America was subject to recurring financial crises. This problem encouraged it to use the British business as a ready source of cash. On the outbreak of the First World War, most of Columbia's American executives left Britain leaving fellow American Louis Sterling in charge. Paradoxically, wartime restrictions on British capital exports meant the US business could no longer rely on its European arm to keep it afloat and this enabled Sterling to retain the profits, investing them in the business, which flourished.

In order to better protect Columbia's growing British, European and imperial assets, The Columbia Graphophone Company Ltd was formed in 1917. Based at its Clerkenwell Road, London premises, the ownership of 137,000 of the 200,000 £1.00 shares was vested in the American parent, to whom an additional cash payment of £15,317.34 was made (essentially profit previously remitted to the US). A board of directors included as chairman former Thomas A. Edison Ltd director Sir George Croydon Marks MP. The sale agreements provided for the sharing of patents, trade secrets and trademarks, together with record licencing arrangements and a division of sales territories.[51] That same year Columbia formed The Hertford Record Company Ltd, which acquired the British assets of the German Carl Lindström AG for £24,000. These assets included labels like Odeon, Coliseum, Jumbo, Favorite and Scala. All this gave Columbia additional record manufacturing capacity; the factory had eighty presses and held many important prewar recordings.[52]

Sterling was not only a brilliant entrepreneur he was also, rightly as it turned out, an eternal optimist. This can be seen in a 1918 interview given during a visit to the United States. He told *Talking Machine World*: "Our figures for the year [1917] show that our business was double that of 1913." And he concluded prophetically "We are optimistic regarding the future. . . . The talking machine industry is certain to enjoy an era of activity and prosperity."[53] That said it wasn't apparent in the 1919 sales figures, which show a trading loss of £40,199. This was due to a combination of factors, including the abrupt ending of war-related government contracts, commodity inflation, bad debts and an inadequate capital structure to finance the growing business; the usual Columbia problem. As Sterling told the 1920 annual meeting, "It was recognised that the largely increased business was inadequately financed by the present capital especially with regard to the largely increased stocks of war materials to which it had become necessary to carry and considerable accounts receivable and outstanding."[54]

Table 9.6.   The Columbia Graphophone Company Ltd: Turnover and Profit/Loss, 1917–1921

Year	Profit	Profit/Loss
1917	£271,292 [$1,356,460]	£2,392 [$11,960]
1918	£278,962 [$1,294,810]	£14,089 [$70,445]
1919	£456,875 [$2,284,375]	–£40,199 [–$200,995]
1920	NA	NA
1921	NA	–£177,008 [–$885,040]

Source: Figures derived from board minutes, 1917–1922, and Louis Sterling to F. D. Bartow, of J. P. Morgan & Co, New York, 1 November 1926 (Columbia board papers, EMI).

A 1920 Gramophone Company trade intelligence report told of the difficulties Sterling experienced in the transition to peacetime manufacturing and trading in the midst of unprecedented inflation and disrupted markets.[55] Table 9.6, which is an incomplete table of Columbia Graphophone Company Ltd turnover and profit/loss, shows the impact of these wholly exceptional market conditions.

Despite the losses, Columbia's affairs in Britain were relatively secure and in the event it, unlike many competitors, survived the major 1921–1922 economic recession. That said, as events in the United States were to show, the parent company fared less well. In a 12 May 1919 letter, Victor recording manager Calvin G. Child told Gramophone Company International Artists manager Sydney Dixon:

> Some of the DuPont family, not the DuPont Powder Company, but some wealthy members of the family have put money into the Columbia Company and they are spending it, to use the old expression "like drunken sailors." They have said to their Directors "Look at these advertisements of the Victor Talking Machine Company, they state their catalogue cost twenty million dollars, we have got to have names to bring our standing in line with them."[56]

Although DuPont family members joined the board, their money had only a short-term effect. In May 1919, *Talking Machine World* noted that the US Columbia common $100 stock was trading at $250. It also observed that the business had unfilled orders to the tune of 90,000 machines and several million records.[57] Unfortunately, the DuPont money didn't help in the medium to long term and Columbia continued to experience financial problems, which required further refinancing. The result of all this was another renaming, this time American Graphophone became the Columbia

Manufacturing Company. Finally, in February 1922, in the midst of the international recession, the business was once again placed in receivership; it filed assets of $18,667,931 against which were liabilities of $23,910,405, leaving a shortfall of $5,242,474. The business was salvaged and reconstructed, this time as Columbia Phonograph Company Inc.[58]

The travails of Columbia in America played into Sterling's hands and, in November 1922, he headed a management buyout of the British concern. That month merchant banker and venture capitalist Edward (later Sir Edward) de Stein financed the £100,000 deal through his firm Constructive Finance & Investment Company Ltd. The following year de Stein and the Columbia British board took The Columbia Graphophone Company Ltd to a stock floatation. The share capital was £200,000 in 400,000 shares with a par value of 10s each. For de Stein it wasn't simply a financing deal, he joined the Columbia board as did his brother-in-law Michael Herbert a partner in Morgan Grenfell, then the London arm of New York banking house J. P. Morgan. For the next thirty years de Stein played a key role in the integration of the international record industry. He also played a major role brokering the deal that brought about the formation of Electric and Musical Industries Ltd (EMI Ltd) in 1931 and became a founding EMI director.[59]

The management buyout of the British Columbia business occurred just as the postrecession market in records and machines took off. In addition, sales were helped by a number of technological innovations. In 1924, for example, Columbia introduced its much-improved "New Process" silent surface records and in 1925 electrical recording was introduced.[60] This was a giant leap forward for the industry, enabling the business to remake its catalogues and develop not only new mechanical but also electrical gramophones, the first of which appeared in 1929. Columbia also played an important role in the export trade. As Louis Sterling told the London correspondent of *Talking Machine World* in April 1927, "93 foreign countries . . . now rely on us [Columbia factories] for their recorded music. Last year we exported to these countries 225,419 gramophones and 8,903,544 records valued at £1,625,515."[61] As a consequence, during the years 1923 to 1929, the Columbia business was one of the glamour blue chip high-tech stocks on both the London and New York Stock Exchanges. The share price of the 10s ordinary and £1.00 preference shares reflected this confidence and the growth in their value made Sterling, who at one point owned 40,000 ordinary shares, a very rich man.[62] The success of the British end of the business can be gauged from the, albeit incomplete, runs of Columbia record and machine production by both units and values

Table 9.7. The Columbia Graphophone Company Ltd: The British Business, 1922–1931

Year	Capital		Assets		Profit		Dividend	Cash/War Bonds		Return on Capital
1922–1923	£200,000	[$1,000,000]	£257,451	[$1,287,255]	£56,689	[$283,445]	Nil	£66,593	[$332,965]	28.34%
1923–1924[a]	£200,000	[$1,000,000]	£360,973	[$1,804,865]	£76,367	[$381,835]	15% + 5%	£103,404	[$517,020]	38.19%
1924–1925	£200,000	[$1,000,000]	£459,537	[$2,297,685]	£126,619	[$633,095]	20% +20%	£116,123	[$580,615]	63.19%
1925–1926	£550,000	[$2,750,000]	£932,655	[$4,663,275]	£150,825	[$754,125]	20% + 20%	£158,741	[$793,705]	27.42%
1926–1927	£695,417	[$3,477,085]	£1,770,201	[$8,851,005]	£180,442	[$902,210]	40%	£142,862	[$714,310]	25.6%
1927–1928	£791,046	[$3,955,230]	£2,647,028	[$13,235,140]	£491,305	[$2,456,525]	60%	£260,327	[$1,301,635]	62.1%
1928–1929	£1,369,550	[$6,847,750]	£3,567,350	[$17,836,750]	£505,120	[$2,525,600]	45%[b]	£138,996	[$694,980]	37%
1929–1930	£1,369,550	[$6,847,750]	£5,307,573	[$26,537,865]	£564,668	[$2,823,340]	40%	£7,140,318	[$35,701,590]	41%
1930–1931[c]	£1,582,871	[$7,914,355]	£4,197,209	[$20,986,045]	£133,293	[$666,465]	30%	£234,588	[$1,172,940]	8.42%

Source: Data extracted from Louis Sterling to F. D. Bartow of J. P. Morgan & Co, New York, 1 November 1926, and from board and general meetings (Columbia board papers, EMI). Also Deloitte, Plender, Griffiths & Co, "Report Upon the Profits and Assets of the Columbia Graphophone Co Ltd," 29 July 1930 (merger papers, EMI).

[a]In early 1923, the Columbia board changed the date of its financial year for 31 December to 31 March. These figures are therefore for a period of 15 months.
[b]For the 1928 dividend, this payment was accompanied by a bonus distribution of 982,093 fully paid-up shares paid for out of reserves cash and war bonds.
[c]Figures for 1930 are derived from "Electric and Musical Industries Ltd Application for Listing on the New York Stock Exchange," 8 July 1931 (merger papers, EMI).

Table 9.8. Columbia Graphophone Company Ltd: Record Sales by Label, 1922–1931

Year	Columbia	Regal	Other	Total	Value
1922–1923	1,445,399	3,319,627	19,841	4,784,867	NA
1923–1924	2,787,907	3,408,932	153,316	6,350,155	£219,029
1924–1925	5,274,916	3,609,370	72,137	8,956,423	£271,082
1925–1926	6,634,282	3,749,327	46,724	10,430,333	£265,439
1926–1927	8,991,283	2,817,535	57,068	11,865,886	£297,560
1927–1928	NA	NA	NA	17,667,000	NA
1928–1929	NA	NA	NA	18,048,000	NA
1929–1930	NA	NA	NA	17,920,000	NA
1930–1931	NA	NA	NA	15,484,000	NA

Source: Extracted from an unsigned "General Commentary" (merger files, EMI).

Table 9.9. Columbia Graphophone Company Ltd: Machines, Records and Other Goods, 1922–1931

Year	Machines		Miscellaneous	Total Value, Including Records
	Units	Value		
1922–1923	NA	NA	NA	NA
1923–1924	17,957	£111,855 [$559,275]	£30,102 [$150,510]	£360,986 [$1,804,930]
1924–1925	35,584	£163,545 [$817,725]	£28,984 [$144,925]	£463,611 [$2,318,055]
1925–1926	43,649	£183,840 [$919,200]	£31,318 [$156,590]	£480,597 [$2,402,985]
1926–1927	69,799	£275,133 [$1,375,665]	£36,412 [$182,060]	£609,105 [$3,045,525]
1927–1928	NA	NA	NA	NA
1928–1929	NA	NA	NA	NA
1929–1930	NA	NA	NA	NA
1930–1931	NA	NA	NA	NA

Source: Data derived from Columbia factory output book, 1923–1927 (Columbia papers, EMI), and "Gramophone Records: A Review of United Kingdom Sales, 1905–1956," Table 2, 2; Economic and Statistics Department, March 1957 (statistics files, EMI). They do not include figures for Parlophone records.

Table 9.10. Columbia Graphophone Company Ltd: Annual High Share Prices, 1924–1930

Year	Ordinary Price	Preference Price
1924–1925	£1.22 [$6.10]	£0.95 [$4.75]
1925–1926	£2.65 [$13.25]	£1.02 [$5.10]
1926–1927	£7.56 [$37.80]	£1.13 [$5.65]
1927–1928	£15.50 [$77.50]	£1.17 [$5.85]
1928–1929	£7.25 [$36.25]	£1.12 [$5.60]
1929–1930	£2.06 [$10.30]	£1.25 [$6.25]

Source: Data from *The Stock Exchange Yearbook*, 1918–1931. It appears that in these years, the publishers cited the year-end price of shares.

The management buyout was the beginning of an aggressive acquisitions policy. In July 1925 the Columbia share capital was increased to £300,000 in £1 7 per cent preference shares and £250,000 ordinary 10s shares. Although the preference shares were issued at par, the extra 100,000 ordinary shares were issued at £1.10s each. In the event the issue was hugely oversubscribed.[63] The additional capital was used to acquire a majority stake in the former American parent company The Columbia Phonograph Company Inc, for which Sterling paid £714,000. To accommodate this, Columbia International Ltd was established in November 1925. With a one million pounds share capital, it became a holding company for Columbia overseas assets. The Columbia Phonograph Company Inc and its predecessors in business had been long-term loss makers. However, with fresh management and Sterling at the helm this loss-making leviathan was turned around and made profitable, that is until the Great Depression began in 1929 and ended the record industry in its then form.[64]

In 1926 The Columbia Phonograph Company Inc acquired the record business of General Phonograph Corporation, a US descendent of Carl Lindström AG, owners of The Okeh Phonograph Corporation and manufacturers of Okeh and Odeon records in the United States.[65] General Phonograph was not just the publisher of American- and European-sourced Parlophone and Odeon recordings, it had important catalogues of

Table 9.11.   Columbia Phonograph Company Inc
and Predecessors in Business: Profit/Loss, 1920–1929

Year	Profit/loss
1920	$7,303,734 [£1,460,747]
1921	−$4,678,262 [−£935,652]
1922	−$3,394,854 [−£678,971]
1923	NA
1924	NA
1925	−$318,250 [−£63,650]
1926	−$875,311 [−£175,062]
1927	$270,215 [£54,043]
1928	$760,140 [£152,028]
1929	$716,848 [£143,370]

Source: Data from New York Times, 10 February 1922 and 9 March 1922. See also Louis Sterling to F. D. Bartow of J. P. Morgan & Co, New York, 1 November 1926. According to Sterling, the 1923 and 1924 figures are missing because the firm was in receivership. Furthermore, in 1927, the capital was written down by $1 million so as to write previous losses from the balance sheet. See also Deloitte, Plender, Griffiths & Co, "Report Upon the Profits and Assets of the Columbia Graphophone Co Ltd," 29 July 1930 (merger papers, EMI).

American jazz, country and other popular music, which became available to the British company via licencing agreements.[66] Also in 1927, Columbia invested £163,000 in the New York-based radio network United Independent Broadcasters, which it used as a vehicle for advertising new Columbia records. Although the investment was only short term, it did result in the venture changing its name to the Columbia Broadcasting System (CBS).[67] 1927 also saw an agreement between Columbia and The Kolster Radio Corporation, which allowed Columbia to enter the new fields of electrical gramophones and radiograms. Under its terms a new range of Columbia machines was developed incorporating Kolster radio sets.[68] Columbia Graphophone also had its own British research laboratories headed by electrical engineer Isaac (later Sir Isaac) Shoenberg. In 1929, on the back of important developments in the laboratories, Columbia announced its entry into the radio manufacturing business.[69]

Runs of US Columbia machine sales have not survived for this period, but it has been possible to reconstruct two short runs of record sales. These were derived from a General Phonograph Corporation Inc report to its board in 1924 and a series of Columbia royalty accounting statements to Western Electric. If nothing else, table 9.12 shows the vulnerability of the industry to broader economic changes, with a collapse in sales from 1929 onwards.

Table 9.12. General Phonograph Corporation and Columbia Phonograph Corporation Inc: Unit Record Sales, 1918–1930

Year	General	Columbia
1918	193,857	NA
1919	1,335,979	NA
1920	2,155,850	NA
1921	3,977,170	NA
1922	4,417,509	NA
1923	6,016,095	NA
1924	4,575,832	NA
1925	NA	NA
1926	NA	NA
1927	—	17,828,330
1928	—	16,480,016
1929	—	12,305,099
1930	—	5,583,930

Source: Data derived from "Report to Board of Directors Fiscal Year 1924, General Phonograph Corporation & Subsidiaries" and "Columbia Phonograph Co Inc, Quarterly Royalty Statements to Electrical Research Products in 1928 to 1935." Lawrence Collection, New York Public Library, Rodgers & Hammerstein Center, New York.

With 1925 purchase of Carl Lindström AG Columbia acquired a well established record and machine business with a range of continental manufacturing facilities and European markets and through NV Transoceanic Trading an extensive worldwide network, including manufacturing and recording facilities, especially in South America, India and China.

In 1911 Carl Lindström AG proposed a merger to The Gramophone Company Ltd, but the deal was vetoed by Victor and lapsed.[70] When the business came up for sale again in the 1920s, The Gramophone Company Ltd was an ardent suitor right down to the sale to rival Columbia; this deal saw Louis Sterling outflank Alfred Clark and he clearly savoured the moment. If these two important acquisitions were not enough, Columbia continued its buying spree. In 1927 it bought Nipponophone, the largest Japanese record company for £250,000 and in 1929 the record division of Pathé Frères. There were other ventures, including new Australian manufacturing and distribution facilities and smaller European acquisitions.

Although the picture these figures paint is rosy, the lack of surviving turnover figures is significant. Sterling was used to manipulating assets and, according to a 1927 memorandum of a talk he had with Alfred Clark, combined Columbia profit for 1927 was nearer £1,000,000 rather than the figure cited in table 9.13.[71] Nonetheless with these kinds of figures Columbia was a much sought after stock and Louis Sterling and Edward de Stein became very wealthy men on the proceeds. In 1927 The Columbia Graphophone Company Ltd became the first British registered business to gain a quotation on The New York Stock Exchange, and by the 1929 crash most of the shares were owned by Americans. Also by that date, The Columbia Graphophone Company Ltd was the most important and dynamic leader in the international record business and Louis Sterling the industry world leader.[72]

Having put together a profitable worldwide organisation it was Sterling's bad luck to be denied the necessary time to integrate it. The October

Table 9.13.   The Columbia Group Profits: Capital Employed and Return on Capital, 1927–1929

Year	Profit	Capital Employed	Return on Capital
1927	£639,629 [$3,198,145]	£2,705,660 [$13,528,300]	23.6%
1928	£823,919 [$4,119,595]	£3,143,783 [$15,718,915]	26.2%
1929	£872,546 [$4,362,730]	£4,284,378 [$21,421,890]	20.3%

Source: In September 1928 Columbia capitalised part of its reserves, distributing £1,200,000 worth of fully paid-up shares in the business among shareholders, *New York Times*, 7 September 1928. Data are profit after preference share and tax deductions and are taken from Deloitte, Plender, Griffiths & Co, "Report Upon the Profits and Assets of The Columbia Graphophone Co Ltd," 29 July 1930 (merger papers, EMI).

1929 collapse of the stock markets in the United States and the rest of the world brought about the Great Depression, which practically destroyed the worldwide record and machine industry. Markets dried up as quickly as they had formed and instead of a rationalisation of his organisation Sterling was, in the spring of 1931, forced into a partnership with his major rival The Gramophone Company.

NOTES

A line from the 1919 popular song "I'm Forever Blowing Bubbles," composed by a group of musicians known as Jaan Kenbrovin with lyrics by John William Kellette. It featured in the Broadway musical *The Passing Show of 1918* and was recorded by most record companies. Popular in the months between the Armistice and the signing of the Versailles peace treaty, the lyrics summed up the wishful hopes of a better world emerging from the war. It is now the anthem of West Ham AFC, the London-based soccer club.

1. "Louis Sterling, Columbia Head, Gives Interesting View on Gramophones Future," *Talking Machine World* 22, no. 8 (August 1926): 140.

2. Clarion records was a small British cylinder record company. In a 1922 letter to W. D. Carter, its manager expressed the hope that Clarion would produce disc records "in the near future" but added, "I am venturing to enclose our latest list of cylinder records and notice of reduction in price." A copy of this letter and a 1919 Clarion record catalogue are in possession of the author. Edison started a postwar British export trade, but the remaining market for cylinder records was tiny and largely composed of enthusiasts. Edison did export disc records and phonographs to Britain. Although a good product, they used a nonindustry standard format and found few takers. Edison ceased making records in 1929.

3. For an account of the "Victor Talking Machine Company v Starr Piano Company" case, see *Talking Machine World* 17, no. 3 (March 1921): 33–35. See also a copy of the judgment in Department of Justice antitrust investigation, 60-20-7 (US National Archives, College Park, Maryland).

4. For more on this, see chapter 11.

5. Trade catalogues for Garrard Engineering and Manufacturing Company Ltd, 1932; Langton & Company Ltd, Maxitone, 1929 to 1934; Brown Brothers, 1926–1927; C. Gilbert & Company Ltd; Sheffield and Hull are in possession of the author.

6. For more on the development of Barnett Samuel and Sons Ltd, see chapter 9.

7. For details, see "Epitomes 1918–1931" (board papers, EMI).

8. For details of needle manufacturers, see trade advertisements in *Talking Machine World*, *Talking Machine News* and *Sound Wave*. See also Lord & Thomas and Logan Ltd, "Gramophones," in *Merchandising Survey of Great Britain* (London: Lord & Thomas and Logan Ltd, 1930), 7:61.

9. This figure is taken from an article on a proposed 17 per cent luxury tax, in which it was argued would raise £100,000 per annum. Cited in "From our European Headquarters," *Talking Machine World* 14, no. 8 (August 1918): 99–100.

10. "A Go-Ahead Industry," *Talking Machine News* 28, no. 9 (January 1931): 570.

11. Data from *Merchandising Survey*, 1–12.

12. Duophone was not the first manufacturer of unbreakable records; before the war, Nicole records and Neophone produced similar discs.

13. William Manson was a highly experienced industry hand and manager of The Gramophone Company's Australian branch. He said, "The boom which the industry has been experiencing will undoubtedly slow down and directly the demand for cheap records falls there will be a debacle." William Manson to James Muir, 23 July 1928 (British branch files, Gramophone Company Ltd, EMI).

14. Muir to Manson, 27 August 1928 (British branch files, Gramophone Co Ltd, EMI).

15. Data taken from *Merchandising Survey*, 7:1–12, and *The Music Seller Reference Book 1928–1929* (London: Evans Brothers Ltd, 1929), 11. The twelve were British Brunswick Ltd, The British Homophone Company Ltd, The Columbia Graphophone Company Ltd, The Crystalate Gramophone Record Manufacturing Company Ltd, The Decca Record Company Ltd, The Dominion Record Company Ltd, The Duophone & Unbreakable Record Company Ltd, Edison Bell Ltd, The Goodson Record Company Ltd, The Gramophone Company Ltd, The Metropole Gramophone Company Ltd and The Vocalion Gramophone Company Ltd, with its Universal Music Company Ltd subsidiary.

16. See Edison Bell advertisement, *Talking Machine World* 14, no. 8 (August 1918): 100.

17. Joseph Batten, *Joe Batten's Book the Story of Sound Recording* (London: Rockliff, 1956), 56–59.

18. See "Prospectus," 2 September 1928, Edison Bell (International) Ltd company file, BT31/131162 (Companies House, London).

19. See "Birthday Party at Frascati's for J. E. Hough," *Talking Machine News* 16, no. 6 (October 1918): 210, 226.

20. See minutes of The Gramophone Company Ltd executive committee, 4 November 1920: "Report that the arrangements for the flotation of a new company to take over the Edison Bell had fallen though and that J. E. Hough and his co-directors had found it necessary to put in capital themselves" (Board papers, EMI).

21. See "Death of Mr J. E. Hough," *Talking Machine News* 23, no. 11 (April 1925): 8, and "Edison Bell Ltd," *Talking Machine News* 24, no. 6 (October 1926): 376. For further details, see *The Story of Edison Bell* (London: J. E. Hough Ltd, 1924).

22. *Merchandising Survey*, 9–11.

23. For more on the career of this remarkable man, see John Gilbert, "Obituary: P.A.G.H. Voigt," *The Gramophone* 38, no. 12 (April 1981): 136.

24. For an account of the introduction of electrical recording into Britain, see Frank Andrews, "The Birth of Electrical Recording," *The Hillandale News* 144 (June 1985): 199–204.

25. Edison Bell (International) Ltd file (Companies House, London) and Edison Bell Ltd entries in *The Stock Exchange Yearbook*, 1927–1933. See also, "Edison Bell Ltd: Some Historical Notes," *Talking Machine News* 31, no. 11 (March 1933): 4, and Frank Andrews, "Introduction," in *Edison Bell Winner Records*, ed. Karlo Adrian and Arthur Badrock (Bournemouth, UK: Bayly, 1989). For a history of the Edison Bell businesses and its labels, see Frank Andrews, "Genuine Edison Bell Records," *The Hillandale News* (December 1984; March, April and August 1985), 141–45, and Frank Andrews, *Edison Phonograph: The British Connection* (Rugby: City of London Phonograph and Gramophone Society, 1986).

26. For more on the early history of this firm, see chapter 5. See also "Visit to Crystalate Factory," *Talking Machine News* 20, no. 4 (August 1922): 238–40.

27. This first Imperial catalogue was made up of pressings from earlier Sound Recording Company labels, Grammovox and Popular, supplemented by pressings from other Crystalate clients, mainly Ariel, Chappell, Guardsman, Olympic, but included many others.

28. For more on the record-making activities of Jack Payne, see chapter 11.

29. Crystalate also had important US interests. In 1927, it acquired a stake in The Regal Record Company Inc, a subsidiary of The Plaza Music Company; it purchased Regal outright in 1928. The following year, Crystalate and others established The American Record Corporation; from this source came additional American masters for the Imperial catalogue.

30. As a result of licencing deals, US record companies exported metal masters to The Crystalate Manufacturing Company Ltd, The Edison Bell works, The Metropole Gramophone Company Ltd, The Goodson Record Company Ltd, The Dominion Gramophone Record Company Ltd and Pathé Frères Pathéphone Ltd during the 1920s.

31. In 1925, the US Vocalian record business of The Aeolian Company was taken over by The Brunswick-Balke-Collender Company Inc. When electrical recording was introduced in 1925, Brunswick eschewed the expensive Western Electric process adopting its own "light ray" (or "Pallotrope") system of recording, but this proved ineffective. It was abandoned and a more conventional system adopted.

32. Pressed by his father-in-law, recording engineer William Sinkler Darby left The Gramophone Company in 1921 to join US Brunswick. He returned to London participating in the unsuccessful British Brunswick Ltd. As a result of its failure, he and his father-in-law lost much of their money (William Sinkler Darby file, EMI). Information derived from interviews with the late Kathleen Darby, Darby's daughter.

33. Initially, Warner Brothers formed a British branch for its Brunswick business, which included the cheaper Panachord label. These were pressed by Decca Records, which eventually acquired the business, changing the name to Brunswick Ltd. See also "Duophone Takes Control of British Brunswick," *Talking Machine World* 24, no. 8 (August 1928): 42, and "Warner Brothers Takes Over," *Talking Machine World* 26, no. 5 (May 1930): 113. For comments about Darby and Roberts, see Alfred Clark, "Memorandum of Talk With Louis Sterling, Columbia Company, Savoy Grill Room, 20 June 1927" (Columbia papers, EMI).

34. This venture has no links to Universal Music Inc, which was formed in the 1930s as the music arm of Universal Pictures.

35. See article on the Aeolian-Vocalion venture, *Talking Machine World* 16, no. 12 (December 1920): 546. Prior to 1921, Aeolian released vertical cut (using the Pathé method) records to avoid action by the US patent pool. After the Starr Piano case, it started using the Berliner-Johnson zigzag cut.

36. See minutes of The Gramophone Company Ltd executive committee meeting, 15 July 1920: "Vocalion has had 16 automatic presses installed and the propose to increase this number to 120—that they have as yet to install a matrix plant the [Vocalion] Hayes [factory]—that they accepted orders to press Scala and Coliseum records to sell at £0.3s retail" (board papers, EMI).

37. The Gramophone Company Ltd board minutes, 9 January 1924 (board papers, EMI).

38. For more on this business, see "The Vocalion Gramophone Company Ltd" company registration file, BT31/203093 (The National Archive, Kew).

39. See "Introduction of Broadcast Records," *Talking Machine World* 23, no. 8 (August 1927): 135, and *Merchandising Survey*, 76–77.

40. For more on the early years of this business and its wartime experience, see chapter 9.

41. See Edgar Samuel, "Decca Days—The Career of Wilfred Sampson Samuel, 1886–1958," *Journal of Jewish History*. Information and data used in this section are derived from Jenny Davenport, "Sir Edward Roberts Lewis (1900–1980)," in *Dictionary of Business Biography*, ed. David J. Jeremy and Christine Shawe (London: Butterworth, 1984), 757–60, and Peter Martland, "Sir Edward Roberts Lewis," in *Oxford Dictionary of National Biography*, ed. H. C. G. Matthew and Brian Harrison (Oxford: Oxford University Press, 2004).

42. Edward Lewis, *No CIC* (privately published, 1957). The CIC was the Capital Investment Committee, established after the Second World War to prioritise share issues so as to manage scarce capital resources. See also Samuel, "Decca Days," and Martland, "Frank Samuel," in *Oxford Dictionary of National Biography*.

43. Samuel, "Decca Days."

44. See "The Decca Gramophone Company Ltd" and "The Decca Record Company Ltd" in *The Stock Exchange Yearbook*, 1929 and 1930.

45. For more on the artists, see chapter 11.

46. In 1932 Lewis acquired Warner Brunswick Ltd (itself the successor to British Brunswick Ltd); thereafter, "Brunswick" and "Panachord" were pressed by Decca.

47. For a biographical note on Oscar Preuss and his remarkable career, see Peter Martland, *Since Records Began*, 116.

48. See Frank Andrews and Michael Smith, "Introduction," in *Parlophone Records 12-Inch "E" Series 1923–1956* (Wells-Next-the-Sea, Norfolk: City of London Phonograph and Gramophone Society Ltd, 2000).

49. In 1928 the Hertford factory was sold to The Metropole Gramophone Company Ltd and production of Parlophone Odeon records transferred to the Columbia factory in London. This information has been gathered from The Parlophone Company Ltd, minute book, business files and agreements (Parlophone papers, EMI).

50. For more on the early history of this important company, see chapters 1, 2, 4 and 8.

51. See Columbia Graphophone Company Ltd company registration file, BT31/145983, Companies House, London, and "agreement for sales," "assignment of leasehold premises, book debts etc" and "assignment of goodwill and trademarks," all dated 27 April 1917 (Columbia Graphophone Company Ltd, formation files, EMI).

52. For details of this acquisition, see Columbia board minutes, 1 November 1917 (Columbia papers, EMI). For more details on the complexities of this, see chapter 9.

53. "Conditions in Talking Machine Industry in England," *Talking Machine World* 14, no. 4 (April 1918): 55.

54. Annual meeting, Columbia Graphophone Company Ltd, 18 June 1920 (Columbia board and annual meetings, EMI).

55. See minutes of The Gramophone Company Ltd executive committee 10 June 1920: "that their [Columbia] first orders for the May supplement containing 36 recordings amounted to only 50,000 and that at present they only had one mill at work and no biscuit [the material used to make records]" (Gramophone Company, executive committee minutes, 1920, EMI)

56. Calvin G. Child to Sydney W. Dixon, 12 May 1919 (Victor papers 1919, EMI).

57. *Talking Machine World* 15, no. 5 (May 1919): 27.

58. See the *New York Times*, 29 December 1923, and *Talking Machine World* 18, no. 2 (February 1922), and 20, no. 1 (January 1924).

59. For further details of de Stein's career, see "Sir Edward Adolphe Sinauer de Stein," in *Oxford Dictionary of National Biography*.

60. The first commercially available electrically recorded discs were released by the Chicago-based Marsh Laboratories in 1924 under the Autograph label. Among the artists to record using this early system were jazz musicians Jelly Roll Morton, Mugsy Spanier and King Oliver together with theatre organists Jesse Crawford and Milton Charles, several of which were released in Britain on The Winner label. The author is grateful to Frank Andrews for sharing this nugget of information.

61. "Interview With Louis Sterling," *Talking Machine World* 23, no. 4 (April 1927).

62. The par value of Sterling's 40,000 Columbia 10s ordinary shares was £20,000; however, at their peak, they traded at £15.50, giving them a valuation of £620,000. William Manson said in 1928, "Columbia shares seem to have had a wonderful boosting on the Exchange, but I am afraid that those who paid such high prices will eventually be very sorry for themselves." Manson to Muir, 23 July 1928 (British branch, Gramophone Co Ltd, EMI).

63. According to *Talking Machine World* 21, no. 5 (May 1925): 26, 66a. "The issue of 300,000 7 per cent preference shares at £1 each was taken within five minutes of opening the lists."

64. For an account of the acquisition, see "Louis Sterling and Associates Acquire Control of the Columbia Phonograph Co Inc," *Talking Machine World* 21, no. 3 (March 1925): 1.

65. For further details, see "Memorandum for Mr O'Brien," citing *Moody's Manual of Industrials 1930*, Department of Justice, Washington, DC, 15 June 1931 (antitrust investigation, 60-20-7, US National Archives, College Park, Maryland).

66. See "Columbia Co Buys Okeh-Odeon Record Division of General Phonograph Corp," *Talking Machine World* 22, no. 10 (October 1926): 18.

67. See Louis J. Paper, *Empire: William S. Paley and the Making of CBS* (New York: St. Martin's Press, 1987): 21.

68. See "Memorandum for Mr O'Brien," Department of Justice, Washington, DC, 15 June 1931 (antitrust investigation, 60-20-7, US National Archives, College Park, Maryland).

69. See "Columbia Enters the Radio Field," *The Sound Wave* 23, no. 9 (September 1929): 494.

70. For more on this, see chapters 5 and 6.

71. Alfred Clark, "Memorandum of Talk With Louis Sterling, Columbia Company, Savoy Grill Room, 20 June 1927" (Columbia papers, EMI).

72. "Application for Listing on the New York Stock Exchange," 3 November 1928 (Columbia papers, EMI).

10

HIS MASTER'S VOICE: 1918–1931

"All Alone, Feeling Blue"

> I have come to the conclusion that these two companies must,
> as soon as it can be done, be brought under a single manage-
> ment. To my mind as long as we do not do this we are going
> to be weak as compared with any competitor who does.
>
> —Alfred Clark to Eldridge Johnson,[1] 1919

Two days after the First World War ended The Gramophone Company
Ltd held its 1918 annual meeting in London. Inevitably there was a
heady atmosphere of rejoicing at a great military victory, but this was tem-
pered with relief at the end of a terrible war and worry at the uncertainties
of the future. In addressing shareholders company chairman Trevor Williams looked to that future with extraordinary prescience, highlighting key
problems facing his and other British businesses:

> It is of vital importance for the Company to conserve its cash position.
> The time is within sight—indeed, we may say it is upon us—when
> we shall have to revert from Government work to ordinary peace
> conditions, and be as ready as may be humanly possible to speed up
> the manufacture of gramophone goods to meet the very large demand
> which already exists and is likely to increase. The transfer stage, or what
> is commonly known as the period of reconstruction, will entail anxieties
> and difficulties for all concerned, but those anxieties and difficulties will
> be lighter in proportion to the size of our cash working capital.[2]

The biggest problem confronting The Gramophone Company
was the rebuilding of its war-shattered foreign trade. In 1913 overseas
branches accounted for more than 60 per cent of business, but by the end
of the war this had fallen to 40 per cent.[3] The war had also seen the loss of

the company's German and Russian branches, which had previously been hugely profitable. In addition, its assets in the former Austro-Hungarian Empire were subject to wartime sequestration and remained so for several years after its end.[4] Other overseas branches faced daunting problems, ranging from rampant inflation and wildly fluctuating exchange rates to unstable often hostile national governments and high discriminatory tariffs. All this meant the world into which The Gramophone Company traded was quite different to the relatively stable pre-1914 days and to the postwar experience of the industry in the United States. This chapter tells the story of that extraordinary journey.

★   ★   ★

Compared with many other British businesses The Gramophone Company had a number of factors working in its favour when the war ended. For example there was managing director Alfred Clark's farsighted decision at its start to keep the skilled labour force of engineers in employment at the company's Hayes factories. Then there were the lucrative wartime munitions contracts he negotiated, which had kept the business financially afloat. These contracts ended in December 1918 and Clark (with his skilled workforce freed from these commitments) made the swift transition to gramophone manufacturing, which had originally been planned to commence the week war broke out back in August 1914.[5] This new capacity gave The Gramophone Company complete control over all its manufacturing processes. Furthermore, before the war Clark created a new organisation and planned to expand the business, especially in imperial and extra European markets. The postwar period saw these plans largely come to fruition, but the results proved mixed.[6]

The end of munitions contracts left The Gramophone Company with a number of pressing problems. It was always going to be a difficult period and it was; the fiscal year 1919–1920 shows the collapse of turnover and profit. The figures speak for themselves. If the business had maintained 1913–1914 levels of activity in real terms (by taking inflation into account) it needed to earn £2.7 million in the year 1919–1920, whereas actual turnover was £1.7 million, with profits of £350,000 rather than the £150,000 achieved. Therefore, in real terms, the company's 1919–1920 activities represented only about one half those of 1913–1914.

After the end of hostilities, The Gramophone Company tried to recover its German branch and other assets in enemy countries, but this proved a long drawn out process and it was not resolved until 1931 (see below). Although the company received £300,000 in compensation the German assets had been written out of the balance sheets at the end of the war.[7] The immediate postwar problem was price inflation. By 1919 prices were double those of 1914, with labour and production costs up by factors well above that level. Nothing illustrates the rampant raw material inflation better than the price of shellac, the most costly ingredient in the manufacture of records. Before the war shellac cost around £4 per hundredweight (50.9 kilos), but by 1920 the price was in excess of £27 and during the whole period 1918 to 1931 it never fell below £10 per hundredweight.[8]

It was not simply the loss of assets and inflation, for the business (if it was to flourish again) needed recapitalising. Fresh capital was also required to buy in and stockpile equally inflated raw materials and to pay for marketing and distribution. The company also needed to invest in new buildings and up-to-date plant and equipment at its Hayes factories and to rebuild its worldwide sales and manufacturing facilities. One indication of the need for recapitalisation was the immediate postwar period consumer boom, which stimulated demand for both records and gramophones. Frustratingly, the lack of capital caused a serious supply deficit leading to the loss of valuable business. In normal times an issue on the London capital markets would have solved the problem, but these were not normal times. For, due to the war and its immediate aftermath, financial markets were in disarray and could not be relied on. Furthermore, the costs of commissions and underwriting fees were at unprecedented levels.

With limited possibilities of raising capital in London, The Gramophone Company turned to its American affiliate The Victor Talking Machine Company. During the war years this business had become a major manufacturing concern with assets in 1918 three times greater than those of The Gramophone Company. In 1921 Victor had a turnover of $51,281,276 compared to The Gramophone Company equivalent of $9,744,955, a more than fivefold difference.[9] The possibility of the Gramophone and Victor companies merging interests had been explored several times during the turn-of-the-century pioneering phase of the industry.[10] During these discussions it was always assumed that The Gramophone Company would buy out Victor interests, though in the event nothing came of these moves. In the main the two ventures stuck to a number of key agreements that worked well and kept open the possibility of a future fusion.[11] The dramatically altered postwar relationship and its causes were highlighted by Victor vice president Charles Haddon in 1918. He wrote, "Our business with The Gramophone Company has been reduced to an insignificant amount as a result of the war." In the last year of the war, according to Haddon, Victor exports to Britain were limited to "a few hundred dollars a month," consisting of matrix shells, small model machines and drawings of devices.[12] This wartime curtailment was a function of the intense pressure on British-bound shipping and the limited amounts of raw materials available for nonwar purposes. Also, following the US entry into the war in 1917, Victor turned much of its manufacturing capacity over to government contracts. As a consequence there was a significant drop in machine production; in 1917 Victor manufactured 573,012, the following year the figure was 315,624.[13]

The Victor Company also experienced management problems when, beginning in 1915, its president, Eldridge Johnson, became ill with a serious depressive disorder that rendered him incapable of conducting business. In a 1921 letter, Clark claimed the illness had lasted from 1915 to 1917. He maintained he had visited Johnson to find the poor man so ill he could only remain with him for a few minutes. In such circumstances, the discussion of business matters proved impossible.[14] At this critical time Victor and the other members of the American record oligopoly was the subject of a US Department of Justice antitrust investigation into allegations of price fixing. The investigation also examined the Victor-Gramophone relationship, specifically the division of the world into exclusive trading territories.[15] The resultant conviction stung Victor, and to free it from future investigations asked The Gramophone Company to be released from the controversial territorial clauses. These were replaced with less formal agreements, which were maintained until the mid-1950s.[16] By the end of the summer of 1919 Eldridge Johnson had recovered sufficiently to make the journey to Britain where he discussed future relationships between the Victor and Gramophone companies.[17] As far as Alfred Clark was concerned this meant one thing, a merger of some kind.

Before the year was out a deal had been reached, and in May 1920 the cash rich Victor Company acquired a substantial stake in the British business. It took the form of 850,000 new one-pound Gramophone Company ordinary shares, which increased the capital to £1,700,000. In the event Victor paid the premium price of £1.25 per share and the move provided the British venture with the cash it needed. Initially, only the first 20 per cent amounting to £212,500 was subscribed and, as agreed, the new shares attracted no dividends for three years.[18] This investment gave Victor a 47 per cent holding and therefore not a controlling interest in the business; the balance of power lay with the owners of the 100,000 one-pound preference shares.[19] As part of the deal Victor appointed Eldridge Johnson and one other director to the board, with Alfred Clark and former auditor Colin

Cooper (then a new Gramophone Company director) joining the Victor board. In practice the US directors rarely appeared for London board meeting and Clark and Cooper spent only a short period of each year in the United States. In these circumstances, the US and British directors had little influence over each others business. The relationship was therefore limited to Victor receiving annual dividends and, as capital was needed, paying further instalments of the share subscription. The early hope of integrating the two businesses was never pursued. This changed in 1926 when Eldridge Johnson and other Victor shareholders sold the business to a consortium of New York bankers, who took the company to market in early 1929; when it was acquired by Radio Corporation of America (RCA), then jointly owned by General Electric and Westinghouse.[20]

★   ★   ★

During the 1920s the British record and machine industry were threatened not simply by uncertain economic conditions but also by the new medium of radio (popularly known as wireless). Although wireless broadcasting began in 1922, the initial take-up of radio receiving sets was slow in comparison to the United States. When the British Broadcasting Corporation (BBC) received its first public service broadcasting charter in 1926 only about one quarter of British households had a radio, however, by the time EMI was formed in 1931 that figure had risen to around one third.[21] In the early and mid-1920s many thought broadcasting would kill the record industry as the principal source of home entertainment, but it didn't. Judging by The Gramophone Company's public statements about radio it is clear that during this period the attitude remained curiously uncertain. Overall, they suggest the minds of directors and executives remained firmly rooted in the core business and disinclined to take on the new products of the radio age. Radio first became an issue for The Gramophone Company in September 1922 when Marconi's Wireless Telegraphy Company Ltd approached the board suggesting cooperation in the manufacture and sale of a combined gramophone and wireless; the proposal was rejected.[22] At the annual meeting held a few weeks later chairman Trevor Williams told shareholders, "Your board is satisfied that wireless telegraphy in the present state of the art is in no way likely to adversely affect our business. . . . Such development will be watched with interest, and the future may show influence upon the gramophone industry far other than prejudicial."[23]

The following year Williams, in the face of adverse press speculation about the impact broadcasting was having on the record industry, attempted a rebuttal. He sought to highlight the remarkable growth in profits over the previous year, they were the largest since 1907, and said (somewhat disingenuously), "Broadcasting has undoubtedly come to stay, and it has been our policy all along to give assistance to broadcasting companies and encouragement to their development."[24]

At the 1924 annual meeting Williams first noted the death of Francis Barraud, the artist who had painted the picture of "His Master's Voice," before attempting to calm what he said were the: "unnecessary misgivings amongst our shareholders," which had depressed share prices. He said:

> Broadcasting is a thing quite apart from the gramophone industry, though in certain directions the two industries might usefully be combined. Broadcasting, if it affects our trading at all, does not do so in the competition sense. The last two years only show that the greater the vogue for broadcasting, the larger is the demand for our goods, though I do not for a moment suggest that any question of cause and effect arises in this connection.[25]

In contrast to this optimism, a February 1924 British branch report to the board laid out the problem, "From reports received from various places, it appears certain that owing to the demand for wireless sets, sales of gramophones have been affected."[26] The following year the message was much more upbeat, and with some cause. For in 1925, the company introduced a range of products based on the new process of electrical recording. It was not just new recordings, there was also a new range of mechanical gramophones designed specifically to play these recordings. Also, during 1925, The Gramophone Company had pushed through a private act of Parliament prohibiting unauthorised publication of off-air recordings of performances of artists under contract to record companies.[27]

Although the mid- to late 1920s were a boom time for The Gramophone Company the issue of radio did not go away. By 1929 the profitability of the record side of the business was wearing a little thin and subsequently went into free fall as the Great Depression bit. At this point David Sarnoff, then executive vice president of RCA, became a Gramophone Company director replacing the Victor representatives. He paid an early visit to London to discuss future relations between his and the British business.[28] He envisaged The Gramophone Company RCA link as creating a potentially lucrative worldwide partnership in the fields of electronics and home film entertainment, specifically radio and eventually television.[29] The Gramophone Company had already made some moves in this direction. It had, for example, begun to manufacture radios, electrical gramophones and radiograms and had for a time ventured into filmmaking; it was also engaged in television research. Sarnoff wanted them to go much further, pressing the board to use its large cash reserves to acquire a major position in the British radio and electrical manufacturing industries. The pressure worked and although still somewhat reluctant, the board agreed to buy The Marconiphone Company Ltd, one of the largest manufacturers of radios in Britain. Marconi's Wireless Telegraphy Company Ltd owned this business and its main shareholder was the radio inventor and pioneer Marchese Guglielmo Marconi. He joined The Gramophone Company board, though he was little more than a figurehead. As it turned out the Marconiphone business was seriously overpriced, appallingly managed and making serious losses. When EMI was formed in 1931, The Gramophone Company was still turning it around. In the pit of the Great Depression management decided to focus all EMI manufacturing on the Hayes factories. As a consequence, the British Marconiphone and Columbia factories were closed and the products became EMI brands. After 1931 the Hayes factories pressed all EMI record labels, HMV, Columbia, Odeon, Parlophone, Parlophone Odeon, Regal–Zonophone and records derived from a special Electrola catalogue as well as records for export.

Although the purchase of Marconiphone may have been flawed, it gave The Gramophone Company (and later EMI) a valuable stake in the British radio patent pool and an important subcompany, the Marconi Osram Valve Company Ltd (MOV), then one of the largest British radio valve (known as tubes in the USA) and electric lamp manufacturers. At a time of huge growth in the sale of radio and electrical goods, the revenues from the patent pool and MOV were important to EMI's 1930s survival.[30] This and the large royalties EMI paid in licence fees to other patent holders convinced the business of the need to create a world-class electrical research and development laboratory. This became The Central Research Laboratories and demonstrated just how far the record industry had come since the late-nineteenth-century inventors and pioneers.

★   ★   ★

Table 10.1 highlights the extraordinary journey The Gramophone Company made in the thirteen years between 1918 and 1931. At the end of the war, Gramophone Company accounts showed a £300,000 reserve for immediate postwar capital needs to be used to restart the record and gramophone business. At the start of 1919 £105,000 was allocated to cover the cost of manufacturing 135,000 gramophones and nearly £200,000 to

buy raw materials and pay for other manufacturing costs.[31] The postwar
consumer boom lasted until early 1921, with demand for product growing
to the point that it became difficult to fill orders (see above); demand was
so great that the price of goods was not a factor. In September 1919 shellac
costs pushed the already war-inflated price of records up by a further 6d and
the proportion of recycled shellac used in the record mixture was increased;
this resulted in a poorer sound quality and greater wear.[32] In 1921, the
world economy collapsed into a serious recession lasting eighteen months
causing mass unemployment, which severely curtailed consumer spending
on luxury products like records and gramophones. This collapse is reflected
in the disastrous profits for the accounting year 1921–1922 shown in table
10.1. Even so, things might have been much worse. Alfred Clark reported
the declared £26,119 profit as being the result of a £72,387 tax refund and
a windfall government allowance from wartime munitions activities. Without this timely reenforcement the company would have reported losses
amounting to nearly £50,000.[33]

As table 10.1 shows, turnover for 1921–1922 was, perhaps surprisingly, maintained in both the domestic and international business against a
background of collapsing profits. This collapse can be explained by a number of factors, including heavy losses on foreign exchange transactions and
a 10 per cent cut to the retail price of machines, made to shift inventory
and stimulate trade. There was also European competition from the company's former German branch, selling the same records but at discounted
prices.[34] One consequence of this deep recession was the time it took
before recovery and growth kicked in again.[35] Also shown in Table 10.1
is the relatively static turnover, profit and return on capital figures for the
years 1923–1924 to 1926–1927; though these years do show an additional
£250,000 added to the asset base, indicating significant investment in both
the British and overseas branches. The return on capital figures reveal an
early and mid-1920s capital base of £1.7 million. This was more than sufficient to produce good returns, peaking at an impressive 46 per cent in
1926–1927. However, the significant increase in capital (partly used to buy
Marconiphone) failed to bring the hoped for benefits to the business and,
as the figures show, there was a sharp falling off with the 1930–1931 figures
indicating the precipitous descent into the Great Depression. The impressive mid to late 1920s growth spurt shows the extent of demand for these
well-made products, especially the new electrically engineered recordings
and the spin-off range of reentrant horn mechanical gramophones (sold by
Victor as the "Orthophonic range"), which were designed to produce the
best sound quality from the new records. Furthermore, between 1925 and

Table 10.1. The Gramophone Company Ltd: Turnover, Profit, Capital and Assets, 1918–1931

Year	Turnover		Profit		Capital		Return on Capital	Assets	
1918–1919	£876,196[a]	[$4,380,980]	£215,750	[$1,078,75]	£600,000	[$3,000,000]	35.9%	£1,120,126	[$5,600,630]
1919–1920	£1,719,322	[$8,596,610]	£142,398	[$711,990]	£850,000	[$4,250,000]	16.7%	£1,169,663	[$5,848,315]
1920–1921	£1,708,026	[$8,540,130]	£147,962	[$739,810]	£1,700,000	[$8,500,000]	8.7%	£1,179,450	[$5,897,250]
1921–1922	£1,948,991	[$9,744,955]	£26,119	[$130,575]	£1,700,000	[$8,500,000]	1.5%	£1,495,493	[$7,477,465]
1922–1923	£1,938,245	[$9,691,225]	£140,307	[$701,535]	£1,700,000	[$8,500,000]	8.2%	£1,544,939	[$7,724,695]
1923–1924	£2,115,466	[$10,577,730]	£283,769	[$1,418,845]	£1,700,000	[$8,500,000]	16.7%	£1,680,336	[$8,401,680]
1924–1925	£2,211,975	[$11,059,875]	£229,646	[$1,148,230]	£1,700,000	[$8,500,000]	13.5%	£1,719,710	[$8,598,550]
1925–1926	£2,247,053	[$11,235,265]	£294,294	[$1,471,470]	£1,700,000	[$8,500,000]	17.3%	£1,932,296	[$9,661,480]
1926–1927	£2,603,374	[$12,016,870]	£338,008	[$1,690,040]	£1,700,000	[$8,500,000]	20%	£2,034,263	[$10,171,315]
1927–1928	£3,229,022	[$16,145,110]	£780,555	[$3,902,775]	£1,700,000	[$8,500,000]	46%	£2,497,074	[$12,485,370]
1928–1929	£4,160,349	[$20,801,745]	£1,132,414	[$5,662,070]	£3,340,000[b]	[$16,700,000]	34%	£3,349,625	[$16,748,125]
1929–1930	£5,195,782	[$25,978,910]	£1,200,913	[$6,004,565]	£3,340,000	[$16,700,000]	36%	£4,187,660	[$20,938,300]
1930–1931	£4,176,657[c]	[$20,883,285]	£200,998	[$1,004,990]	£3,340,000	[$16,700,000]	6%	£6,112,935	[$30,564,675]

Source: Data from annual reports, appendix to "Future Prospects for the Entire General Business of The Gramophone Company Ltd, 1921" (statistics files, EMI), and The Gramophone Company Ltd entries in *The Stock Exchange Yearbook* between 1917 and 1931.

[a]Turnover figures are for records and machines only. If war contracts turnover of £1,078,501 is added, then total turnover is £1,954,697. It has not proved possible to isolate from the overall profit the proportion derived from munitions contracts.

[b]The additional capital was required for investment in overseas manufacturing facilities and to purchase the Marconiphone business. It was offered to existing shareholders at par ("Gramophone Bonus Issue," *The Times,* 13 June 1929).

[c]Turnover data taken from "Comparative Net Sales and Cash Collections for the Year Ended 30th June 1931" and does not include £498,490 Marconiphone turnover but does include the unquantified Marconiphone losses (board papers, EMI).

1928, a total of 83,763 HMV portable gramophones were sold in Britain.[36] In 1927 The Gramophone Company introduced its first electrical gramophone and radiograms. These were aimed at the very rich, though by 1930 prices had come down and were well within reach of the comfortable middle classes; prices continued to fall across the 1930s, and the quality of the technology improved.[37]

Table 10.2 below gives details of Gramophone Company ordinary and preference shares performance in the years 1917 to 1931. Analysis

Table 10.2.   The Gramophone Company Ltd: Share Prices and Dividend, 1917–1931

Year	Ordinary Shares		Preference Shares		Dividend
	High	Low	High	Low	
1917–1918	£2.06 [$10.30]	£1.26 [$6.30]	£0.83 [$4.15]	£0.77 [$3.85]	15%
1918–1919	£2.25 [$11.25]	£1.31 [$6.55]	£0.95 [$4.75]	£0.72 [£3.60]	15%
1919–1920	£2.25 [$11.25]	£1.41 [$7.05]	£0.74 [$3.70]	£0.61 [$3.05]	15%
1920–1921	£1.53 [$7.65]	£0.52 [$.2.60]	£0.73 [$3.65]	£0.64 [$3.20]	15%
1921–1922	£1.62 [$8.10]	£0.77 [$3.85]	£0.94 [$4.70]	£0.64 [$3.20]	6%
1922–1923	£1.83 [$9.15]	£1.18 [$5.90]	£0.98 [$4.90]	£0.92 [$4.60]	15%
1923–1924	£1.79 [$8.95]	£1.37 [$6.85]	£0.99 [$4.95]	£0.91 [$4.55]	15%
1924–1925	£2.72 [$13.60]	£1.56 [7.80]	£0.98 [$4.90]	£0.92 [$4.60]	15%
1925–1926	£3.12 [$15.60]	—	£0.98 [$4.90]	—	20%
1926–1927	£9.50 [$47.50]	—	£0.98 [$4.90]	—	32%
1927–1928	£15.50 [$77.50]	—	£1.17 [$5.85]	—	35%
1928–1929	£13.12 [$65.60]	—	£0.98 [$4.90]	—	45%
1929–1930	£4.78 [$23.90]	—	£1.00 [$5.00]	—	50%
1930-1931	£1.98 [$9.90]	—	£0.99 [$4.95]	—	15%

Source: Data regarding high/low share price range are taken from "Memorandum Concerning Share Price: 1903–1925" (board papers, EMI). The remaining share and dividend data are derived from The Gramophone Company Ltd entries in *The Stock Exchange Yearbook* between 1917 and 1931. Unfortunately, this gives share price at year end rather than a high/low range.

suggests a close mirroring of broader economic performance and business trends. They also moved in line with changes to dividend payments. Like Columbia and other publicly quoted record company shares, they featured prominently in the late 1920s gramophone bubble, peaking in 1928 with the one-pound ordinary shares trading at £15.50. The fall was equally rapid, with the final quote of £1.98, a massive fall on the peak.

Reviewing broader performance of Gramophone Company shares suggests its rival The Columbia Graphophone Company had a larger market share. This surge in the fortunes of Columbia can be shown by comparing its share price with those of The Gramophone Company. At the peak of the gramophone bubble, Columbia's 10s shares were trading at more than £15, whilst The Gramophone Company one-pound shares traded at a similar price. The return on capital shows similar disparity, as table 10.3 indicates.

The largest annual return on capital achieved by The Gramophone Company was 46 per cent in 1927–1928, but this does not compare favourably to Columbia's 63.19 per cent in 1924–1925 and 61.2 per cent in 1927–1928. These figures suggest Columbia was significantly outperforming Gramophone. However, that needs placing in context as additional market share was gained by buying up record companies as well as developing the existing Columbia business. It also had the formidable partnership of Louis Sterling and Edward de Stein, who seemed always just one jump ahead of The Gramophone Company. In contrast, The Gramophone Company had access to US capital and both ventures had established reputations. Yet Clark equivocated over the issue of the company's former German branch and, as a result, remained outside the key German market till 1925. This enabled the

Table 10.3. The Gramophone Company and The Columbia Graphophone Company: Comparative Return on Capital, 1922–1931

Year	Gramophone	Columbia
1922–1923	8.2%	28.34%
1923–1924	16.7%	38.19%
1924–1925	13.3%	63.19%
1925–1926	17.3%	27.42%
1926–1927	20%	25.6%
1927–1928	46%	62.1%
1928–1929	34%	37%
1929–1930	36%	41%
1930–1931	6%	8.42%

Source: The data commence in the fiscal year 1922–1923 when The Columbia Graphophone Company Ltd separated from its US parent and established as an independent venture. For further details, see chapter 9.

new owners of the former German branch to establish it as a major player in Germany. The Gramophone Company also allowed the opportunity to buy the extensive Carl Lindström AG business to slip through its fingers and fall into the Columbia camp.[38] These debacles forced The Gramophone Company to set up again in Germany, but it had to start from scratch in what had been one of its most successful prewar markets.

Under performing and cash rich, with an increasingly conservative management and a large centralised organisation, The Gramophone Company was, by the late 1920s, confronted by the fact that its core business could not be relied on to provide the necessary growth in the future. It had to reinvent itself as an electronics-driven business. David Sarnoff's insistence, in 1929, on an expensive marriage with Marconiphone and then the 1931 merger with Columbia were not easy changes and marked the personnel of the company for years after. However, without these fundamental changes it is doubtful whether the business could have survived the Great Depression.

★   ★   ★

The end of the First World War saw the British branch of The Gramophone Company (like the rest of the record industry) at a low ebb and things got worse with raw material shortages, disrupted distribution and selling networks and an unprecedented inflation. In addition, many of the most experienced prewar selling staff remained on active service, and in other ways the war had taken its toll, with several employees casualties, either prisoners of war, wounded, missing or killed. For example, Sydney Dixon had been sales director before 1914, but war service left his health so completely shattered he was unable to return to his former job and became head of International Artists until his sudden death in 1921.[39]

Soon after the end of hostilities William Manson, who had previously been manager of the British Zonophone business, was appointed overall head of the British branch. He integrated the HMV and Zonophone selling businesses, however, when he became general manager of the Australian branch in 1925 the two were once more separated. Manson was an experienced record industry hand and a good manager, having begun his career with music wholesalers Barnett Samuel and Son. His successors were Cecil Maryon who took charge of Zonophone and Albert T. Lack who took over the HMV business. Lack was another highly experienced industry figure and formerly British manager of the Russian branch from 1912 till his escape from the Bolshevik regime in 1918.[40]

In the immediate aftermath of the war Manson had to deal with many problems, not least the creation of a new selling organisation. June 1921 saw one initiative come to fruition; the opening of the first HMV store in London's Oxford Street. It was not the company's first retail business as there had been a profitable shop in Regent Street before the war. However, the 1921 venture was different, as the business was formed with the clear intention of breaking into the retail trade. The opening of the first HMV shop was marked with fanfare and performed by the English composer Sir Edward Elgar, then the most important living British musician and Gramophone Company recording artist. As they developed, what became the HMV chain provided a showcase for the British branch stable of artists and other products like gramophones. For many years the HMV shops only stocked HMV and Zonophone records (and after 1931 Columbia, Regal and Parlophone Odeon records) and the range of HMV (later Marconiphone and Columbia) mechanical and electrical machines, radios and radiograms. By the time EMI was formed in 1931 there were six HMV shops, four in London, one in Harrogate and another in Wolverhampton. The turnover of HMV stores peaked in 1928–1929, with an impressive £168,916. By the start of the twenty-first century the number of HMV stores in the United Kingdom had grown to 200, with a further 350 stores worldwide.[41]

★   ★   ★

Table 10.4 shows the extent to which the British branch of The Gramophone Company contributed to overall earnings and profitability in the years down to 1931. The figures indicate the proportion of earnings generated following the postwar boom years of 1918–1920 settled back to the prewar average of around 40 per cent. Even in the years when the figures experience downturns, 1923–1925 and 1929–1930, they are not massively out of step with the balance of the period. The impact of the two revenue strands within the British business, HMV and Zonophone records and machines, is illustrated by the proportion of income each generated. Table 10.4 also shows how Zonophone nearly matched HMV in 1918–1919 then fell back to below 20 per cent in 1920–1921 before falling precipitously to between 5 and 8 per cent, a ratio sustained until the onset of the Great Depression. Although this is largely accounted for by the faster growth in sales of the HMV range of records, it may also be due to Zonophone's mid-1920s withdrawal from the machine market. It also suggests that consumers, when they had surplus wealth, bought the more expensive HMV products

Table 10.4.   The Gramophone Company Ltd: British Branch Earnings, 1918–1931

Year	HMV	Zonophone	Total Earnings	Percentage of Group Profit
1918–1919	£279,570 [$1,397,850]	£256,910 [$1,284,550]	£536,480 [$2,682,400]	61.2%
1919–1920	£702,890 [$3,514,450]	£373,403 [$1,867,015]	£1,076,293 [$5,381,465]	63%
1920–1921	£657,373 [$3,286,865]	£130,079 [$650,395]	£787,452 [$3,937,260]	40.4%
1921–1922	£627,000 [$3,135,000]	£120,122 [$600,610]	£747,122 [$3,735,610]	38.5%
1922–1923	£817,652 [$4,088,260]	£146,929 [$734,645]	£964,581 [$4,822,905]	45.6%
1923–1924	£573,952 [$2,869,760]	£103,019 [$515,095]	£676,971 [$3,384,855]	30.6%
1924–1925	£717,615 [$3,588,075]	£93,855 [$469,275]	£811,470 [$4,057,350]	36.1%
1925–1926	£1,003,956 [$5,019,780]	£46,081 [$230,405]	£1,050,037 [$5,250,185]	40.3%
1926–1927	£1,354,652 [$6,773,260]	£92,330 [$461,650]	£1,446,982 [$7,234,910]	44.8%
1927–1928	£1,834,065 [$9,170,325]	£84,987 [$424,935]	£1,919,052 [$9,595,260]	46.1%
1928–1929	£2,150,620 [$10,753,100]	£125,531 [$627,655]	£2,276,151 [$11,380,755]	43.8%
1929–1930	£2,014,324 [$10,071,620]	£175,366 [$876,830]	£2,189,696 [$10,948,480]	32.3%
1930–1931	£1,781,269 [$8,906,345]	£113,084 [$565,420]	£1,894,353[a] [$9,471,765]	45.4%

Source: Data from "Epitomes," 1918–1931 (board papers, EMI). These figures do not include the earnings from HMV shops.

[a]Data from "Comparative Net Sales for the Financial Years Ended 30th June 1931"; the final figure includes £101,463 for needles and gramophone accessories (board papers, EMI).

as they did in the mid- to late 1920s boom; or in this highly competitive market they bought machines elsewhere. Alternatively, it could be that the business took the decision not to invest in the Zonophone range and allowed the brand to wither away. A further explanation might be that the Zonophone share of the volume markets was eaten away by the growth of cheap aggregate brands offered by other companies in the 1920s.

In contrast to the figures in table 10.4, the five years of data for the Columbia aggregate label, Regal, (cited in chapter 9) presents a quite different profile to Zonophone. These two labels were sold through the same wholesale network and retailed at the same price, 2s.6d for 10-inch records and 4s for 12-inch. There the similarity ends, as Regal more than main-

tained its position as a major label within the Columbia range. Although
derived from an incomplete run, the Regal data reveals a remarkable showing. For two out of the five years, 1922 to 1924, Regal outsold Columbia
by margins of 45.5 and 81.8 per cent and during the other years, 1924 to
1926, its proportions were 68.4 and 56.5 per cent, falling to 31.3 in 1926 to
1927 the last year of stand-alone Regal and Columbia figures. Clearly, and
in contrast to Zonophone, Regal released new recordings throughout the
1920s. These evidently appealed to its customers and the market position
this brand held was such that Regal was able to beat off competition from
the new cheap records.[42]

★   ★   ★

Just before the war Alfred Clark built a gramophone factory at Hayes,
which would have given him control over the manufacture of all Gramophone Company products. Although these plans were disrupted by the
war, the manufacture of gramophones began immediately after hostilities
ended. Clark believed this would provide a springboard to the business
becoming a major domestic manufacturer and exporter. There were other
factors supporting this, including tariff protection and the German trade
ban. Potential markets were good as prewar British machine sales were
around 500,000 per annum, with The Gramophone Company accounting for a mere 20,000 or 4 per cent.[43] In the event, as table 10.5 shows,
the hoped for gains failed to materialise at least in the domestic market.
Although the figures were better than prewar they were not encourag-
ing especially when compared to the broader market, the size of which
can be estimated from the British censuses of production in 1924 and
1930. The 1924 census shows 192,500 machines manufactured for the
domestic market plus imports of 64,500, making a total of 257,000. Of
these only 31,897 or 12.4 per cent were Gramophone Company models.
In 1930, 481,450 machines were manufactured for the British market
plus 41,218 imports, totalling 522,668. Of these only 72,829 or 13.9 per
cent were sold by The Gramophone Company. Certainly 1930 was a
great improvement on 1924 and much better than prewar sales, as were
the two previous years when around 100,000 Gramophone Company
machines were sold in Britain.[44] Table 10.5 show The Gramophone
Company failed (with the exception of a few Zonophone machines) to
break into the lucrative mass markets. There was a strong market for its
cheaper portable models, but beyond that it stuck to the prewar formulae
of selling into low-volume, high-value domestic markets. It is also worth

Table 10.5.   The Gramophone Company Ltd: British Branch Unit Sales of Machines, 1918–1931

Year	HMV	Zonophone	Totals
1918–1919	3,085	Nil	3,058
1919–1920	28,726	Nil	47,132
1920–1921	21,627	18,406	24,404
1921–1922	19,865	2,777	20,352
1922–1923	26,599	487	27,012
1923–1924	31,747	413	31,897
1924–1925	28,846	150	31,701
1925–1926	47,094	2,855	47,428
1926–1927	64,903	3,345	64,908
1927–1928	98,057	Nil	98,057
1928–1929	100,428	Nil	100,428
1929–1930	78,829	Nil	78,928
1930–1931	73,523	Nil	73,523

Source: Data from "Epitomes," 1918–1931, and appendix to "Future Prospects for the Entire General Business of The Gramophone Company Ltd, 1921" (board papers and statistics files, EMI).

noting that the mid-1920s fall off in sales of Zonophone machines coincided with the departure in 1925 of William Manson, the British branch manager of both HMV and Zonophone product ranges. As early 1920s sales show, he tried to make headway in the market for cheaper machines and his successors may well have abandoned this policy.

This failure to make substantive headway in domestic markets may be a function of price rigidity, but it could also indicate a supply problem. Gramophone Company machines were sold through an exclusive dealership network; of which there were 1,185 in 1923.[45] These were often a single high-class music outlet located in large towns and cities. In addition to HMV branded goods they would have sold pianos, sheet music and musical instruments and were usually located at the better end of towns or in department stores, which were not the kind of outlets frequented by the mass of consumers. It might have been possible to increase sales if The Gramophone Company had created more dealerships. However, in the 1920s, the business was concerned its products should be seen as high-class and all the advertising pandered to this end of the market. It also used the His Master's Voice trademark, which was recognised as a quality brand and appeared on all non-Zonophone advertising, as well as its stellar stable of recording stars. In addition, royal warrants together with other royal associations, such as the records they made, were prominently displayed in advertising and in the shops of its exclusive dealerships.

Sales of HMV and Zonophone records provided the British branch of The Gramophone Company with a cash revenue stream, but it was unstable because of British economic circumstances, particularly during the years between 1918 and 1925. For example, the company experienced the full force of the 1921–1922 recession. If that were not enough, the whole HMV and Zonophone range of records were subject first to inflation-driven price rises then deflation-driven price cuts. Furthermore, revenue fell in the fiscal year 1920–1921, with the collapse in the value of large contingency stocks of shellac and other raw materials and under the impact of price reductions. In addition, there were the significant one-off compensation costs to dealers for record returns after the reconfiguration of its two major record labels in 1920 and again in 1924. That said, by 1925 the instability had largely ended (at least for the time being) and the whole industry was reshaped that year by the introduction of electrical recording. Replacing the existing mechanical record cutting process, the new technology was revolutionary and everything changed. For instance, electrical recording rendered existing record catalogues obsolete and forced record companies to remake existing titles.[46] Furthermore, the inherent limitations of the mechanical system had made realistic recordings of large-scale musical works such as symphonies, complete operas and even live performances difficult if not impossible to achieve, and there were only an unrepresentative handful of such records available in pre-1925 record catalogues. The new technology made the making of such recordings possible. Even popular music benefited, with leading Gramophone Company dance bands like Jack Hylton, the Savoy Orpheans and others to make a successful transition. The new sound enabled these and other popular dance bands to redefine their art and sales of the new records boomed.

In the years after the introduction of electrical recording The Gramophone Company experienced a number of practical problems; the most pressing was the need for suitable London-based studio facilities to make the new high-tech records. For several years The Small Queens Hall and The Kingsway Hall in Central London were pressed into service, as well as other locations suitable for recording medium and large-scale orchestral works and other classical and popular music. And, within months of the recording process coming into use, The Gramophone Company began making historic live recordings at The Royal Opera House, Covent Garden. The first were made at the June 1926 farewell of Dame Nellie Melba (released on HMV DB943 and in 1931 to mark her death HMV DB1500). These were followed in 1928 with six extracts from Mussorgsky's *Boris Godounov*, by the Russian bass Fyodor Chaliapine (HMV DB1181–83).[47]

To make high quality location recordings The Gramophone Company constructed a mobile recording unit in 1927. It was used in its first year of operation to record the choir of the Temple Church in London under the direction of George Thalben-Ball. Among the recordings was Mendelssohn's *Hear My Prayer* with the aria "Oh for the wings of a dove" (HMV C1329). The soloist was fourteen-year-old boy treble Ernest Lough and the record an unlikely runaway success, becoming the first British recording to realistically claim sales of one million copies.[48]

Despite these important advances in the art of sound recording and the growth in its consumer base, The Gramophone Company suffered from a lack of London-based recording studios. In 1929 Trevor Osmond Williams, then head of International Artists, proposed the construction of state-of-the-art studios at Abbey Road, in the St John's Wood district of London. These became the world's first purpose-built recording studios. In October 1931 they were formally opened as an EMI facility by Sir Edward Elgar and the London Symphony Orchestra. Since then Abbey Road studios have been the artistic home of the world's most important performing artists.[49]

As a consequence of these dramatic changes, the post-1925 HMV catalogues were extraordinarily rich and diverse, even more so when matched to the remarkable stable of popular and classical artists recording at this time. It was a truly golden age of recorded sound. Added to all this was the growth in consumer spending in a rapidly expanding economy. This combination provided the British branch of The Gramophone Company with a boom market of unprecedented proportions, as demonstrated in tables 10.6 and 10.7, which lasted till the onset of the Great Depression in 1929. It is against this extraordinary background that the 1918 to 1931 activities of the British branch of The Gramophone Company must be judged.

★   ★   ★

Table 10.6 reveals the proportion of British branch income derived from records sales across the period 1918 to 1931. Apart from sales of needles and other miscellaneous items, the balance reflects the proportion of revenue generated by sales of machines. The figures suggest the proportions between record and machine sales fell within a range of 55 to 65 per cent. Compared to the prewar proportions, which showed a similar pattern, very little appears to have changed. The data in table 10.6 also suggests that whilst selling records provided the business with an important high-volume low-value cash product, selling low-volume high-value machines was a more lucrative long-term investment to both the manufacturer and retailer.

Table 10.6. The Gramophone Company Ltd: British Branch Earnings from Record Sales, 1918–1931

Year	HMV	Zonophone	Total	Percentage of Total Branch Income[a]
1918–1919	£225,072 [$1,125,360]	£243,198 [$1,215,990]	£468,270 [$2,341,350]	87.3%
1919–1920	£318,927 [$1,594,635]	£270,608 [$1,353,040]	£589,535 [$2,947,675]	54.8%
1920–1921	£360,674 [$1,803,370]	£130,077 [$650,385]	£490,751 [$2,453,755]	62.3%
1921–1922	£369,600 [$1,480,000]	£120,122 [$600,610]	£489,722 [$2,448,610]	62.2%
1922–1923	£452,059 [$2,260,295]	£146,928 [$734,640]	£598,987 [$2,994,935]	62.1%
1923–1924	£407,999 [$2,039,995]	£103,019 [$515,095]	£511,018 [$2,555,090]	75.5%
1924–1925	£438,822 [$2,194,110]	£93,857 [$469,285]	£532,679 [$2,663,395]	65.6%
1925–1926	£578,691 [$2,893,455]	£48,100 [$240,500]	£626,791 [$3,133,955]	59.7%
1926–1927	£756,879 [$3,784,395]	£52,207 [$261,035]	£809,086 [$4,045,430]	55.9%
1927–1928	£1,148,578 [$5,742,890]	£84,986 [$424,930]	£1,233,564 [$6,167,820]	64.3%
1928–1929	£1,195,187 [$5,975,935]	£125,532 [$627,660]	£1,320,719 [$6,603,595]	58%
1929–1930	£1,147,223 [$5,736,115]	£175,367 [$876,835]	£1,322,590 [$6,612,950]	60.4%
1930–1931	£924,585 [$4,622,925]	£112,199 [$560,995]	£1,036,784 [$5,183,920]	54.7%

Source: Data from "Future Prospects for the Entire General Business of The Gramophone Company Ltd, 1921"; "Epitomes," 1918–1930; and "Comparative Net Sales for the Financial Year Ended 30th June 1931" (board papers and statistics file, EMI). Zonophone data include the small number of instruments sold during this period (small numbers apart from the exceptional year 1919–1920) but exclusive of sales of needles and other accessories.

[a]The balance of revenue was derived from sales of machines and miscellaneous items like needles.

Table 10.6 identifies British branch record sales earnings (therefore exclusive of machines) both in cash and proportionate terms. This reveals how, after the instability of the 1918–1924 period, total earnings grew on a year-by-year basis till the onset of the Great Depression. Interestingly, the HMV and Zonophone revenue streams reveal quite distinct patterns. In the two years following the war Zonophone sales matched those of HMV then after the recession-led collapse sales fell till 1926–1927, subsequently rising till the onset of the Great Depression. Table 10.7 showing unit sales of

Table 10.7.   The Gramophone Company Ltd: British Branch Unit Record Sales, 1918–1931

Year	Celebrity	Black	Plum	Misc	Zonophone	Total
1918–						
1919	70,421	NA	NA	NA	3,200,000	4,916,935
1919–						
1920	173,981	506,712	946,174	Nil	3,077,198	4,704,065
1920–						
1921	160,953	140,188	835,953	120,333	1,021,754	2,279,181
1921–						
1922	453,266	447,408	981,029	Nil	1,390,959	3,272,662
1922–						
1923	505,427	531,586	1,447,291	28,758	1,643,475	4,156,537
1923–						
1924	400,569	543,266	1,095,735	61,546	1,217,566	3,318,682
1924–						
1925	472,414	455,236	2,102,622	74,095	1,269,383	4,373,750
1925–						
1926	382,862	425,119	3,360,165	27,914	783,943[a]	4,980,003
1926–						
1927	457,597	538,426	4,908,852	27,584	1,067,462	6,999,941
1927–						
1928	522,400	1,051,845	7,117,081	63,091	1,143,736	9,898,153
1928–						
1929	528,781	929,351	7,802,188	18,483	1,707,716	10,986,519
1929–						
1930	344,463	602,273	8,204,576	24,332	1,238,681	11,414,325
1930–						
1931	NA	NA	NA	NA	2,370,000	8,189,000

Source: Data from "Epitomes," 1918–1931, and appendix to "Future Prospects for the Entire General Business of The Gramophone Company Ltd, 1921" (board papers and statistics files, EMI). See also F. W. Gaisberg, "Memorandum to Alfred Clark," 7 July 1938 (artists' files, EMI).

[a]One reason for the decline of Zonophone records during this year was the deletion of a large part of the existing catalogue and a generous dealer return policy.

Zonophone records confirm this erratic path. One problem was pricing. In October 1919 the price of Zonophone records increased from 2s.6d to 3s for 10-inch with 12-inch records rising from 4s to 5s. In addition the price of the small number of premium 10-inch Celebrity Zonophone records increased from 3s.6d to 4s. In March 1920 there was a further and as it turned out final wave of price increases, to 4s and 6s.6d and Celebrity Zonophones to 5s. In October 1923 Zonophone record prices were reduced to prewar levels with the 10-inch at 2s.6d Celebrity series at 3s.3d and the 12-inch at 4s. This price structure was maintained till late 1931.[50]

In a rapidly rising market it is difficult to understand why Zonophone performed so erratically, especially when compared to other same price aggregate brands like Regal, or even Imperial and the various Edison Bell labels. However some answers can be gleaned by reviewing the 1925 Zonophone catalogue, the last to be published before the introduction of electrical recording. It was an old catalogue with most recordings dating from the pre-1918 period. There were even records by music hall performer Billy Williams, who died in 1915. The thirty premium-priced Celebrity Zonophone records by Scottish entertainer Sir Harry Lauder no doubt had a market, but they too were largely old recordings and old repertoire that could have little appeal to new consumers. Overall the Zonophone catalogue was made up largely of staples derived from British and US recordings, often of military and brass band music performed by names like "Black Diamonds" (a generic term for the house band or items recorded by a variety of military bands) and with popular songs usually performed by cover artists. To be sure rising stars like Jack Hylton had a showing in this catalogue, but not the scintillating recordings he produced on the HMV Plum label at this time. Even after the introduction of electrical recording Zonophone was slow to act, and it was not until June 1926 that 450 old mechanical records were culled from the catalogue. This was accompanied by a generous dealer returns policy, which accounts for the decline blip in both tables 10.6 and 10.7.[51] Unfortunately, the rebuilding of a new Zonophone catalogue was a muted affair. For example, the November 1926 and January 1927 supplements contained the usual fare of British and Victor derived recordings. The American recordings included the Associated Glee Clubs of America, which was advertised as performances with "over 1,000 male voices" and were a vehicle to show off the new electrical recording. Beyond that it was British brass and military band music and mainly covers of dance music together with a few songs, with named and well-known artists like Elsie Carlisle and Bert Firman's Dance Orchestra the exception.[52] From this it is clear the British branch pinned its hopes on the 10-inch HMV midpriced Plum label records to carry the popular dance and other types of music, with its stable of high profile named artists providing consumers with the incentive to buy. In these circumstances Zonophone was and remained something of a backwater, but a backwater capable of delivering modest but respectable results.

★   ★   ★

The sales profile of Gramophone Company records during the years 1918 to 1931 was mixed, though as table 10.7 shows, overall performance was good with year-on-year growth, even during the 1921–1922 recession;

though the selling year 1923–1924 shows a decline probably accounted for by radio which, for a while, sapped confidence in the whole industry. Overall the HMV sales growth was more stable than Zonophone, even with the price instability of the early 1920s and the costs involved in re-formating those recordings pressed into just one side of the disc into the standard pressing into both sides. Clearly record sales provided the business with a steady cash revenue stream. Using HMV as his yardstick, managing director Alfred Clark might have seen the success of his new organisation. However, a more detailed examination of the HMV records reveals serious inconsistencies that could have stacked up trouble for the future if the Great Depression had not swept all before it.

As shown in chapter 7 the prewar Celebrity recordings were largely made up of the great singers and instrumentalists of the age. They provided The Gramophone Company with a flagship product at premium prices that ranged from 7s.6d to £1.10s.0d. In 1919 important changes were made to the price structure of Celebrity records. Unlike the rest of the HMV/Zonophone product range, prices were cut to bring them roughly into line with Victor prices; with 10-inch selling at 5s.6d and 12-inch 7s.6d.[53] Before the war only the wealthy could afford Celebrity records and averaged no more than 1 per cent of total sales. As the figures in table 10.7 show, by the end of the war little had changed, with this class of record accounting for roughly 1.4 per cent of total sales in the year 1918–1919. Thereafter, until 1924, when most Celebrity records were reconfigured with a recording pressed into both sides of the disc, the proportions underwent a significant rise. This was due largely to price reductions and the growth in interest in this kind of record by musically educated war veterans. This translated into real percentage increases, from 3.7 per cent in 1919–1920, 7 per cent in 1920–1921, 13.8 per cent in 1921–1922 and 12.2 per cent in 1922–1923.

The change from single to double-sided Celebrity records in 1924 was significant, marking as it did the start of a new HMV 10-inch DA and 12-inch DB series of red label records. This premium label was the home to The Gramophone Company's international artists down to the late 1950s, when the serial was finally scrapped in favour of long-playing red label records. The 1924 prices reflected a shift from a low- to a higher-volume product, with 10-inch DA records retailing at 6s and 12-inch DB records 8s.6d. The first catalogue consisted of blocks of doubled up pressings of existing recordings featuring familiar artists like Caruso and McCormack and newer ones by the likes of soprano Amelita Galli Curci. Interestingly, as early as 1926 The Gramophone Company created a "Historic Number 2 catalogue" consisting of those early Celebrity and other recordings. This recognised the historic nature of its Celebrity back catalogue and a belief there was still commercial life in them. This important supplementary catalogue never enjoyed high unit sales, but remained a part of the HMV range until 1946.[54]

A combination of changing tastes and the coming of electrical recording brought about a shift in the kind of Celebrity recordings purchased in the years after 1925, with a decline in sales of single vocal or instrumental records and a growth in the sale of multidisc recordings of orchestral and operatic works, which were often derived from previously unrecorded parts of the repertoire. Adding to the allure of these recordings was the use of the finest European and American orchestras and musicians, all held under exclusive contracts to The Gramophone Company (either directly or through Victor licenced material). These included The Berlin Philharmonic, The Chicago Symphony, The London Symphony, The New York Philharmonic and The Vienna Philharmonic, with conductors such as Otto Klemperer, Hans Knappertsbusch, Serge Koussevitsky and Arturo Toscanini. Demand was so great that by the onset of the Great Depression much of the basic orchestral repertoire had been recorded and despite the economic collapse recording complete works continued throughout the 1930s.[55] The high cost of these large-scale recordings was generally recouped through international sales, which more than compensated for limited sales in the domestic market. Furthermore, many of these recordings were derived from US Victor matrices, for which only a 10 per cent pressing fee was charged. It was a good deal all round, but mainly for British consumers.[56] This change in consumer tastes can be seen in table 10.7, which shows the sale of Red Label Celebrity records decline in 1926–1927, probably due to the combined influence of radio and consumers waiting for the new electrical recordings. Then during the gramophone boom of the next three years sales first rose then stagnated before falling back in 1929–1930 as the Great Depression took hold; in 1928–1929 the proportion of Celebrity records sold fell to 4.8 per cent.

★   ★   ★

In 1918 The Gramophone Company created a new record series, a 10-inch E and 12-inch D Black label with a recording pressed into both sides of the disc; they cost 5s and 7s. In 1920 the preexisting HMV Black label catalogue with a recording pressed into one side of the disc (a catalogue going back to the early days of the business), was reconfigured and integrated into the new catalogue. It was an expensive change involving compensation for

records already in the distribution and retail chain. The cost was borne by
the business and can be seen in the 1920–1921 sales figures. In February
1920 the retail price of Black label records rose to 6s.6d for a 10-inch and
8s.6d for a 12-inch record. In October 1921 prices were reduced to 5s.6d
and 7s and in October 1923 further price reductions followed to 4s.6d and
6s.6d, where they remained till 1931.[57]

The Black E & D series was a versatile label consisting of light and
popular classical works (including complete recordings of musical comedy
and Gilbert and Sullivan operas) by artists who were not in the international
Celebrity category and whose records could be offered at a lower price.[58]
There were also recordings of the basic repertoire by important artists of the
day, including composer and conductor Sir Edward Elgar, English tenor
Walter Widdop, violinist Isolde Menges, Danish tenor Lauritz Melchior
and the young German soprano Elisabeth Schumann. The label also featured recordings by The Philadelphia Orchestra under the baton of Leopold
Stokowski. Early releases included several important works. For example,
there was the first complete recording of Lisa Lehmann's song cycle "In a
Persian garden," a musical adaptation of verses from Edward FitzGerald's
translation of *The Rubáiyát of Omar Khayyam* (HMV D450–52). Originally
published in 1916, the set came complete with its own illustrated album.[59]
In addition it listed some music hall performances derived from the old
single-sided Black label catalogue, including recordings by Albert Chevalier, Dan Leno, Sir Harry Lauder and Violet Lorraine.[60]

Table 10.7 shows how the richness of this series and its price advantage was translated into sales; initially mirroring Celebrity sales then
pulling away in 1927–1928 to peak at more than one million records or
double Celebrity sales for that year. In 1928–1929 sales fell back slightly,
but remained significantly ahead of Celebrity sales. In 1931, in the wake
of a depression-led rationalisation of the HMV product range, the E &
D Black label series was discontinued. Existing recordings were given a
red label and sold at the same lowered price of Celebrity records.[61] The
series of records served a useful purpose, offering high-quality music by
well-known performers at prices that were significantly cheaper than Celebrity records. It is possible that many musically educated veterans who
had come to know records during the war and who remained consumers contributed to the development of this label. Like Columbia's own
cheaper labels, the E & D series helped popularise classical music bringing
it to the homes of many who would otherwise never have been able to
afford to purchase such records.[62]

★   ★   ★

Inaugurated in 1912, the HMV Plum label series was a successful midpriced double-sided record. Initially, its 10-inch record, prefixed B, cost 3s.6d and the 12-inch, prefixed C, priced at 5s.6d. The success of this label before and during the war guaranteed its postwar position, though in August 1919 prices rose to 4s and 6s. Further increases followed in 1920 to 5s and 7s. Thereafter prices fell, in 1921 to 4s and 6s, and in 1923 to 3s and 4s.6d.[63] Thereafter, until 1931, the price remained unchanged. During the years 1918 and 1931, the Plum label catalogue was the most eclectic in the HMV range, containing recordings of at times groundbreaking modernity, including a 1920 series of lectures on melody by British composer Walford Davies (HMV C1063–71). It was also the vehicle for important recordings of complete works, like the 1930 recording of Puccini's opera *Madama butterfly* (HMV C1950–65) featuring Irish soprano Margaret Sheridan, the Australian tenor Lionello Cecil and the orchestra of la Scala, Milan conducted by Carlo Sabjano. Even this nonpremium priced set of sixteen records cost £3.19s.6d, or more than the weekly wage of a skilled working man.

This label also embraced "middlebrow" music for interested but not necessarily musically sophisticated consumers. "Middlebrow" covered the vast array of popular light classical repertoire, ranging from the brass and military band music that had always been a feature of this label, to songs of empire by performers like the bass baritone Peter Dawson, together with the light orchestral music of British composers such as Eric Coates. The 1927 million-selling recording of *Hear my prayer* (HMV C1329) fell into this category. Also available were the recordings of important popular singers including Americans Paul Robeson and Frank Crumit, together with the entertainer Gracie Fields and the sophisticated offerings of playwright, actor and entertainer Noël Coward. The sheer breadth of records offered on the Plum label made it the front line brand as is shown in table 10.7.[64] As a proportion of total HMV/Zonophone sales the performance of the Plum label records started from a low of 19 per cent in 1919–1920, it then rose to 36 per cent in 1920–1921 falling back to 30 per cent in 1921–1922. It recovered to 35 per cent in 1922–1923, 33 per cent in 1923–1924, 48 per cent in 1924–1925, 67 per cent in 1925–1926, 70 per cent in 1926–1927, 72 per cent in 1927–1928, 71 per cent in 1928–1929 and 72 per cent in 1929–1930. These figures show that once the industry began to grow after the 1921–1922 depression, the Plum label revealed its potential as a midpriced selling vehicle for the British branch of The Gramophone Company.

The coincidence of this growth with the new dance band gramo-phone boom of the mid to late 1920s is clear. Underpinning the primacy of the Plum label was an outstanding roster of British dance bands under contract to The Gramophone Company. These included the Savoy Orphe-ans, together with the bands led by Jack Hylton, Ray Noble,[65] Ambrose and others. In addition, there were many American bands accessed through the Victor licence. It is also noticeable that under the weight of the Great Depression sales of Plum label records decreased at a faster rate than the Celebrity and Black record labels, suggesting that, despite the presence of complete multidisc operas and orchestral works, much of the Plum label consumer base came from the industrial working classes, who were affected by the slump at a much earlier stage than other consumers.

★   ★   ★

By 1929 The Gramophone Company had been transformed into a major British consumer electrical manufacturer. It was a sizeable concern, with British manufacturing facilities covered nearly sixty acres accommodating more than one million square feet of working space, with employment for more than 8,000 workers; double the number employed in the factories and nearby offices in 1918.[66] Maximum monthly record output at the factory was around 4,000,000, though by 1930 the figure was 2,437,000. Interest-ingly, the 1930 factory-gate price of each record was 6d or 5 per cent more than the same Columbia product.[67] The factories continued to manufacture machines, with 87,000 made in 1925, 140,000 in 1926, 224,000 in 1927 and 270,000 in 1928. Of these more than half went for export.[68]

The first suggestions of merging The Gramophone Company and The Columbia Graphophone Company and their worldwide interests were noted in firmly denied 1927 press speculation. At the time Columbia was still acquiring much of the non-Gramophone-Victor recording businesses around the world. The Gramophone Company too was expanding, with new factories, plant and selling branches in Australia, India and in Europe. Both businesses were also developing record-making technology and with research facilities, looking out beyond the narrow confines of the record businesses to consumer electrical goods like radio and both were engaged in television research.

A number of obstacles stood in the way of a merger, not least the very poor personal relations between Alfred Clark and Louis Sterling; in truth they detested one another. In addition Clark was utterly focused on The Gramophone Company and had very few outside interests. By contrast

Sterling had developed, through his partnership with financier Edward de Stein and his extensive knowledge of the music and related businesses, strong personal and institutional links to a number of other business and financial ventures. For example, in 1928 he acquired a controlling interest in and became chairman of music publisher Chappells.

There were other differences between Sterling's view of The Gramophone Company and that of Clark. Shortly before his death in 1958, Sterling was interviewed by David Bicknell, then head of EMI's International Artists. During this conversation Sterling said The Gramophone Company was, by the late 1920s, a mature business making poor returns on capital and very little profit. Table 10.8 compares Columbia and Gramophone Company record sales, although based on incomplete Columbia data it brings the situation into sharp focus. Sterling believed Clark paid far too much for Marconiphone, which had been a major loss-maker. Compared to the entrepreneurial flair he brought to Columbia, Sterling felt The Gramophone Company was in poor shape and believed Clark was part of the problem. By this time Clark was very conservative in his thinking and manoeuvring to become chairman of any new merged venture. To this end, in 1930, he forced founding Gramophone Company chairman Trevor Williams to step down in his favour.[69]

The most forceful proponents of the Columbia-Gramophone merger were the American interests in both companies. By 1931 most Columbia shares were American-owned, whilst RCA Victor owned 47 per cent of Gramophone Company shares. In the end these American interests were

Table 10.8.   Columbia Graphophone Company Ltd & Gramophone Company Ltd: Unit Sales of Records, 1918–1931

Year	Columbia	Gramophone
1918–1919	NA	4,916,935
1919–1920	NA	4,704,065
1920–1921	NA	2,279,181
1921–1922	NA	3,272,662
1922–1923	4,784,867	4,156,537
1923–1924	6,350,155	3,318,682
1924–1925	8,956,423	4,373,750
1925–1926	10,430,333	4,980,003
1926–1927	11,865,886	6,999,941
1927–1928	17,667,000	9,898,193
1928–1929	18,048,000	10,986,519
1929–1930	17,920,000	11,414,325
1930–1931	15,484,000	8,189,000

Source: Columbia figures do not include Parlophone Odeon records.

decisive. Some members of the Columbia board with strong links to US bankers J. P. Morgan (who controlled the Columbia depository stock) persuaded Sterling that merger was in the best long-term interests of the business. Clark prevaricated on two grounds. First he claimed Columbia was overvalued and second that the still outstanding German wartime compensation case prevented the merger. Owen D. Young, the head of General Electric and joint owner of RCA Victor (who therefore had an interest in The Gramophone Company), headed a US governmental delegation to Germany to reschedule German debt and war reparations. He broke the logjam and in early 1931 The Gramophone Company received £300,000 in compensation, which was paid out to existing shareholders.[70]

There could be no more arguing and in June 1931, in the pit of the Great Depression, Electric and Musical Industries Ltd (EMI Ltd) was formed. It is worth noting that every Gramophone Company ordinary one-pound shares was exchanged for a one-pound share in EMI Ltd. In contrast, every 10 shilling ordinary share in The Columbia Graphophone Company Ltd was also exchanged for a one-pound share in EMI Ltd. Although the rationale behind the merger were international economies of scale in manufacturing and the creation of a venture capable of competing with other international players in the fields of radios and electronics, the reality was both businesses were in a depression-induced tailspin which would have wiped them out had they not merged resources. It was a curious end to two important pioneering businesses, but in truth (as was shown over the next years) stand alone record companies simply could not survive.

NOTES

A line from the 1924 Irving Berlin hit song "All Alone." In 1926, the HMV catalogue contained three recordings of this song performed by The Savoy Orpheans (HMV B1915), Salon Orchestra (HMV B1931) and De Groot and his Piccadilly Orchestra (HMV B1134).

1. Alfred Clark to Eldridge Reeves Johnson, 12 December 1919 (Clark correspondence, Johnson Victrola Museum).
2. "Chairman's Report," annual meeting, 13 November 1918 (meetings file, EMI).
3. See appendix, "Future Prospects for the Entire General Business of The Gramophone Company Ltd" (board papers, 1921, EMI).
4. Between 1918 and 1931, The Gramophone Company pursued a tortuous litigation against the German state and the new owners of DGAG. Eventually, the metal matrices (or at least copies of them) were returned and, in 1931, £300,000 paid in compensation (see MAT files, EMI).
5. For further details, see chapter 8.

6. For further details, see chapter 8.

7. For more on the writing off of assets in enemy territory and in Russia, see chapter 8.

8. Data from The Gramophone Company Ltd annual reports 1913 to 1921 and managing directors' conference minutes 1917 to 1927 (meetings file and board papers, EMI).

9. Victor data from "Report of the President to Stockholders of the Victor Talking Machine Co, 1922," and J. & W. Seligman, "An Analysis of the Victor Talking Machine Co, 1928." Gramophone Company data from "The Managing Director's Annual Report to the Board, 1922" (Johnson Victrola Museum and board papers, EMI).

10. For more on this, see chapters 2 and 3.

11. For further details of these agreements, see chapter 5.

12. Charles K. Haddon to James M. Beck, 18 April 1918 (US Department of Justice anti-trust investigation, Southern District of New York, 60-23-0, US National Archives, College Park, Maryland).

13. For details of this, see Charles K. Haddon to Alfred Clark, 17 May 1918 (Victor files 1918, EMI). See also Peter Martland, "A Business History of The Gramophone Co Ltd: 1897–1918," especially chapter 4 (unpublished Cambridge University PhD dissertation, 1993). For Victor production figures, see Robert W. Baumbach, *Look for the Dog* (Woodland Hilles, CA: Stationary X-Press, 1981), 8.

14. Alfred Clark to John Broad, 27 September 1921 (advertising files, EMI).

15. See "Jesse Isidor Straus et al (Trading as R. H. Macy & Co) v Victor Talking Machine Co," US District Court, Southern District of New York, 243 US 490 (1917) (copy in 60-23-0, US National Archives, College Park, Maryland).

16. For details, see Peter Martland, *Since Records Began* (London: Batsford, 1997). See also Martland, "A Business History," chapter 4.

17. The correspondence makes it clear that Johnson wanted Clark to return to the United States so as to become Victor general sales manager. See "Eldridge Reeves Johnson to Alfred Clark," 19 November 1919, and "Eldridge Reeves Johnson to E. E. Shumaker," 29 August 1927. This letter provides an interesting insight into Clark's ruthlessness and Johnson's opinion of the man. As he observed, "his [Clark's] character is utterly and hopelessly selfish" (Clark correspondence, Johnson Victrola Museum).

18. "Shareholder Circular," 26 May 1920, and the chairman's statement at the 9 June 1920 extraordinary general meeting, during the course of which he explained the need for extra capital. The meeting approved changes to the articles of association relating to capital (meetings files, EMI).

19. "Shareholder Circular."

20. For details, see J. & W. Seligman, "An Analysis of the Victor Talking Machine Co, 1928," and "Report of the Directors to Be Presented to Shareholders," 13 November 1929 (meetings files, EMI). By 1929 RCA had interests in record making, Victrola and radio manufacture and broadcasting; it owned the National Broadcasting System (NBC) together with filmmaking, distribution and exhibition through its ownership of Radio-Keith-Orpheum (RKO). It also had important research laboratories.

21. For data concerning wireless telegraphy licence take-up in Britain between 1923 and 1937, see *BBC Handbook 1938* (London: BBC, 1938), 73.

22. Board minutes, 13 September 1922 (board papers, EMI).

23. "Chairman's Report," annual meeting, 8 November 1922 (meetings files, EMI).

24. "Chairman's Report," annual meeting, 14 November 1923 (meetings file, EMI).

25. "Chairman's Report," annual meeting, 12 November 1924 (meetings file, EMI).

26. "Epitomes," February 1924 (board papers, EMI).

27. "Chairman's Report," annual Meeting, 11 November 1925 (meetings files, EMI).

28. See minutes, 6 March and 13 March 1929 (board papers, EMI).

29. The RCA Victor files at EMI contain a variety of Sarnoff thoughts on those RCA ideas that might work in Britain (RCA Victor files, EMI).

30. For an account of the MOV business and its products, see Barry Vyse and George Jessop, *The Saga of Marconi Osram Valve* (Pinner, UK: Vyse, n.d.).

31. "Report to the Managing Director on Finance and Outside Contract Work November 1918," 9 December 1918 (board papers, EMI).

32. For details of price increases, see minutes, 23 July 1919 (board papers, EMI).

33. Alfred Clark, "Memorandum to the Board," 5 October 1921 (board papers, EMI). See also "Memorandum re Decreased Profits for the Half Year Ended 31st December 1920 as Compared With Corresponding Half Year of 1919" (board papers 1920, EMI).

34. These factors are all referred to in the "Chairman's Address," annual meeting, 25 October 1921 (meetings file, EMI).

35. Though the board minutes record that in April 1922 the sum of £100,000 was invested in 5 per cent Treasury Bonds (board papers, 1922, EMI).

36. At the 1925 annual meeting, Trevor Williams said of these new instruments: "The effect of the improvement is startling—the scale range of reproduction is nearly doubled, the actual proportion being five and a half octaves against three in the old instrument" (meetings file, EMI). The HMV 101 and 102 portables were the best-selling lines. In 1927 the 101 cost £7.00. For further details of HMV instruments, see "His Master's Voice Gramophone Catalogue, 1927." See also Alfred Clark interview, *Talking Machine News* 28, no. 10 (29 March 1931).

37. According to the 1931 HMV catalogue of instruments, radiograms ranged in price from £33.50 and £99.75, the 1939–1940 catalogue shows a range from £17.85 to £46.20.

38. For more on this debacle, see chapter 9.

39. See Sydney Wentworth Dixon, in Martland, *Since Records Began*, 64.

40. The Manson period and its integration of the Zonophone and HMV business had consequence. For example, the HMV trademark appeared on Zonophone records sold between 1919 and 1925. When the businesses were separated, Zonophone dropped the logo.

41. For details regarding HMV stores at the time of the 1931 merger, see "Comparative Net Sales and Cash Collections for the Year Ended 30th June 1931" (board papers, EMI). For further details, see Martland, *Since Records Began*, 266–69, and http://www.hmv.co.uk.

42. The role of Regal within Columbia's British business is discussed in chapter 9.

43. The reasons for this are discussed in chapter 6.

44. Data from "Musical Instrument Trade," *Third Census of Production Final Report, 1924* (London: HMSO, 1924), 397–400, and "Musical Instrument Trade," *Fourth Census of Production Final Report (Part IV)* (London: HMSO, 1930): 249–59.

45. Executive committee minutes, 8 February 1923 (board papers, EMI).

46. For more on this important issue, see chapter 11.

47. See J. R. Bennett and Eric Hughes, *The International Red Label Catalogue: HMV "DB" (12-Inch)* (London: Oakwood Press, n.d.), 49, 60–61, 73. For details of the opera and the version sung by Chaliapine, see entry for Modest Petrovich Moussorgsky Boris Godounov in *Kobbé's Complete Opera Book*, 10 ed., ed. The 10th Earl of Harewood (London: The Bodley Head, 1987), 714–23.

48. See HMV royalty ledger, which shows British sales of 650,000 in the six months after its release. See also memorandum from F. W. Gaisberg to Alfred Clark 7 July 1938. In it Gaisberg asserts in the decade after 1927, the record enjoyed combined Gramophone Company and Victor Company sales of 818,476. It remained in the catalogue till the end of 78-rpm record production and has since been rereleased in other formats (artist file and royalty ledger, EMI). See also Michael Smith and Frank Andrews, *The HMV Plum Label Catalogue: "C" Series (12-Inch)* (London: Oakwood Press, 1974), 51.

49. For an account of the Abbey Road studio project, see Brian Southall, *Abbey Road* (Wellingborough, Herts: Omnibus, 1985), chapters 2 and 3.

50. Pricing data taken from *Talking Machine World* 17, no. 3 (March 1920) 18; no. 10 (October 1921); and 20, no. 12 (December 1923).

51. For further details of this move, see *Talking Machine News* 24, no. 2 (June 1926): 160.

52. The Zonophone catalogue for March 1925 together with monthly supplements for November 1926 and January 1927 is in the author's collection.

53. For details of the price reductions of Celebrity records, see *Talking Machine News* 17, no. 4 (August 1919): 256.

54. For details of the early transfer releases, see Bennett and Hughes, *The International Red Label Catalogue.*

55. For details of the artists performing on the HMV Celebrity label, see the HMV record catalogues, 1926–1931.

56. Cited by David Bicknall in a lecture, "Fred Gaisberg," given to the British Institute of Recorded Sound, London, 19 May 1972.

57. Details of retail prices in *Talking Machine News* 16, no. 5 (September 1918): 188; 17, no. 4 (August 1919): 256; 17 no. 9 (February 1920): 482; 19, no. 6 (October 1921): FP; and 21, no. 6 (October 1923): 382.

58. Also republished were historical political speech records by former Liberal Prime Ministers H. H. Asquith, David Lloyd George and others.

59. This recording was advertised as being made "under the direction of the composer Lisa Lehmann." Other works, such as extracts from "The Fringes of the Fleet," by Sir Edward Elgar and Rudyard Kipling, and "The Starlight Express," by Elgar and Algernon Blackwood (both recorded by the composer), were originally published in the single-sided format but later transferred to the E & D series.

60. For further details, see Michael Smith, *The HMV "D" & "E" Catalogue* (London: Oakwood Press, 1971). See also F. W. Gaisberg, memorandum to Alfred Clark, 7 July 1938 (artist files, EMI).

61. Smith, *The HMV*; Gaisberg, memorandum.

62. The background to this important label is discussed in "Introduction," in Smith, *The HMV.*

63. For details of Plum label retail prices, see *Talking Machine News* 17, no. 4 (August 1919): 256 and 17, no. 10 (February 1920): 482; 19, no. 6 (October 1921); and 21, no. 6 (October 1923).

64. For more on this, see chapter 11. See also "Introduction," in Andrews and Bayly, *Catalogue of HMV,* and "Introduction," by Leonard Petts, in Smith and Andrews, *The HMV Plum.*

65. For further details about Ray Noble, see Martland, *Since Records Began,* 210.

66. See "The Coming of Age of His Master's Voice at Hayes," *The Sound Wave* 23, no. 8 (August 1929): 432, 434. See also Gaisberg, memorandum.

67. "Monthly Epitomes to the Board of The Gramophone Company," February, March and April 1925 (board papers, EMI); "General Commentary, 1930" (merger file, EMI).

68. "Interview With Alfred Clark," *Talking Machine News* 29, no. 11 (March 1931).

69. "Interview With Sir Louis Sterling," 1958 (Louis Sterling file, EMI). See also "Chairman's Address," annual meeting, 1930 (meetings file, EMI).

70. The merger papers (EMI) have survived in some quantity, providing a fascinating insight and blow-by-blow account of the workings of international business and finance in the middle of the Great Depression.

11

COMING OF AGE: 1918–1931

"Just a Memory among My Souvenirs"

> The new electrical recording is a landmark of scientific achievement. It is early yet to prophesy concerning its future developments.
>
> —Fred Gaisberg,[1] 1928

O f all the artefacts to survive the years between the end of the First World War in 1918 and the start of the Great Depression in 1929 records provide the most immediate, intimate and vivid contact with that now distant and vanished age. Like an insect preserved in amber recordings are a time capsule of performance art, therefore really do provide "a memory among my souvenirs." Often described by that overworked cliché "the jazz age," this final chapter explores the extraordinary musical creativity of those years through the lens of sound recording. It examines not just developments in the art of record making, but also changes in consumer taste and the role recorded music played in the lives of people, and it looks at the experiences of some artists who made records during those remarkable times.

★ ★ ★

Like many in Europe at the end of the First World War the pioneer recording engineer Fred Gaisberg was depressed and disillusioned, and with good reason. In November 1918 just six days before the war ended his brother, William Conrad Gaisberg, who was head of The Gramophone Company's London recording studios, died in the flu pandemic then sweeping the world. He contracted the illness after exposure to poison gas whilst visiting the

Western Front to record a Royal Garrison Artillery gas shell bombardment of German lines in front of the city of Lille; which became one of the first actuality recordings on discs (HMV D378).[2] Following his loss, Fred Gaisberg seriously considered quitting the industry and returning to the United States. However, he didn't, and his spirits lifted as the record industry returned to peacetime activities. Gaisberg's decision was important, for in the years that followed he played a central role rebuilding his company's postwar record catalogues, though he and other recording engineers faced new technical and artistic challenges in turbulent circumstances.[3]

Fred Gaisberg wrote of the period 1914 to 1918, "The four war years were not productive of any advance in music or the recording art. It was a sterile period of suspended animation."[4] Although true of Europe that statement did not describe the United States, where there were innovations; though because of wartime disruptions it took a while for them to cross the Atlantic. In 1921, for example, as a part of the Gramophone-Victor linkup, Victor sent a top recording engineer Raymond Sooy (brother of Harry O. Sooy) to London, where he worked with his British-based counterparts making records and instructing them in the new ideas and techniques; especially in the art of recording jazz and dance bands and other popular music records.[5] Raymond Sooy's memoirs provide important insights into the art of the recording engineer in those final days of mechanical recording. They show engineer tasks continued to include artist management in cramped studios. Of the recording engineer, Sooy said, "He must be a very quick thinker and patient—he must know how to meet and handle all kinds of temperamental people, and govern himself under some very trying conditions." Trying to manage orchestra and bands in the near impossible conditions they worked in, he noted:

> It was necessary . . . to place the musicians who were playing the cello, oboe, clarinet, cornet, trombones and some of the other instruments, on high stools, so that they could concentrate their tones directly towards the recording horns. They had to be placed so close together that it was almost impossible to play. The violinist, while playing, would often run their bows up the bell of the clarinets which were being played directly above them or in one of the other musician's eyes, which would cause a heated argument.[6]

Despite the important empirical innovations in record making he and others pioneered, little had in the reality changed from the prewar rough-and-tumble accounts of record making by Gaisberg and other early engineers.[7]

However, after the war the art of sound recording did change and a portent of this occurred in London on 11 November 1920, the second anniversary of the Armistice. On that day, amid the splendour of Westminster Abbey and in the presence of King George V, Prime Minister David Lloyd George and the combined leadership of the British armed forces, the body of an unknown British warrior from the battlefields of northern Europe was buried with pomp and ceremony in that final resting place of Britain's great and good. Parts of the funeral service were recorded by two British engineers Lionel Guest and H. O. Merriman and released by Columbia. To make this first recording of a public event, the pair used microphones and electric amplifiers. It was a primitive affair even by the standards of the time and the results were poor, but nonetheless the Guest and Merriman experiment showed the way forward.[8]

Curiously, although record companies on both sides of the Atlantic had in-house research facilities, the development of a practical system of electrical recording came from outside the industry. Although a number of experimental recordings using electrical amplification were made in the early 1920s, it was not until 1925 that the breakthrough occurred. Just as Edison's 1877 invention of sound recording was a spin-off of experimental work relating to telephone transmissions, research into solving the problem of fading signals in long-distance telephone conversations led to the Western Electric recording system. In April 1925 Alfred Clark, whilst visiting Victor in the United States heard the new recordings. He sent an enthusiastic cable to London executives extolling the amazing sound quality of the new records and telling of the agreement he had signed with Western Electric.[9] The process was soon taken up by almost the entire British recording industry, but to secure existing catalogues it was introduced with little fanfare.[10] Columbia, for example, released its first electrical recording in Britain during the summer of 1925. It was derived from a Western Electric experimental recording and in a September 1925 review in *The Sound Wave* the editor commented

> This wonder record just issued by Columbia (No 9048) of the remarkable singing of the Associated Glee Clubs of America, making a combined choir of 850 male voices, is something that was considered absolutely impossible only a few short years ago. Those who demanded this kind of thing were laughed at. Those who believed in it and predicted it were considered hopeless optimists.[11]

It was an expensive innovation, as Western Electric charged a one penny royalty per record sold. In 1935 Alfred Clark estimated that in ten years

EMI and its predecessors in business had paid Western Electric around £500,000, equal to worldwide record sales of 120,000,000.[12]

Overnight electrical recordings rendered obsolete not just the existing record catalogues but also the mechanical process, recording studios and the industry's most experienced sound engineers. Although the first three were easily overcome the old engineers were out of a job; with the notable exception of Charles Gregory at Columbia, who retrained as an electrical engineer.[13] The innovation brought about a revolution in recording studio management. For until the advent of electrical recording, studio personnel consisted of an engineer and an assistant, with the engineer doubling up as artist and repertoire manager. However, after the changeover, the tasks were separated, providing experienced mechanical sound engineers like Fred Gaisberg, Arthur H. Brooks, Joe Batten, Oscar Preuss and others with the means to continue their careers as artist and repertoire managers. The change was nonetheless dramatic, as Fred Gaisberg dryly reported in 1928, "Down at Hayes we have a staff of sixteen young electrical engineers specially trained for their departmental duties, and I need hardly add that they are one and all possessing scientific qualifications."[14]

During the period 1925 to 1931, these artist and repertoire managers engaged with the possibilities of the new technology and the reinvention and redefining of their job. Assessing the doyen of this group, Fred Gaisberg, in his new role (he called it artistic director) during these years and those leading up to his retirement in 1939, a colleague David Bicknell noted his importance within the industry and wider musical circles:

> No longer was he an engineer but the artistic director and master of his profession. During the remaining twelve years of his career Fred's influence—perhaps power would be a better word—in the world of international music increased steadily. It was found firstly on the status and worldwide ramifications of the [Gramophone] Company and secondly on the fact that during those years it was almost impossible for a musician to make a successful international career without records being included in the HMV celebrity catalogue and Fred was the man who decided whether they went there.[15]

It was certainly a demanding job requiring many new and novel innovations. For example, an important goal of all the major international companies was to record the basic classical repertoire and complete operas. It was therefore necessary to make contracts with top British and European orchestras, conductors, opera houses and operatic stars. That said, recording these large musical forces required new skills. It also required the breaking down of scores into manageable four to four and a half minute blocks; the limit of a 12-inch 78-rpm record. This sometimes required the insertion of holding notes and other novel end-of-side breaks; it also required the management of conductors in the often highly charged atmosphere of the recording studio or other venues. After cutting their teeth with difficult and temperamental singers like soprano Dame Nellie Melba, these old hands may well have found conductors less of a problem; though Arturo Toscanini was notoriously brittle when it came to the end-of-side breaks.

It was into this new exciting and vibrant creative world of the late 1920s that a new generation of artist and repertoire managers entered the profession, among them were David Bicknell and Walter Legge.[16] Both worked for The Gramophone Company, Bicknell as an assistant to Gaisberg and Walter Legge initially wrote album and analytical notes, and notes for published lists of new records. He later became editor of the in-house monthly magazine *The Voice* and as such first entered the recording studio. In his memoirs Legge said he learned his trade standing on the shoulders of figures like Fred Gaisberg, Oscar Preuss and music critic Ernest Newman, and working with artists such as organist Albert Schweitzer, conductor Sir Thomas Beecham and singer John McCormack. In 1931 (in the depths of the Great Depression), Legge launched the subscription-based Society series of previously unrecorded classical works. The success of this venture cemented his reputation as a precocious talent. After the Second World War, Legge created the modern role of record producer. Legge claimed Gaisberg told him that "we are in the studio to record as well as we can wax what the artist habitually do in the opera house or on the concert platform" and suggested Gaisberg (who was an accomplished photographer) made "sound photographs." In contrast Legge saw himself creating a new form of performance on record, with the listeners seated in the equivalent to the best seat in the house. He was a kind of recording Cecil B. de Mille.[17]

★ ★ ★

Before the First World War it was customary for record companies to circulate details of new record releases first to dealers (usually through the trade press) and then to the public by advertising in local, regional and national newspapers and also in magazines. All this made the British record industry large and important advertisers. Furthermore, record companies published annual catalogues, to which new releases were added via monthly supplements. For those interested in classical music and with a pocket deep enough to invest, there were specialist catalogues; these included

The Gramophone Company's *International Artists Catalogue* (for Celebrity recordings), which was first published in 1914. In 1920, the same company published *Opera at Home*. This was a series of thumbnail plots of operas and available recorded selections. It was an immediate success and had, by 1924, sold 20,000 copies and gone to three editions, each containing updates of the latest HMV operatic record releases.[18]

The first regular record reviews appeared in the national press a year or so after the war ended. One of the first reviewers was Robin Legge of the *Daily Telegraph*. He succeeded in interesting the individual who, more than any other, developed the ideas of record reviews and consumer power in this field of culture and commerce; the writer Compton (later Sir Compton) Mackenzie. Mackenzie's first *Daily Telegraph* record review appeared in September 1922, soon after he acquired a gramophone.[19] Although these record reviews had some effect in pressuring manufacturers to expand the range of available records, specialist magazines proved more effective. Consumers, particularly the more musically sophisticated (and especially men), had often come to appreciate recorded music during war service. As discussed in chapter 8, it was during these years that individuals like Christopher Stone and his comrades used recorded music as a source of solace and a means of passing time. Many kept their interest after the war, and took recorded music seriously as a medium for listening to music.

In 1923, as a result of the interest generated by his articles, Mackenzie and Archibald Marshall (who was another reviewer) published *Gramophone Nights* in which they created a series of programmes based on readily available classical recordings. Published before the advent of popular radio, it was intended as a sort of after-dinner drawing room entertainment; they had in fact invented the format for later radio record programmes. The authors were quick to criticise the quality of many orchestral records, which they described as "those murderous assaults on the ear." They also more reasonably pointed out that: "poor material soon wears out, and the public are not going to pay for records of rubbish."[20] Others quickly entered the field, not least Dr. Percy A. Scholes, music critic of *The Observer*, musical educator and lexicographer. He published *The First Book of the Gramophone Record*, which appeared in 1923 and went to a second edition in 1927. In this work he summed up the case for music on record: "By means of the gramophone people everywhere can enjoy the Queen's Hall Orchestra, or Chaliapin, or the London String Quartet, or Sammons, or Samuel, or Busoni. No other agency of musical reproduction for years to come is likely to reduce the popularity of the gramophone." *The Second Book of the Gramophone Record* followed in 1928. These works were intended for the serious musician and assumed much musical knowledge. However, through the medium of his small books, Scholes did more than most to establish recorded music as an important and effective teacher of music.[21]

In April 1923 Compton Mackenzie launched *The Gramophone* as a monthly record review magazine, a role it continues to perform to the present. It also provided a forum for reviewing and debating the merits of the latest machines. With a start-up capital of £2,000, the magazine was aimed at the educated but not necessarily musically sophisticated individual. With ongoing developments in wireless broadcasting many saw the magazine as a high risk venture, but it worked and settled to monthly sales of around 5,000. Mackenzie was editor and his brother-in-law Christopher Stone was London editor.[22] One of the contributors was his wife Faith, joined later by a host of others, including Percy Scholes. Mackenzie was supported by major manufacturers, who became advertisers and supplied review records. The first edition contained twenty-one pages plus advertising copy and (using various guises) Mackenzie wrote most of the articles. He also wrote a "Prologue," which he later thought read like "the preliminary announcement of a school magazine that is being published as a rival to *the* school magazine." In it he summed up the philosophy that underpinned the venture: "Our policy will be to encourage the recording companies to build up for generations to come a great library of good music."[23] The success of *The Gramophone* was based not just on educated middle-class male war veterans, but also on those skilled and semiskilled working-class consumers who had traditionally bought recorded music. To appeal to as wide a readership as possible, *The Gramophone* published a broad range of record reviews including popular music, which was the largest sector of the market. There were also important jazz reviews, designed to appeal to those middle-class intellectuals rather than the broad mass of consumers. There was even a "Collector's Corner," recognising the emergence (by the mid-1920s) of record collectors.[24] The magazine also acknowledged those who had, through the fortunes of war, little spare cash to spend on records, though they were rather patronisingly described as "the new poor." They were offered a regular column of reviews of good quality recorded music available at 2s.6d.

In a move prefiguring Walter Legge's later venture by eight years, Mackenzie formed The National Gramophonic Society, to publish previously unrecorded chamber music on a subscription basis. Although The National Gramophonic Society did not last, it showed the commercial viability of chamber music recordings.[25] The greatest opportunity for *The Gramophone* and the consumers it championed came in the golden five or six years after the introduction of electrical recording in 1925, years when annual record sales in Britain rose to a staggering sixty million.[26]

★   ★   ★

One of the major research issues encountered in writing this book has been the paucity of surviving sales data relating to individual recordings. In part this is due to the standard nonroyalty contracts on which most artists were engaged during the period under review. In addition, most medium and small record companies went out of business in the 1930s and their papers were destroyed. On the positive side, there survives a wealth of data in The EMI Group Archive for the period 1918 to 1931. This collection comprises royalty payments for all the businesses that merged in 1931 to form EMI Ltd. It is therefore largely, but not entirely, from these sources that the present assessment is based.

In its volume entitled "Gramophones," Lord & Thomas and Logan's 1930 *Merchandising Survey of Great Britain* detailed consumer trends indicating the proportions of British record sales by genre. When placed with the data cited in chapter 9, which shows overall British record sales of around 60,000,000 in 1930, it is possible to create a table (table 11.1), showing both proportions and what that meant in terms of sales figures.

That more than 52 per cent of consumers preferred to buy popular dance and vocal records is perhaps unsurprising, though the figure for operatic and serious music sales is something of a surprise as the overall figure of 16.5 per cent is in line with more modern proportions of classical record sales. The sales data of serious music, defined in the survey as large scale orchestral, chamber and solo instrumental works, seems to be strange and at odds with the excellent late 1920s sales of complete works by large orchestral forces boasted by Sterling and Clark.[27] Overall sales of

Table 11.1.   Consumer Preference as to the Popularity of Records by Genre, 1930

Type of Record	Per Cent	Sales
Dance	29.3	17,580,000
Vocal	23.1	13,860,000
Operatic	16.1	9,660,000
Humorous	15.5	9,300,000
Serious music	0.4	240,000
Bands	0.3	180,000
No particular preference	15.3	9,180,000

Source: Merchandising, 7. See also chapter 9 for details of overall British sales during this year.

240,000 represents a substantial revenue stream for the concerns exploiting this particular market, although as these works often consisted of two or more premium-priced records they required a significant consumer investment, which would have limited sales. The figures in table 11.1 also show that the strong pre-1914 sales of brass and military band music records had, by the late 1920s, been largely replaced by dance band and other kinds of popular music. The Lord & Thomas and Logan survey also asked record dealers to give their own estimate of the comparative popularity of different genres of record.

Table 11.2 shows the combined forces of dance, jazz and vocal amounted to 52 per cent of all sales, with operatic and instrumental records accounting for a further 24 per cent. It is a pity that the same categories were not used for both surveys, though the similarity of data suggests dealers and consumers were arguably in agreement.

Table 11.2.   Dealer Survey of the Most Popular Record by Genre, 1930

Type of Record	Per Cent
Dance, ordinary	22.0
Jazz	14.0
Orchestral	18.0
Vocal	16.0
Humorous	12.0
Instrumental	12.0
Operatic	6.0

Source: Merchandising, 73.

Another source identifying particular best-selling records is a 1938 memorandum prepared by Fred Gaisberg for EMI chairman Alfred Clark. In it Gaisberg provided details of the top-selling British HMV and Zonophone records. These are given in table 11.3.

The data cited in table 11.3 is weakened by the inclusion of four recordings with rounded up figures, which appear to be best estimates. That said, this list is of great interest not just for the sales figures but also the kinds of music they represent. Five of them, the three Zonophone's together with Ben Selvin's Novelty Orchestra and Leopold Stokowski and The Philadelphia Orchestra, were derived from American Victor recordings, whilst the rest were British sourced. What remains quite astonishing in table 11.3 is the data relating to The Gramophone Company's best-selling British-made record of the 1920s, indeed till the 1950s; The Temple Church choir recording of Mendelssohn's "Hear my prayer" (HMV C1329). One feature of this record was the cost. It was a 12-inch midpriced HMV Plum

Table 11.3. Best-Selling HMV and Zonophone Records: 1920–1938

Artist	Title	Catalogue Number	Release Date	Sales
Temple Church	"Hear My Prayer"	HMV C1329	1927	804,036 to 1938
The Savoy Orpheans	"Valencia" and "The Student Prince"	HMV B2272	1926	750,000 to 1935
Ben Selvin's Novelty Orchestra	"Dardanella"	HMV B1089	1920	500,000 to 1925
Gracie Fields	"My Blue Heaven" and "Because I Love You"	HMV B2733	1928	500,000 to 1935
International Novelty Orchestra	"Cuckoo" and "Lena"	Zono 5002	1926	323,797 to 1932
Maurice Gunsky	"Why Do I Always Remember?" and "Lay My Head Beneath a Rose"	Zono 2864	1928	232,670 to 1932
Bud Billings	"Wanderer's Warning" and "Will the Angels Play Their Harps for Me?"	Zono 5422	1929	216,831 to 1932
Stokowski & the Philadelphia Orchestra	Hungarian Rhapsody No. 2 (Liszt)	HMV D1296	1927	170,000 to 1932

Source: FWG to AC, 7 July 1938 (statistics files, EMI). International Novelty Orchestra was a generic term used by Zonophone for releases of Victor-derived light orchestral music. Sales from "Hear My Prayer" are for the years 1927 to 1938; see HMV royalty ledger (EMI). Ben Selvin's "Dardanella" was deleted in December 1925. The Savoy Orpheans' record of "Valencia" coupled with "The Student Prince" was deleted in March 1935, and Gracie Fields's record of "My Blue Heaven" coupled with "Because I Love You" was deleted in January 1935. For further details, see Frank Andrews and Ernie Bayly, *Catalogue of HMV "B" series records.*

label record retailing at 4s.6d. At the time it would have taken an average skilled male worker nearly half a day to earn such a sum. That a piece of religious music recorded by a church choir rather than popular music by a dance band could achieve British sales in excess of 800,000 was without precedent. If world and cumulative sales to date are added then, as EMI records claim, it was the first authenticated British-made one-million-selling record. However, it proved a spectacular one off. Although by 1931 the HMV catalogue boasted no fewer than thirteen 10- or 12-inch Temple Church choir recordings none sold more than a few thousand copies.[28]

Consumer interest in records with a religious or sacred subject remains an important though much neglected subject. By the time "Hear my prayer" was released in 1927, this genre of music was already a well-established feature of record catalogues. One example was Stephen Adams

"The Holy City." In the 1920s and early 1930s two fine premium-priced recordings of this sacred song were made, one by British contralto Dame Clara Butt (Columbia 7375) (who was rather unkindly described by the American music critic James G. Huneker as: "the greatest contralto ever born in captivity"), and the other by American tenor Richard Crooks (HMV DB1798). Good sales could not always be guaranteed, but Columbia scored an equally important success with its 1927 American recording of Scottish-born gospel singer William MacEwan's rendition of the hymn "The old rugged cross" coupled with "Lets talk it over bye-and-bye" (Columbia 4148). By 1933 British sales of this record exceeded 250,000, at a time when all but a handful of the most successful dance and popular music records enjoyed sales of 100,000 and most record companies considered sales in excess of 10,000 copies a "hit."[29]

The Gaisberg list of top-selling records cited in table 11.3 provides a useful matrix to assess the most popular genres of records sold in the 1920s and early 1930s. Popular singers provided three of Gaisberg's Gramophone Company recordings, two by country and western singer Bud Billings and one by popular tenor Maurice Gunsky. These were American performers and the three records cited were unexpected "freak" hits. However, Gracie (later Dame Gracie) Fields was in a different league and one occupied by a handful of largely, but not entirely, British vocalists. Prior to 1931, their records provided the record industry with one of its most important engines of growth. Born in Rochdale in the industrial North of England, Gracie Fields served a long apprenticeship in musical revue. She arrived as a major entertainer in the mid-1920s, and was one of a small number of British entertainment giants active in the interwar years. Apart from her undoubted talent, she reflected a comforting image of the British industrial working classes as cheerful and stoic in all circumstances, especially during the Great Depression. Her first HMV record, "My blue heaven" (HMV B2733) was released in 1928 and appeared on Gaisberg's list as selling around 500,000. It proved so popular that the company claimed its factories had to work overtime to meet demand.[30] From 1927 till the mid-1930s, when Gracie Fields left for other record companies, practically every HMV monthly supplement included details of her latest records. Such was the appeal of this extraordinary artist that in 1933 HMV marked the manufacture of the four millionth Gracie Fields record (which was pressed by the singer herself) with a filmed celebration. The manager of the British branch of HMV claimed "the production of these [4,000,000 records] has given continuous employment to 120 people in the His Master's Voice record factory at Hayes for the last 4½ years."[31]

Gracie Fields was not alone in the field of 1920s vocal stardom. The decade threw up a host of outstanding performers who also made records. These included stars from the lighter London stage and film such as Noël Coward, Gertrude Lawrence and Evelyn Laye. It also brought to maturity established gramophone artists like the bass-baritone Peter Dawson, whose records dominated the HMV Plum label catalogue throughout this period; between 1928 and 1938 1,189,244 of his records were sold in Britain.[32] One of the most successful and popular American recording stars in Britain during the 1920s was entertainer Frank Crumit. Although he never performed in or even visited Britain, the recorded output of this artist, first for Columbia then Victor and finally Decca, encompassed popular, folk and novelty songs. In the year between 1924 and 1932 a total of 684,380 Frank Crumit records were sold by HMV; his 1926 Victor-derived recording of Percy French's whimsical "Abdul abulbul amir" (HMV B3208) remained in the HMV catalogue until the 1950s. Another great transatlantic entertainer was the actor, singer, film star and civil rights campaigner Paul Robeson. An African American, Robeson starred as Joe in the 1928 Drury Lane production of Jerome Kern and Oscar Hammerstein II musical *Show Boat*. This established him with British audiences and the recording he made of "Ol' man river" (HMV C1505) with Paul Whiteman and his orchestra sold more than 200,000 copies.[33] Robeson lived and worked mainly in Britain until the outbreak of the Second World War in 1939. He made extensive concert tours and made many successful records often of songs featured in his British-made films. Overall, more than one million Robeson records were sold in Britain between 1928 and 1938. This is even more impressive given these were also the years of the Great Depression.[34]

The contrast with the great German soprano Lotte Lehmann could not have been more complete. She made her first records in 1923, and although she enjoyed a long and highly successful record making career she made very little money from her early endeavours. In a 1975 interview she said: "You know, at that time [when she made her first records] I never had a penny. And I was always paid for each side I sang. So I never made any money with my old recordings. . . . I didn't give a hoot what it was, what I had to sing. They said, 'Now today, lets do this and this.' I said 'Fine, Fine.'"[35] Nonetheless, these early examples of Lehmann's art contain some of her finest performances on record.

Amongst the most successful and prolific recording artist's active in Britain during the period 1918 to 1931 was African American close harmony duettists Turner Layton and Clarence Johnstone. Their first Columbia record "Hard Hearted Hannah" coupled with "It had to be you" (Columbia 3511) was made in 1924 and thereafter, until they split in 1935, their records were a staple of the Columbia catalogue. Rarely a month went by without several releases. The remarkable popularity of Layton and Johnstone was such that cumulative sales of their many hundreds of records exceeded eight million, mostly in the period 1924 to 1931.[36] The novelty song was a peculiarity of the British trade and rarely travelled beyond these shores. Some were derived from music hall, or even from dance band orchestrations of hit songs. One of the most successful was music hall artist Charles Penrose 1927 recording of "The laughing policeman" (Columbia 4014). A replacement of an earlier mechanical recording, which had sold in modest numbers, by 1933 120,000 copies had been sold. Although Penrose made several other laughing records, none proved as successful; though his "Laughing policeman up to date" (Columbia 5532) did sell more than 91,000 copies.[37]

★   ★   ★

The lack of sales data from small and medium-sized British record companies active between 1918 and 1931 has already been noted; despite this it has been possible to deduce something of the most successful popular music and records of the two years 1928 and 1929. *The Music Seller Reference Book: The Year's Music and Records 1928–29* contains an alphabetical listing of around 7,500 British releases during those years. At the time and for years after record company releases of the most popular music and songs were performed either by the artist identified with the piece (which was fine if that artist was under contract to your record company), or as cover versions by other performers, or as orchestrations for dance band recordings. This important listing shows all recorded variants and therefore permits a mapping of what was popular in Britain during that period. In the absence of British best-selling record charts, which did not start until 1951, table 11.4 identifies the twelve titles popular enough to generate at least twenty different recordings. This creates a list that is probably as close as it is possible to get to the best-selling popular music on record at the eve of the Great Depression.

　　With an incredible forty variations, table 11.4 shows "Sonny Boy" as the runaway success. Yet it is a curiously mawkish song about the death of a child, and might therefore be considered a very odd piece of popular music. Composed for American entertainer Al Jolson by songwriters Buddy De Sylva, Lew Brown and Ray Henderson, Jolson cleverly featured it three times in the 1928 Warner Brothers film *The Singing Fool*. Its extraordinary

Table 11.4.   The Most Recorded Popular Music and Songs in 1928–1929

Songs or Music	Number of Recordings
"Sonny Boy"	40
"I Can't Give You Anything but Love Baby"	27
"My Inspiration Is You"	25
"Carolina Moon"	25
"Broadway Melody"	23
"Just Like a Melody out of the Sky"	23
"Me and the Man in the Moon"	22
"Roll Away, Clouds"	22
"Wedding of the Painted Doll"	22
"I Kiss Your Hand, Madame"	21
"Jeannine, I Dream of Lilac Time"	21
"Just a Little Fond Affection"	21

Source: The data used in this table have been taken from "Gramophone Record Titles (Arranged Alphabetically)," *The Music Seller Reference Book: The Year's Music and Records 1928–29* (London, Evans Brothers Ltd, 1929), 17–152.

success shows a development in existing patterns of recording hit songs from live musical shows by the original cast; Jolson simply moved the goalposts by singing for the new talking pictures to communicate his art to this new and "hidden" audience in movie theatres not just across America but throughout the world. The idea of forty versions of a single hit song seems improbable, but a breakdown shows eighteen vocals, sixteen dance band or orchestral and six piano or organ versions. Of the vocal renditions, three were Brunswick recordings, including Al Jolson's version (Brunswick 3879), whilst HMV released seven versions, including one by John McCormack (HMV DA1027) and another by Paul Robeson (HMV B2948). Columbia issued five versions, including one waxed by the ubiquitous Layton and Johnstone (Columbia 5198), whilst there were three Regal, four Parlophone and two Zonophone renditions. The balance was made up of offerings from the rest of the trade.[38]

Although eight of the remaining eleven songs were not identified with a specific musical show or film, they all had melodies capable of orchestration for dance music records. Of the remaining three songs two, "Broadway Melody" and "Wedding of the painted doll," were featured in the 1929 MGM musical film success *Broadway Melody*.[39] "Roll away, clouds" in contrast was featured in a stage musical, *Virginia,* which had its London premiere in October 1928.[40] This marriage of hit songs to the new medium of talking pictures stimulated record sales sourced from the cinema, which in turn helped the careers of the new Hollywood musical performers like Maurice Chevalier, Jeanette MacDonald and Marlene Dietrich.[41]

Furthermore, spin-off songs remained an important feature of the industry throughout the Great Depression and beyond; and eventually brought Hollywood film companies into the modern record industry.[42]

★ ★ ★

In the early years of the twentieth century, classical music recordings were largely limited to vocalists and those instrumentalists whose art was recordable by the mechanical process. However, by 1914, empirical developments in the process had widened the range of recordable music resulting in the appearance of what were often cut-down versions, orchestral or small ensemble music. Down to the Great Depression, the number of companies engaged in making classical records remained small. Indeed the trade in this kind of music was dominated by the major firms, namely The Gramophone Company, Columbia Graphophone and Parlophone, though some important classical recordings on the smaller labels like Edison Bell, Vocalion, Polydor (the Deutsche Grammophon export label) and Brunswick and, after 1929, Decca.

Earlier chapters showed how the prewar market for classical records was dominated by a relatively small group of performers, mainly in the form of Celebrity records published by firms like Columbia Graphophone and The Gramophone Company. There were some prewar differences with Gramophone Company premium-priced Celebrity series had records pressed into just one side of the disc, while its rival Columbia often had recording pressed into both sides. Whatever the format, they were expensive and enjoyed relatively small sales, though they gave wealthy and interested consumers access to a whole range of important classical music.

As Gaisberg noted, the war years were largely a period of marking time for the British industry and its classical record catalogues. To be sure The Gramophone Company and Columbia received American-derived recordings, but few European-made classical recordings appeared. That said, it was during the war years that British composer Sir Edward Elgar began his recording career and great conductors like Sir Thomas Beecham and Sir Henry Wood contributed to the art, supported by lesser figures such as Albert W. Ketèlbey. Even in the midst of war new performers appeared and whilst recordings of large scale works like operas were attempted singers and instrumentalists remained the bread and butter of the postwar classical record catalogues. Of the new artists Fred Gaisberg spotted the big one in 1918. At the time he was working in Italy from where he wrote enthusiastically to his brother, who managed The Gramophone Company London recording studios, about a new singer he had heard.

> Sabjano [the Italian music director] will be writing to you about a new tenor named Gigli who has been singing in Rome and here [in Milan] and making an awful hit. I have heard him and today I made a test of his voice. I tell you he is wonderful and don't hesitate to follow Sabjano's advice about securing him because he is going to have a great career. You can describe him as a 2nd Caruso except he has greater vocal flexibility. It is a real lyric voice that rings out all over the place and give [*sic*] you the impression of illimitable [*sic*] reserve. He is about 24[43] and robust health average height and shows extraordinary intelligence for a tenor. Columbia have already made him an offer so we are not alone in the ring. We lost Schipa and for goodness sake don't let us lose Gigli.[44]

Sabjano's letter backed Fred Gaisberg's assessment, asserting Beniamino Gigli was a first class tenor who would "be at the high [*sic*] of his career when Caruso is *passe* and a memory."[45] Like the records Gaisberg made of Caruso in 1902, those he made of Gigli in 1918 preceded him around Europe and the Americas making him a star in lands he had never seen.[46] Gigli signed his first record contract in 1918 and a second, jointly with Victor, after his 1921 American debut and a third in 1931, again jointly with Victor. These earned him a decent living and between 1925 and 1929 he achieved worldwide earnings of £15,032.93. Gigli also enjoyed an outstanding operatic and concert career and made several films. He also made a number of complete opera recordings for The Gramophone Company during the 1930s.

Gigli was in many ways lucky, for in 1921 the great Italian tenor and best-selling international recording artist Enrico Caruso, with whom he had been compared by Gaisberg and Sabjano, died at the early age of forty-eight. Caruso had signed his first royalty-based contract with Victor in 1906 and his last in 1919.[47] Constant visibility remains a continuing feature of the performing arts or entertainment generally, and interest declines once an artist retires and stops making records or dies, as do record sales. The reverse occurs in only in the rarest of cases and Caruso was one such artist.[48] The point was made by Fred Gaisberg who noted Caruso sales figures in The Gramophone Company territories for the period 1906 to 1937 as set out in table 11.5.

Table 11.5 shows 1,362,045 Enrico Caruso records were sold in the seventeen years 1906 to 1923, whilst 2,043,437 records were sold in the thirteen years 1923 to 1937. Therefore two thirds more records were sold

Table 11.5. Sales of Enrico Caruso's Records in The Gramophone Company's Territory, 1906–1937

Type of Record	Number Sold
10-inch single-sided	420,761
12-inch single-sided	941,284
Total sales 1906–1924	1,362,045
10-inch double-sided	861,043
12-inch double-sided	1,182394
Total sales 1924–1937	2,043,437

Source: Between 1902 and 1906, Caruso had fee-based contracts receiving a fixed fee per recording. These figures do not include post-1914 German and Russian sales and are derived from memorandum from F. W. Gaisberg to Alfred Clark, 7 July 1938 (artist file, EMI).

in the latter and shorter period, all of which were postmortem. Further, apart from the years 1923 to 1925, modern electrical recordings of the old Caruso repertoire were available, made by the new generation of tenors like Beniamino Gigli. There are some mitigating factors in all of this, not least price. Sales were boosted in 1919 when the price of all Celebrity records, including those of Caruso, was cut. There was a further boost in 1923 when these records were reconfigured to having a recording pressed into both sides of the disc, effectively halving the price. Royalty ledger figures for the six year to 1929 show the boost given by the reconfiguration, with sales of 103,836 for the year 1924 thereafter settling to around 70,000 per year to 1929. Also between 1923 and 1930 the record industry boomed, giving Caruso's recordings an extra push. It is worth adding that Caruso was a phenomenon and a one-off; someone who defined his art for generations to come. The boom did not last and sales of his records collapsed during the Great Depression. That said, as Gaisberg noted, the period 1906 to 1937 saw sales totalling 3,405,482 in the territory controlled by The Gramophone Company, generating royalties payable to the artist (and later his estate) of £162,435 and this does not include his Victor earnings; clearly when it came to royalty earnings Caruso was in a class of his own.[49]

In the early postwar years British interest in opera was at an all-time low. Things were so bad that in 1921 there was no season at the Royal Opera House, Covent Garden.[50] The causes of this are not too difficult to discover. To start with, many prewar aristocratic subscribers and patrons had died (or had been killed in the war) or were no longer able to maintain the old ways. The passing of this world was noted by Dame Nellie Melba, who had dominated Covent Garden from the late nineteenth century. In her 1925 memoirs *Melodies and Memories* she wrote of her first postwar appearance at Covent Garden, as Mimi in *La Boheme,*

> I find myself looking into the great space of the auditorium, and feeling once again that I am singing to an audience of ghosts. Lady de Grey had gone, Alfred de Rothschild had gone, and so many others, all gone; and yet I felt them there. I seemed in my imagination to see their faces again, looking out from the shadows of their boxes, and it was for them rather than for this great audience that I sang.[51]

The brutal truth was that between 1914 and 1918 the social and musical milieu in which Nellie Melba flourished had perished in the trenches of France and Flanders. Reluctantly, Melba recognised she was out of her time and at the end of her career. Of the former she observed, "Can you imagine in the old days, men walking into Covent Garden on a Melba night, or on any other night, and sitting in the stalls, in shabby tweed coats?"[52]

The postwar world Melba so detested also produced electrical recordings, which allowed the most realistic recordings of her voice and art to be made. Unfortunately for her, the old mechanical process often failed to capture the unique silvery, almost childlike, quality of her voice. In June 1926, the new technology was used to record parts of her farewell performance live from the stage at Covent Garden. At sixty-seven she was past her best, but few sopranos, whatever their age, have been able to match the ethereal beauty of the voice that was Melba. These few records, including her farewell speech, were released (HMV DB453 and DB1500) as a unique souvenir of a remarkable musical life lived in extraordinary times, and showed the importance of records as the preserver of the very best of musical culture.[53]

The 1920s saw a new generation of great classical singers come to the fore. Many came from continental Europe and their recordings first appeared in Britain via pressings of German records like Parlophone, Odeon and Polydor. Polydor were later pressed by Decca, and Parlophone and Odeon became part of the Columbia conglomerate and subsequently EMI. Among these new artists were the Austrian Richard Tauber, the Germans Friedrich Schorr, Elena Gerhardt, Frida Leider, Lotte Lehmann and Elisabeth Schumann, the Dane Lauritz Melchior and Norwegian Kirsten Flagstad. In 1924 the tenor John McCormack returned to the British concert stage after a ten-year absence in the United States. Thereafter, he refocused his record making activities on Britain and made his final recordings as late as 1942. As a crossover artist McCormack enjoyed substantial sales particularly from his recordings of popular songs, with sales for the decade 1924 to 1933 totalling 606,859. His two best-selling records were the 1927 Victor sourced "Mother

Machree" coupled with "I hear you calling me" (HMV DA958), a remake
of an earlier mechanical recording, which sold an impressive 60,542 copies
in the six years prior to 1934 and his 1930 film spin-off record "The rose of
Tralee" coupled with "Ireland mother Ireland" (HMV DA1119) which sold
58,194 in four years. The contribution made by these and other artists to the
recorded art of the interwar years is a remarkable testament to the international appeal of great classical music on record.[54]

The 7,500 records listed in "Gramophone record titles" *The Music
Seller Reference Book: The Year's Music and Records 1928–29,* included all
the new classical recordings. Only two had multiple recordings and one of
these was Schubert's "Serenade," of which six records were released. The
others were a selection of the Liszt Hungarian rhapsody, which generated a
total of nine recordings. Gaisberg's 1937 list of best-selling records had just
one classical recording, and that was Liszt's Hungarian rhapsody No. 2 with
sales of around 170,000 copies.

With the coming of electrical recordings in 1925 interest in single
records of great singers waned and the music of great orchestras and conductors came to the fore. Record companies responded to this demand by
creating a basic catalogue of recordings of complete works, which required
artistic directors like Fred Gaisberg and Arthur H. Brookes to work closely
with conductors. As a result, the art of figures like Sir Edward Elgar and Sir
Thomas Beecham was made available to new audiences in Britain and around
the world. Though the only reason record companies could afford to make
these recordings was the knowledge they would enjoy international sales.[55]

The combination of new technology and cheaper prices encouraged
record companies to make recordings of the finest continental European
instrumentalists such as pianist Alfred Cortot, violinist Jacques Thibaud
and cellist Pablo Casals. Their extraordinarily vivid recordings of Haydn's
Trio in G (HMV DA895–96), Beethoven's Trio in B flat major (HMV
DB1223–27) and the Schubert Trio No 1 in B flat (HMV DB947–50)
proved great sellers and remained in the record catalogues for decades. At
the same time these same years saw the appearance of two young violinists, Jascha Heifetz and Yehudi Menuhin. Their records challenged those
of existing virtuoso performers like Fritz Kreisler. At the same time, the
new process captured the art of established recording artists like pianist Ignacy Jan Paderewski and the Russian composer pianist Serge Rachmani-
nov and these newer records outsold the more expensive recordings they
had made earlier in the century. By the start of the Great Depression such
developments enabled consumers to access a broad range of outstanding
classical music recordings, performed by the greatest exponents of the age.

It also enabled a small number of recording artists to make a decent living from their records. By 1931 British multinational record companies active in this field had catalogues of such quality that many recordings remained available into the modern era.

★   ★   ★

Classical music recordings enjoyed a golden age during the period between the end of the First World War and the onset of the Great Depression, but the real engine of growth and prosperity in the record industry was popular, especially dance band music. It was during this time that dancing became a modern mass entertainment, with dance halls opening in every British town and city. In these circumstances dancing and dance bands, whether performing live, via broadcasting, or on records, dominated popular music and entertainment. So much so that by 1930 a large proportion of the sixty million records sold in Britain were of popular, mainly dance music.

The origins of postwar dance music can be found in the prewar world of new American musical forms like ragtime. However, during the war jazz emerged to become America's greatest cultural achievement and its unique contribution to modern popular music. Black Americans developed jazz, which emerged out of New Orleans early in the twentieth century. As the pull of urban industrial life attracted poor rural populations, jazz spread up the Mississippi river to Chicago, then to New York and the East Coast. The pioneers included great Black American musicians like Jelly Roll Morton, W. C. Handy, Eubie Blake, Sidney Bechet, "King" Oliver, "Kid" Ory, Louis Armstrong and many more, and they all made important recordings. Although jazz was the music of Black America, the first jazz records, made by Victor in February 1917, were recorded by a group of white musicians known as The Original Dixieland Jazz Band. Released in May 1917, these records made an impact that was nothing short of sensational and they threw the American record industry into turmoil. Victor simply did not know what to make of them. For example, a month after their release Calvin Child, head of recording at Victor, wrote in reply to a query by Eldridge Johnson about music his son had heard:

> This dance music changes from day to day and this may be something entirely new which we should get after at once. However, I rather imagine it is something on the order of the Jass Band work in which the clarinets and drums are featured to a great extent, the melody being given to the clarinets and the after beats to the drum with very marked rhythm. We have a doubled sided record No 18255.[56]

The record cited was The Original Dixieland Jazz Band's "Dixieland Jass Band one-step" and "Livery Stable Blues." Victor's publicity for these records did not understate its potential: "The Jass Band is the very latest thing in the development of music. It has sufficient power and penetration to inject new life into a mummy, and will keep ordinary human dancers on their feet till breakfast time."[57]

Jazz in its various forms first took the United Sates by storm and then, after the war, Europe. The phenomenal speed in which the new music spread was due in no small part to the advent of recorded music. Although it took until July 1919, more than two years after their US release, before Original Dixieland Jazz Band records appeared in Britain; and then only two records were released by The Gramophone Company, "At the jazz band ball" and "Ostrich walk" (HMV B1021) and "Bluin' the blues" and "Sensation Rag" (HMV B1022). This release coincided with the band's sensational tour of Britain and Europe, introducing jazz to wildly enthusiastic audiences and, before returning to the United States, they recorded for Columbia in London.[58]

Although British interest in jazz and its twin the twelve bar blues attracted dedicated enthusiasts, it remained a niche market and was not taken up by the record buying public. Instead they took to dance music, a homogenised hybrid of jazz. The most successful exponents of this came from the United States as did most of the early and best dance bands, with leaders like Paul Whiteman and Ben Selvin. It has been suggested that people like Whiteman and Selvin tamed and harmonised jazz making it acceptable to mass audiences. Whatever the truth, Paul Whiteman called the hybrid "symphonic syncopation." It is never easy to define with precision what must in the end be a qualitative judgement. However, in 1926, the British dance band leader Jack Hylton, by highlighting the tensions at play in syncopated dance music, did just that. He wrote: "Syncopation is the compromise between rhythm and harmony, between savagery and intellectualism. It is the music of the normal human being, and because of this it will live—progressively of course and gradually evolving into new forms—but it will live."[59] Jack Hylton was right about progressive development, which by the start of the Second World War saw jazz and dance music grow into many distinct styles including "Hot Jazz," "New Rhythm," "Big Band" and "Swing," all of which had their own specialist record catalogues containing records by British, European and American practitioners. It is the music pioneered by these and the host of other bands, conductors and musical arrangers who joined them that dominated the record industry during the 1920s.

The recordings of US dance bands not only attracted British consumers they also had a profound influence on British musicians, who eagerly copied the new performance styles and built on them to develop their own. As a result, records became an important mechanism not just for the transfer of musical culture but also as a teacher of new musical forms. This was assisted by the 1911 Copyright Act, which created the compulsory licence. If a composer agreed to allow one record company to use his music he could not refuse others. The composer, of course, earned fees every time the music was recorded.

Of the many successful British dance bands two were based in London's Savoy Hotel, just off the Strand in the middle of the capital's theatreland. One was the Savoy Havana, which was originally directed by American saxophonist Bert Ralton then by Reginald Batten, and the more famous Savoy Orpheans under the direction of Debroy Somers[60] who was succeeded by Carroll Gibbons; the American musician Rudy Vallée played saxophone in both bands. The Savoy bands first recorded for Columbia and then, after 1924, for The Gramophone Company. They were a good catch and an immediate success, selling a total of 73,343 10- and 12-inch HMV Plum label records in the month of February 1925 alone.[61] It was the beginning of a period of extraordinary creativity, for by the mid 1920s the record industry was awash with dance bands and their leaders who became unlikely pop stars of their day. Every record company big or small had its own roster of dance bands either named bands under contract, though often used under a variety of different names, or session bands labelled with a generic title, or bands whose recordings had been acquired through licencing deals with American companies. Even small British record companies like Vocalion with its 8-inch Broadcast records and Edison Bell with its The Winner and 8-inch Radio label used a number of names for the Harry Bidgood dance band and Harry Hudson's many different combinations of recording session musicians.[62] Harry Roy, who later recorded for Parlophone, began his record career at Vocalion with his brother Syd and their band the Crichton Lyricals. Their records were released on a range of cheap labels like Guardsman, Coliseum, Aco, Crown, Beltona, Imperial and Scala.

More substantial record companies like Columbia could afford the big boys, the most popular band leaders of the day. In 1925 Jack Payne ran a six-piece band at the Hotel Cecil in London, which the BBC broadcast live via its studios at nearby Savoy Hill and on the back of this he directed the BBC dance orchestra between 1928 and 1932. As a consequence of the rapid take-up of radio from the second half of the 1920s, Payne became one of the most popular dance band leaders in Britain. When he left his replacement was Henry Hall. Jack Payne made his first recordings in 1925 for The Gramophone Company on its Zonophone label. In 1927 he moved to Columbia's Regal label and the following year there was a further move, this time to the Columbia premium label. With access to a brilliant musical arranger Ray Noble, Payne became one of the biggest names in British dance music and his records a mainstay of Columbia's monthly supplements from 1928 until 1932 when he joined Imperial records. In his Columbia years, Jack Payne and the BBC dance orchestra released a total of 202 records. Of these sixty-four sold more than 10,000 copies, then the standard measure for a "hit" record, with six selling more than 40,000, and one, "The Stein Song" coupled with "Moonshine is better than sunshine" (Columbia CB62), almost made it to the rarefied heights of 100,000. These six top-selling Jack Payne records achieved cumulative sales of 342,201 and were made up of those in table 11.6.

Table 11.6.   Jack Payne and the BBC Dance Orchestra: Top-selling Columbia Records, 1928–1932

Title	Catalogue Number	Unit Sales
"On Her Doorstep" and "Fairy on the Clock" (side 2, Debroy Summers band)	Col 5634	43,886
"Sunny Side Up" medley	Col 5659	42,405
"Happy Days Are Here Again" and "Lucky Me, Lovable You"	Col CB9	41,149
"Stein Song" and "Moonshine Is Better Than Sunshine"	Col CB62	94,688
"When Its Springtime in the Rockies" and "I'm Falling in Love"	Col CB106	72,926
"Over the Garden Wall" and "There's a Good Time"	Col CB 132	47,127

Source: Data are derived from Jack Payne royalty sheets (artist file, EMI); *The Columbia Compete Catalogue, 1931*; and Frank Andrews, *Columbia 10-Inch Records, 1904–30.*

The Gramophone Company also had a roster of top line dance bands under exclusive contract. In 1928 its house band, the New Mayfair Dance Orchestra, came under the direction of the gifted, classically trained twenty-five-year-old Ray Noble, who subsequently became The Gramophone Company's musical director. Formerly Jack Payne's arranger, Noble came to the New Mayfair Dance Orchestra an established British songwriter, arranger and conductor; with these credentials he attracted top musicians into the band. Its vocalists included Al Bowlly; and in the early days the British jazz trumpet and cornet player Nat Gonella. Noble and the New Mayfair Dance Orchestra produced hit after hit, not just in Britain but also in continental Europe and even in the United States where British dance bands traditionally fared badly.[63] Whatever the recorded fare or manifestation it appeared under on the record label the New Mayfair Dance Orchestra proved highly versatile, with recordings ranging from Noble's own orchestrations of the latest dance tunes and songs to musical tie-ins from the talkies. Noble also orchestrated medleys, which weaved together melodies from musical shows like *Funny Face* and *Virginia* (HMV C1588) and selections from musicals such as *Rose Marie* (HMV C1756). He greatly influenced the art of musical arrangement and his wide-ranging skills as a manager, composer, arranger and conductor brought him fame in Britain, continental Europe and in the United States, where he went to continue his career.[64]

During the decade 1921 to 1931 The Gramophone Company enjoyed the services of Jack Hylton, the most important of all British dance band leaders. Born in the village of Great Lever, near Bolton in the industrial north of England, Hylton's mother was a schoolteacher whilst his father had a varied career as cotton spinner, railway worker and later a grocer and publican. Like Ray Noble, Jack Hylton was a gifted, classically trained musician and a successful businessman who retained a close interest in classical music and musicians.[65] Hylton's recording career began in 1921 with The Queen's Hall Dance Orchestra and his first records were made for The Gramophone Company, some appeared on the HMV Plum label and others on Zonophone were listed as Jack Hylton's Jazz Band. At the time British record companies were trying but failing to replicate the American dance band sound of Paul Whiteman. Hylton told The Gramophone Company that they had to abandon improvisation and use written scores like a classical orchestra. Hylton made some dance band arrangements and gathered together musicians who could sight-read. The resulting success gave Hylton his first billing on record labels, and in 1923 Jack Hylton and his Orchestra was born.

Hylton's formulae for success was to play live around the country, take regular European tours and use broadcasting sparingly. By the mid-1920s work was pouring in at such a rate that he even created a Jack Hylton brand, with another band using the same syncopated Hylton sound touring the country under the leadership of his then wife. Then there was the Kit Cat band, which was led by American clarinettist Al Starita; this sometimes recorded as Jack Hylton's Hyltonians.[66] He also appeared in London shows like *London Revue* in 1925 and *Shake Your Feet* in 1927. Such was his success that by the late 1920s the band had become a musical phenomenon. Table 11.7 shows sales data from the early and midphase of Hylton's time with The Gramophone Company and indicates just what a draw he was.

If Jack Hylton earned a decent return on record sales in 1926, by 1929 with worldwide earning of £22,565 he was in a league of his own. In an attempt to understand the phenomenon they were dealing with,

Table 11.7.   Sales of Records by Jack Hylton and His Orchestra: 1923–1926

Year	Record Sales	Earnings	
1923	190,818	£795	[$3,975]
1924	332,436	£1,385	[$6,925]
1925	485,803	£2,024	[$10,120]
1926	790,449	£3,294	[$16,470]

Source: Data, which are worldwide sales, are derived from "Jack Hylton's Orchestra," n.d. (artist file, EMI).

The Gramophone Company produced the data from which table 11.8 is derived. It compares sales of his records from July to December 1929 with those of the same period in 1928; 1929 proved the sales peak for the record industry, before the Great Depression began.

Table 11.8.   Sales of Records by Jack Hylton and His Orchestra: July–December 1928 and 1929

Record Size	July–December		Increase
	1928	1929	
10-inch Plum	724,401	1,479,180	754,779
12-inch Plum	104,174	184,933	80,759
Total	828,575	1,664,113	835,538

Source: Derived from W. L. Streeton to Albert Lack, n.d. (artist file, EMI).

A company memorandum reveals total British HMV December 1929 sales of 1,888,766 records of which 439,876 or 23.3 per cent were Jack Hylton records. These were made up of 337,567 10-inch and 102,309 12-inch records. Between 1923 and June 1930 world sales totalled 7,050,205, earning the artist royalty payments of £48,443. The British record industry did not see another act like his until The Beatles in the 1960s.[67] In 1930 Gramophone Company executive W. L. Streeton attempted to place this extraordinary achievement into perspective. He wrote, "I ascribe this increase partly to the continued improvement which has taken place in the entertainment value and musical quality of Hylton's band: to the increased popularity of dance numbers, caused by talking films and to the extraordinary pains which Hylton has taken to make his records interesting, particularly those records containing comedy effects."[68] The key is evidently the pains and professionalism Jack Hylton invested in record making. This is clear in a March 1930 letter he wrote to Streeton:

On Thursday last Mr Anderson brought me up a master of "Moanin' Low." On hearing it I found right in the very first eight bars the trombone player "duffed" his passage and again later in the trumpet chorus there are many cracks, as well as some of his hot playing being in the wrong chord. Also in my opinion, the record was amplified far too much.

I told Mr Anderson that I would like to hear the other tests which he had brought me and on playing them over I preferred number 3. He took them back and came to see me again in the evening and asked me to make a repeat of the title, as your office was under the impression the band was not brought up sufficiently.

I should be most glad if we could make a ruling once and for all, that we must consider the artistic performance of a record more than its strength.

I consider that the record of "Body and Soul" being brought up so much has not done the sales any good, in fact, it has probably brought the recording of another company to the attention of the public, which would not have been the case had our record had the atmosphere that this number required.[69]

The letter shows just how involved Jack Hylton was in the process of selecting the music he wanted to record, the process itself and the final selection and quality control of the records. It also reveals the perfectionist in the artist. He evidently regarded his performances, and particularly his recordings as works of art. He saw correctly that the public judgement of him as an artist was largely based on his records. That judgement was positive during the period July 1927 to April 1929, when The Gramophone Company released a total of 163 Jack Hylton records. Of these forty-seven, or nearly 30 per cent, enjoyed British sales in excess of 10,000. During this period, no other British band released anything like the number of records as Jack Hylton, nor did any approach his proportion of "hit" records.[70] A list of all Jack Hylton's hit records is beyond the field of this present work.[71] However, table 11.9 lists the seven records that sold in excess of 50,000 copies between 1927 and 1929.

Reviewing these records, the interesting feature is the three top-selling records were not of Hylton's syncopated dance music, rather two were waltzes (HMV B5136 and B5391) and the third is a sing-a-long medley of old songs (HMV C1592). This reveals the eclectic nature of Jack Hylton's art. He was first and foremost a commercial artist with a good ear for what the public wanted. In June 1930 Jack Hylton recorded "The stein song" coupled with "On the sunny side of the street" (HMV B5844), which became his best-selling record. Released in July 1930, within three months it had sold 175,918 copies (compared to sales of 94,668 for Columbia's

Table 11.9. Jack Hylton's Best-Selling Records, 1927–1928

Title	Catalogue Number	Sales
"When You Played the Organ" and "When Day Is Done"	HMV B5136	114,851
"Selection of Good Old Songs"	HMV C1592	83,773
Serenade from *Millions d'Arlequin* and "Persian Rosebud"	HMV B5391	81,486
"Souvenir" and "Leonora"	HMV B5356	80,980
"Hallelujah" and "Sometimes I'm Happy"	HMV B5332	60,433
"My Inspiration Is You" and "In Old Vienna"	HMV B5530	54,289
"Ramona" and "Sunshine"	HMV B5474	50,202

Source: Data derived from schedule A, "Re Jack Hylton and His Band," W. L. Streeton to Mr Hutchinson, 18 March 1929 (artist file, EMI).

Jack Payne version) and at a time when record sales were collapsing under the weight of the Great Depression.[72] In part Jack Hylton was successful because he was a good businessman who knew his own value. This can be seen in the 1931 decision he took to leave HMV and accept a better offer from Edward Lewis at Decca. Although Decca survived the depression, Hylton did not prosper and returned to HMV in 1935. Jack Hylton continued to make records until 1940, when in difficult wartime circumstances he gave up the business, and thereafter worked as a highly successful theatrical impresario.

Jack Hylton provides an appropriate end point to this book, for he epitomised better than most the optimistic 1920s. Hylton brought to mass audiences the new ideas of popular music and with it new methods of artist management and organisation in the entertainment industry. No one during the years down to 1931 exploited creative talents better than Jack Hylton. He conceived the thoroughly modern idea of regular national and European tours, together with strategic use of recording and broadcasting and, critically, keeping ahead of the competition by using the best available music, arrangers and musicians. The success he enjoyed in the rapidly rising market for his kind of music placed him in a position to force record companies to deal with him, and people like him, as equals, and he is therefore one of the few recording artists able to negotiate from a position of strength. In doing so, he and those other fortunate performers laid the foundations on which the modern recording and the broader entertainment business were built.

* * *

This account of the founding and formative years of the British record industry should be seen as the prologue to its post Second World War transformation, which took a form that lasted till the start of the twenty-first century. By the 1920s the industry was firmly established and already beginning to change, broadening and developing its product base, both the machines and recordings. The industry embraced electrical recording, began manufacturing electrical gramophones and radiograms. In addition, the major manufacturers joined the growing electrical appliance industry and established research and development facilities. These laboratories worked on important projects relating to improved recording techniques, stereophonic sound, radio, radar, television and sound films and other communications hardware. All these projects and many more bore fruit before, during and after the Second World War.

Coincidentally, 1929, the last year of growth for the British record industry before the onset of the Great Depression, was also the year of Emile Berliner's death. His 1888 address to the Franklin Institute, during which he gave the first public demonstration of his gramophone and disc records, launched the technology that proved the key element in the modern record industry. Between that first demonstration and his death Berliner's invention, as he predicted, was transformed from a crude toy into a vehicle for spreading music and culture worldwide. Based on these wholly novel technologies, the British record industry created an important new art form and with it markets, providing previously undreamt of opportunities for home entertainment. In addition, it offered some new opportunities to earn a good living and important new ways of spreading art and culture.

As this book shows, the products of this new British industry quickly gained a central place in the lives of many ordinary people, surviving recessions, a world war, innovations in technology and musical taste, to find itself at the end of the 1920s the prime provider of music in the home. If it had not been adaptable and capable of continuously reinventing itself, it would not have survived the stern tests of the years of the 1930s and 1940s.

In 1931, at the deepest point of the Great Depression, the consolidation of the international industry finally came to fruition. Originally proposed before the First World War, the depression-led merger of The Gramophone and Columbia Graphophone Companies created Electric and Musical Industries (EMI) Ltd. This created the organisation that with Decca were the only British record manufacturers to survive the 1930s. If that was not enough, in the years after 1931 the record industry faced not just the Great Depression but intense competition from radio and the movies. Crushed between these powerful forces, the industry suffered an almost complete collapse with British record sales in 1938 hovering around the same level they had been in 1906. Compounding all of this, just as the industry started to show signs of recovery it was, like much else in Britain, engulfed by the Second World War and once again languished. So deep was the pit into which it had fallen, the industry took until the late 1950s to recover the levels of activity, turnover and profit of the late 1920s. However the industry did survive and succeeded in reinventing itself, just as it did after the First World War, with new technology, new musical forms and new and expanding consumer markets to exploit. This in itself should provide guidance and inspiration for the industry as it faces the challenges of the early twenty-first century.

NOTES

Written and composed by Edgar Leslie and Lawrence Wright (using the name Horatio Nicholls), "Among My Souvenirs" was a popular 1927 hit, with most British record companies having at least one version in their catalogues.

1. Fred Gaisberg, "Round the Recording Studios, No II Mainly About Pioneers," *The Gramophone* 5, no. 11 (April 1928): 451–54.

2. For an account of this unique recording expedition to capture the sounds of battle, see "Recording the Guns on the Western Front," *The Voice* 2, no. 12 (December 1918): 4.

3. See Jerrold Northrop Moore, *A Voice in Time*: 149–52.

4. "All Roads Lead to La Scala," cited in Jerrold Northrop Moore, *A Voice in Time: The Gramophone of Fred Gaisberg, 1873–1951* (London: Hamilton, 1976), 160.

5. For an account of this importation skill transfer, see "The Memoirs of Raymond Sooy," *Communicate* (June/July 1974): 20–21. Raymond Sooy's memoirs, together with those of his brother Harry O. Sooy "Memoir of My Career at Victor Talking Machine Company," can be accessed via http://www.davidsarnoff.org. Compare also Sooys's vibrant 1917 Victor recording of *Tiger Rag* (Victor 18255), by the Original Dixieland Jazz Band, with the staid flat sound of the same recording made in London by Columbia (Columbia 748) in May 1919.

6. Cited in Sooy, "Memoirs," *Communicate*.

7. Although the profession of recording engineer based on mechanical cutting lasted until 1925, up to that date only one serious work was published on the subject *The Reproduction of Sound* (London: W. B. Tatterall, 1918), by Henry Seymour. In it, the former NPC engineer largely eschews the art of disc record making and instead focuses on the mechanics and processes of the by then dead art of cylinder record making.

8. An illustrated article concerning this important recording was published in the *Illustrated London News* 157, no. 4261 (18 December 1920): 1030.

9. See minutes of a special executive committee, 29 April 1925 (executive committee meetings file, 1925, EMI).

10. Edison Bell held out against the US system and its royalty payments and began making electrical recordings in 1926 using an in-house process developed by its brilliant electrical engineer P. G. A. H. Voigt (see chapter 9).

11. William B. Parkin, "Making Gramophone History," *The Sound Wave* 19, no. 9 (September 1925): 640.

12. Alfred Clark to the board of EMI, "Memorandum Concerning Central Research Laboratories," 1939 (board papers, 1939, EMI). The exchange rate used is $5.00 to the pound.

13. For details of Gregory's career after the introduction of electrical recording, see "Fifty Year of Recording," *Sound Wave* (Spring 1945); F. W. Gaisberg, "Charlie Gregory's Fifty Years of Talking Machines," undated manuscript (Gregory file, EMI); F. W. Gaisberg, "A Tribute to Charles Butler Gregory," *The Voice* 31, no. 1 (Spring 1946); Herbert C. Ridout, "An Appreciation of Charles B. Gregory," *The Gramophone* 23, no. 11 (March 1946): 123.

14. Gaisberg, "Round the Recording Studios."

15. David Bicknell, "Fred Gaisberg," a lecture to the British Institute of Recorded Sound, 19 May 1972.

16. For a personal account of his life in the record industry, see David Bicknell typescript, "Some Reflections on the Past," 21 August 1970 (David Bicknell file, EMI). See also Peter Martland, "David Bicknell," in *Oxford Dictionary of National Biography*, ed. H. C. G. Matthew and Brian Harrison (Oxford: Oxford University Press, 2004), and Martland, *Since Records Began* (London: Batsford, 1997), 166.

17. See Elisabeth Schwarzkopf, *On and Off the Record: A Memoir of Walter Legge* (London: Faber, 1982): 58–60; Alan Sanders, *Words and Music* (London: Duckworth, 1998); Martland, "Walter Legge," in *Oxford Dictionary of National Biography*; and Martland, *Since Records Began*, 169.

18. The preface to each edition was written by a distinguished musician or musical administrator. These were Henry Coates, H. V. Higgins and Sir Hugh Allen.

19. For more details, see Compton Mackenzie, *My Record of Music* (London: Huchinson, 1955), 66–67, and Anthony Pollard, *Gramophone: The First 75 Years* (Harrow, UK: General Gramophone, 1998), 14–32.

20. Compton Mackenzie and Archibald Marshall, *Gramophone Nights* (London: Heinemann, 1923), 8. See also Mackenzie, *My Record of Music*, 68.

21. Percy A. Scholes, *The First Book of the Gramophone Record* (Oxford: Oxford University Press, 1923 and 1927), and *The Second Book of the Gramophone Record* (Oxford: Oxford University Press, 1928). Scholes also published other works, including the *Oxford Dictionary of Music* and the multivolume *Columbia History of Music*. He was a government advisor on teaching music in schools and, in 1933, wrote a pamphlet, *Practical Lesson Plans in Musical Appreciation by Means of the Gramophone*.

22. Mackenzie preferred living on islands and was, in 1923, ensconced on the tiny island of Herm in the Channel Islands: he later moved to the Outer Hebrides.

23. For an account of the formation and early years of *The Gramophone*, see *My Record of Music*, chapter 8, and Pollard, *Gramophone*, 11–32.

24. See P. G. Hurst, "The Record Collector" *The Gramophone Jubilee Book* (Harrow, UK: General Gramophone Publications, 1973): 171–77 (first published in April 1942).

25. For further details about The National Gramophonic Society, see "Record Societies" in Pollard, *Gramophone*, 44–46.

26. For contemporary consumer comments on electrical recording, see letters, "new recordings," *The Gramophone* 3 no. 9 (February, 1926): 429–30.

27. This is discussed in chapters 10 and 11.

28. For further details, see 1931 *HMV Record Catalogue*, The Temple Church and Ernest Lough artist files and HMV royalty ledgers (EMI).

29. Data from Frank Andrews, *Columbia Records 10-Inch Series*, and Columbia royalty register (EMI).

30. For details about Gracie Fields recording career, see "Gracie Fields," HMV press release, 1933 (artist file, EMI).

31. For an account of this event, which was filmed for the newsreels, see "Greatest Day in Life of England's Greatest Comedienne," 14 February 1933, HMV press release (artist file, EMI). During the years 1928 to 1933, a total of 2,012,302 of her records were sold. Data calculated from the royalty ledgers (EMI).

32. Calculated from the royalty ledgers (EMI).

33. See also Robert Seeley and Rex Bunnett, *London Musical Shows on Record, 1898–1989* (Harrow, UK: General Gramophone, 1989), 194.

34. For more about Robeson's recording career, see Martland, *Since Records Began*, 208–9. Data calculated from royalty ledgers (EMI).

35. John Harvith and Susan Edwards Harvith, eds., "Lotte Lehmann" in *Edison, Musicians and the Phonograph* (New York: Greenwood, 1987), 71.

36. For more about Layton and Johnstone, see Martland, *Since Records Began*, 124, 126. Sales data calculated from royalty ledgers (EMI).

37. Sales data are calculated from royalty ledgers (EMI). For further details, see "Messrs Penrose and Whitlock: 'The Two Old Sports,'" *Talking Machine News* 17, no. 5 (September 1919): 208.

38. Royalty ledgers (EMI). "Messrs Penrose and Whitlock."

39. The merits of *Broadway Melody* and its hit songs are discussed in "A Talk on Talkies," *The Sound Wave* 23, no. 5 (May 1929): 258.

40. For details of the musical *Virginia*, see Seeley and Bunnett, *London Musical Shows*, 229.

41. Although Dietrich's *Blue Angel* recordings enjoyed success in Britain and on the European continent, they failed to make an impact in the US. In July 1931 Victor wrote to London: "We had a poor sale on the Dietrich record and would not be interested in a contract obligation, nor would we be disturbed if she should record for some other record company" (Marlene Dietrich, artist file, EMI).

42. For contemporary comment on this phenomenon, see "A Talk on Talkies," and "The Talking Film," *The Sound Wave* 23, no. 7 (July 1929): 361–62.

43. He was in fact twenty-eight years old.

44. F. W. Gaisberg to William C. Gaisberg, 17 May 1918 (artist files, EMI). See also F. W. Gaisberg, "Beniamino Gigli, Italy's Greatest Tenor," *The Gramophone* 16, no. 2 (June 1938): 3–4.

45. Carlo Sabajno to William C. Gaisberg, 18 May 1918 (artist file EMI).

46. The soprano Amelita Galli Curci had a similar experience but in reverse. She made her name in the United States during the later war years, and her records sold in enormous quantities in the US and Britain. In 1924 she made a debut tour of Britain but was not a great success. Her first appearance was at London's largest venue, The Royal Albert Hall, and it did not suit her voice: the illusion was shattered and thereafter her popularity waned.

47. See also chapter 7. This final contract guaranteed him $100,000 advance per year for ten years and 10 per cent royalty payments on records sold beyond the guarantee (artist file, EMI).

48. This phenomenon was noted in the executive committee minutes of 15 September 1921, which showed July 1921 Caruso records sales of 2,600 and August sales (the tenor died on 2 August) of 40,000 (board papers, EMI). I am grateful to Tony Locantro for highlighting this point. He argues that the only other artists whose record sales grew postmortem are Maria Callas, Elvis Presley, The Beatles and Michael Jackson.

49. This calculation uses an exchange rate of $4.05 to the pound, which was the exchange rate in 1938. Postmortem worldwide sales of Caruso's records show that in 1921, the year of his death, he earned $422,981 [£100,709] and the following year royalties fell to $125,177 [£29,804]. The two years in question were years of recession, which substantially reduced sales of all records. Victor celebrity record sales for 1922 were six million units, half those of the previous year. These figures are derived from "Caruso's Records Still in Big Demand," *Talking Machine World* 25, no. 4 (April 1928): 34a, and Michael W. Sherman, *Victrola Records: The Collector's Guide to Victor Records* (Dallas, TX: Monarch Record Enterprises, 1992), 168.

50. For comments on this issue, see Sydney W. Dixon to Calvin Child, 7 March 1921 (Victor correspondence, EMI). Dixon, then manager of International Artists at The Gramophone Company, deplored the King and Queen's lack of interest in opera, observing, "They would rather visit a hospital or workhouse than hear Caruso or Galli Curci." His solution was for Child to "send us a musically inclined millionaire as Princess of Wales."

51. Dame Nellie Melba, *Melodies and Memories* (London: Butterworth, 1925), 215.

52. Melba, *Melodies and Memories*.

53. Melba, *Melodies and Memories*, 215. Melba was not the only great singer to be recorded during performances from Covent Garden during the later 1920s. For more details, see chapter 10.

54. The art and recorded music of the great interwar singers are discussed in J. B. Steane, *The Grand Tradition, Seventy Years of Singing on Record 1900 to 1970* (London: Duckworth, 1978).

55. Compared with operatic and instrumentalists who made records, the British composer and conductor Sir Edward Elgar's Gramophone Company contracts were modest. His first in 1914 included a £50 advance and a 5 per cent royalty. His second in 1916 provided for an annual £100 retaining fee, a £21 recording session attendance fee and a 5 per cent royalty. The contract stipulated four sessions per year and renewal options. Between 1914 and 1921, Elgar received nearly £2,000 in fees and royalties and between 1916 and 1921 nearly 19,000 of his records were sold (Elgar file, EMI).

56. Calvin G. Child to Eldridge R. Johnson, 13 June 1917 (Calvin G. Child file, Johnson Victrola Museum).

57. Cited in Victor monthly record supplement, May 1917.

58. Although the Original Dixieland Jazz Band records were released in Britain in 1919, two years earlier continental Europe saw the arrival of the first jazz musicians in the form of the US army's 369th US Infantry Band led by Lieutenant James Reese Europe. It was made up of African American servicemen who were also professional jazz musicians. On its return to the US in February 1919, the band recorded for Pathé, using its vertical cut recording system, which made the records unplayable on most American talking machines. Tragically, in May 1919, an event occurred that turned Jim Europe into a lost pioneer of jazz. He was murdered by a member of the band. See *James Reese Europe: The Complete Pathé Recordings* (IAJRC CD 1012) and Reid Badger, *A Lifetime in Ragtime: A Biography of James Reese Europe* (Oxford: Oxford University Press, 1994).

59. Jack Hylton, *Melody Maker* (London, January 1926).

60. Born William Somers (1890–1952), after a career in military bands, joined The Aeolian Company as a house conductor. He also honed his skills as an arranger. In 1923 Somers formed the Savoy Orpheans and made it a leading dance band with an HMV recording contract. He left in 1926 and went on to enjoy a career in commercial radio.

61. The Gramophone Company epitomes note that "the increase in units and decrease in value [of records sold] is accounted for by the increase in Plum Label [records], which is mainly due to the Savoy Dance Records." The total number was 281,652. "Epitomes," March and April 1925 (board papers, EMI).

62. Harry Bidgood appeared under a variety of names, including "Harry Bidgood and his broadcasters," "Primo Scala and his novelty accordions" and "Primo Scala and his banjo band."

63. The orchestra also recorded as The New Mayfair Orchestra, The New Mayfair Novelty Orchestra and in cut down from The New Mayfair Quartet.

64. Among the popular songs Ray Noble (1903–1978) wrote are "The Very Thought of You" and "Love Is the Sweetest Thing." For more about Ray Noble, see Martland, *Since Records Began*, 210–12.

65. For a while, classically trained violinist (later conductor) Hugo Rignold worked for Hylton. For an assessment of Jack Hylton's life and career, see Roger Wimbush, "Here and There," *The Gramophone* 42, no. 12 (April 1965): 472.

66. This ensemble included future band leader Ted Heath and Billy Ternent, who also worked as Jack Hylton's principal arranger. Another Hylton sponsored band was The Piccadilly Revels Band.

67. Undated and unsigned note (artist file, EMI).

68. Undated and unsigned note.

69. Jack Hylton to W. L. Streeton, 8 March 1930 (artist file, EMI).

70. "Re Jack Hylton and His Band," W. L. Streeton to Mr Hutchinson, 18 March 1929 (artist file, EMI).

71. For Jack Hylton's discography, see Dennis Pareyra, "Jack Hylton Compete Discography," official Jack Hylton website, http://www.jackhylton.co.uk.

72. News report in *Talking Machine News* 29, no. 10 (March 1931).

APPENDIX:
CURRENCY CONVERTER

Between the end of the Civil War in 1865 and the outbreak of the First World War in 1914 the US British exchange rate was $4.85 to the pound. In practice business accounts rounded this up to $5.00 to the pound. Between 1914 and 1924 the pound floated on international exchanges trading at around $4.20 to the pound. Between 1924 and 1931 the value of the pound was fixed at the pre-1914 level of $4.85 to the pound. Again business accounts rounded this up to $5.00 to the pound. These conventions have been followed in this book.

Until 1971 the British pound was divided into twenty shillings and each shilling into twelve pence. After that date decimal currency was introduced with the pound divided into 100 new pence.

A currency conversion for the period 1865 to 1914 and 1924 to 1931:

12 pence = 1 shilling = $0.25 = 5 new pence
4 shillings = 1 dollar = 20 new pence
10 shillings = $2.50 = 50 new pence

GLOSSARY

The record and machine industry used a variety of terms to describe its products. Some of these terms were proprietary and others generic. To confuse matters the same terms came to have different meanings in the United States and Europe. The following glossary provides an explanation of those differences.

Talking Machine: a generic term used on both sides of the Atlantic to describe all kinds of instruments; though it was used more by the trade than consumers.

Phonograph: Thomas Edison used the word phonograph to describe his 1877 "Speaking Machine." In the United States it became a generic term to describe all kinds of talking machines. In Britain and Europe it was used to describe cylinder machines.

Graphophone: was a proprietary term used to describe the machines manufactured by The American Graphophone Company and sold by Columbia Phonograph Company General. It fell from general use in the early twentieth century, but was used by The Columbia Graphophone Company Ltd in 1917 when it became a limited liability company.

Gramophone: a proprietory term used by Emile Berliner to describe the machine on which his disc records were played. After 1900 it fell from general use in the United States (the reason for this is discussed in chapter 1), but remained a proprietary name of The Gramophone Company Ltd and its products until 1910, when a court ruled it to be generic. In the text it is capitalised when referring to the pre-1910 period and lower case after that date.

BIBLIOGRAPHY

MANUSCRIPTS

Companies House, London, England.
Edison National Historic Site, West Orange, New Jersey.
EMI Music Archive, Hayes, Middlesex, England.
Johnson Victrola Museum, Dover, Delaware.
Library of Congress, Washington, DC.
Museum of American History, Smithsonian Institution, Washington, DC.
The National Archive, Kew, London.
The New York Public Library, New York.
Sony Music Archive, New York.
US National Archive and Record Center, College Park, Maryland.

OFFICIAL PUBLICATIONS

All works published in London unless otherwise stated.
"Addis v The Gramophone Co Ltd," *All England Law Reports 1908–1910* (1910): 1–9.
"American Graphophone Co v Edward H. Amet," US Circuit Court, Northern District of Illinois, *Transcript of Record* (1896).
BBC Handbook, 1938. London: BBC, 1938.
"Berliner Gramophone Co v Frank Seaman," US Circuit Court, Western District of Virginia, *Transcript of Record* (Harrisonburg, 1901).
"Boosey v Whight," *All England Law Reports 1900* (1901), 122.
Census of Production 1907 (Cmd. 5254) (HMSO, 1910).
Fourth Census of Production Final Report (Part IV) (HMSO, 1930).
"Frank Seaman v Berliner Gramophone Co," US Circuit Court, Western District of Virginia, *Transcript of Record* (Harrisonburg, 1900).
Jesse Isidor Straus et al (trading as RH Macy & Co) v Victor Talking Machine Co, US District Court, Southern District of New York, 243 US 490 (1917).
Law on Copyright Committee (Cmd. 4976) (HMSO, 1909).

Report on Import Duties Act Presented to Parliament (1934) (HMSO, 1934).

Third Census of Production Final Report (HMSO, 1924).

Thirteenth Census of the United States Taken in the Year 1910, vol. 10, "Manufactures" (Washington, DC, 1911).

Twelfth Census of the United States Taken in the Year 1900, vol. 10, "Manufactures" (Washington, DC, 1901).

United States Supreme Court Reports 1917, vol. 243 (Washington, DC, 1917).

CONTEMPORARY PRINTED SOURCES

Newspapers and Journals

The Advertisers' ABC. London, 1886–1914.

The Columbia Record. Bridgeport, CT, 1901–1909.

Daily Mail. London, 1896–1931.

Directory of Directors. London, 1880–1931.

Electrical Engineering. New York, 1890.

Electrical World. New York, 1887.

English Mechanic and World of Science. London, 1897.

The Era Annual. London, 1918.

Financial Times. London, 1900–1931.

The Gramophone. Harrow, 1923 to date.

Journal of the Franklin Institute. Philadelphia, 1888–1914.

Journal of the Society of Arts. London, 1878–1914.

Melody Maker. London, 1926.

The Music Seller Reference Book 1928–1929. London, Evans Brothers Ltd, 1929.

New York Times. New York, 1900–1931.

New York World. New York, 1887.

North American Review. New York, 1878.

Opera News. New York, 1937.

The Phonogram. New York, 1891–1893.

The Phonoscope. New York, 1896–1902.

The Phono Trader and Recorder. London, 1904–1931.

Scientific American. New York, 1877–1896.

Sound Wave. London, 1906–1931.

The Stock Exchange Official Intelligence. London, 1890–1934.

Talking Machine News. London, 1903–1935.

Talking Machine World. New York, 1904–1929.

The Times. London, 1900–1931.

Transactions of the British Association for the Advancement of Science. London, 1888.

The Voice. Hayes, Middlesex, 1917–1934.

The Voice of Victor. Camden, NJ.

Who Was Who. London, 1897 to date.

Articles

Barker, W. G. "Before 1910: Kinematograph Experiences." *Proceedings of the British Kinematograph Society* 1 (1936).

Berliner, Emile. "Berliner's Gramophone." *The Electrical World* (November 1887): 255–56.

———. "Etching the Human Voice." *Journal of the Franklin Institute* 125, no. 6 (June 1888): 435–47.

———. "The Development of the Gramophone." *Journal of the Franklin Institute* 176 (August 1913): 189–99.

———. "The Gramophone." *Scientific American* 74, no. 20 (16 May 1896): 311.

———. "The Improved Gramophone." *The Electrical World* (August 1888): 80.

———. "The Improved Gramophone." *The Electrical World* (January 1891): 6–8.

———. "Improvements in the Gramophone." *The Electrical World* (June 1889).

———. "Technical Notes on the Gramophone." *Journal of the Franklin Institute* 160 (December 1895): 419–37.

Edison, Thomas A. "The Phonograph and Its Future." *North American Review* 177 (May–June 1878): 526–36.

———. "The Talking Phonograph." *Scientific American* 37 (22 December 1877): 384.

Edmunds, Henry. "The Graphophone." *Journal of the Society of Arts* 36 (7 December 1888): 39–48.

Fewkes, Jesse Walter. "A Contribution to Passamaquoddy Folk-Lore." *Journal of American Folk-Lore* 3, no. 11 (October–December 1890): 257–80.

———. "On the Use of the Phonograph in the Study of the Languages of American Indians." *Science* 15 (May 1890): 267–69.

Gouraud, Colonel George E. "The Phonograph." *Journal of the Society of Arts* 36 (30 November 1888): 23–33.

Houston, Edwin J. "The Gramophone." *Journal of the Franklin Institute* 125, no. 5 (January 1888): 44–55.

Johnson, Edward H. "A Wonderful Invention-Speech Capable of Indefinite Repetition From Automatic Records." *Scientific American* 37 (17 November 1877): 304.

"Le nouveau phonographe d'Edison," "Le Parfaite phonograph," "Nouveau Phonographe d'Edison." *La Science Illustrée,* 16 June 1888 and 8 September 1888.

Morton, Turner. "The Art of Advertising." *Pearson's Magazine* 20, no. 119 (November 1905): 488–93.

Oesterreicher, S. I. "The Production of Sound by Machinery." *American Machinist* 32 (10 June 1909): 974–77.

Preece, William H. "The Phonograph." *Journal of the Society of Arts* 26 (10 May 1878): 535–39.

Reddie, Lovell N. "The Gramophone, and the Mechanical Recording and Reproduction of Musical Sounds." *Journal of the Royal Society of Arts* 66 (8 May 1908): 633–49.

Sooy, Raymond. "The Memoirs of Raymond Sooy." *Communicate* (June/July 1974).

Sousa, John Philip. "The Menace of Mechanical Music." *Appleton's Magazine* 8, no. 3 (September 1906): 278–84.

Tainter, Charles Sumner. "The Graphophone." *The Electrical World* (14 July 1888): 16–18.

Viall, Ethan. "Manufacturing Wax Cylinder Records." *American Machinist* 35 (23 May 1912).

Whittle, John. "A Record Life, 1927–1975: A Lecture Given Under the Chairmanship of Sir Joseph Lockwood" (18 May 1975), *Recorded Sound: Journal of the British Institute of Recorded Sound* 65 (January 1977): 656–61.

Other Printed Works

Barnett, Captain Harry Theodore. *Up-to-Date Gramophone Tips*. Guernsey, Channel Islands: Gramophone, 1923.

Batten, Joseph. *Joe Batten's Book: The Story of Sound Recording*. London: Rockliff, 1956.

Bottone, Selimo Romeo. *Talking Machines and Records*. London: Pitman, 1904.

Brophy, John, and Eric Partridge. *Songs and Slang of the British Soldiers: 1914–1918*. London: Partridge, 1930.

Bryson, Herbert Courtney. *The Gramophone Record*. London: Benn, 1935.

Buick, Thomas Lindsay. *The Romance of the Gramophone*. Wellington, New Zealand: Ernest Dawson, 1927.

Caruso, Dorothy. *Enrico Caruso: His Life and Death*. London: T. Werner Laurie, 1946.

Dawson, Peter. *Fifty Years of Song*. London: Hutchinson, 1951.

Du Monsel, Theodore Achille Louis. *The Telephone, the Microphone and the Phonograph*. New York, 1879.

"Dyer." *Intensity Coils: How Made and How Used With a Description of the Electric Light, Electric Bells, Electric Motors, the Telephone, the Microphone and the Phonograph*. London: Thoburn, 1883.

Dyer, Frank Lewis, and Thomas Commerford Martin. *Edison, His Life and Inventions*. New York: Harper & Brothers, 1910.

Edgar, George, ed. *Careers for Men, Women and Children*. London: Newnes, 1911–1912.

Elwes, Hervey. *Thoughts on Music*. London: Gramophone, 1926.

Freer, Cyril C. *The Inner Side of Advertising*. London: Library Press, 1924.

Gaisberg, F. W. *Music on Record*. London: Hale, 1946.

Ganot, Adolphe. *Elementary Treatise on Physics*. Translated by Edmund Atkinson. London: Longmans, 1886.

Gaydon, Harry A. *The Art and Science of the Gramophone*. London: Dunlop, 1926.

Giraud, S. Louis, ed. *Daily Express Community Song Book, No 3, Songs That Won the War*. London: Express Newspapers, 1930.

The Gramophone Co Ltd. *Celebrity Records by International Artists*. Hayes, UK: Gramophone, 1914.

———. *Opera at Home*. Hayes, UK: Gramophone, 1920, 1922 and 1925.

J. E. Hough Ltd. *The Story of Edison Bell to 1924*. London: Hough, 1924.

Johnson, William W. *The Gramophone in Education*. London: Pitmans, 1936.

Klein, Herman. *The Reign of Patti*. New York: Century, 1920.

Lauder, Harry. *Roamin' in the Gloamin'*. London: 1928; reprint, E. P., 1976.

Lewis, Edward. *No CIC*. London: Privately published, 1957.

Lord & Thomas and Logan Ltd. *Merchandising Survey of Great Britain: Gramophones*. Vol. 7. London: Lord & Thomas and Logan Ltd, 1930.

McClure, J. B. *Edison and His Inventions*. Chicago: Rhodes & McClure, 1879.

McCormack, Lily. *I Hear You Calling Me*. London: Allen, 1950.

McKendrick, John Gray. *Waves of Speech and Sound*. Basingstoke, UK: Macmillan, 1897.

Mackenzie, Compton, and Marshall Archibald. *Gramophone Nights*. London: Heinemann, 1923.

Mackenzie, Sir Compton. *My Record of Music*. London: Huchinson, 1955.

Mackenzie-Rogaan, John. *Fifty Years of Army Music*. London: Methuen, 1926.

Melba, Dame Nellie. *Melodies and Memories*. London: Butterworth, 1925.

Miller, Francis Trevelyan. *Thomas A. Edison*. London: Paul, 1932.

Mitchell, Ogilvie. *The Talking Machine Industry*. London: Pitmans, 1923.

Moore, Gerald. *Am I Too Loud*. London: Hamilton, 1962; reprint, Harmondsworth, UK: Penguin, 1979.

National Radio Exhibition Catalogue. London: National Radio Exhibtion, 1928.

Robertson, Alec. *The Golden Treasury of Recorded Music*. Hayes, UK: Gramophone, 1927 to 1930.

Ronald, Sir Landon. *Myself and Others*. London: Sampson Low, 1931.

———. *Variations on a Personal Theme*. London: Hodder, 1922.

Ruffo, Titta. *La mia parabola*. Milan, Italy, 1937; reprint, Rome, Italy, 1977.

Scholes, Percy A. *The First Book of the Gramophone Record*. Oxford: Oxford University Press, 1924 and 1927.

———. *The Oxford Companion to Music*. Oxford: Oxford University Press, 1939.

———. *The Second Book of the Gramophone Record*. Oxford: Oxford University Press, 1925.

Seymour, Henry. *The Reproduction of Sound*. London: Tattersall, 1918.

Stark, Malcolm. *The Pulse of the World: Fleet Street Memoirs*. London: Skeffington, 1915.

Stone, Christopher. *Christopher Stone Speaking*. London: Mathews & Marot, 1933.

Tewkesbury, George E. A. *Complete Manual of the Edison Phonograph*. New York: National Phonograph Co, Foreign Department, 1897; reprint, Kent, UK: G. L. Frow, n.d.

Wile, Frederick William. *Emile Berliner: Maker of the Microphone*. Indianapolis, IN: Bobbs Merrill, 1926.

Wilson, G. *Gramophones Acoustic and Radio*. London: Gramophone, 1932.

Wilson, H. L. *Music and the Gramophone*. London: Allen & Unwin, 1926.

Young, J. Lewis. *Edison and His Phonograph*. London: 1893; reprint, Bournemouth, UK: Talking Machine Review, 1970.

SECONDARY SOURCES

Adams, R. J. G. *Arms and the Wizard*. London: Cassell, 1978.

Adrian, Karlo, and Arthur Badrock. *Edison Bell Winner Records*. Bournemouth, UK: Bayly, 1989.

Aldridge, Benjamin L. *The Victor Talking Machine Co*. New York: RCA, 1964.

Alford, B. W. G. *W. D. and H. O. Wills and the Development of the British Tobacco Industry 1786–1965*. London: Methuen, 1973.

Andrews, Frank. "The Birth of Electrical Recording." *The Hillandale News*, no. 144 (June 1985): 199–204.

———. *Columbia 10-Inch Records 1903–30*. Rugby: City of London Phonograph and Gramophone Society, 1985.

———. *Edison Phonograph: The British Connection*. Rugby: City of London Phonograph and Gramophone Society, 1986.

———. "Genuine Edison Bell Records." *The Hillandale News*, nos. 141, 142, 143, 145 (December 1984; March, April and August 1985).

———. *The HMV Plum Label Catalogue: "C" Series (12 Inch)*. London: Oakwood Press, 1974.

———. *Sterling Records*. Bournemouth, UK: Bayly, 1975.

Andrews, Frank, and Arthur Badrock. *The Cinch Record*. Wells-Next-the-Sea, UK: City of London Phonograph and Gramophone Society Ltd, 2000.

———. *The Complete Regal Catalogue (February 1914 to December 1932)*. Malvern: City of London Phonograph and Gramophone Society, 1991.

Andrews, Frank, and Ernie Bayly. *Billy Williams' Records*. Bournemouth, UK: Talking Machine Review, 1982.

———. *Catalogue of HMV "B" Series Records*. Wells-Next-the-Sea, UK: City of London Phonograph and Gramophone Society Ltd, 2000.

———. *The Zonophone Single Faced Record Discography*. Wells-Next-the-Sea, UK: City of London Phonograph and Gramophone Society Ltd, 1999.

Andrews, Frank, and Michael Smith. *Columbia Graphophone Company Ltd, English Celebrity Series and 10-Inch and 12-Inch D, LB, L and LX Series, YB, RO, ROX Series. D-40,000*. Wells-Next-the-Sea, UK: City of London Phonograph and Gramophone Society Ltd, 2002.

———. *Parlophone Records, 12-Inch "E" Series 1923–1956*. Wells-Next-the-Sea, UK: City of London Phonograph and Gramophone Society Ltd, 2000.

Arnold, Bruce. *Orpen: Mirror to an Age*. London: Cape, 1981.

Badger, Reid. *A Life in Ragtime: A Biography of James Reese Europe*. Oxford: Oxford University Press, 1994.

Badrock, Arthur. *The Parlophone Red Label Popular Series*. Cupar, Scotland: City of London Phonograph and Gramophone Society Ltd, n.d.

Barnum, Frederick O., III. *His Master's Voice in America*. Camden, NJ: General Electric Company, 1991.

Bauer, Robert. *The New Catalogue of Historical Records 1898–1908/9*. London: Sidgwick & Jackson, 1947.

Baumbach, Robert W. *Look for the Dog: An Illustrated Guide to Victor Talking Machines 1901–1929*. Woodland Hills, CA: Stationary X-Press, 1981.

Bayly, Ernie, and Michael Kinnear. *The Zon-o-Phone Record: A Discography of Recordings Produced by the International Zonophone Company and Associated Companies in Europe and the Americas, 1901–1903*. Victoria, Australia: Kinnear, 2001.

Bennett, J. R., and Eric Hughes. *The International Red Label Catalogue: HMV "DB" (12-Inch)*. London: Oakwood Press, n.d.

Bolig, John R. *Caruso Records: A History and Discography*. Denver, CO: Mainspring Press, 2002.

Boulton, David. *Jazz in Britain*. London: Allen, 1958.

Bowley, A. L. *The Change in the Distribution of the National Income 1880–1913*. Oxford: Clarendon Press, 1920.

Brady, Erika, Maria La Vigna, Dorothy Sara Lee, and Thomas Vennum, eds. *The Federal Cylinder Project*. Washington, DC: Library of Congress, 1984.

Briggs, Asa. *The History of Broadcasting in the United Kingdom*. London: Oxford University Press, 1961–1979.

———. "Mass Entertainment: The Origins of a Modern Industry." Twenty-Ninth Fisher Lecture in Commerce. Adelaide, Australia: Griffin Press, 1960.

Brooks, Tim. "Columbia Records in the 1890's: Founding the Record Industry." *Association of Recorded Sound Collections Journal* 10, no. 1 (1978): 5–36.

Bruce, Robert V. *Alexander Graham Bell and the Conquest of Solitude.* Boston: Little, Brown, 1973.

Burns, R. W. *British Television: The Formative Years.* London: Peregrinus, 1986.

Burt, Leah S. "Record Materials. Part 1: Chemical Technology in the Edison Recording Industry." *Journal of the Audio Engineering Society* 25, nos. 10/11 (October/November 1977): 712–28.

Carstensen, Fred V. *American Enterprises in Foreign Markets: Studies of Singer and International Harvester in Imperial Russia.* Chapel Hill: University of North Carolina Press, 1984.

Carter, Sydney H. *Blue Amberol Cylinders.* Bournemouth, UK: Talking Machine Review, 1978.

Caruso, Enrico, Jr., and Andrew Farkas. *Enrico Caruso: My Father and My Family.* Portland, OR: Amadeus, 1990.

Chandler, Alfred D., Jr. *Strategy and Structure.* Cambridge, MA: Harvard University Press, 1966.

———. *The Visible Hand.* Cambridge, MA: Harvard University Press, 1977.

Chandler, Alfred D., Jr., and Herman Daems. *Managerial Hierarchies.* Cambridge, MA: Harvard University Press, 1980.

Chandler, Alfred D., Jr., and Richard S. Tedlow. *The Coming of Managerial Capitalism: A Casebook on the History of American Economic Institutions.* Homewood, IL: Irwin, 1985.

Chew, V. K. *Talking Machines 1877–1914: Some Aspects of the Early History of the Gramophone.* London: HMSO, 1967.

Cliffe, Peter. *Fascinating Rhythm.* Baldock, UK: Egon, 1990.

Coase, R. H. "The Nature of the Firm." *The Firm, the Market and the Law.* Chicago: University of Chicago Press, 1988.

Collier, James Lincoln. *The Making of Jazz.* London: Hart-Davis MacGibbon, 1978.

Coover, James, ed. *Music Publishing: Copyright and Piracy in Victorian England.* London: Mansell, 1985.

Duckinfield, Bridget. *O Lovely Knight: Biography of Sir Landon Ronald.* London: 1991.

Edge, Ruth, and Leonard Petts. *A Guide to Collecting His Master's Voice "Nipper" Souvenirs.* Hayes, UK: EMI Group Archive Trust, 1984.

Ehrlich, Cyril. *The Music Profession in Britain Since the Eighteenth Century.* Oxford: Clarendon, 1985.

———. *The Piano: A History.* London: Dent, 1976.

Fagan, Ted, and William Moran. *Encyclopedic Discography of Victor Records.* Westport, CT: Greenwood, 1982.

Frow, George L. *The Edison Disc Phonograph and Diamond Discs.* Sevenoaks, UK: Frow, 1982.

Frow, George L., and Albert F. Sefl. *The Edison Cylinder Phonographs 1877–1929.* Sevenoaks, UK: Frow, 1978.

Fussell, Paul. *The Great War and Modern Memory.* London: Oxford University Press, 1975.

Gelatt, Roland. *The Fabulous Phonograph.* London: Cassell, 1956.

Godbolt, Jim. *A History of Jazz in Britain 1919–50.* London: Quartet Books, 1984.

Hall, Peter, and Colin Brown, eds. *Hayes on Record.* Hayes, UK: EMI Group Archive Trust, 1992.

Harewood, The Earl of, ed. *Kobbé's Complete Opera Book.* 10th ed. London: Bodley Head, 1987.

Harvith, John, and Susan Edwards Harvith, eds. *Edison, Musicians and the Phonograph.* New York: Greenwood, 1988.

Hatcher, Danny H., ed. *Proceedings of the 1890 Convention of Local Phonograph Companies.* Reprint, Nashville, TN: 1974.

Hurst, P. G. "The Record Collector." In *The Gramophone Jubilee Book.* Harrow, UK: General Gramophone, 1973.

Ingham, John N., ed. *Biographical Dictionary of American Business Leaders.* Westport, CT: Greenwood, 1983.

Israel, Paul. *Edison, a Life of Invention.* New York: Wiley, 1998.

Jeremy, David J., and Christine Shawe, eds. *Dictionary of Business Biography.* London: Butterworth, 1984.

Johnson, E. R. Fennimore. *His Master's Voice Was Eldridge R. Johnson.* Dover, DE: Fennimore Johnson, 1974.

Jones, Geoffrey, ed. *British Multinationals: Origins, Management and Performance.* Aldershot, UK: Gower, 1987.

———. "The Gramophone Company: An Anglo-American Multinational, 1898–1931." *Business History Review* 59 (Spring 1985): 76–100.

Jowett, Garth. *Film: The Democratic Art.* Boston: Little, Brown, 1976.

Juxon, John. *Lewis and Lewis.* London: Collins, 1983.

Kilgarriff, Michael. *Sing Us One of the Old Songs: A Guide to Popular Song 1860–1920.* Oxford: Oxford University Press, 1998.

Kinnear, Michael. *Nicole Record.* Victoria, Australia: Kinnear, 2001.

Knight, Frank H. *Risk, Uncertainty and Profit.* New York: Houghton Mifflin, 1921.

Koenigsberg, Allen. *Edison Cylinder Records 1889–1912.* New York, APM Press, 1987.

———. *The Patent History of the Phonograph 1877–1912.* New York: APM Press, 1990.

Lane, Michael R. *Baron Marks of Woolwich: International Entrepreneur, Engineer, Patent Agent and Politician (1858–1938).* London: Quiller, 1986.

Ledbetter, Gordon T. *The Great Irish Tenor.* London: Duckworth, 1977.

Low, Rachael. *The History of the British Film Industry 1906–1914.* London: Allen & Unwin, 1949.

Maas, Jeremy. *The Victorian Art World in Photographs.* London: Barry & Jenkins, 1984.

Marco, Guy A., ed. *Encyclopedia of Recorded Sound in the United States.* New York: Garland, 1993.

Martland, Peter. "Caruso's First Recordings: Myth and Reality." *Association of Recorded Sound Collections Journal* 25, no. 2 (Fall 1994): 193–204.

———. "David Bicknell," "Alfred Clark," "Frederick William Gaisberg," "Walter Legge," "Sir Edward Roberts Lewis" and "Sir Louis Sterling." In *Oxford Dictionary of National Biography.*

———. "The Edison Records of John McCormack." *Record Collector* (May 1991).

———. Introduction to A. F. Wagner, *Recollections of Thomas A. Edison.* London: City of London Phonograph and Gramophone Society, 1991.

———. "The Okhrana: Guardians of Recorded Culture." *Intelligence and National Security* 6, no. 3 (July 1991) 627–28.

———. *Since Records Began: EMI the First 100 Years.* London: Batsford, 1997.

Matthew, H. C. G., and Brian Harrison, eds. *Oxford Dictionary of National Biography: From the Earliest Times to the Year 2000.* Oxford: Oxford University Press, 2004.

Millard, Andre. *Edison and the Business of Innovation.* Baltimore: Johns Hopkins University Press, 1990.

Milward, Alan S., and S. B. Saul. *The Development of the Economies of Continental Europe 1850–1914.* London: Allen & Unwin, 1977.

Mitchell, B. R. *Abstract of British Historical Statistics.* Cambridge: Cambridge University Press, 1962.

Mitchell, Ogilvie. *The Talking Machine Industry.* London, 1922.

Moore, Jerrold Northrop. *Elgar on Record: The Composer and the Gramophone.* London: Oxford University Press, 1974.

———. *A Voice in Time: The Gramophone of Fred Gaisberg, 1873–1951.* London: Hamilton, 1976.

Nevett, T. R. *Advertising in Britain.* London: Heinemann, 1982.

Newville, Leslie J. "Development of the Phonograph at Alexander Graham Bell's Volta Laboratory." *United States National Museum Bulletin* (1959): 218.

Niver, Kemp R., and Bebe Bergstein. "James H. White: Primitive American Film-Maker." In *Performing Arts Annual 1988,* 74–95. Washington, DC: Library of Congress, 1989.

Paper, Louis J. *Empire: William S. Paley and the Making of CBS.* New York: St. Martin's Press, 1987.

Petts, Leonard. *The Story of Nipper and the HMV Picture.* Bournemouth, UK: Talking Machine Review, 1973.

Phelps Browne, E. H., and Margaret H. Browne. *A Century of Pay: The Course of Pay and Production in France, Germany, Sweden, the United Kingdom and the United States of America, 1860–1960.* London: Macmillan, 1968.

Phillips, Jeremy. *Introduction to Intellectual Property Law.* London: Butterworth, 1995.

Pollard, Anthony. *Gramophone: The First 75 years.* Harrow, UK: General Gramophone, 1998.

Pope, Daniel. *The Making of Modern Advertising.* New York: Basic Books, 1983.

Pretzner, William S., ed. *Working at Inventing: Thomas A. Edison and the Menlo Park Experience.* Dearborn, MI: Henry Ford Museum & Greenfield Village, 1989.

Priestley, Brian. *Jazz on Record.* London: Elm Trees, 1988.

Priestley, J. B. *The Edwardians.* London: Heinemann, 1970.

Radic, Therese. *Melba: The Voice of Australia.* Basingstoke, UK: Macmillan, 1986.

Read, Oliver, and Walter Welch. *From Tin Foil to Stereo.* Indianapolis, IN: Sams, 1959.

Rosenberg, Nathan. *Inside the Black Box: Technology and Economics.* Cambridge: Cambridge University Press, 1982.

———. *Perspectives on Technology.* Cambridge: Cambridge University Press, 1976.

Rosenberg, Nathan, and L. E. Birdzell Jr. *How the West Grew Rich: The Economic Transformation of the Industrial World.* New York: Basic Books, 1986.

Rosselli, John. "The Opera Business and the Italian Immigrant Community in Latin America, 1820–1930." *Past and Present* 127 (May 1990): 165–82.

———. *The Opera Industry in Italy From Cimerosa to Verdi: The Role of the Impresario.* Cambridge: Cambridge University Press, 1984.

Rust, Brian. *The American Dance Band Discography, 1917–1942.* New Rochelle, NY: Arlington House, 1975.

———. *British Music Hall on Record.* Harrow, UK: General Gramophone, 1979.

———. *The Dance Bands.* London: Allan, 1972.

———. *Gramophone Records of the First World War.* London: David and Charles, 1974.

———. *Jazz Records 1897–1942.* Chigwell, UK: Storyville, 1974.

Rust, Brian, and Allen G. Debus. *The Complete Entertainment Discography From 1897 to 1942.* New York: Arlington House, 1989.

Sadie, Stanley, ed. *The New Grove Dictionary of Music and Musicians*. London: Macmillan, 2001.

Samuel, Edgar. "Decca Days: The Career of Wilfred Sampson Samuel 1886–1958." *Jewish Historical Studies* 30 (1987–88): 235–74.

Sanders, Alan, ed. *Walter Legge: Words and Music*. London: Duckworth, 1998.

Saul, S. B. "Industrialisation and Deindustrialisation? The Interaction of the German and British Economies Before the First World War." Annual lecture to the German Historical Institute, 1979.

Schwarzkopf, Elisabeth. *On and Off the Record: A Memoir of Walter Legge*. London: Faber, 1982.

Scott, Michael. *The Great Caruso*. London: Hamilton, 1988.

Seeley, Robert, and Rex Bunnett. *London Musical Shows on Record: 1889–1989*. Harrow, UK: General Gramophone, 1989.

Sheffield, G. D., and G. I. S. Inglis, eds. *From Vimy Ridge to the Rhine: Great War Letters of Christopher Stone*. Marlborough, UK: Crowood, 1989.

Sherman, Michael W. *The Collector's Guide to Victor Records*. Dallas, TX: Monarch Record Enterprises, 1992.

———. *The Paper Dog*. New York: APM Press, 1987.

Smith, Michael. *The Decca Record Company Ltd, Decca 78-rpm Records 1929 to 1954*. Wells-Next-the-Sea: City of London Phonograph and Gramophone Society Ltd, 2002.

———. *His Master's Voice "BD" Series*. Hastings, UK: Tamarisk Books, 1992.

———. *The HMV "D" and "E" catalogue*. London: Oakwood Press, 1971.

Smith, Michael, and Frank Andrews. *The HMV Plum Label Catalogue*. London: Oakwood Press, 1974.

Southall, Brian. *Abbey Road*. Wellingborough, UK: Omnibus, 2002.

Steane, J. B. *The Grand Tradition*. London: Duckworth, 1974.

Swinnerton, Frank, ed. *Arnold Bennett: The Journals*. Harmondsworth, UK: Penguin, 1971.

Teichova, Alice, Maurice Levy-Leboyer, and Helga Nussbaum, eds. *Historical Studies in International Corporate Business*. Cambridge: Cambridge University Press, 1989.

Todman, Daniel. *The Great War: Myth and Memory*. London: Hambledon, 2005.

Tritton, Paul. *The Godfather of Rolls Royce: The Life and Times of Henry Edmunds MICE, MIEE*. London: Academy Books, 1993.

———. *The Lost Voice of Queen Victoria*. London: Academy Books, 1991.

Vyse, Barry, and George Jessop. *The Saga of Marconi Osram-Valve: A History of Valve-Making*. Pinner, UK: Vyse, 2000.

Wagner, Alfred F. *Recollections of Thomas A. Edison*. London: City of London Phonograph and Gramophone Society, 1991.

Watts, Len, and Frank Andrews. "Pathe Records in Britain." *Hillandale News*, nos. 13 and 14 (October 1989 to April 1990): 258–63, 289–95, 320–26, and 8–11.

Welch, Walter L. "Edison and His Contribution to the Record Industry." *Journal of the Audio Engineering Society* 25, nos. 10/11 (October/November 1977): 660–65.

Welch, Walter L., and Leah Brodbeck Stenzel Burt. *From Tinfoil to Stereo: The Acoustic Years of the Recording Industry*. Gainesville: University Press of Florida, 1994.

Wile, Raymond R. "The American Graphophone Company and the Columbia Phonograph Company Enter the Disc Record Business, 1897–1903." *Association of Recorded Sound Collections Journal* 22, no. 2 (Fall 1991): 207–21.

———. "The Development of Sound Recording at the Volta Laboratory." *Association of Recorded Sound Collections Journal* 21, no. 2 (1990): 208–25.

———. "Etching the Human Voice: The Berliner Invention of the Gramophone." *Association of Recorded Sound Collections Journal* 21, no. 1 (1990): 2–22.

———. "Growing Hostilities Between Edison and the Phonograph and Graphophone Developers." *Association of Recorded Sound Collections Journal* 22, no. 1 (1991): 8–34.

———. "Introduction." In *Proceedings of the 1890 Convention of Local Phonograph Companies.* Reprint, Nashville, TN, 1974.

———. "Phonograph Production Figures." *Antique Phonograph Monthly* (March 1973).

Williamson, Oliver E. "The Modern Corporation: Origins, Evolution, Attributes." *Journal of Economic Literature* 19 (December 1981): 1537–68.

Winter, J. M. *The Great War and the British People.* Basingstoke, UK: Macmillan, 1985.

———. *Sites of Memory, Sites of Mourning: The Great War in European Cultural History.* Cambridge: Cambridge University Press.

Worth, Paul W., and Jim Cartwright. *John McCormack: A Comprehensive Discography.* New York: Greenwood, 1986.

UNPUBLISHED MANUSCRIPTS

Andrews, Frank. "Edison Bell in 1899" (undated).

Clark, Alfred. "His Master's Voice: A Record" (circa 1939).

Edge, Ruth. "An Early History of the Australian Branch of The Gramophone Company" (undated).

Gibbs, Patricia. "Trevor Williams 1859–1946" (1968).

Martland, Peter. "A Business History of The Gramophone Company, 1897–1918" (unpublished Cambridge University PhD dissertation, 1993).

Petts, Leonard. "Loss of the German (DGAG) Co 1914–30" (undated).

Wadey, T. C. "Edison's European Phonograph Business: A Business History of the National Phonograph Co Ltd, 1902–1912" (Oxford Brookes University MBA dissertation, 1998).

Wile, Raymond R. "Berliner Record Sales" (undated).

———. "Launching the Gramophone in America 1890–96" (undated).

INDEX

United Kingdom census of production, 1924 and 1930 and *Report on Import Duties*, 1934, 241-243, 283

United States Census of Manufacture, 20-21, 34n80, 36n108, 89

United States Gramophone Company, 17, 19, 22

The Universal Talking Machine Company (The Universal Talking Machine Manufacturing Company), 21

Vallée Rudy, 322

Velvet Face records, 75, 84, 245, 247

The Victor Talking Machine Company, xix, 20, 25-27, 34n71, 34n74, 35n90, 36n102, 56, 75, 78, 113, 116, 123-124, 126-128, 132-140, 149-150, 153n70, 158, 168-170, 183, 185, 191, 193-194, 196-198, 213, 215, 238-249, 256, 262, 263n3, 271-274, 276, 289-291, 294-296, 297n9,n17, 302-303, 309, 312, 316-318, 320-321. *See also photospread*

Victory records, 248

Victrola, 27

The Vienna Philharmonic Orchestra, 291

The Vocalion Gramophone Company Ltd (The Universal Music Company Ltd, Vocalion records, Aeolian Vocalion records), 238, 249-251, 265n36, 315, 322

The Voice, 223, 305

Voigt, Paul Gustavus Adolphus Helmut, 247, 264n23

The Volta Associates, 5-7

The Volta Bureau, 6

The Volta Graphophone Company, 6, 29n20

The Volta Laboratory, xiv, 5-6, 29n19

Volta Prize, 5

Wagner, Alfred Fenner, 88-89, 95n56, 188

Weatherly, Frederic E. and Wood, Haydn, 226

West Orange laboratory and factories (Edison Phonograph Works), 8-9, 14, 38-39, 42-43, 63n9, 63n13, 80-81, 83, 88-90, 108

Western Electric, 247, 261, 303, 304

Westinghouse, 273

White, James Henry, 77, 80, 86, 88, 95n61, 119n32, 190

Whiteman, Paul, 312, 321, 324

Widdop, Walter, 292

Wile, Raymond, 20, 29n14, 33n55, 33n57, 35n84

Williams, Billy (stage name of Richard Banks), 91, 191, 203n51, 289

Williams, Edmund Trevor Lloyd, 47-49, 53-57, 64n50, 67n93, 124, 126, 136, 146, 149, 206, 216-218, 269, 273-274, 295

Williams, Romer, 57, 67n93, 136, 152n43, 216

Williams, Trevor Osmond, 286

Williamson, Oliver, 127

The Winner Records, 75, 84, 94n50, 95n51, 206-207, 210, 229, 245, 247, 322

Winter, J. M., xiv, 221, 225

Wood Sir Henry, 107, 193, 315. *See also photospread*

W. R. Steel (Reddich) Ltd, 240

Young, Jonathan Lewis, 38-40, 62n5, 95n52. *See also photospread*

Young, Owen D., 296

Zonophone records and machines (includes Zonophone-Twin records), 21, 24, 34n81, 50, 60, 69n121, 74, 84, 89, 100-103, 109-110, 118n18, 121n58, 133, 150, 158, 162-169, 174, 175n2, 176n24, 176n39, 193, 275, 280-285, 287-290, 293, 298n40, 309-310, 314, 322, 324. *See also photospread*

ABOUT THE AUTHOR

British historian **Peter Martland** was educated at Corpus Christi College, Cambridge, from where he holds the degrees of Master of Arts and Doctor of Philosophy. He is a research associate of his college, a member of the Faculty of History and a lecturer in history for International Programmes at Pembroke College, Cambridge. Dr Martland is the author of many articles and has published several books including *Since Records Began: The First 100 Years of EMI* (1997) and *Lord Haw Haw: The English Voice of Nazi Germany* (2003). He was part of the team engaged in the research for Christopher Andrew's book *Defence of the Realm: The Authorised History of MI5* (2009). Peter Martland regularly contributes to British radio and television and is a frequent lecturer on both sides of the Atlantic. He lives in Cambridge, England.